THE IVP NEW TESTAMENT COMMENTARY SERIES

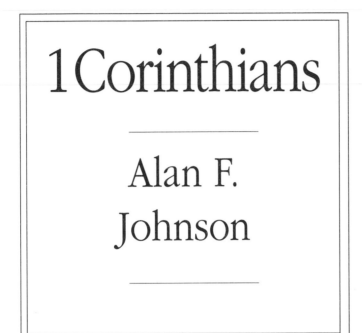

1 Corinthians

Alan F. Johnson

Grant R. Osborne
series editor

D. Stuart Briscoe
Haddon Robinson
consulting editors

INTERVARSITY PRESS
DOWNERS GROVE, ILLINOIS, USA
LEICESTER, ENGLAND

InterVarsity Press, USA
P.O. Box 1400, Downers Grove, IL 60515-1426, USA
World Wide Web: www.ivpress.com
E-mail: mail@ivpress.com

Inter-Varsity Press, England
38 De Montfort Street, Leicester LE1 7GP, England
World Wide Web: www.ivpbooks.com
E-mail: ivp@uccf.org.uk

InterVarsity Press®, U.S.A., is the book-publishing division of InterVarsity Christian Fellowship/ USA®, a student movement active on campus at hundreds of universities, colleges and schools of nursing in the United States of America, and a member movement of the International Fellowship of Evangelical Students. For information about local and regional activities, write Public Relations Dept., InterVarsity Christian Fellowship/USA, 6400 Schroeder Rd., P.O. Box 7895, Madison, WI 53707-7895, or visit the IVCF website at <www.intervarsity.org>.

Inter-Varsity Press, England, is the book-publishing division of the Universities and Colleges Christian Fellowship (formerly the Inter-Varsity Fellowship), a student movement linking Christian Unions in universities and colleges throughout the United Kingdom and the Republic of Ireland, and a member movement of the International Fellowship of Evangelical Students. For information about local and national activities write to UCCF, 38 De Montfort Street, Leicester LE1 7GP.

USA ISBN 0-8308-1807-3
UK ISBN 1-84474-033-1

Printed in the United States of America ∞

Library of Congress Cataloging-in-Publication Data

Johnson, Alan F.
  1 Corinthians/Alan F. Johnson.
    p. cm.—(The IVP New Testament commentary series)
  Includes bibliographical references.
  ISBN 0-8308-1807-3 (cloth: alk. paper)
  1. Bible N.T. Corinthians, 1st—Commentaries. I. Title: First
Corinthians. II. Title. III. Series.
  BS2675.53.J64 2004
  227'.2077—dc22

                                                            2004000436

British Library Cataloguing in Publication Data

A catalogue record for this book is available from the British Library.

P	17	16	15	14	13	12	11	10	9	8	7	6	5	4	3	2	1
Y	18	17	16	15	14	13	12	11	10	09	08	07	06	05	04		

To all my former students,
for their patience in looking beyond these feet of clay
to catch some glimmer of the One who said,
"I came not to be served but to serve and to give my life . . ."
To those who have gone far beyond their teacher
in intellectual and spiritual excellence

General Preface

In an age of proliferating commentary series, one might easily ask why add yet another to the seeming glut. The simplest answer is that no other series has yet achieved what we had in mind—a series to and from the church that seeks to move from the text to its contemporary relevance and application.

No other series offers the unique combination of solid, biblical exposition and helpful explanatory notes in the same user-friendly format. No other series has tapped the unique blend of scholars and pastors who share both a passion for faithful exegesis and a deep concern for the church. Based on the New International Version of the Bible, one of the most widely used modern translations, the IVP New Testament Commentary Series builds on the NIV's reputation for clarity and accuracy. Individual commentators indicate clearly whenever they depart from the standard translation as required by their understanding of the original Greek text.

The series contributors represent a wide range of theological traditions, united by a common commitment to the authority of Scripture for Christian faith and practice. Their efforts here are directed toward applying the unchanging message of the New Testament to the ever-changing world in which we live.

Readers will find in each volume not only traditional discussions of authorship and backgrounds, but useful summaries of principal themes and approaches to contemporary application. To bridge the gap between commentaries that stress the flow of an author's argument but skip over exegetical nettles and those that simply jump from one difficulty to another, we have developed our unique format that expounds the text in uninterrupted form on the upper portion of each page while dealing with other issues underneath in verse-keyed notes. To avoid clutter we have also adopted a social studies note system that keys references to the bibliography.

We offer the series in hope that pastors, students, Bible teachers and small group leaders of all sorts will find it a valuable aid—one that stretches the mind and moves the heart to ever-growing faithfulness and obedience to our Lord Jesus Christ.

Author's Preface

No one who has pored for hundreds of hours over 1 Corinthians can remain unchanged. My life has been transformed by the words of Paul in this ancient letter.

A wise earlier commentator has captured the important thing to remember about the detailed study of Scripture: "Scripture teaches its own use, which consists in *action*. To *act* it, we must understand it, and this understanding is open to all the upright of heart (Johann Albrecht Bengel [1687-1752] 1971:xii). According to the opening page of German explanation of the Nestle Greek New Testament, for many years the reader saw the Latin motto

Te totum applica ad textum: "Apply yourself totally to the text:
rem totam applica ad te.   Apply the text totally to yourself."
(J. A. Bengel, *Vorrede zur Handausgabe des Griech.* N.T. 1734, cited in Nestle 1957:3)

In particular I have learned not only how the cross of Christ changes our eternal destiny but how the pattern of the self-effacing, self-giving life of Christ should permeate the whole of our life in all spheres of our existence. In 1 Corinthians Paul works through his theology of the cross as lifestyle. To retrace in detail this nascent, unfolding theology of self-giving love is to be confronted among other things with one's own shortcomings in living out the Christian life.

Paul applies this transforming insight to the nature and life of the

Christian community. We are to be self-effacing servants of one another, submitting ourselves to one another, preferring one another above ourselves, doing everything to build up the other into the image of Christ. There is no place for status seeking and self-promotion. Even the perceived weaker members are essential, invaluable, worthy of honor in Christ's body.

If some small glimmer of this great truth emerges in these pages, pointing others to its source in Paul's amazing letter, I will be greatly encouraged.

Someone has well said that for a man the closest thing to a woman's experience of giving birth to a child is to give birth to a book. I have found this to be true. Others have assisted immeasurably with the birthing. First, my wife of forty-nine years, Rea, kept me working on the manuscript day and night for a number of years even when I wanted to quit. She gave me the time to do it at great personal expense to herself. She also read the whole piece carefully and offered many helpful suggestions.

Thanks also to those who make possible the Tyndale House Research Center in Cambridge, England. The collection, its accessibility and the encouraging community have been invaluable. With gratitude I acknowledge Wheaton College and Graduate School for generously giving me time away and support to enable this project to emerge. And without the tireless and self-giving labor of one of my beloved colleagues, Zondra Lindblade, the project would not have reached its conclusion.

What can an author say in appreciation for the publisher's patience in waiting for the completed piece and, in particular, for the helpful suggestions and skill of the editors, Jim Hoover and Grant Osborne? These people have removed many of my infelicities and made me look better than I am.

Finally, may the Lord who gave this infallible word to Paul and enabled me to grasp dimly some small part of it be honored and blessed eternally. May he bless you also as you pore over Paul's words and consider my fallible words of comment.

Commentaries are like travel guidebooks. They are not to be used as substitutes for but as useful pointers to the real-life experience of reading and being changed by Paul's letter itself.

Introduction

Paul's Corinthian letters have long been considered among the most important windows into the life of the early-first-century church. The first letter especially has attracted preachers, teachers and laypersons alike to its richly diverse landscape of problems found in any young, struggling church that is populated, as was Corinth, with people from an upwardly mobile culture infused with radical diversity of ethnic, religious, economic and social composition. Where else do we turn for a glimpse of the internal problems of an actual early church and how the apostle addresses these issues and seeks to correct them? Do we not turn to this letter for help on how to deal with church factions and splits; the proper attitude toward church leaders and the nature of their ministries; Christians suing other Christians in law courts; issues of sexual immorality, marriage, divorce and remarriage; freedom to participate in pagan rituals; gender and worship; the Lord's Supper observance; spiritual gifts; the importance of Christian love; and the resurrection of the dead?

Yet understanding the problems the Corinthians presented and the careful way Paul sought to respond to and correct these matters has frequently shed more obscurity than light on the text. Often the reason for this lies in a failure to understand the social and cultural context of Roman Corinth into which Paul addressed his words to the church. It is my conviction that by bringing the best studies of the ancient world of Corinth to bear on the biblical text, we are in a better position to understand what Paul wrote to the Corinthians and how that instruction can be properly applied to the modern church. Of course this will not mean that everything the apostle has written will become crystal clear in its meaning—human language defies such absolute clarity—but my hope is that light will nevertheless be cast on a large part of the letter for the modern reader.

As you prepare to read this commentary with an awareness of its historical and cultural context, I offer a summary of what I judge to be the best contemporary scholarship on the setting of 1 Corinthians. Space constraints allow only the briefest conclusions, without supporting argumentation on controversial matters. The brief list of sources at the end of this introduction, however, will help the interested student to probe the scholarly discussions that are merely summarized here.

□ Roman Corinth in the Time of Paul

While not bereft of Greek culture, the city of Corinth in Paul's day was significantly *Roman* in character and life. This meant that the city's architecture looked Roman, it was governed by a Roman civic structure, and it was inhabited largely by Roman people—a small contingent of Caesar's military veterans, many freedmen and women, and urban plebeians.

Greco-Roman in character yet a Roman colony answerable to Rome, Corinth, not Athens, became the capital city of the whole province of Achaia. Its official language was Latin. More prosperous and larger than any city in Greece (70,000-80,000), Corinth was of strategic cultural and political significance. Modern missionary-evangelization strategy might well take note of how important this city and its church were to Paul's strategy of spreading the gospel.

The Roman character of the city dated to the events around 44 B.C., when Julius Caesar ordered the Roman colonization of the city, probably because of its strategic commercial potential (see below). The city had been destroyed in 146 B.C. by the Romans. In the recolonization of the city by Julius Caesar, Roman freedmen and their families, eager to further their financial success and status, seized the opportunity to migrate to the newly formed colony. Corinth became like a modern boomtown in the American West in the Gold Rush days, a San Francisco of ancient Greece. Within fifty years the city boasted of many residents who had acquired considerable wealth, some of them graverobbers who sold the famous Corinthian bronze and pottery pieces in Rome for handsome sums.

As a Roman colony, Corinthian citizens voted, had their own city council and elected city officials annually. Citizens of the city could own property, initiate lawsuits (cf. 1 Cor 6:1-8) and maintain their identity based on cultural inheritance. The word *cosmopolitan* aptly describes the mix of people who inhabited this great city in Paul's day. Yet being closely allied with Rome, which brought great benefits to them, they were highly susceptible to changes and trends in Rome itself. For example, modifications in religious practices in Rome were immediately felt in Corinth as well.

Corinth's Market-Service Economy Of great importance to our study of 1 Corinthians is the commercial culture that was prominent in Paul's Corinth. In the first century the city was a bustling commercial crossroads for Europe and Asia. Ships from the west traveling from Italy through the Corinthian Gulf would head for the port of Lechaeum, Corinth's eastern harbor. Those from the east could harbor at Cenchreae, which faced eastward toward the Saronic Gulf, which eventually led to the Aegean Sea and Asia.

An ancient cargo roadway a few miles to the north connected the western sea lanes with the eastern across the isthmus at its narrowest point. Small ships could be pulled along the road from one side to the other (about a mile); larger ones would unload their cargoes and they would be transported on the roadway to waiting ships on the other side. While this sounds inefficient to us, it saved the businessmen considerable cost and enhanced safety for the sailors, who did not need to make the long trip around the dangerous southern tip of the Peloponnese. This made Corinth unequaled in all of Greece in commercial success and abundance of goods. Today the roadway has been cut down hundreds of feet to sea level to form a deep gorge connecting the two seas and allowing large ships to pass through, much like the Panama Canal.

Additionally, Corinth itself became a manufacturing city. Pottery, lamps, roof tiles and sculpture from Corinth were prized in Rome, as was its famous "Corinthian bronze" metal that rivaled gold in its appearance. How much of this metal was still being made at Corinth in Paul's day is quite uncertain. Perhaps the trade was more of a collectors' business of selling products from the previous classical period, since the smelting furnaces that have been unearthed in the area are mostly from an earlier time.

Strabo, the geographer, writes in 7 B.C. about the commercial prosperity of the city:

> Corinth is called "wealthy" because of its commerce, since it is situated on the Isthmus and is master of two harbors, of which the one leads straight to Asia, and the other to Italy; and it makes easy the exchange of merchandise from both countries that are so far distant from each other. . . . To land their cargoes here was a welcome alternative to the voyage to Malea for merchants from both Italy and Asia. (*Geography* 8.6, 20-23)

The highly competitive market-service economy bred unprincipled profiteering, not unlike the U.S. business culture of the early twenty-first century. Apuleius describes Corinth as "a city of unprincipled profit-takers who would stop at little or nothing to outdo their rivals" (*Metamorphoses* 10.19, 25). The implications of this for the problems in the church are discussed below under the heading "Social Status Inconsistency."

Tourism Not only was Corinth the first Greek city to have Roman gladiatorial contests, but the highly popular biennial Isthmian Games were held there. These events, ranked just below the Olympian Games, were one of the three or four great Panhellenic festivals of Greece. Visitors to these games brought excitement and more wealth to the tradespeople and merchants of the city. Included in the games were not only athletic events, in which women also participated, but oratorical and musical contests as well. The president of the games, who also funded them, gave multiple civic dinners for those who had Corinthian citizenship (the Roman citizens). This civic right may have presented a problem for some Christians, since the gods were celebrated and sacrificial food eaten at the dinners (1 Cor 8:9-10).

Paul would have arrived in Corinth the first time (A.D. 50) just after the games were held (49). They would have been going on during his second visit (55-56). He may have made tents for some of the crowd that flooded into the city (cf. Acts 18:3). Paul's analogy of the race and the crown of "perishable" vegetables no doubt immediately resonated with inhabitants of Corinth (1 Cor 9:24-27). Some would also see a possible connection between the "liberated" women in the Corinthian church and the fact that women participated in war chariot races and sometimes triumphed over male competitors (1 Cor 11:2-16).

There is some recent evidence that the Isthmian Games may have been moved back to their original site in Isthmia, a short distance from Corinth, a short time after Paul left Corinth in the 50s. At this time a convention was established whereby the president of the games invited a special segment of Corinthian society to Isthmia for an elite dinner. Would this have put special pressure on Christians to compromise their faith for the sake of conformity or status enhancement?

Religious Life in Corinth A cursory reading of chapters 8—10 of the letter would suggest that Christians were surrounded with idolatrous temples of various sorts ("many 'gods' and many 'lords,'" 8:5). Archaeological and literary evidence shows that Corinth had temples or sanctuaries devoted to the gods Aphrodite (two varieties), Isis and Serapis, Artemis, Dionysus, Poseidon, Apollo, Helius, Pelagrina, Necessity, Fates, Demeter, Maid, Zeus, Asklepius, Hermes, Athena and Hera Bunaea. Additionally, there were edifices for mystery religions, such as the Eleusinian mysteries, and for Roman imperial cult worship.

Two features of these religions require brief comment. It is reported that in classical times over a thousand temple prostitutes descended daily from the temple of Aphrodite on the Acrocorinth (high mountain to the south) in a column. They circled through the city and returned to the temple. As they walked, the writing on the bottom of their sandal soles could be read: *akolouthei moi*, "follow me!" Whether this tradition is true is uncertain, but Roman Corinth in Paul's day was probably neither better nor worse morally than other major cities in Greece.

The other significant factor in certain religions in Corinth, especially the widely promoted imperial cult (worship of the emperor), was their use to promote the status of freedmen. The emperor worship cult was rejuvenated in Corinth in A.D. 54, shortly after Paul left the city. Did this contribute to the problems of idolatry that developed in the Corinthian church, especially since the Isthmian Games held biennially at Corinth were regularly sponsored by the imperial cult worship? Even if the games were removed from Corinth after Paul left, the close proximity of Isthmia would have involved many of the Corinthians, including Christians, in the dinners that were held in connection with the games. Furthermore, the imperial temples would have remained and attracted adherents. The following important aspect of Corinthian life will explain this further.

Social Status Inconsistency One of the interesting and important features uncovered by those who study the social behavior of ancient communities is that at Corinth the culture allowed a rapid rise in social status for many people. Power (to achieve goals), education, wealth, knowledge, religious and moral purity, family and ethnic group position, and local community status were prized goals in this highly status-conscious society.

Freedmen (former slaves), for example, could raise their status considerably by achieving a measure of wealth or by active participation in religious practices. Such rapid change in social status is called "status inconsistency" because it fosters a fragile sense of insecurity as one attempts to project an image of higher status and to protect this image from assault by others. Rhetors also could enhance their status or the status of others (who paid them) by making brilliant speeches. This "spin" skill was not unlike that of today's PR people, who create images designed to promote their client's status in the public mind. Virtual reality comes to replace actual reality.

The atmosphere of Corinth had resemblances to our own postmodern mood, which looks not for truth but for applause, success and adulation and thrives on social constructivism, competitive pragmatism and radical pluralism. Market forces gave rise to a form of social reconstruction that dominated the Corinthian mindset. Boasting and self-promotion became common, acceptable cultural expressions (cf. 1:29, 31; 3:21; 4:6-7; 5:2, 6; 8:1-2). This spirit of the culture fed into many of the problems Paul addresses in his letter.

□ Paul, the Author

No serious challenge to Paul's authorship of the letter has ever been raised. However, the question of the integrity of the letter has been discussed (see below). This is not the place for an extended examination of Paul as a person and letter writer, but several factors related to his background and the influences that shaped his life are perhaps pertinent to understanding the letter.

Paulos is the Greek form of the Latin *Paul(l)us.* It was normal for Roman citizens to have three names: a given name, a name indicating the ultimate founder of the Roman family and a family name. Paul was either his family name or more likely his *signum,* an additional family name used when among Gentiles.

Born in Tarsus, a city more Asian than western, from parents who were both Roman citizens (and citizens of Tarsus) and Jews who had most probably migrated from Palestine (Acts 22:3; Phil 3:5), Paul had descended from the tribe of Benjamin (Rom 11:1). In Tarsus, in addition to his Hebrew school training, he would have been exposed in the university to the literature of the Greek poets and especially to the heart of Greek education, rhetoric. In Jerusalem he would have encountered the Pharisees and their teachings, especially the great rabban Gamaliel I (Acts 22:3; cf. 5:34). Pharisees were given over to study and zealous observance of the law of Moses, especially with regard to food, tithing and the additions to the law found in the "oral law" (traditions of the fathers). As a Pharisee in distinction to Sadducees, he also was taught to believe in the resurrection of the dead (Acts 23:6-8; cf. 1 Cor 6:15; 15).

Paul became a persecutor of the followers of Jesus as Messiah (Acts 8:1; Gal 1:13; cf. 1 Cor 15:9). His turning to Christ in A.D. 33, when he was in his late thirties (Acts 9:23, 26; Gal 1:15-16; Phil 3:7-10), his missionary-apostleship calling (Gal 1:16) and his contact with the Christian tradition and community before him (Rom 1:3-4; Gal 1:18) were radical reshaping influences on his life. He may well have been married, as was the norm for his Jewish culture, but he was single when he wrote 1 Corinthians (cf. 1 Cor 7:8; 9:5).

To sum up, although Paul no doubt could identify with the Greco-Roman culture in which he was raised at Tarsus and bore the impress of responsibilities of Roman citizenship, the greatest influence on his life was his rabbinic, Pharisaical Jewish background. Today scholars are increasingly convinced that Paul's Jewish background places him squarely in the mainstream Pharisaical Judaism of his day. He was not a cheap or second-class Jew.

□ The Occasion and Date of the Letter

I believe the reason Paul deals with the issues he does in the letter is not that he wanted to go over things that he had already taught the Corinthians or that he lacked time for when he was with them. Rather, in 1 Corinthians Paul is addressing circumstances that arose in the two years after he left Corinth. The city and the church were quite susceptible to rapid change and were neither static nor tranquil.

Paul's Journeys and the Founding of the Church For the purposes here, the tracing of Paul's life after his conversion to Jesus as Messiah and Lord will skip over events preceding his stay at Antioch (cf. Gal 1—2). While we are not certain of every detail or precise date in some instances, the overall sketch of his journeys and his letter writings may be summed up in the chronological chart on the next page.

The founding of the church as described by Luke presents a situation of immediate opposition by some Jews in the synagogue. This forced Paul to begin meetings in the house next door belonging to Titius Justus, a Gentile "God-fearer" who had joined the synagogue. There Crispus, the synagogue leader, and his whole household became followers of Jesus as Messiah and Lord (Acts 18:1-11). While in Corinth Paul continued to face Jewish opposition, which led to his being brought before Gallio for his favorable ruling on the matter (Acts 18:12-18).

The Letters to Corinth and Their Dating "While Gallio was proconsul of Achaia, the Jews of Corinth made a united attack on Paul and brought him to the place of judgment [bēma]" (Acts 18:12). The key to the dating of Paul's life and subsequently to the writing of his letters lies in identifying the precise date for his appearance before Gallio during Paul's founding visit to Corinth. Fortunately, we have an imperial edict inscription of Claudius that was found in Delphi in 1905 and mentions Gallio. The relevant part of the inscription is as follows: "Tiberius Claudius Caesar Augustus Germanicus, 12th year of tribunician power, acclaimed emperor for the 26th time, father of the country, sends greetings to [————]. For long have I have been well-disposed to the city of Delphi and solicitous for its prosperity. . . . Now since it is

Chronology of the Life of Paul

City	Date	Writings
Antioch	45-46	
Galatia	46-48	
Macedonia	48-50	
Corinth (founds church)	50-51 (18 mos.)	**1 and 2 Thessalonians**
Jerusalem	51	
Antioch	51-52	
Ephesus	52-54 (2 yrs.)	**Galatians** (A.D. 53)
		"prev. letter" (1 Cor 5:9)
		1 Corinthians (fall 54)
(quick "painful visit" to		"angry, sorrowful let-
Corinth, 2 Cor 2:1)		ter" to Corinthians
		(2 Cor 1:13)
Macedonia	54-55	**2 Corinthians** (55?)
Illyricum	55	
Corinth	55-56 (3 mos.)	**Romans**
Jerusalem	56-61 (?)	
Rome	62-64	**Ephesians,**
		Colossians,
		Philippians,
		Philemon
Spain	64	**1 Timothy, Titus?**
Aegean	64-66	**2 Timothy?**
Death in Rome	67	

said to be destitute of citizens, as my friend and proconsul L. Junius Gallio recently reported to me."

From other evidence it may be said that the twenty-seventh acclamation of Claudius took place between April and July of 52. Therefore the twenty-sixth acclamation would have occurred between April and July of 51. The Delphi letter was probably written in 52. The proconsul position was a one-year appointment (though Gallio did not complete his full term). The impression left from Acts 18:12-18 is that we see Gallio early in his term of office and late in Paul's eighteen-month stay in Corinth. If this is accepted, we may date Paul's appearance before Gallio as likely between July and October 51 (though 52 is possible).

An incidental note about Gallio, not without significance, is the effect that his ruling concerning the "messianic" Jews who believed in

Jesus as Crispus and others had in Corinth. Since Gallio was the supreme ruler of all Greece when he issued this judgment about early Christians that in effect exonerated them from criminal charges, at least for a time, his decision would no doubt have benefited not only the further evangelization of Corinth but also beyond to all of Greece. Furthermore, the ruling would have allowed Christians in Corinth and elsewhere to buy nonsacrificial meat in the markets, as Jews were permitted to do (cf. 1 Cor 8—10).

This Gallio dating would place the writing of Paul's four letters to the Corinthians at these probable dates:
* the "previous letter" (cf. 1 Cor 5:9)   53
* 1 Corinthians   54
* the "anguished" letter (2 Cor 1:23—2:11)   54 (?)
* 2 Corinthians   55 (?)

Comparing the date when Paul left Corinth after founding the church (51) and when he wrote 1 Corinthians yields the remarkably short period of about two and half years. During this time, changes occurred and issues arose that threatened the authenticity and integrity of the new community.

Paul's Purpose in Writing the Letter We have every reason to believe that Paul was deeply concerned for the church's well-being. Certain moral practices that can be traced to ingrained cultural patterns in the wider Corinthian society were threatening the stability of the church and needed to be corrected. "Brothers and sisters, I could not address you as spiritual but as worldly. . . . For since there is jealousy and quarreling among you, are you not worldly? Are you not acting like mere human beings?" (3:1-3 TNIV).

Many characteristics of the cultural life of first-century Corinth were seeping into the life of the Christian community. Instead of being transformed by Christian values and viewpoints, they were behaving like their counterparts in the pagan society around them. Status seeking, self-promotion, a competitive drive for adulation and success, even use of the Christian church as a means of self-promotion and advancement are themes that reoccur throughout the letter. There was a spirit of self-satisfaction and boasting, a spirit of having arrived and not needing anything else (4:6-8). Those without status were being marginalized, neglected and even humiliated in the church's meetings (11:17-34; 12:21-26). A wrong notion of Christian freedom, more like the "freedom" of the surrounding culture, was prevailing in their relationships with each other and toward the wider culture (6:12; 8:9; 10:23).

News of these developments reached Paul through three sources. Chloe's household brought Paul word of the dissension in the church (1:11). The Corinthians themselves wrote Paul a letter raising a number of questions (7:1, 25; 8:1; 12:1; 16:1, 12). Finally, the visit of Stephanas, Fortunatus and Achaicus brought not only refreshment to Paul but likely also further reports as well as possibly the letter from the Corinthians (16:17-18). There is good reason to believe that his information sources for what was going on in Corinth were reliable.

Therefore Paul writes in order to correct the non-Christian behavior that has manifested itself in the life of the community since he left over two years earlier. His strategy is to develop a theology of the cross bringing a new value system that emphasizes self-expending love and respect for the less-esteemed other, especially the other who is unlike ourselves. Paul's own life is held up as a transparent agency of this kind of life, in which the crucified and risen Christ is portrayed in thought, act and utterance. The letter is something of a stopgap measure until Paul can come and spend enough time with the Corinthians to more fully correct the problems (11:34).

We should resist the common error of reading 2 Corinthians back into this letter. The further problems that 2 Corinthians addresses may have some overlap, but that letter should be viewed as addressing new developments. Unfortunately Paul's 1 Corinthians letter does not seem to have met with great success, as he had to make an emergency trip to Corinth shortly afterward and write another "grievous" letter (now lost) before there was encouraging evidence that they were following Paul's instructions.

☐ Social Composition and Theologies of the Corinthian Church

A great deal of discussion has recently taken place over the questions of Paul's own social position and the social composition of the fledgling Corinthian church. Earlier views depending heavily on a particular emphasis on 1:26 described the congregation as poor, slaves and of the lower classes. "Think of what you were when you were called. Not many of you were wise by human standards; not many were influential; not many were of noble birth." In the early 1960s certain studies swung the pendulum back a bit and argued that the Christian community was a socially diverse group. In the 1970s this was pushed even further toward a "radically diverse" social constituency. In the 1990s certain studies emphasized that there were a number of higher-status people in the church such as rhetors, members of the ruling class and Sophists. These, it is thought, though small in number, influenced the church disproportionately. It would seem that the church was made up of people from all the social strata of Corinth: free Roman citizens, merchants, freedmen and women, slaves, educated, many poor, rulers, wealthy land-estate owners, wealthy but lower in status, and benefactors and patrons. As I noted before, they were called by God from a highly competitive, upwardly mobile Roman culture in this bustling city. Included in the composition of the church were Jews, God-fearers and Gentiles.

Paul was probably in the upper 1-2 percent of the population in educational level. Additionally he was an artisan (leatherworker). This could be looked down on in Corinth's society (4:10-13), but it might also be seen as a source of pride of skill. Nevertheless, Paul did not seek status but deliberately practiced downward mobility. This stance of practicing humility and servanthood was contrary to the culture in Corinth and unfortunately also in the church. Paul pointed to Christ crucified in shame and humiliation not only as the God-appointed means of our salvation but also as the model for our individual and community life.

Paul certainly used theology in his response to the problematic behaviors of the Corinthian Christians. But did *they* base their practices explicitly on particular theologies? Or were their lifestyle aberrations due to mere assimilation of values and practices from the surrounding Roman culture of Corinth? Probably more the latter, though in quotes in a few places in the letter they seem to argue from some theological position (6:13; 8:1; 4; 15:12).

Paul on the other hand definitely bases *his* case on a theology of

Christ crucified and raised from the dead. Each problem at Corinth is addressed from a theological premise directly or indirectly related to this theology of the cross whereby Paul promotes a new way of being and living in the world. In this way he weds theology to transformative ethical action. "Thus in the cross there is revaluation of all things in this reality in a lasting and binding way, because the crucified One makes known once and for all only the God who in the depths, in the deathly misery, in lostness and nothingness intends to be God and Savior" (Becker 1993:208).

Paul clearly rejects the Corinthians' interpretation of Christian freedom (6:12; 10:23). Freedom from the law (Gal 2:4; 5:2-3) for the Corinthians meant freedom to eat known idol food in the temple dining rooms and in the presence of those who were conscious of the idol in the food (8:10; 10:28). Also they were free to engage in extramarital sexual contacts with courtesans or prostitutes (6:13-20). In the former case Paul argues that the supposed knowledge of some that idol food is just plain food, since there are no "idols" in the world, is leading to a serious damage of other Christians who eat the food conscious that it is idol food. Their freedom is not under the control of Christian love.

In the latter misuse of freedom Paul argues theologically from an anthropology of the body: our bodies, though perishable now, are the property of God through redemption; they are even now united to the risen Christ. They cannot therefore be united with prostitutes without committing adultery against Christ (6:13-20). Paul's theology of the body is crucial to his rebuke of the Corinthians' misuse of the body. He rejects the dualism that allows them to separate their spiritual relation to Christ from the use of their bodies.

Freedom for Paul, then, is freedom for service to others and the community. Love must have priority over individual desires. Further theological issues are briefly sketched below under "Major Theological Themes."

☐ Integrity and Unifying Theme of the Letter

Three main views of the integrity of the letter may be mentioned. Some have suggested that 1 Corinthians may be stitched together from three separate letters the apostle wrote (e.g., 6:12-20; 10:1-23, etc.). Another view is that Paul wrote the letter in two different sittings: first, after Chloe's report came to him (1—4); second, after the Corinthians' letter and the further report of Stephanas were received (5—16). Both of these views are to be taken seriously as reflecting careful attention to content and style differences in the material, but ultimately they are not persuasive because of lack of agreement on the separate letters—and such theories are really not needed in the light of careful exegesis.

A number of modern scholars have more convincingly argued for the unity of the entire letter (Fee, Hays, Becker, Mitchell, Collins, Thiselton). But precisely how we are to understand the unifying theme is variously understood. Margaret Mitchell argues that the letter should be read as an extended appeal for unity. Anthony Thiselton, while abandoning for the most part his earlier thesis that "realized eschatology" binds everything together, now argues that secularized infiltration into the church of self-promotion, competitive pragmatism, radical pluralism and status elevation through spiritual gifts of the Holy Spirit permeates the letter. Paul's emphasis on grace, the cross and the resurrection provide the antidote for such worldly corruption of the church.

Paul proclaims a "different value system of grace, gifts, the cross and resurrection as divine verdict, criterion, and status bestowal within the new framework of respect and love for the less esteemed 'other.' Glorying in the Lord and receiving status derived from identification with the crucified Christ (1:30-31) lead to a new value system demonstrable in a wide array of life issues" (Thiselton 2000:40). Such a unifying theme binds together what otherwise might look like a series of unrelated topics and issues in the letter.

This commentary utilizes the twenty-seventh edition of the *Novum Testamentum Graece* (Nestle-Aland) as found in the UBS *Greek New Testament,* fourth revised edition, 1993.

□ Paul and "Rhetoric"

Extensive discussions have been published not only on the importance and nature of Greco-Roman rhetoric in Paul's day but also on Paul's letters as forms of rhetorical speech. There is no question that a certain form of Greco-Roman rhetoric played a role in the partisan contentiousness in the Corinthian church. This should not in itself make us discount the more positive use of rhetorical style that Paul himself may have on occasion employed to persuade his audience to follow the truth of the gospel.

But did Paul use rhetorical style at Corinth? The answer must be clearly no, if by "rhetorical style" we mean a cleverly devised presentation designed to emotionally move people to Paul's point of view and ultimately to praise him as a high-status rhetor. But excluding this motive, does Paul follow the pattern of the Greco-Roman declamation in this letter? In response let a balanced viewpoint prevail. Paul wants to present the truth of Christ crucified and risen and its full, transformative implications for the church's behavior and life, not to win a case but to touch the whole person. In doing this Paul does not polarize rhetoric against tradition but instead appeals to Scripture, reason and common custom, all in the light of a theology of the cross presented in a transformative speech-act form. Such speech not only *says* something true but *does* something in the saying. Paul's approach may display elements found in Greco-Roman rhetoric, but we should avoid pressing his argument at every turn into the straitjacket of rhetorical form. I believe Mitchell's treatment falls into this category; as helpful as her treatment is, it finally reduces Paul's thought into an assumed framework. This commentary will utilize insights from such rhetorical studies but will emphasize a historical and exegetical understanding of the text. "Paul sees his apostleship not as *an instrument of power* but as *a call to become a transparent agency* through whom the crucified and raised Christ becomes portrayed through lifestyle, thought and utterance" (Thiselton 2000:45).

☐ Major Theological Themes and Contemporary Relevance

Christ crucified, Christ risen, Christ coming again permeates the whole epistle (1:6; 10:3; 12:12; 15:23; 16:22). This story is central to the authenticity, life and mission of the church. Paul is, however, interested in more than the redemptive significance of Christ for the Christian church. He wants to set forth Christ crucified as a pattern for reevaluation of all things in the culture that may be brought over into the Christian community. Paul calls for a transformation of cultural values in all areas such as leadership, honor-respect, rhetorical expressions, suing in the courts, the eating of idol food in temples and in homes, the meaning and expression of ministries of the Spirit. All is to be brought under the transforming light of Christ crucified and raised for us through God's grace. Something of this sense is captured by Matt Redman (1995) in the gospel song "Once Again":

Jesus Christ, I think upon your sacrifice,
You became nothing, poured out to death.
Many times I've wondered at your gift of life,
And I'm in that place once again.
And I'm in that place once again.

And once again I look upon
The cross where you died,
I'm humbled by your mercy
And I'm broken inside.
Once again I thank you,
Once again I pour out my life.

Apocalyptic Relevance That the "new creation" age has dawned is evident for Paul (1:8; 10:11; 11:26). But there is also the need to remain connected to the present age's realities of bodily life in this world (sex, marriage, temptations to infidelity and idolatry, and the need for bodily discipline) and the mission of the church to the non-Christian world (9:19-23). We have the promise of Christ's coming and of our resurrection to form in us a proper attitude toward our present body (6:14; 15:32-34). The "already, not yet" framework is part of Paul's appeal. We are tempted to live outside the realm of everyday bodily existence in a form of "realized eschatology," but Paul calls us back to earthly life, empowered by the indwelling Holy Spirit and the model of suffering servanthood in Jesus Christ.

The Primacy of Love Paul sees every problem that has arisen in Corinth as related in some way to a failure of authentic Christian love (chap. 13). What is this love? How does it manifest itself? Why is it absolutely essential to the Christian church and its mission in the world (cf. 16:13)?

Gospel and Culture Paul's interface with the effects of the Corinthian culture, both positive and negative, on the life of the Christian community is highly instructive for our own approach to the contemporary cultures we interface with in the modern world. His approach is neither totally conservative nor totally progressive. Paul rejects outright certain features of Corinthian culture (e.g., idolatry, sexual activity outside monogamous heterosexual marriage, competitive status seeking, discriminatory dining practices, party contentions). But, on the other hand, he accepts other cultural practices within the transformative context of the crucified and risen Christ (e.g., Greco-Roman gender markers of hairstyles/coverings, leadership, power and status as transformed by servanthood, boasting but 'in the Lord,' slavery as service to Christ).

☐ Major Background Studies in 1 Corinthians

Below I list the works that I found most helpful in preparing these introductory remarks. In these works the student can go far beyond the brief summary in this introduction. Complete documentation for each can be found in the bibliography at the end of this commentary.

C. K. Barrett 1968; Jürgen Becker 1993; Donald Engels 1990; John H. Kent 1966; Wayne A. Meeks 1983; Jerome Murphy-O'Connor 1983, 1996; Anthony Thiselton 2000; Bruce Winter 2001; Ben Witherington III 1995.

Outline of 1 Corinthians

16:1-24 _____ Final Matters and Conclusion of the Letter

16:1-12 _____ Mutuality and Hospitality

16:13-20 _____ Advice and Greetings

16:21-24 _____ Paul's Postscript in His Own Hand

COMMENTARY

☐ Paul's Introduction to His Letter (1:1-9)

Have you ever tried to find the perfect church that has everything you want and does everything just the way you like? Well, I have tried unsuccessfully for many years. It is said that when Dr. Harry Ironside was pastor of Moody Memorial Church in Chicago, a young woman approached him and said, "I'm looking for a perfect church, and when I find it, I'll join it." He replied, "You can look, but I don't think you'll find one. But if you do, and you join it, it won't be perfect anymore because you will be a part of it!"

While we may not find any perfect churches, we do occasionally find vital churches, congregations that are dynamically alive and maturing in relationship to the triune God and to one another and in mission to outsiders. Many today are searching for deeper meaning in the worship of God and in service than their present church fellowship provides.

In such a quest we need something that is quite rare in our day. We need a solid theology of the church. In 1 Corinthians Paul aids us greatly in building a theology that is wed to and issues in authentic Christian experience and practice.

Paul's Corinthian correspondence was written to a first-century church that had serious problems on a number of fronts. Yet though it was a congregation with prominent warts, a messy group in imminent danger of failure, the church was a divine fellowship (1:9) that Paul was convinced could, under Christ, correct its faults and become a vital, maturing people for God. But would they respond? We will find out at the end of the letter.

As in other introductions to his letters, Paul begins by striking chords that will be crucial to his purpose later in the epistle. Four themes in verses 1-9 resonate throughout the remainder of the letter. First, Paul's authority and divine call as *an apostle of Jesus Christ* is highly significant to his case in all that follows (v. 1). Second, the real position of the Corinthian church is as a separated people, holy before God (*sanctified in Christ Jesus and called to be holy*, v. 2). Third, Paul recognizes the rich bestowal of spiritual gifts on them (vv. 4-7). Fourth, the eschatological note of the return of Christ checks and balances their tendency toward excessive enthusiasm for the present manifestation of spiritual gifts (*as you eagerly wait for our Lord Jesus Christ to be revealed . . . on the day of our Lord Jesus Christ,* vv. 7-8).

In these themes we may find the scriptural background for the historic Nicene claim that the church is characterized essentially as one, holy, universal and apostolic. In our day, as in Paul's, what we believe about the church is crucial to the whole enterprise of Christian mission and discipleship. Yet how neglected a theme it is!

This section has three descriptive functions as it introduces Paul's letter. First, it identifies the author (v. 1). Second, the recipients are addressed (vv. 2-3). Third, Paul offers a lengthy thanksgiving that is quite revealing regarding the true nature of the church (vv. 4-9).

The Author (1:1) Paul follows the ancient form of letters in which A (sender) addresses B (recipient) and concludes with a prayer in the opening sentence (vv. 1-3). The author identifies himself as "Paul." In the book of Acts he is described as a Jewish rabbi who came to believe in Jesus as Messiah and Lord (Acts 8:1-3; 9:1-31; 22:1-21; 26:1-23; Gal

---

1:1 On Paul's name, see introduction. Current opinion on the background of the word *apostle* (*apostolos*) leans toward the Old Testament Jewish sense of a commissioned agent (Hebrew *shaliah*), one who is legally authorized to act as the representative or proxy of another and who carries that person's full authority. More

1:13-15; Phil 3:4-6). Paul's background in Judaism is the most significant influence on his thought and expression beyond his experience of God's forgiveness through Jesus. No serious question has ever been raised about the authorship of this epistle, even by extreme critics.

Paul refers to himself as *called to be an apostle of Christ Jesus by the will of God*. This emphasizes his divine call to be an authoritative representative of Jesus Christ in the same sense of the original twelve apostles. Some at Corinth apparently challenged this calling and thus attempted to make Paul's voice irrelevant (cf. 4:3, 10-20; 9:3).

Sosthenes was apparently well known to the Corinthians. He is probably the same synagogue ruler who was beaten by unbelieving Jews before the Roman governor Gallio on Paul's first visit to the city (Acts 18:17). He is now designated with the common term *brother,* which unites him with the family of God but also distinguishes him from the *apostle,* Paul. Sosthenes may have been the amanuensis (secretary) who wrote the letter (cf. 16:21).

The Recipients (1:2-3) Paul addresses them as *the church of God in Corinth*. What really is the church? Is there a universal church or only particular, local churches? What is the minimal constitutive reality of a genuine particular church? These are extremely important and debatable questions for the modern church. A definitive discussion cannot be undertaken at this point, but what Paul has to say here and below (vv. 4-9) should serve as significant input to any theology of the church that might be framed.

First, Paul emphasizes the church as a divine creation (v. 2, *the church of God*). The Corinthians are first of all God's people because of the divine grace given to them (v. 4, *because of his grace given you in Christ Jesus*). They are united to one another as they are united to Christ. But what is important is that the church is given to us by divine grace. Therefore the church does not arise first of all through human organizational activity. Thus when we think "church" we should first of

specifically, the concept relates to the Old Testament sending convention, in which the term is applied to persons of profound religious and theological significance, such as prophets (Rengstorf 1964:415; Agnew 1986).

all think of divinely called people who belong to God through their faith in Jesus Christ's redeeming work (cf. 15:1-2). This people is gathered for the worship of the triune God. We are God's people. This is what the church is all about. All else is secondary.

This redeemed people is not merely some ideal, mystical entity; it must have visible, concrete manifestation in regions of the empire (Rom 16:16, 23; Col 1:24), as well as in a particular province (*what I told the Galatian churches to do,* 16:1; cf. 16:19; 2 Cor 8:1) or in a particular family home (*Aquila and Priscilla . . . and . . . the church that meets at their house,* 16:19; Rom 16:3-5; Col 4:15; Philem 2). "In other words, the universal church, the church of the living God (I Tim 3:15), which is the body of Christ (Eph 1:22), because Christ is its head (Col 1:18), is manifested, emerges phenomenologically, comes to concrete realization in the various particular churches in which the faithful gather to express their faith, celebrate the presence of the Spirit, and commune with their fellow Christians" (Boff 1986:20). To speak of the church as divine gift *and* empirical reality is to speak of the church as a continuing miracle and at the same time as a place of parking lots, budgets, potluck dinners, heated debates on who will be the next pastor, and so on.

Paul describes further the identity of God's people: they are *sanctified in Christ Jesus and called to be holy* (v. 2). This means that God's people as a group are set apart by God's gift of grace to fulfill his ultimate purposes. *Sanctified* and *holy* are from the same root Greek word that stresses not so much their moral character as their identity as belonging to the triune God and his present and eschatological (future)

1:2 *Called to be holy (hagioi)* is found only once elsewhere, where the NIV translator has given it an alternate but accurate rendering, "called to be saints" (Rom 1:7).

In Christ Jesus occurs 164 times in Paul and has been understood as a sort of participation-communion with Christ or a Christ "mysticism" (Deissmann 1957:140-57). Others have reacted against this sense of Paul's words and would, like Hans Conzelmann, stress the more objective salvation or justification aspect: "'In Christ' thus [in this objective view] means that here, in him and not in me, salvation has taken place: therefore it is true for me" (1969:210). Others have argued for a both-and approach. "Far from divorcing a 'juridical' hermeneutic from a 'participation' hermeneutic, Paul integrates them to protect ontology from disintegrating into realized eschatology and so preserves the apocalyptic perspective of the lordship of Christ" (Beker 1984:275; cf. Sanders 1977:458-61). This latter view is much more in keeping not only with verse 9 but with the diversity of Paul's use of the expression

purposes for the church (cf. Eph 1:9-14; 2:7).

Of course to be identified as God's purchased possession is also to sense a calling to exhibit the Owner's own character and will. Thus all of us are to be in our daily life what God has by grace given to us to be in his sight: pure, holy, saints. Are we conscious of this when we are traveling and meet and talk with strangers?

Just how amazing this statement of our status before God is can be fully appreciated only later, when we see the messy condition of the actual Corinthian congregation, a group that was plagued with divisions, sexual immorality, discrimination, divorce and other sins. Nevertheless, Paul calls them to become more of what they are already *in Christ Jesus*—in communion with him, with his saving work on their behalf and with all who confess his name. The church is pure by divine grace and is in the process of becoming holy like its Lord. We must not forget that we are all persons with sinful pasts. This is part of our story as God's people. A continuing healthy remembrance of this past is a prerequisite to our growth in genuine Christlike holiness (cf. 6:9-11). A good time to remember this is when we take the bread and wine at the Communion table.

Finally, in this commendation the author gives another mark of the true church, its universality: *together with all those everywhere who call on the name of our Lord Jesus Christ—their Lord and ours* (v. 2). We may in passing note two things here for our instruction. First, the main purpose or goal of the church is its relationship with Jesus Christ himself. "For any real renewal of the church to take place, the renewal of

---

elsewhere (cf. 2 Cor 5:19).

Everywhere (*en panti topō,* literally "in every place") is perhaps a reflection of the phrase "in all the places of Israel" (i.e., Jewish meeting places) found in some synagogue inscriptions. Of course there is no evidence at this early period of buildings used exclusively as Christian meeting places. Homes were used for church gatherings (1 Cor 16:19; cf. Rom 16:5). "The phrase gives expression to an idea of the church that is governed by world mission" (Conzelmann 1975:23).

To *call upon the name of the Lord* is an expression derived from the Greek Old Testament (Ps 98:6; Joel 3:5), with *Lord* applied to Jesus. It may therefore have roots in earlier Jewish Christianity and carry significant christological overtones of deity. Given that it is used to identify "Christians" (Acts 9:14, 21; 2 Tim 2:22), there is no reason to deny that *those . . . who call upon the name of the Lord* includes their prayers as well as their trust in and acclamation of Jesus as Lord (contra Conzelmann 1975:23).

men's commitment to Christ and knowledge of him is of first priority" (Clark 1972:104). Second, this deepening relationship to Jesus is inseparably linked to our recognition of and fellowship with the whole community of God's people—*all those everywhere.*

For us today not only geographical diversity but ethnic, national, economic and cultural plurality worldwide are involved in this recognition. But beyond this we are also a part of a universal church that is manifested in particular and different structural and traditional ways of calling *on the name of our Lord Jesus Christ.* We must feel a sense of oneness with every other confessing and worshiping believer in Christ, regardless of their identification with our group. God's rays of grace are diffused as in a prism through many different but complementary channels. It is not our national origin or denominational sameness but our embracing of Christ's lordship *(their Lord and ours)* that is our true identity and the basis of our universal unity as God's people.

If we are together sanctified in Christ, how can we be strangers or enemies to one another? Has not the time come for us to call for a broadly based ecumenical fellowship with all those who confess and worship Jesus as Lord? My true identity as a Christian is valid only in relation to the other who is different from me (or my tradition). This "other" has gifts that I both lack and need to mature in Christ. "The time is ripe for a new evangelical alliance, embracing Bible believing Christians from all branches of Christendom" (Bloesch 2004). I am continually reminded in my travels abroad—to India, Europe, the Mideast, England and elsewhere—of how small is the Christian world and how rich is our common faith in Christ, regardless of our different cultural and racial backgrounds.

Finally Paul greets them with a familiar formula, *Grace and peace to you from God our Father and the Lord Jesus Christ* (v. 3). *Grace (charis)* was customarily used in Greek letter addresses, whereas *peace (shalom)* was and is the common greeting among Semitic peoples (cf. Num 6:24-26). Paul enriches these standard cultural terms with transformed Christian significance.

The Thanksgiving (1:4-9) Another common part of the beginning of ancient letters was the *proemium* or preface. Paul, following secular style, phrases the preface as he often does, in the form of a thanksgiving (cf. Rom 1:8-9; Phil 1:3-6; 1 Thess 1:2-3; 2 Thess 1:3-4; 2 Tim 1:3-7; Philem 4-6). It is especially interesting to consider how Paul transforms the standard thanksgiving for a Christian purpose and applies it to the immediate context of the Corinthian church and its needs. If we think of 1 Corinthians 1:2-3 as a description of what the church *is* by God's calling, we may see verses 4-8 as a brief statement of what the church *has* by God's grace, followed by what the church exists *for* by God's faithfulness (v. 9).

Paul's joy over what God was doing among the Corinthians is itself an amazing testimony to the apostle's maturity. He first of all looks beyond the problems and his criticisms to the genuine evidence of God's grace at work among them. Such an approach is reminiscent of the words of Jesus to the seven churches in Asia. In five churches there were problems, but in all except one case the Lord begins with genuine commendation before proceeding to criticism (Rev 2—3).

As a young man in theological training I was deeply impressed by the counsel of Joe Blinco of the Billy Graham Evangelistic Association regarding how to criticize constructively, avoiding the cynical type of criticism often leveled at Billy Graham. "First of all," he said, "stand back in awe of the working of God. Then, offer suggestions on how certain things should be changed." This seems to be Paul's approach. Before he administers his somewhat harsh words of correction, he genuinely compliments them "so that the Corinthians may willingly accept and drink down the cup of saving medicine, its rim being coated with sugar" (Colet 1985:75).

He gives thanks for the grace of God given to them, especially as seen in the wealth of spiritual gifts they had received in Christ. Yet this wealth, rich as it was, was only a foretaste of the fullness to be experienced at the revelation of Jesus in his second coming. The same Christ will strengthen them in their daily lives until that day. All this will occur not because of the Corinthians' proud achievements but because of God's covenant faithfulness that has brought them into a shared relationship with Christ.

Paul is continually thankful to God because of the divine *grace given you in Christ Jesus* (v. 4). *Grace* is a favorite word of Paul in all his letters (100 times), especially in Romans (24 times), Ephesians (12 times) and the two Corinthian epistles (28 times). *Grace* is Paul's word for God's free, unmerited, saving action toward us in Jesus Christ. When he wants to stress that salvation arises from God's initiative and not from human achievement, he uses the word *grace* (cf. Rom 11:6). Interchangeable with "gift" in some contexts (1 Cor 16:3; cf. Rom 3:24), the word also refers to God's enabling power or gifts to us for serving him (1 Cor 3:10; 12:9; cf. Rom 12:3, 6; 15:15). That Paul has this further aspect of grace in mind is evident in the following verses.

In light of the Corinthians' tendencies toward pride in spiritual gifts, they are reminded that they were *enriched* (made rich, cf. Rom 2:4; 11:33; Phil 4:19) *in him* (Christ, v. 5). *Knowledge* and *speaking* (eloquence) were especially prized gifts for some in the congregation (cf. 1 Cor 8:1-11; 12:8; 13:2, 8; etc.). Paul acknowledges the legitimacy and value of these gifts but only as they are grounded "in Christ." Later he will deal with their abuse.

Thus the Corinthians' genuine response to the testimony of Paul about Christ was *confirmed* (*keep you strong* in v. 8 is the same Greek word) among them by the gifts of the Holy Spirit that they received (v. 6). Perhaps this should lead us to put more emphasis than many do on the significance of spiritual gifts properly expressed, as evidence not only of individual response to Christ's gospel but also of a community's heartfelt embrace of the lordship of Christ. This would shift our focus away from individual accomplishments to service as the true evidence of spiritual maturity in Christ.

Paul further states negatively what he has just affirmed in verses 4-6: *Therefore you do not lack any spiritual gift* (v. 7). This is an amazing testimony to God's grace. All that was available to a people from God was available to the Corinthians. Lacking no possible manifestation of the Spirit, richly blessed with all manner of the Spirit's working, they nevertheless were arrogant, morally lax, divided and unbalanced in the exercise of and preference for the expression of the spiritual gifts. Possessing God's rich working is no guarantee that the goal of such gifts,

---

1:8 *To the end* (*heōs telous*) could mean "totally" or "completely" (cf. 2 Cor 1:13). But most translators and commentators feel that here the sense given in the NIV is correct

namely Christlikeness in love, will be realized. It may reasonably be said that the troubles in Corinth were due not to a deficiency of gifts but to a lack of proportion and balance in valuing and using them (Barrett 1968:38).

Somewhat abruptly Paul introduces a clear reference to the second coming of Jesus: *as you eagerly wait* (cf. Rom 8:23) *for our Lord Jesus Christ to be revealed* (v. 7). There are three eschatological terms in verses 7-8 which all point to the same event. First, *to be revealed (apokalypsis)*, is a Pauline expression for Jesus' return to the earth (2 Thess 1:7), as are the parallel terms *the day* or *the day of our Lord Jesus Christ* (v. 8; cf. 2 Cor 1:14; Phil 1:6, 10; 2:16), and *the end* (v. 8; cf. 1 Cor 15:24; also Mt 10:22; Lk 21:9; Rev 2:26). More frequent in Paul are the terms *manifestation (epiphaneia,* 1 Tim 6:14; 2 Tim 4:1; Titus 2:13), and *coming (parousia,* 15:23; 1 Thess 2:19; 3:13; 4:15; 5:23; 2 Thess 2:1, 8). While all Bible scholars are not agreed, it is difficult to argue against the conclusion that all these terms are equivalent and together refer with different emphases to the one event of the Lord's return to the world.

But why refer to this event here? No doubt to bring further balance to a defective view of God's kingdom present at Corinth. Throughout the letter, but especially at 4:8, this emphasis on the present realization of the future kingdom of God (realized eschatology) surfaces. Thus promise of the second coming not only encourages persecuted and suffering Christians, it also checks excessive enthusiasm for spiritual gifts and blessings in the present. Only the return of Christ will bring into the world the fullness of redemption (13:10). If according to Corinthian theology all is realized now, why *wait eagerly* for the Lord's return? Those of us today who, like the ancient Corinthians, are tempted toward a health-, wealth- and success-oriented Christianity need to take seriously Paul's point about expecting Christ's return. This emphasis may be especially significant in a culture that has coined the term "dinks" for a growing group of young couples (*d*ouble *i*ncome, *n*o *k*ids).

and that Paul substitutes the less common *heōs telous* for the common *eis telous*.

Finally, the thought of blamelessness at the Lord's coming leads Paul to stress once again the note of God's grace by calling attention to his faithfulness, which is the basis for their existence as those divinely called into *fellowship* with the Son of God (v. 9). The Corinthians' confidence, despite their shortcomings, is to rest not in their own faithfulness and successes but in God's covenant loyalty and love that apart from their deeds has called them into participation with Christ.

In the Johannine understanding, fellowship is first of all association with Christ and then a sharing in or sharing with the people of God (1 Jn 1:3, 6-7). But it is difficult to get church community from Paul's use of the word (cf. 2 Cor 13:13; 8:4; 9:13; Gal 2:9; Phil 1:5; 2:1; 3:10; Philem 6). Instead he wants to stress Christ-centeredness.

The following summary of verses 1-9 from the pen of an early-twentieth-century expositor is superb.

As we look back over the introduction, it is the name of Christ that gives unity and meaning to every sentence. Nine times in the nine short verses does this name appear. To be his apostle, Paul has been called; in fellowship with him believers are sanctified, as by calling upon him they are saved; in him, as with God the Father, grace and peace find their source; by him are bestowed the spiritual gifts which confirm the testimony of Paul and equip his fellow Christians for life and service; his return is the center of their hopes; the day of that reappearing will be the consummation of their joy; participation in his life is the essence of their experience, the explanation of their character, the assurance of their destiny. Surely, to those who are members of his Church, Christ should become increasingly all in all. (Erdman 1928:21)

☐ The Problem of Factions: Putting Clergy and Congregation in Their Place (1:10—4:21)

Divisions in the church are always sad, but perhaps they are saddest when they arise out of conflicting loyalties to faithful servants of God. Paul himself faced this kind of problem in Corinth, where various factions within the church claimed loyalty to Paul, Apollos, Cephas and even Christ. Let us look closely at how he handled this situation to see if there are insights we can gain for today.

After the brief introduction (1:1-9), Paul now turns to one of the major problems among several reported informally to him by *Chloe's household* (v. 11), the problem of factionalism within the congregation. The section is lengthy (1:10—4:21) and has been the focus of numerous discussions. Why were there divisions in the church? What were the disagreements about? What was the root of the problem? What difference did it make anyway? How does Paul go about correcting the problem? Is there any similarity to discords and divisions found today in the local or worldwide church?

Anyone who has gone through a church split, as I have, knows the pain and brokenness that result for individuals, families and children. All testify to the loss of the peace of the congregation, not to mention the damage outwardly to the testimony of the church of Christ. Divisive cliques and factionalism can break up the strongest and best Christian ministries and institutions. Paul treated the issue quite seriously, and we need his emphasis and perspective as we face similar threats today, not only to specific local churches but to the worldwide Christian body.

We may rightly object that until very recently efforts toward unity in the worldwide church have been led by theological modernists; we conservatives in general have been reluctant to get involved in ecumenical dialogue. Instead we have divided ourselves more and more over theological trivia, personality preferences, and political and social ethical agendas. Paul's treatise on factionalism (1:10—4:21) is the best remedy the contemporary church has for this insidious malady with its many faces. But it is important first to understand as best we can the exact nature of the problem at Corinth, as well as Paul's proposed corrective, lest we simply read our own problems of division (such as denominationalism) into the statements of Paul. Why is ecumenism so important? Is not a healthy, biblical ecumenism essential to the church's renewal? Is not unity necessary so that God's purposes may take precedence over our own petty differences?

Charles H. Talbert offers a helpful overall summary of this section of the letter (1987:10-11; cf. Dahl 1977:40-61). First Corinthians 1:1—4:21 has a preparatory function. It both defends Paul's authority as the founder and father of the whole church at Corinth and calls the believers to emulate him. Further, it lays a foundation for the answers to be given to many of the issues raised later in the letter from the church.

In 1 Corinthians Paul answers an official letter with six questions (1:7, 25; 8:1; 12:1; 16:1, 12) brought to him by the delegation of Stephanas, Fortunatus and Achaicus (16:17). Before he can answer their questions he must deal with other information that had come to him informally through *Chloe's household* (1:11, probably through her slaves). They reported that there were rivalries or factious parties in the church, caused by boastful, exclusive attachments to various preachers (1:12; 3:21; 4:6; cf. 11:18).

Some Christians at Corinth seem to be outright opposed to asking Paul anything (4:18-21), citing his inadequacy (he didn't teach us any hidden wisdom and is therefore an unfaithful steward of God's mysteries, 2:6; 3:1-4; 4:2) and their own independence (2:15-16; 4:15, 19-20) based perhaps on their overrealized eschatology (4:8-13). Given this unofficial information, Paul begins his letter with an appeal to unity that has to include a rehearsal of his personal apostolic authority as well as the theological underpinnings for his response to their six questions.

Paul's reminder of his authority in the Corinthian church includes the following points.

1. God by his own will has called me to be an apostle (1:1).

2. The confirmation of my preaching is neither in my clever, sophistic speech nor in my status and wisdom, but in the power of God that was evidenced when I preached the gospel to you (1:6; 2:1, 4-5).

3. My failure to teach you secret wisdom (about spiritual gifts, 2:12) was not due to any unfaithfulness as an assistant to Christ (4:1-3) but to your own immaturity (3:1-4).

4. All preachers, missionaries and Christian teachers are to be viewed as equal (3:8), necessary in God's plan, each with a different task assigned by the Lord (3:5-15). It is wrong to exalt and boastfully favor one of Christ's assistants over against another (4:6).

5. Nevertheless, as the one who founded the church at Corinth, I am your spiritual parent, and you should pattern you life after mine (4:15-16).

6. As an agent of God's kingdom, I operate with God's power, not

with empty words. Those who arrogantly oppose me will have to face this divine power when I come to Corinth (4:18-21).

Paul's theological foundation for most of what will follow is twofold. First, he teaches a theology of the cross. His view involves an emphasis on God's power and wisdom as crucially revealed in the crucifixion of Christ Jesus, over against all forms of human wisdom and strength (1:17-25; 2:1-2). The cross metaphor also focuses on the kind of discipleship the cross demands from followers of Jesus (4:9-12; cf. Gal 2:20). For Paul, the whole understanding of Christian existence and experience is grounded in the fate of the crucified Christ. "The full force of Paul's insights is missed if we interpret him as teaching that we can have life *despite* death and strength *despite* weakness: for Paul, the remarkable meaning of the enigma of the cross is that life comes *through* death and strength *through* weakness" (McGrath 1988:30). This lesson for the whole church has been signally evidenced by the long list of the martyrs of the church, including many in our own day.

Second, closely tied to this cross theology is Paul's eschatological reservation or qualification. In 4:8-13 and occasionally elsewhere he speaks of the Corinthians' overrealized eschatology. They were behaving as if the age to come were already consummated and the full power of the resurrection life had already broken into the existence of the believer. By emphasizing the centrality of the cross, Paul draws attention to the dialectic of the cross and the resurrection/second coming in Christian experience: there is a tension between the "now" of the Corinthians' enthusiasm and the "not yet" of the resurrection/second coming (1:7; 4:5).

The Corinthian Christians (and many today!) live as though they were already in the age to come beyond the resurrection—beyond suffering, beyond tragedy, beyond poverty, beyond hard times. The apostles live within the limits of the present evil age, while the Corinthian "kings" are ignorant that the glory of the church and its leaders is, like the glory of Christ himself, veiled behind weakness and sufferings.

Any serious attempt to understand Paul's thought in 1:10—4:21 must somewhere deal with (1) the specific words he uses to describe the problem, (2) the slogans the Corinthians were using, (3) the sense and the reason for the emphasis on wisdom, and (4) the particular way

Paul uses certain expressions such as "spiritual" *(pneumatikoi)* and "the man without the Spirit" *(psychikos)*. Rather than break these out as a separate unit for discussion, here it may be better to treat them in the order in which they come up in the text itself.

The Problem and Paul's Appeal (1:10-13) Paul appeals directly to the whole church for unity with a three-pronged challenge: (1) *that all of you agree,* (2) *that there may be no divisions among you* and (3) *that you may be perfectly united in mind and thought* (v. 10). *Appeal* (request, plead) words usually come later in Paul's letters, after he has set forth his doctrinal teaching (e.g., Rom 12:1; Eph 4:1; Phil 4:2), but in 1 Corinthians two appeals come early (1:10; 4:16; cf. 16:15). This may suggest to us that the problem at Corinth was not basically theological but ethical (Baird 1964:39). Paul's appeal for unity is strengthened by a reference to the authority of Jesus: *I appeal to you, brothers, in the name of the Lord Jesus Christ, that all of you agree with one another* (literally, that you all say the same thing). This seems to point to the divisive sloganeering mentioned later (v. 12).

The second appeal includes the word *divisions* (*schismata,* a tear, crack or split), which occurs only in this epistle in the New Testament, though the verbal form occurs elsewhere and has the sense of groups divided by strongly held differences of opinion (Acts 14:4, 23:7). In 1 Corinthians the noun also occurs in 11:18, of divisions among them at the Lord's Supper. And it appears in 12:25, of the absence of divisions among bodily members; this harmonious functioning comes about because of God's creative wisdom in complementing the various parts so that there is no jealousy but instead mutual care for one another. Both these latter passages are instructive as to the nature of the problem at Corinth and the more exact sense of the word *divisions.*

Scholar L. L. Welborn has pointed in another direction. He extensively documents the ancient political use of the same word for a "cleft in political consciousness" or "civil strife" and cites *1 Clement* as a con-

---

1:10 *In the name of our Lord Jesus Christ* (NIV) should be rendered "through *[dia,* not *en]* the name . . ." The use of this preposition *(dia)* with "the name of Christ" occurs

firmation of this sense at Corinth. Clement asks the Corinthians, "Why are there quarrels and anger and dissension and divisions *[schismata]* and war among you?" (46:5). "The terms with which *schisma* is associated make it clear that it is neither a religious heresy nor a harmless clique that the author has in mind, but factions engaged in a struggle for power" (1987:87).

In 1 Corinthians 3:3 Paul combines "jealousy" and "quarreling" ("hot debate") to describe the spiritual source of divisions. Both words are used in the secular literature of the time to refer to bitter, destructive party rivalries that precipitate civil disorder *(stasis)*. Assuming this to be a correct association, what we have then at Corinth is a case of the world-spirit creeping into the church and threatening to destroy it as an expression of the unity of Christ's body (cf. 3:16-17). North American evangelicals especially face this problem in their divisions over doctrinal differences and the co-opting of Christian unity by political party allegiances.

The third part of 1:10 appeals further: *and that you may be perfectly united in mind and thought.* This is a variation of the thought in the first part of the verse. *Perfectly united* translates a word used literally elsewhere for "mending nets" (Mk 1:19) and metaphorically in a secular usage for putting the social order back together after a revolution (Herodotus 5.28; see Barrett 1968:42). *Mind* and *thought* (judgment, opinion) are very close in meaning. Both stress the need for thinking that is united and Christian in its orientation. Paul appeals for a type of mindset that opposes factionalism, seeks Christ's purposes and is thus truly spiritual (1 Cor 2:16—3:4; cf. Rom 12:2). It is not necessary to infer from this that the factions represented theological divisions. The roots of the divisions had more to do with socioeconomic background, personality and status than with doctrine, as the following verse indicates.

The bases for Paul's appeal are two: (1) the report from *Chloe's household* (v. 11), and (2) three rhetorical questions that expose the non-Christian character of the behavior in Corinth (v. 13). Before bearing down further on the problem, Paul unites the believers with the ad-

---

only here, to emphasize the origin of Paul's apostolic authority. Otherwise *en* is normally used (1 Cor 5:4; 6:11; Eph 5:20; Phil 2:10; 2 Thess 3:6).

dress *My brothers* (v. 11, which TNIV renders correctly as "My brothers and sisters").

Chloe's household brought a report that made clear to Paul that *quarrels* (*erides,* "bitter disputes") were present in Corinth. Chloe is a prominent woman, no doubt known to the Corinthians but unknown to us beyond this mention. Who then makes up her household? They could be family members, but then why not use the father's name, as Paul does elsewhere (Rom 16:10-11)? More likely the reference is to the wider concept of household, which includes servants and slaves (freedpersons). "If Chloe's people were representatives of the lower classes, it would be understandable that Paul, in responding to their report, should stress that in Corinth there are not many who are wise, powerful, or of noble birth" (1:26; Theissen 1982:94).

In other cases of the use of the Pauline word *quarrels* ("discords") found in the New Testament there is an explicit connection with the non-Christian, self-centered, sinful flesh (Rom 1:29; 13:13; 1 Cor 3:3; 2 Cor 12:20; Gal 5:20, etc.). "*Erides* refers to battle strife in the *Iliad,* and *contention* or *rivalry* in the *Odyssey*" (Baird 1964:30).

Paul now explains more exactly in verse 12 what he meant when he used the word *quarrels.* He is not talking about private, individual disputes but about party factions, the group practice of rallying around preferred preachers and denigrating or outright rejecting all others. Paul captures this in the watchwords or slogans the Corinthians used. *One of you says, "I follow" [I am of] Paul"; another, "I follow Apollos"; another, "I follow Cephas" [or Peter]; still another, "I follow Christ."* Scholars now tend to agree that this does not point to actual separate groups at Corinth, each with different doctrines and practices, but to

---

1:12 *I follow Christ.* Opinion has varied on the nature of this faction. If we discount the marginal gloss view (all manuscripts of 1 Corinthians have these words), and the view that this group represents Paul's true emphasis, we are left with several options. Earlier expositors saw in these people Judaists or Jewish Christians who were opposed to Paul, while some recent interpreters to the contrary regard them as "hyper-Pauline enthusiasts," Gnostics who identify their own self with Christ (Schmithals 1971:121). Margaret Mitchell sees the term as equivalent to the positive expression in 3:23, "and you are of Christ," and therefore as an expression of Paul's true identity: all of you belong to particular groups; I belong to Christ (1991:83 n. 101). Johannes Munck has argued that there were no parties as such but merely cliques within the one congregation. There is no suggestion that the preachers named were themselves the instigators, encouragers or actual leaders of these factions. The leaders were lionized by the factions at Corinth. The fault appears to lie solely with the worldly attitudes of some in the church.

The formal derivation of these slogans seems to clearly reflect the principle behind the formation of ancient political parties. Unlike modern Western political parties, in which individuals represent groups or parties and their platforms and interests, the ancients selected an individual and rallied their support to serve his interests. "Political parties thus took the form of groups of clients and personal adherents pledged to particular leaders" (Welborn 1987:91-92). Two examples illuminate the Corinthian situation.

The first, which shows the positive counterpart of the fractious behavior Paul parodies in 1:12, comes from the orator Aelius Aristides' speech to the Rhodians: "When we visited you, we saw you even in the assembly using not only a single voice, but if I may say so, for the most part even a single word. For often it was enough for you to exclaim, 'Well said!' and 'Crown him!' and such like, with the name of the speaker" (*Oration* 24.56). But it is Dio Chrysostom's pointed account of the conduct of his fellow Prusans at their common gatherings that most recalls Paul's ironic report of discordant voices in the Christian assembly. The orator describes "the shouts of the partisans, uttered in hatred and abuse, . . . outbursts which are not for reasonable men or temperate cities, but rather for those who, . . . as Homer says, 'In rage to midassembly go, and quarrel with one another as their anger bids'" (*Oration* 4.28-29; see also 39.4; Welborn 1987:93). At Corinth the groups

---

harmless squabbles (cited by Conzelmann 1975:34). Another view is that Paul is using irony. By applying the same Corinthian logic to Christ, Paul would be seeking to show the absurdity of their party spirit (Schrage 1991:142-48). While not certain, however, the best explanation sees the "Christ followers" as another real faction, perhaps united in the illusion that they do not need any human leader. Whereas some overvalued certain ministers, this group undervalued the ministry as a whole. Neither a Gnostic-influenced group nor a radical Jewish-Christian party best explains the evidence. Rather these "represent the slogan of hyper spiritual enthusiasts who saw no need for any human leader" (Thiselton 1978:513-14).

were "personality cults," according to the careful study of Andrew Clarke (1993:89-105).

The most curious slogan is the last, *I follow Christ*. This sounds like a group of orthodox spiritual people with the correct emphasis. Why does Paul include them also? While some have argued that these represent early Gnostics, or are exponents of a radically Jewish Christianity, or an ironic touch by Paul, they are in all probability "hyper-spiritual enthusiasts who see no need for any human leader" (Thiselton 1978:514; 2000:133). F. C. Baur correctly saw the connection with this faction and Paul's admonition to the same type of spirit if not the same faction in his second epistle to Corinth: "If anyone is confident that he belongs to Christ, he should consider again that we belong to Christ just as much as he" (2 Cor 10:7; cited by Dahl 1977:41). While their leader was rightly Christ, they affirmed this allegiance in the same exclusive, proud, fleshly spirit that was at the root of those who elevated certain merely human leaders. And they were still not following the *crucified* Christ (1 Cor 1:17-25).

Apollos was an Alexandrian Jew who, after embracing Christ as his Lord and Messiah, distinguished himself by his mastery of the Scriptures as a learned exegete as well as his enthusiasm for clear teaching about Jesus. To Jewish skeptics he set forth a powerful case from the Bible for Jesus' claim to be the Messiah (Acts 18:24-28). Otherwise we know little of him (cf. 1 Cor 16:12; Acts 19:1; Tit 3:13).

Cephas (Aramaic "rock"; Greek *Petros,* "rock") is the name Paul almost always uses for Peter (1 Cor 1:12; 3:22; 9:5; 15:5; Gal 1:18; 2:9, 11, 14; cf. Jn 1:42). He was one of the original twelve Palestinian Jewish apostles of Christ, one who was called especially to the evangelism of his Jewish people (Gal 2:7-8). Some have suggested that since the factions at Corinth were apparently determined by baptism (1 Cor 1:14-17), Peter must have visited the church at some point after its founding. But this is mere conjecture. Besides, the Christ party at Corinth could

---

1:13 *Is Christ divided?* The NIV correctly follows the reading of the more diverse and numerically larger number of New Testament manuscripts. The alternate reading supported by p[46] and a few other Greek manuscripts and versions is *mē memeristai,* "Christ is not divided, is he?" (expecting a negative answer).

not have been baptized by Jesus himself. Furthermore, Paul mentions only two individuals by name plus a handful of Stephanas's "household" that he himself baptized (vv. 14-15). This would make a very small Paul following if all members of a faction had to have been baptized by their leader.

We are on the best track if we do not press the factions into specific doctrinal or lifestyle positions suggested in statements later in the letter. They may have been divided among these lines, but we have no way of knowing this from the text of 1 Corinthians. Paul addresses the church as a whole throughout, not the separate parties. He turns now to expose of the non-Christian attitudes displayed in the Corinthians' political sloganeering.

Three rhetorical questions in verse 13 form the second basis for Paul's appeal for unity: *Is Christ divided? Was Paul crucified for you? Were you baptized into the name of Paul?* (v. 13). Further hints about the causes and nature of the bickering at Corinth are disclosed in these questions and in Paul's response. The answers are in reverse order to the questions, in a pattern ABC/C'B'A'. The answers to the three questions contain Paul's solution to the devastating problem he believes exists in the church at Corinth.

Paul's First Response to the Problem of Factions: The Significance of Baptism (1:14-17) The last question from verse 13 is answered first. The response focuses on the facts regarding who Paul baptized and the significance of the rite. *Were you baptized into the name of Paul?* gently chides the Corinthians, reminding them that they were baptized into the name of Jesus to be *his* disciples, not Paul's followers (cf. Acts 18:8). Paul recalls personally baptizing only *Crispus and Gaius* (v. 14) and the *household* (possibly family but probably slaves) *of Stephanas.*

Acts records that Crispus, the synagogue ruler, and his whole house-

---

1:16 *Yes, I also baptized the household of Stephanas.* Paul's lapse of memory can be explained as due to the presence of Stephanas with him when he writes (Dahl 1977:50).

hold "believed in the Lord" as a result of Paul's preaching on his first visit to Corinth on his second missionary journey (Acts 18:8). We may assume that he was a man of wealth and status in the community because of his position in the synagogue and the reference to his extended household. We know nothing else of him.

Gaius was apparently wealthy and of high social status (a patron?), since not only did Paul write the letter to the Romans from his house, but "the whole church" (not just the smaller house congregations) met in his home in Corinth (Rom 16:23). The combined group was large (Acts 18:10), perhaps as many as one hundred if this was a villa (Snyder 1991:248-49). He may also be the same individual at Corinth referred to as "Titius Justus," who with two names was probably a Roman citizen (Acts 18:7). "Since 'Titius' is a Roman nomen (i.e., *gens* name), the person is likely to have had also a praenomen, which might easily have been Gaius" (Cranfield 1979: 807). It is doubtful that the other references to Gaius in Acts refer to the Gaius from Corinth (Acts 19:29; 20:4). Likewise we may discount the Gaius in 3 John 1.

Paul later identifies Stephanas's household as the "first converts in Achaia" and as having "devoted themselves to the service of the saints"; therefore they were worthy of the church's submission to their leadership (1 Cor 16:15-16). Stephanas himself was also present in Ephesus as a member of the delegation from Corinth (16:17).

Paul's main point in these verses (1:14-16) is to defuse the bickering spirit among the factions by denying that the gospel he preached required people to be baptized in his name or in any way declare themselves to be his followers. However, the fact that he did baptize socially prominent persons helps us to appreciate the role such individuals (the "not many . . . influential" of v. 26) can have in the work of Christ. Persons of wealth and status who use their property and influence to aid the work of the gospel are to be honored and encouraged for their provisions and labor.

Finally Paul states that *Christ did not send me to baptize, but to*

1:17 "Wisdom" or "wise" occurs thirty-four times in Paul's letters; twenty-eight are in 1 Corinthians, twenty-six in chapters 1-3. "Oh, if the crucified Jesus should come

preach the gospel (v. 17). At first this seems to sever the ordinance of baptism from the gospel and to devalue baptism. But the context suggests that Paul's point is that his calling or commission as an apostle was not to baptize people but to preach the gospel message to the Gentiles (Gal 1:16). Others can baptize the repentant, but Paul must preach the crucified Christ. Therefore even those who like Crispus and Gaius could claim a special loyalty to Paul, because his own hand had baptized them, have no claim at all, much less those he had not baptized who were claiming, *I follow Paul*. Paul's emphasis was not on baptism but on the cross of Christ.

This corrective truth encourages us to avoid overemphasizing baptism in God's economy in comparison to proclamation of the gospel message. Baptism has an important place in our response and expression of our faith. But it must not take precedence over the message of the gospel or be administered in a manner that enlists people to follow a particular person or faction within the diverse expressions of the church.

Not with words of human wisdom ["clever rhetoric," "sophisticated speech"], *lest the cross of Christ be emptied of its power* (v. 17). Here we are introduced for the first time to the Corinthians' infatuation with *wisdom* and speech artistry. There have been considerable scholarly discussions of the origin and nature of this sophisticated speech and its connection to the problems at Corinth that Paul addresses throughout the letter and in particular to the issue of factions or parties in the church. I have mentioned something of this discussion in the introduction. Unlike our culture, the Romans were interested in rhetorical skill and performances of persuasion in speeches. Certain orators were able to win wide acclaim and status in the ancient world. Perhaps more like our pop music stars of today, such orators won large followings, moving them emotionally to embrace their views when they spoke with such exquisite eloquence.

This cultural appetite for speech eloquence combined with an intense desire, also fostered by the social structure, to improve one's status or honor in the eyes of others. It was desirable to advance through

into our heart, how quickly and sufficiently learned should we be" (Thomas à Kempis *Imitation of Christ* 25.6).

stages or levels of new knowledge acquisition, associated with reveling in the eloquence of speech forms, argument and emotional effect generated by orators who brought such "wisdom."

But how does this empty the cross of its power? "If everything rests on human cleverness, sophistication, or achievement, the cross of Christ no longer functions as that which subverts and cuts across all distinctions of race, class, gender, and status to make room for divine grace alone as sheer unconditional gift. . . . To treat the gospel of the cross of Christ as a vehicle for promoting self-esteem, self-fulfillment, and self-assertion turns it upside down and 'empties' it of all that it offers and demands" (Thiselton 2000:145-46). The following section of Paul's letter (1:18—2:5) takes up this emphasis on the vanity of self-promotion through rhetoric and wisdom achievement without the cross and expands on its fallacies from several angles.

Paul's Second Response to Factions: Christ Crucified for You (1:18—2:5)

Corporations spend huge sums of money designing logos. Advertising agencies are hired to conceive a logo which will express the qualities that the corporation wants to be associated with it in the public mind. These are usually qualities such as stability, reliability, progressiveness, or aggressiveness. This design will appear on their letterheads, on their products, and be prominently displayed at their national and local headquarters. . . .

An organization which chose as its logo a hangman's noose, a firing squad, a gas chamber or an electric chair would accordingly seem to have taken leave of its senses. It would be sheer madness to choose an instrument of execution as a symbol of an organization. . . .

And yet exactly such a symbol is universally recognized as the logo of Christianity. Christians are baptized with the sign of the cross. Churches and other places of meeting do not merely include a cross, they are often built in the shape of a cross. Many Christians make the sign of the cross in times of danger or anxiety.

The graves of Christians are marked with crosses. (McGrath 1992:115-16)

For Paul the cross is the ground and criterion of Christian and apostolic identity. Not only are its saving benefits as the road to life and well-being jeopardized, but the cross's transformative reshaping of our identity is rendered ineffective when the cross is not central or is misunderstood or misapplied. This section of Paul's letter suggests that Christians were seeking to promote their own status inside the Christian community, and possibly outside as well, by introducing into the church the worldly wisdom of speech eloquence and personal success. More than that, they saw the gospel of Christ and their Christian leaders as the means for their own advancement and "boasting"!

Paul aims to correct this fatal misunderstanding with an extended meditation on the meaning of the cross in order to show that prideful confidence in the achievement of human wisdom is antithetical to the logic of the cross (1:18—2:5). He asks how the gospel of Christ can be a form of worldly wisdom when (1) its message concerns a crucified Christ (1:18-25), (2) the gospel's recipients at Corinth were far from the elite, "wise" or influential of the society (1:26-31), and (3) Paul's own preaching at Corinth was not characterized by cleverness designed to impress an audience (2:1-5).

The decisive act of God in Christ's death has brought about a reversal of the world's values concerning status, success, self-achievement and boasting. The cross confounds all human wisdom and redefines wisdom in a new and paradoxical way. Therefore our whole way of seeing the world is turned upside down. The cross becomes the lens for an epistemological revolution, a conversion of the imagination. For anyone who grasps the paradoxical logic of this text, the world can never look the same (Hays).

God's Foolishness and Human Wisdom (1:18-25) Paul's unstated question for the Corinthians would go something like this. How can the gospel of Christ be a form of worldly *wisdom* when it proclaims (*message*, v. 18) a *crucified* leader, Jesus? Isn't such a proclamation *foolishness* in terms of the world's evaluation of what counts for wisdom and knowledge? Paul argues that in fact God has decided to decisively reject the *wisdom of the world* (those of status, political power, oratorical skill) and instead to set forth his own wisdom in the proclamation of the crucified Messiah. By doing what appears from the world's viewpoint to be foolishness, God has dethroned human wisdom, and through the proclamation of the crucified Jesus he has been pleased *to save those who believe.*

The *message of the cross is foolishness to those who are perishing* (on the way to ruin, or as in the words of a movie, "on the road to perdition"), *but to us who are being saved* (on the road to being saved) *it is the power of God* (v. 18). The proclamation of the gospel breaks into the world and divides all people into two groups: those on the road to perdition and those on the road to salvation. This captures the salvific reality of the crucified Christ.

The power of God for those *being saved* (through faith, v. 21) gives the epistemological parallel that emphasizes the transformation of the life-view, the way we see reality. No longer do human achievement, status, self-interest and success without suffering and self-expenditure to serve others define reality for those *who are being saved* (present tense of a process not yet finished). Instead, living for others in the cruciform model of Jesus ("This is my body, which is for you," 11:24) constitutes our true identity (see chap. 13).

Dietrich Bonhoeffer's classic words of challenge to move us to an authentic Christianity are worth repeating here. "Wisdom or grace without the cross is what is sold on the market like a cheapjack's wares. Cheap grace means justification of sin without the justification of the sinner, . . . forgiveness without requiring repentance, baptism without church discipline . . . the world goes on in the same old way . . . grace without the cross, grace without Jesus Christ" (quoted in Thiselton 2000:157).

I will destroy the wisdom of the wise (v. 19; Is 29:14, Septuagint) is the first of fourteen clear quotations from the Old Testament in the letter. God will destroy what the Corinthians have prized! In the context of the Isaiah passage the nation of Judah has refused to listen to the wisdom of God proclaimed through the prophets. Instead they are planning their own escape from danger by making an alliance with Egypt. "The Lord says: 'These people come near to me with their mouth and honor me with their lips, but their hearts are far from me.

1:20 Richard Hays calls attention to the recent attempts of some to recast Jesus into a Cynic philosopher (e.g., Burton Mack and John Dominic Crossan): in other words,

Their worship of me is made up only of rules taught by men.'" Then follow the words Paul selects. "Therefore once more I will astound these people with wonder upon wonder; the wisdom of the wise will perish, the intelligence of the intelligent will vanish" (Is 29:13-14). Because the rulers of Judah listened to the learned of the politically dominant class, God will do an astounding thing. He will reverse and set aside this wisdom by his own acts. This divine decision has dramatic consequences in the light of the cross.

Where is the wise man? begins a series of contrasts between human wisdom and the foolishness (to the world) of the gospel proclamation. Here Paul envisages a destruction of philosophers such as the Sophists, whose system of thought exalted self-achievement, success, excellence and boasting (pride in accomplishments) without suffering and without loving service to others. In our age these are the modern pundits, the Oprahs. Not all philosophers fit this negative category. Nor should we despise legitimate construal and analysis that combines reason with faith, seeking genuine understanding of truth unaccompanied by claims of absolute truth or applause seeking.

The scholar is simply an expert or professional. The term could refer, as in the NIV, to the religious or Jewish expert in the law, but the expression should not be limited to this, especially in the Roman context, where it may apply to different status-seeking "wisdom" expressions such as that of the Sophists. *The philosopher of this age* is a debater (perhaps an allusion to the different factions in Corinth?). The word occurs only here in the New Testament and Septuagint. It seems to refer to persons who engage in extended discussions of particular issues. They are the pop orators of the day. *This age* refers to "this world order" or the perspective of the age.

Paul's point that may relate to us is that those persons who are highly acclaimed by the world as the pundits, commentators, experts, pop philosophers of the day all belong to *this age* and are nothing in the light of God's great act accomplished in the crucified Messiah. God has swept the pundits of this world all away with his own wisdom.

---

we should see Jesus as a wise teacher of philosophical truth, not as God's foolishness that reverses human wisdom by the cross (Hays 1999:116).

Has not God made foolish the wisdom of the world? Paul asks (v. 20). God has indeed done this by the startling act of redemption effected by the despised, weak Jewish carpenter who was crucified as a criminal. By this act God has reversed the world's values. The self-styled, success-oriented, status-seeking wisdom and rhetorical skill of the wise has been dethroned and *made foolish* itself. So why would you want to bring this alien view of life into the church and split into factions over it? Paul might well ask.

The wisdom of the world with its hubris has failed to lead them to grasp the truth about God *(know him);* therefore *God was pleased through the foolishness of what was preached [kērygmatos] to save those who believe* (v. 21). The NIV correctly renders the word Paul uses but captures only half the truth. Both the content of the message—Christ crucified for our sins and raised from the dead (vv. 22-25; 15:3-4)—and the form of communication are in view (not in persuasive rhetorical display of "human wisdom" but simple "placarding" of the Crucified One, 2:1; Litfin 1994:198-99). This would include various speech forms (for example, preaching, dialogue, lecture, life) but exclude others (rhetorical declamations, philosophical disputations). Proclamation without the rhetorician's persuasive flourish is foolishness to those infatuated with human self-reliance and self-sufficiency, but in reality it is the wisdom of God, for it was the place where God himself defeated those very powers that crucified Jesus. God's great act shatters both the world's system of authority and values and its prized claim to knowledge.

Jews demand miraculous signs (semeia, wonders, miracles; v. 22) because they already had access to *wisdom from God* in the Scriptures and needed only confirmations of the times in which they were living (cf. Mt 12:38-39; 16:1-4; Jn 2:18). *Gentiles,* on the other hand, *look for wisdom,* the kind Paul has already described as acclaim-seeking and expressed especially in rhetorical excellence. *But we preach [kēryssō,* "proclaim"] *Christ* [as] *crucified* (v. 23). This is the heart of Paul's message and his whole understanding of God's matchless wisdom. All else follows from this central core; without it, all else is a rabbit trail that leads nowhere, a powerless gospel. But a crucified Christ is a *stum-*

1:23 *Skandalon* is difficult but probably does not mean a *stumbling block* but a

bling block to Jews. The word is difficult but probably does *not* mean "stumbling block" but rather means the affront, outrage or shock (cf. Gal 5:11) caused by the Messiah's dying on a tree (cross), which signifies a person's being cursed by God (Deut 21:23; Gal 3:13). Also the weakness and disgrace of a cross death nullify the worldly power and acclaim expected of the Messiah (Mk 15:30-31; but cf. Is 53).

But to those whom God has called (the believers, v. 21), *both Jews and Greeks, Christ the power of God and the wisdom of God* (v. 24): this is how Christ is to be seen by those who belong to him. God's power is revealed in the crucified Jesus, God's wisdom is inseparable from the cross. "Any version of the gospel that substitutes personal success for the cross is a manipulative counterfeit" (Thiselton 2000:172).

The last verse (25) in this section further compares "God's foolishness" ("the foolish thing," i.e., the crucified Christ), and "God's weakness" (the self-effacing way of the cross) with "human wisdom" (the self-promoting, status building, rhetoric enhancing way of the world) and "human strength" (self-achievement, boastful success and self-help) that breeds the "party splits" in the community. God's great act of self-effacement on the cross outshines anything attained or attainable by human wisdom or strength.

God's Calling Excludes Human Boasting (1:26-31) To further bolster his case against human wisdom and achievement as the way for Christians to express their faith in Christ, Paul points to the social composition of the redeemed community in Corinth as it was when he wrote. *Think of what you were when you were called* (when you became believers, v. 21) asks them to notice that few of them were members of the elite *(of noble birth),* the *influential* (powerful) or the *wise* (recognized, acclaimed) *by human standards* (that is, as the world counts cleverness). God did not call them to be his people because they were acclaimed, influential or elite in the eyes of the world. Why would they now want to make social status the criterion of spirituality and create factions around their self-achieved status improvement?

God in fact called them to himself in that very low social condition, those who were not worthy of the world's attention *(foolish, weak,*

"snare" or "trap, temptation, affront" (Thiselton 2000:171; Danker 2000:926).

lowly, despised nobodies), in order to show his love for the unworthy, the undeserving, those who could not claim any self-help or status (from the world's viewpoint). In a deliberate strategy *God chose* these "nobodies" for shaming the *wise,* the *strong,* the "somebodies" by human standards.

So the grace message of the cross is contradictory to the Corinthian believers' seeking now to be upwardly mobile for spiritual reasons. Ben Witherington is right when he says,

> Salvation in Christ is not a human self-improvement scheme, but a radical rescue from a form of slavery out of which one cannot earn or buy one's way. Paul must establish this theology of grace at the very outset of his arguments because it is on the basis of that theology that he will undercut all factors that promote factionalism. Grace is not only the great unifier but also the great leveler in the Christian community, which if taken seriously nullifies the importance of all cultural devices used to create social stratification. It can also stifle rivalries about and between Christian teachers, since it makes possible the rejoinder, "was Paul (or Apollos or whoever) crucified for you?" (1995:118)

In Roman society your value was determined by your education, wealth and breeding. Paul shows that you cannot become an insider in the world's status game by becoming a Christian, but you can become an insider in God's eyes by finding your status in Christ (Thiselton 2000:179). *So that no one may boast before him* (v. 29) is an allusion to Jeremiah 9:23-24, which will be directly quoted in verse 31. This is God's ultimate purpose in the proclamation of the gospel of the crucified Christ: to overthrow all human claims of achievement, all boasting in one's human success and acclaim in participating in God's wisdom and power (salvation), to highlight the glory of grace as sheer gift.

It is because of him that you are in Christ Jesus (v. 30) follows this thought further by emphasizing that this sheer gift of grace is from God himself alone. To be *in Christ* is not a mere mystical experience; it is the objective reality of having been united to Christ by the Holy Spirit

---

1:31 Alternatively to Jeremiah 9:24, the source of the quote could possibly be from the text of 1 Samuel 2:10 (LXX, 1 Kingdoms 2:10), a portion absent from the Hebrew

and thus sharing in his resurrected life, the new creation (2 Cor 5:17) and the new community that is his body (1 Cor 12:12-13).

The new *wisdom from God* is Jesus Christ himself, who has become for Christian believers their *righteousness, holiness and redemption* (v. 30). The way of Jesus Christ crucified is the true path to acceptance and self-worth in God's new community. This way is the way of receiving the gifts of *righteousness, holiness and redemption* that are freely given through Christ apart from self-achievement and self-promotion. These four qualities belong together; they both characterize Christ himself and are imparted to his people.

Wisdom of the self-effacing, self-giving life of Jesus is signified by the cross (11:24, "This is my body, which is for you"). See Paul's further exposition of this wisdom in 2:6-16. *Righteousness* is God's vindicating action in our behalf, effected in the cross, whereby we are forgiven and reconciled to God (6:11; cf. Rom 3:21-22; 2 Cor 5:21). *Holiness* (consecration, sanctification) is a term related to "saints" and "holy" in the New Testament; it can refer either to moral expression in keeping with God's own holy character and will (1 Thess 4:7) or to drawing near to God in intimate relation with him, having been purified and set apart (Heb 10:22; 12:14).

Redemption ("buying back a slave or a captive, i.e., 'making free' by payment of a ransom; acquittal," Danker 2000:117) describes our release from sin's captivity and our being freed or liberated ones through Christ. These realities reverse our low estate in social terms of the world; instead of weakness there is now righteousness (acquittal), instead of being despised there is holiness (acceptance into God's intimate fellowship), and instead of nothings (nobodies) we become the redeemed, holy people of God. Glorying in these divine gifts is the only "boasting" of any ultimate value.

Let him who boasts ("takes pride in") *boast in the Lord* closes the section with a direct quote from Jeremiah 9:24. The passage has been moving toward this climax of finding our ground of boasting not in our own achievements of learning, wealth and status improvement but in

---

text of the verse that emphasizes in a positive sense the reversal of status (Hays 1997:34-35).

God's grace expressed through the crucified Christ. Since all Christians possess this priceless worth and status, there is no need to compete for honor by forming factions around our favorite speakers. All such is contrary to the realities of God's great reversal of human wisdom found in the crucified Savior.

Isaac Watts (1748) understood Paul's teaching when he wrote the great hymn "When I Survey the Wondrous Cross":

When I survey the wondrous Cross
on which the Prince of glory died,
my richest gain I count but loss,
and pour contempt on all my pride.
Forbid it, Lord, that I should boast
save in the death of Christ, my God;
all the vain things that charm me most,
I sacrifice them to His blood.

Paul's Preaching the Cross at Corinth (2:1-5) For his final demonstration of the antithesis between human status seeking and the gospel, Paul turns to his own manner of evangelizing the Corinthians when he first came among them. Contrary to what they were prizing (oratorical skills, success, acclaim), he did not come as a Sophist would come to them, *with eloquence* (high-sounding rhetoric) *or superior wisdom* (display of cleverness, 2:1).

Instead his proclamation (wider than only preaching) of the "mystery" of God (see NIV alternate reading), namely, *Jesus Christ* as the *crucified* One, was in keeping with the sole focus on the cross because Paul consistently, deliberately presented himself not self-confidently but in self-effacement, not in strength as a "successful" person but in *weakness and fear, with much trembling* (v. 3). "Paul's own personal bearing mirrored his message" (Hays 1997:35; 1999:119).

All of this contrasts with the Sophists, who competed with great showmanship of rhetoric at the Isthmian Games. Paul came among the

---

2:1 On Greco-Roman rhetoric and the gospel, see especially the fine studies of Winter 1997; Litfin 1994; Witherington 1995.

There are two textual traditions on the word *mystērion,* "mystery," or *martyrion,* "testimony, witness." The manuscript evidence is quite divided. Most modern versions, following earlier practice, translate it "testimony" or "message" (Tyndale, KJV,

Corinthians as a humble servant, focusing his *testimony about God* exclusively on *Jesus Christ and him crucified*. "To know nothing but Christ and him crucified is to know everything significant" (Baird 1964:45). Furthermore, far from being personally impressive in his persona or manner of preaching, Paul sensed his own *weakness . . . fear . . . trembling* (v. 3; cf. 2 Cor 10:10; 11:6). These terms refer not to Paul's physical condition but to his usual manner of delivery of the message, in all humility, as in the presence of God (Job 4:14; Ps 2:11), as one who was confident in the Spirit's power to convict, regenerate and sanctify, and totally without confidence in his own abilities of speech and persuasion. In other word, his modus operandi was the modus operandi of the cross.

If his preaching had been highly successful at Corinth and the response was not due to his powers of speech and intellect, it could be attributed only to a *demonstration of the Spirit's power* (Acts 18:7-11). But what does Paul mean by this *demonstration of the Spirit's power* ("in demonstration or proof of Spirit and of power; or proof consisting in possession of the Spirit and power," Danker 2000:109)? Some see a reference to miraculous signs and wonders that accompanied Paul's preaching as well as the gifts of the Spirit poured out on the Corinthians when they believed (1 Cor 1:7; 2 Cor 12:12; Gal 3:5). Today there is a sentiment in certain sectors of the worldwide church that to be effective, the preaching of the gospel must be accompanied with similar signs and wonders (Hays 1997:36). Others would stress that Paul means the convicting power of the Holy Spirit as the Word of God is proclaimed.

To what extent the apostolic signs (2 Cor 12:12) are to continue to accompany the gospel presentation in every age is subject to debate among Bible-believing Christians. In any case Paul is emphasizing that it is not mere rational argument or oratory that persuades us to believe in Jesus Christ but the mysterious operation of God's powerful Spirit.

By bypassing the Sophists' approach, Paul aimed to ground the new

---

RSV, NIV, NEB, TNIV). The NRSV has "mystery." The later is a frequent term in Paul's writings to express the gospel of Christ (1 Cor 4:1; esp. Col 2:2; 1:27; 4:3). The very early reading of *mystērion* in p[46] should be taken quite seriously. For arguments favoring "testimony" see Fee 1987:91; for "mystery" see Thiselton 2000:207, 210.

believers' *faith* (confidence) response to the gospel message not on human sophistry or cleverness but on the power of God (v. 5). As C. K. Barrett wisely remarks, "The supernatural conviction and force that accompanied the preaching furnished a better proof of its truth than any logical process" (1968:65). Paul may have known of others who came to the Corinthians whose efforts relied on the power of argumentation and the persuasion of rhetoric (2 Cor 11:4-6, 13). However, there is no evidence that in 1 Corinthians that he has such opponents in mind. Rather, Apollos and Peter are referred to as respected, complementary servants of God along with Paul (3:5-9, 22).

Today's proclamation of the gospel must also pay close attention to the essential correlation of the cross message and a cross method of presentation. That is, the gospel must still be presented with humility and dependence not on dramatic emotional appeals or high-powered sales techniques but on the powerful working of God's Spirit. "All the weight of proclamation must fall on what God has done, not on how we respond to God. . . . We have become so accustomed to anthropocentric preaching and theology that we hardly know how to talk in theocentric terms, but this text insists that we must—and models how we might do it" (Hays 1997:37).

Lidie H. Edmonds (1891) clearly sought to confess this emphasis of Paul when she wrote:

My faith has found a resting place,

Not in device nor creed;

I trust the ever living One,

His wounds for me shall plead.

I need no other argument,

I need no other plea,

It is enough that Jesus died,

And that He died for me.

God's Revealed Wisdom for the Mature and Why Paul Did Not Teach It at Corinth (2:6—3:4) In this section Paul responds further to the question he raised in 1:13, "Was Paul crucified for you?" To head off the overly enthusiastic following by the Corinthians of their favorite spiritually "wise" Christian ministers, Paul has pointed them to Christ crucified as the expression of God's true wisdom (1:24, 30). In every day as in Paul's, the test of true ministers of God is their ability to turn those who hear them away from following themselves to following the crucified God (2:1-5).

However, Paul now seems to say that for those who are truly *mature* Christians—not very recent believers, nor believers unskilled in the exercise of Christian love—there is a "wisdom" that can be taught and discussed. This wisdom is God's foreordained secret and mysterious wisdom, which was not known in history until Christ appeared. No human being ever thought of it; even the most clever Sophist (wise-speech expert) or world leader never dreamed of it. Further, not even an inspired prophet like Moses or Isaiah ever disclosed it. But now God has revealed this wisdom in the gospel of the crucified God-man. Such wisdom is not a different wisdom from that of the cross Paul preached initially to the Corinthians but a further elaboration of the theology of this event and its implications, such as might be found in the epistle to the Ephesians or Colossians.

How is such wisdom to be discussed and taught by God's servants? The manner must be consistent with the matter being discussed. Divine truths can be grasped only by the Spirit of God, who indwells believers. Furthermore, God's revelation must be communicated not in language and styles more appropriate to the teaching of secular wisdom but in forms suitable to the Spirit. The person devoid of God's indwelling Spirit is incapable of grasping this divine wisdom, which must be searched out with humility and receptivity by those who are truly *spiritual*—that is, those who have received the gift of the indwelling Spirit.

Finally, Paul explains why he did not speak such divine wisdom to the Corinthians: they were *worldly—mere infants in Christ* (3:1). Their immaturity did not consist in a lack of knowledge but in the jealousy and quarreling among them, which resulted from their unhealthy view of both the ministry as a whole and individual ministers in particular: *I follow Paul . . . I follow Apollos.*

Let's look in more detail at aspects of the divine wisdom (2:6-16) before we look at Paul's view of the ministry (3:5—4:7). In the first section (2:6-10) Paul refers to a divinely revealed wisdom that he did not present to the Corinthians but of which he does speak to the mature (*telios,* complete, perfect, finished). This wisdom is not a different kind of message or subject from the message of Christ crucified that Paul did bring to the Corinthians (2:2). Paul knows of no other divine wisdom except that of Christ and his crucifixion (1:23-24, 30; Col 2:2-3).

There is, however, much more that God has disclosed about himself, his promises and our calling in relation to the crucified Christ than what is initially necessary for us to know to say yes to God's love and grace proclaimed in the fundamentals of the gospel. This wisdom from God is identified first negatively (*not the wisdom of this age or of the rulers of this age*) and then positively (*God's secret wisdom, a wisdom that has been hidden . . . destined for our glory*). While *rulers of this age* could re-fer to the demonic principalities and powers (Eph 6:12; Col 2:15), it is better in this instance to see them as the Roman political (Pilate and Herod, etc.) and Jewish religious-political (Caiaphas, Sanhedrin, etc.) leaders. Had they known who Christ was and what great eternal conse-quences follow rejection of him, *they would not have crucified the Lord of glory* (cf. Jas 2:1). God's wisdom is awesome, rooted in eternity (*be-fore time began*), and though formerly *hidden,* it has now been *revealed to us* and divinely purposed *for our glory* (Eph 3:3-6).

Various expressions for this wisdom are found throughout the sec-tion. It may be helpful to tie these all together:

2:6	wisdom
2:7	God's secret wisdom, a wisdom that has been hidden
2:9	what God has prepared for those who love him
2:10	the deep things of God
2:11	the thoughts of God
2:12	what God has freely given us
2:14	the things that come from the Spirit of God
2:15	all things
2:16	the mind of Christ

Such divine wisdom is for the mature. The mature are all those who,

---

2:6 *Rulers of this age* is understood as demonic rulers by Origen, Theodore of Mop-suestia, Oscar Cullmann, G. B. Caird, Jean Héring and alternately as human rulers by John Chrysostom, Leon Morris, Gordon Fee, Ben Witherington, Richard Hays, Simon Kistemaker. Some commentators argue for both human and demonic dimensions: Walter Wink, Gerd Theissen (1987), Anthony Thiselton.

having believed on Christ, show a readiness to humbly receive as God's wisdom the instructions of the apostles, in particular teachers such as Paul, Peter and Apollos. They are those who patiently allow the Holy Spirit to guide and illumine them in the divine mystery or logic of the gospel of Christ. Additionally, the mature are those who begin and continue to evidence in their lives that they are making progress in expressing the many facets of the divine love in their relationships to others (1 Cor 13).

To clinch his argument that the divine wisdom was not known before in history and is known only by special revelation in the crucified Christ event, Paul quotes from a document that refers to matters that *no eye has seen, no ear has heard, no mind has conceived, what God has prepared for those who love him* (1 Cor 2:9; cf. Rom 8:28). Similar to but not a direct quote from Isaiah (Is 52:15; 64:4), this quotation is like a few others in the New Testament that seem to defy a simple text identification (e.g., Jn 7:38; Eph 5:14).

Paul's focus now turns to the role of the Spirit as the mediator of the christological wisdom (v. 10). This distinctly divine wisdom is revealed only by the Holy Spirit: *God has revealed it to us by his Spirit.* This general statement is further elaborated in verses 10-16. The Spirit reveals this wisdom because he alone *searches all things* (v. 10), not in the sense of conducting a search to find out something but of penetrating, knowing, perceiving. The Spirit knows all things about God, *even the deep things of God,* the humanly unfathomable realities that are impenetrable in God's mind and being (cf. Job 11:7; Rom 11:33). *To us* is emphatic: *to us,* to the weak and despised of the world (1:26-28), not to the Sophists or the philosophers of this world, that no boasting may occur in God's presence. *Us* shows also that Paul is including other apostles and ministers, such as Peter and Apollos. If human beings have secrets that they only can reveal, how much more necessary is it that God's Spirit reveal to our inner being God's secrets about the gos-

---

2:9 The source of the quotation is uncertain. Ancient and modern opinion often suggests the LXX of Isaiah 64:3(4) combined with allusions to other texts, but no entirely satisfactory solution seems to be available. Origen thought it came from the now lost Apocalypse of Elijah (*Commentary on Matthew* 27.9; Migne, PG 13:1769C).

pel of the crucified Christ (cf. Zech 12:1).

The Spirit's relationship to us now comes into focus in three important verbs: We (Christians) have *received* the Spirit sent from God so that we might *understand* (or know) what God has freely given us (the wisdom for the mature of 1 Cor 2:6) and *speak* this wisdom of God in words thought to us by the Spirit. *The spirit of the world* (*kosmos,* not *aiōnos* as in vv. 6, 8) does not refer to Satan (Eph 2:2), nor even to the human spirit of 1 Corinthians 2:11, but to the temper or character of the age at any moment in history and any locality, including worldly impressions of who the wise and successful are and how they express themselves. Instead we have received the eschatological gift of the Spirit (sent) from God (Acts 1:8; 2:4, 17; 10:44; Rom 5:8; 8:9) for the purpose of our understanding the revealed christological wisdom of the gospel.

Furthermore, this revelation from the Spirit must be communicated to others. The evidence of the Holy Spirit's inspiration was *not in words taught . . . by human wisdom* (or "in learned words of human wisdom," Davis 1984:112) *but in words taught by the Spirit* (1 Cor 2:13). The Corinthians apparently prized eloquent speech as a sign of the Spirit's inspiration. Paul instead values language learned from the Spirit as the appropriate vehicle for communicating divinely revealed wisdom. He adds, *expressing spiritual truths in spiritual words* (v. 13). All interpreters struggle with translating Paul's words *(pneumatikois pneumatika synkrinontes)*. The NRSV has: "interpreting spiritual things to those who are spiritual." While this translation is possible, the best sense of *synkrinō* is "to combine, wed or join." If Paul wanted to say "interpret," he had good Greek words available, such as *dianoigō* (Lk 24:32; Acts 17:3) or *diermēneuō* (Lk 24:27; Acts 9:36). Thus the NIV gives the preferred translation if we correct it slightly by using "joining" or "combining" in place of "expressing" (or "explaining," TNIV): "combining Spirit-taught wisdom with Spirit-taught words" captures the sense.

2:12 *Charisthenta* refers not to "gifts" given to us (NRSV) but to the "wisdom of God" in Christ crucified and raised that is revealed and given to us.
2:14 Charles Talbert offers an interesting suggestion: "The presupposition underlying Paul's argument is the common Greco-Roman epistemological conviction: like is known by like (Plato *Protagorus* 337C-338A; *Timaeus* 45C; Philo *On the Change of Names* 6; Plotinus *Enneads* 4.5.7, 23-62; 1.6.9, 30-45). Since the Corinthians who

Paul certainly seems to be claiming that the divinely revealed wisdom of the gospel of the crucified Christ is shared with others by means of language taught to the teachers by the same Holy Spirit who gave the original revelation. This ensures that the communication is a "demonstration of the Spirit and power" that in turn leads to divinely grounded Christian faith among the hearers (vv. 4-5). The observation is certainly correct that Paul throughout this section is not talking about "inspiration" but of "rhetorical adaptation" (divine revelation with rhetorical form, Litfin 1994:219). The Spirit-taught words that embody the communication of the Spirit's revelation of God's wisdom must be scrutinized and investigated by those who have received the indwelling Spirit.

A person who is *without the Spirit* (*psychikos,* "soulish," "natural," "untouched by the Spirit") *does not accept* ("welcome," "greet") as truth *the things that come from the Spirit of God* (the wisdom of God revealed by the Spirit in Spirit-taught words about what God has given to the saints, v. 12, and laid up for them in the future, v. 9). Why does this unenthusiastic response to God's revealed wisdom occur? First, the logic of the crucified Lord eludes them, and they consider it foolishness (1:18, 23). Second, they are unable to grasp that the wisdom of God is found in the straightforward speech of Paul's teaching, because it cannot be understood by human investigation devoid of the Holy Spirit's illumination: *they* (the things God has given and laid up for the saints) *are spiritually discerned* (scrutinized, investigated, examined—there are ten instances of this term in 1 Corinthians, but nowhere else in Paul; it occurs frequently in Luke's writings).

On the other hand the *spiritual man makes judgments about all things*—the things of God's wisdom revealed by the Spirit in Spirit-taught form, verses 9-13. Lydia of Thyatira provides an excellent case in point. When Paul preached Christ to her at Philippi, "the Lord

---

acted as if they had not died to sin were not spiritual, Paul could not teach them matters that are only spiritually discerned" (1987:6).

2:15 The TNIV rendering correctly clarifies the sense of *spiritual man* in verses 14-15: "The person without the Spirit. . . . The person with the Spirit." Thus it not only avoids a gender inaccuracy for the modern reader but clarifies that "spiritual" is Paul's own word designating the Holy Spirit's presence and operation.

opened her heart to respond to Paul's message" (Acts 16:14). With God's help she discerned the divine wisdom in Paul's proclamation. Yet here in 1 Corinthians 2:15 and 3:1 the reference goes beyond the initial grasping of the gospel truth as divine wisdom and includes the thought of maturity as defined in 2:6 and 3:1-4. Exactly what the Corinthians were asserting about the natural person versus the spiritual person in 2:14—3:4 we may never know for sure, since Paul is using a language of redefinition, incorporating the terminology of those he disputes but giving the words a new twist (Davis 1984:128; Thiselton 1978:513). The person without the Spirit ("natural") is the nonredeemed person, while the real spiritual individual is the one who is a genuine Christian, possesses the indwelling Spirit and is learning from him the true wisdom of God.

But how are we to understand the statement that the true spiritual person not only judges all things but *is not subject to any man's judgment* (v. 15)? This is not altogether clear. The Corinthian "super-spirituals" may have taught that as a function of their ability to know all things, they could discern the more valuable ministries among God's servants (or alternately, that they need no ministers at all: "I follow Christ" alone, 1:12; Thiselton 1978:513). At the same time they may have argued also that their high spiritual status rendered expressions of their freedom above the moral scrutiny of others.

We might see the latter in the congregation's apparent celebration of the "freedom" of the man living in incest with his stepmother (5:1-8), those who litigated against their fellow Christians in the pagan law courts (6:1-11) and those who saw no moral problems in using their bodies in unmarried sexual encounters (6:12-20). To this Paul responds by arguing that true spirituality consists in being indwelt by the Spirit, who enables us to respond positively to God's revelation of his deep secrets in the Spirit-inspired words of the apostles (spoken and written). This truly spiritual person cannot be judged by the person *without the Spirit* (v. 14), any man or woman who is devoid of the indwelling Spirit. For the truly spiritual Christian (at least in principle) reflects *the mind of Christ,* whose mind is the unfathomable mind of the Lord God whom no one is capable of instructing (Is 40:13).

Furthermore, the truly spiritual person, having *the mind of Christ,* does in fact judge other Christians' behavior that is contrary to the commands of Christ—such as the worldliness of the Corinthians' discords and divisions over the relative value of human messengers, or their fornication, or their boasting. Yet judgment on the *value* of each Christian's service can be made solely by the Lord Christ himself, and that not in the present but only when Jesus returns and brings everything into full view (4:3-5).

Finally, in the last part of this section on the divine wisdom for the mature, Paul tells them plainly why he could not teach them this wisdom when he was with them (3:1-4). They were not then nor now *spiritual* people; rather, they are *worldly* (made of flesh, fleshy)— *mere infants in Christ* (hence needing milk, not solid food, Heb 5:12-13; 1 Pet 2:2). The term *infants in Christ* occurs only here in the New Testament, but Ephesians 4:13-14 refers to the church as progressing into "maturity, attaining to the whole measure of the fullness of Christ," so that we may be no longer mere "infants."

Every Christian must begin as an "infant," and there is no shame in this stage. But we should grow up in our understanding of and obedience to the divine wisdom disclosed in Christ and his Word. To remain infants is as unnatural and unacceptable in the spiritual realm as in the physical. Paul does not address the Corinthians as those *without the Spirit* (1 Cor 2:14). Rather, he chooses middle terms that recognize they are believers *(worldly, mere infants in Christ)* yet subtly raise questions about their commitment to Christ as well as directly exposing their immature condition.

They were acting as if they were still merely human (*mere men,* vv. 3-4), that is, without the indwelling Holy Spirit and also without the fruit of the Holy Spirit in their lives. The evidence of this was their continued *jealousy and quarreling* (cf. Jas 3:14, 16) over the superiority of their favorite preachers and guest ministers: *One says "I follow Paul," and another, "I follow Apollos"* (v. 4). True spirituality, on the other hand, produces a respect for and a welcoming of the different servants of God whom the Lord has raised up and sent to minister to us, and at the same time a relativizing of all such ministers. It is the Lord Christ alone who is to be highly prized by his people. Respecting yet relativizing God's servants is God's point of view. Do we have this perspective in our Christian communities today?

Paul's Third Response to Factions: God's View of Ministers and the Ministry (3:5—4:21) Who is important? Are favorite pastors, priests, radio or TV preachers, or writers? What do you think of Benny Hinn or Chuck Swindoll or Kay Baxter or James Dobson or Chuck Colson or Charles Stanley or Pat Robertson or J. I. Packer or John Stott or John MacArthur or Bill Hybels? Do you listen to them all, or to just your leader or pastor? Can we say with Paul that they are all important and at the same time that they are all unimportant?

The Corinthians had Paul, Peter and Apollos. Some listened only to Paul, others only to Apollos. How should we think of ministers and the ministry today from God's point of view? The tragic results of a merely human viewpoint on these matters were evident in the sad events surrounding the Jim Jones following in Guyana and the David Koresh group in Waco, Texas. What causes a perverted evaluation of and extreme attachment to leaders? Paul has helpful words to guide the church today to avoid overemphasizing individual Christian leaders and at the same time to steer clear of the opposite error of undervaluing the Christian ministry.

This section is the response of Paul to the first question in 1:13, "Is Christ divided?" Can Christ be portioned out to different leaders? He builds his teaching first around two metaphors: farming a field (3:5-9) and constructing a temple building (3:10-17). Second, Paul turns to a theological treatment of the future judgment to put the worth of servants of God into a realistic perspective (4:1-7).

Lessons from Farming and Building (3:5-23) To correct the Corinthians' harmful boasting in one minister of God over against another, Paul first refers directly to himself and Apollos as servants (*diakonoi,* waiters at tables, helpers) who were mere agents helping them to believe in the saving message of Christ. We should note three features of the agricultural image of farming a field Paul uses in this part of the section.

3:14-15 *Reward/loss* language may refer to ancient building contracts, which allowed for penalties if the work was delayed or unsatisfactory, and for rewards related to the employer's own assessment of the value of the completed work. These verses are frequently cited in the Anglo-Catholic tradition as among texts supporting

1. Each worker is needed and is equal (*one purpose*, v. 8). Each has a different but complementary role in the farming process assigned by the field's owner, God: *as the Lord has assigned to each his task. I planted the seed, Apollos watered it* (vv. 5-6). God's garden is his church (*you are God's field*, v. 9). This garden requires a team of differently gifted servants working together under God's authority to produce the kind of harvest he intends.

2. The servants, though necessary, are relatively unimportant—even Paul and Apollos—because it is *God who made it grow. So neither he who plants [Paul] nor he who waters [Apollos] is anything, but only God, who makes things grow* (vv. 6-7). This viewpoint should deflate the proud, competitive boasting of some at Corinth in favor of Paul over against Apollos, or more probably for Apollos over against Paul. *God* is at center stage. All his servants pale into insignificance if we truly worship him, put him at the center of all.

3. While the servants' tasks are different and they share the same purpose, *each will be rewarded according to his own labor* (v. 8). Certainly they are not rewarded with salvation for their labor, since salvation is a gift of God's grace, but perhaps they will be rewarded with some form of praise from the Lord (3:14; 4:5). This keeps servants and congregations watchful over and responsible for the ministry to which God has called them: *We are God's* (emphatic*) fellow workers; you are God's* (emphatic) *field, God's* (emphatic) *building.* Keep in mind that there will be a future day of judgment for both the servants and the field. Let this realistic viewpoint change the way you pridefully cling to your favorite Christian leaders.

The second image, the construction of a building (eventually a temple, vv. 16-17), has some similar lessons and some new points. First, like the planting of a large garden, the construction of a building requires a team of differently gifted workers (*by the grace God has given me*, v. 10). Paul as an *expert builder* (a competent or skilled builder)

---

the doctrine of purgatory. But the text is not salvation-oriented; it refers to ministers of the gospel as a warning, not to all Christians. Most of the fathers of the church did not understand these verses as pointing to a postmortem intermediate purgation step on the way into Christ's presence.

laid a foundation through his evangelistic efforts at Corinth. This once-only laid foundation was faith in Jesus Christ crucified (1:18; 2:2, 5). Apollos built further on this foundation through his teaching ministry (*someone else is building on it*). The chief builder of temple projects supervised the whole project (Shanor 1988:465). We see Paul doing this in the teaching and warnings that follow, as well as by his continuing life involvement with the Corinthians.

Second, Paul issues a mild warning that each servant of God who labors to build further on the Corinthian church's foundation should be careful how he or she builds. This caution is defined in terms of the selection of building materials: *gold, silver, costly stones, wood, hay or straw* (v. 12). The materials are first of all distinguished according to value, then later according to durability when the building is engulfed in fire (*if what he has built survives,* v. 14). If, as I believe, Paul has the temple building in mind here as well as in verses 16-17, the experience of ancients when fire swept through their towns may be in mind. After a fire often the only structures remaining were the temples and their ornamentation of *gold, silver, costly stones* (Shanor 1988:466-67). Christian servants who labor in God's field should be careful that they are building on the foundation of Christ a high-quality, enduring house where the Spirit of God may dwell in his fullness (*gold, silver, costly stones)* and not a structure of self-aggrandizement, worldly competitiveness and status seeking.

Third, Paul again puts the whole matter into realistic perspective by mentioning the future day of accountability when the quality and durability of what has been built by the servant's labors will be tested (assayed, examined) and if it is approved (*gold, silver, costly stones)* they will receive a *reward* (wage). If the work is burned up in this fiery test (*wood, hay or straw),* the builder will suffer loss but will still *be saved, but only as one escaping through the flames* (v. 15). Ill-advised, misdirected Christian ministry will be weighed and found wanting. Those who have so constructed will suffer loss of praise from Christ (4:5); because salvation is based on grace, not works, they will be saved, yet as if by the skin of their teeth.

The *loss* is reminiscent of the losses suffered by some building contractors responsible for poorly constructed houses (poor in both material and workmanship) that Hurricane Andrew destroyed in Florida in

1992, leaving a number dead and 250,000 homeless. The aftermath exposed to everyone's view the faulty structures. Damages against these builders are still being pursued in law courts at this writing. Fines will no doubt be imposed where appropriate.

Note that the fire can test only the *work,* not the laborers or the foundation (v. 11; 4:3). There is no reference here to the purifying fires of purgatory, as some have maintained. This fire *tests* (not purifies), with a view to approval or disapproval. But what are the materials? Paul does not explicitly tell us. We can deduce that some doctrines are involved, such as the understanding of the cross he has presented (1:18—2:5) or his later teaching on the resurrection of the dead (chap. 15). But he is also surely concerned about servanthood to others and our hidden motives (4:1-5; chap. 13). Beyond this is speculation.

Finally, Paul turns to address the congregation and says explicitly that the building is a temple: *you yourselves* (plural for the church) *are God's temple* (sanctuary, holy of holies) *and . . . God's Spirit lives in you* (Eph 2:21). The church, not the home or building but the community of God's people at Corinth, is the temple of God, the place where God dwells. The individual Christian body is also a shrine of the Holy Spirit in 6:19, but this is not the thought here. Hence the seriousness and gravity of the offense *if anyone destroys* (corrupts, mars, spoils, ruins) *God's temple* (the church). Those who destroy the church will be met with God's judgment: *God will destroy him.* The punishment fits the crime. If you harm God's temple, God will harm you.

But does this harm refer to eternal ruin—condemnation and hell? Or is the reference to the same loss suffered by those who built with poor materials (v. 15)? Leon Morris takes the first view (1985:67), while Jay Shanor argues the latter (1988:470-71). Since the word is not definite, it cannot show clearly whether the harm is annihilation or conscious eternal punishment, on the one hand, or the harm-loss of verse 15. God's temple is *holy* (set apart for God's use and his presence) and is thus God's very own possession (Eph 5:25-27). This is why Paul is so concerned for the church: God is living in this community through his Spirit. It can be corrupted or harmed by strife, division and boasting over human leaders. Paul appeals to the congregation to be responsible in the way they view leaders since they are that temple.

A final sharp warning against boasting closes these lessons from farming and building (1 Cor 3:18-23). There is a sense in which this part can be seen as referring back to 1:18 and thus providing a conclusion for the whole epistle up to this point (Conzelmann 1975:79). How prone we are individually and separately to self-deception: *Do not deceive yourselves.* Some of the Corinthians appear to have really believed that their ideas of what constituted Christian wisdom and who best expressed that wisdom among their leaders were correct. Some Corinthians judged themselves to be *wise* based on what their culture had taught them constitutes true wisdom: *by the standards of this age.* They were viewed by themselves and by others in the congregation as truly wise people.

Yet Paul has shown that their view is completely opposite to God's perspective, *for the wisdom of this world is foolishness in God's sight* (v. 19; cf. 1:20). From God's viewpoint (true reality) the one who would seek to be truly wise *should become a "fool"* (from the world's perspective). That is, they should not abandon their intellect but recognize and adopt the correct wisdom of God regarding both content and method of teaching.

Paul calls to mind two Old Testament passages that support his contention that God has chosen deliberately to set aside the wisdom of the world in his saving plan of redemption in the crucified Christ: *He catches the wise in their craftiness* (Job 5:13), and *the Lord knows that the thoughts of the wise are futile* (Ps 94:11). Only a perspective given Paul by special revelation from God could correct their self-deception about sophistic wisdom. This point of view Paul presents is not immanent in the world; it is not available to be drawn out inductively through reason, even reason informed by Christian faith. So *no more boasting* about human leaders (1 Cor 3:21; cf. 1:31)! Hans Conzelmann's remark is perceptive: "The act, seemingly negative, of refraining from 'human' boasting is, positively speaking, freedom" (1975:80). To this freedom Paul turns in the concluding verses of the chapter.

Paul is not quite finished with the matter. He is not concerned about the Corinthians' attitude toward non-Christian leaders but about how they view their Christian leaders, such as Paul, Peter and Apollos (vv. 21-23). *All things are yours* is the reason they should not boast in human leaders. Instead of the Corinthians belonging to their teachers (as the culture taught), the teachers belong to the Corinthian Christians. This is an inversion of the Sophist-disciple relationship prevalent in Corinth (Winter 2002:42). Instead, Paul rejects the statements of loyalty made by the Corinthians in 1:12 and 3:4 and states that all things, including their Christian teachers (Paul, Apollos, Peter), *the world or life or death or the present or the future—all are yours.* That is, all these belong to you as your servants. So don't follow human leaders; let them minister to and serve you! This is God's perspective. If we had heeded this word, how much needless suffering and damage to the church would have been avoided.

That Paul expands the circle of what belongs to us beyond our teachers to include *the world, life, death, things present, things to come—all things* (v. 22) is quite amazing. That all things belong to us believers as servants for our edification and fulfillment of God's will should change our attitude. We are truly free. Only Christ (and through him God the Father) commands our loyalty and discipleship (*you are of Christ,* v. 23). To the extent that we belong to Christ, we are truly free to use all things without falling into addiction to them.

Finally, Paul says that *Christ is of God.* Christ belongs to God in the sense that his loyalty and obedience is to the Father. Does this imply that Christ is not equal with God or has a subordinate relation to the Father in the Godhead? Not in any sense that would diminish Christ's full deity (Phil 2:6). On the other hand, whether the subordination passages in the New Testament are relative to Christ's earthly mission of redemption (Morris 1985:76) or whether they also hint of something in the very essence of God, the eternal dynamic relation between Father and Son (McGill 1982:chap. 4) is very difficult to settle. See comments also at 11:3 and 15:27-28.

Ministers and Ministry: A View from the Future (4:1-21) Just when we think Paul is finished with this topic that has consumed so much of his attention in the letter, he comes back to make some observations about himself and Apollos (4:1-7), to contrast with biting irony the lifestyle of the Corinthians vis-à-vis the apostles (4:8-13) and to offer a fatherly admonition (4:14-21). This section will finally end his long discourse on leaders and harmful divisions in the church.

Paul first turns once again to describe the minister of God and picks up the threads of his emphasis in 3:5-23 *(so then)* by returning to the thought of servanthood with which he began (3:5). He uses two different words to complement his earlier development. The Corinthians' leaders are to be thought of as *servants of Christ.* The word used here is *hypēretēs,* which refers to "one who stands and acts in the service of a higher will and is fully at the disposal of this will" (Rengstorf 1972:531). In military circles it referred to either the quartermaster or the immediate aide of a commander (an attaché), while in medicine it designated an intern or resident and in the judicial arena could refer to the executioner. All of these uses stress the important but subordinate role of the persons so named, in this instance to Christ.

Paul and Apollos are also to be thought of as those *entrusted with . . . secret things.* The word translated as "entrusted" is *oikonomos,* "steward, manager, administrator" (Lk 12:42; 16:1; Rom 16:23; Tit 1:7; 1 Pet 4:10). This is Paul's second term for Christian ministers. Owners of large land estates often would appoint a slave to manage their properties. Though the position entailed a bit of responsibility in the managing of households, properties and persons, the steward was still in a slave-master relation to the owner. Paul and Apollos are stewards of God's mysteries *(secret things),* that is, God's revealed wisdom in the gospel of Christ, including its deeper dimensions (2:7, 10). What is the most important quality or virtue sought in a steward? Since they have such wide-ranging supervision over all their master's affairs, they must be *faithful* (trustworthy, dependable). All Christians are similarly but in different ways called to this same stewardship (1 Pet 4:10).

Christian leaders are everywhere in the New Testament seen as possessing no special character traits but as having virtues typical of what all Christians should possess. The principle of "little to much" is especially pertinent here. "Whoever can be trusted with very little can be trusted also with much" (Lk 16:10). Each steward must be accountable to his or her own master alone. Only the future day of accountability before God will reveal who has been the dependable servant-steward

---

4:6 *Beyond what is written* has been a challenge to interpreters. Thiselton lists seven different views and adds his own as an eighth: "*He [Paul] urges the sufficiency of the gospel of the cross interpreted within the framework of biblical tradition,* as against

of God's Word. No one and no human court can properly judge such matters in the present. Not even one's own clear conscience is a reliable guide; only *the Lord who judges* is capable of this assessment, and this will be known to us only when *the Lord comes* (1 Cor 4:5).

So the Corinthians are to stop judging their leaders and comparing them to one another, boasting in one and despising another. There are two reasons they are not capable of judging adequately. First, there are many publicly or personally unknown factors in each person's life that, if known, would change our view of them. Second, we cannot see the inner motives that underlie a person's outward actions. Once true motives are known, actions and attitudes may be understood in entirely different ways. Thus Paul says that only Christ, when he comes, will be able *to bring to light what is hidden in darkness and will expose the motives of men's hearts* (v. 5). For the third time in this section (the first two being 3:8 and 3:13-15), Paul calls attention to the absolutely personal judgment of each individual Christian by the Lord himself in that future day. *At that time each will receive his praise from God* (v. 5; Mt 25:21, 23; Rom 14:10-12; 2 Cor 5:12). All in all, Paul has offered a strong apology to the Corinthians for his own behavior and teaching and shown why their criticism of him and his status has been unjustified.

Paul now directly tells the Corinthians why he has embarked on this long exhortation involving himself and Apollos. It was so that they would learn *the meaning of the saying "Do not go beyond what is written"* (1 Cor 4:6). But what does the saying mean? Thiselton identifies and analyzes seven different views and concludes that the saying is quite relevant to Corinth and to us today: "Paul uses (1) *scripture* . . . (2) *tradition* . . . and (3) *reason*. . . . Most of all, he urges the sufficiency of the gospel of the cross interpreted within the framework of biblical tradition, as against . . . trying to add 'wisdom' aspects or notions of being 'people of the Spirit' without the cross" (2000:356). Such a view has merit. The majority of commentators have taken it to refer

---

the misguided and indeed damaging effects of trying to *add* 'wisdom' aspects or notions of being 'people of the Spirit' without the cross" (2000:356).

to going beyond what Scripture teaches in such places like Jeremiah 9:23, Job 5:13, and Psalm 94:11, passages that Paul has already cited in his arguments against boasting (1 Cor 1:19, 31; 3:19-20). Paul would be saying that they should keep to the rules laid down in Scripture concerning pride and boasting: Don't violate these instructions. But this is far from certain.

It may also be possible that Paul refers to some well-known idiomatic saying among the Corinthians as F. F. Bruce suggests (1971:48-49), familiar to them but not to us today. "Do not go beyond what is written!" or "Keep to the book!" would have been intelligible to them and relevant to the comparison Paul drew using himself and Apollos as well as to the following clear statement, *then you will not take pride in one man over against another.*

There follow three penetrating questions that have the effect of a strong rebuke to the Corinthians for judging between the apostles and setting up one leader in opposition to another (1 Cor 4:7). *Who makes you different from anyone else?* The Greek phrase may also mean, "Who concedes you any superiority?" (Danker 2000:231). Any abilities that we possess and others may lack are to be received in humble gratitude as gifts of grace from God, not claimed as tools to promote self-interest or accomplishments that merit our elevation in status. The Corinthians have not understood yet, nor applied this teaching of grace to their relationships with various leaders and one another.

Paul now turns to an underlying theological problem of the Corinthians with its lifestyle consequences (vv. 8-13). The church was infected with some who held an overrealized eschatology (Bruce 1971:49). They had fallen victim to living in the "already" (present) without the necessary counterbalancing tension of the "not yet" (future). In our day certain "health and wealth" or "name it and claim it" approaches to Christianity sound much like this ancient error of the Corinthians. We will do well, therefore, to pay close attention to how Paul deals with this gospel distortion lest we fall prey to and repeat the same excesses ourselves.

Already you have all you want! Already you have become rich! You have become kings! (v. 8). Paul speaks in bitter irony. That this is the case is confirmed in the next words: *How I wish that you had really be-*

come kings. In reality they were not kings. Why then does Paul call them kings? According to Paul's teaching, Christ, having been raised from the dead, is now exercising his messianic kingship in his state of glory (cf. 15:25); when his people in turn are raised from the dead at his parousia (cf. 15:22-23), they will share his glory (cf. Col 3:4). But as suffering preceded glory for Christ, so for his people the same order is prescribed: "we share in his sufferings in order that we may also share in his glory" (Rom 8:17; cf. the hymn quoted in 2 Tim 2:12, "if we endure, we will also reign with him").

Some of Paul's Corinthian friends (cf. 1 Cor 15:12; 2 Thess 2:2; 2 Tim 2:18) "were speaking and acting as if they had already attained the kingdom and the glory simultaneously with the gift of the Spirit" (Bruce 1971:49). "Many of the converts, convinced that they were on a new plane of life, felt that they could do anything: they were kings (4:8), they were in the Spirit, they were dead to the flesh and emancipated, so that their physical conduct might seem to them a matter of indifference; they were altogether superior to the unchanged men around them" (Arthur Darby Nock, quoted by Thiselton 1978:512)

Compare the Corinthians' boast of high status with the status of the nonchosen of Corinth's cultural elite in 1:26-29. *You have all you want* (4:8) may refer to material or spiritual food; they were satiated, filled up so that they had all they wanted. *You have become rich* refers to material wealth or spiritual wealth, or perhaps both (cf. Rev 2:9; 3:17).

Paul will now contrast the lowly lifestyle of the apostles with that of the Corinthians in order to hold up a model for them to compare with their practice and self-image (4:9-13). The behavior that led to their self-deception needed to be confronted with the opposite behavior found in the chosen representatives of Christ in the world. Only if they recognized the discrepancy could there be hope for repentance and change.

God has put us apostles on display at the end of the procession (v. 9). The expression *eschatos apodeiknymi* (proclaim, make, appoint at the end or last) may refer to a triumphal procession where defeated enemies were paraded through the streets as those *condemned to die* (cf. 2 Cor 2:14). They were *at the end* or last perhaps in the sense of the last or final age in a long line of prophets and saints who suffered reproach for the sake of the truth (1 Cor 10:11).

Alternately, if the figure refers to a gladiatorial spectacle in the circus, then "it is almost a kind of mocking gladiatorial salute to the would-be kings, 'Hail, Emperor, greetings from men about to die'" (Marshall 1987:209). As such the apostles had become a *spectacle* (*theatron*, "theater" [Acts 19:29, 31], and what is seen in the theater, a play or spectacle) viewed by *the whole universe* (*kosmos*, "the world"), by *angels* and by *men*, "in the eyes of heaven and earth" (Bruce 1971:50). But Paul is convinced that this situation was no accident; God put them in this position.

This disreputable and humiliating position of Paul and the others is now elaborated and contrasted with the self-image and claims of the Corinthians (4:10-13). The apostles are depicted *as fools . . . weak . . . dishonored*, while the Corinthians are *so wise . . . strong . . . honored*. The Corinthians prize status in their culture; Paul is contrasting the way of the cross displayed in the lives of the apostles.

Furthermore, the apostles are needy (*hungry and thirsty, . . . in rags*), mistreated (*brutally treated* or beaten) and *homeless*. They have chosen to identify with the lower-status position of those who *work hard* (*kopiaō* may refer to manual labor). Chapter 9 will be a longer apologetic for Paul's choice to refuse aid from the Corinthians. This was no doubt a major stumbling block for the Corinthians' relationship to him (Marshall 1987:173-75).

Finally, Paul speaks of himself and the other apostles as the object of much ridicule, abuse and violence: *When we are cursed, we bless; when we are persecuted, we endure it; when we are slandered, we answer kindly. Up to this moment we have become the scum of the earth* (sweepings of the floor), *the refuse of the world* (dirt, scum, filth of all). The terms translated "scum" and "refuse" were both used in the ancient world to refer to a person, usually a criminal, condemned to death as a sacrifice for the purification or cleansing of a city. Josephus and Philo use the term of the lowest classes of the society. The Greek scholar Photius (ninth century A.D.) writes that the word was used of a human

---

4:10 Paul ironically borrows the high-status terminology of the elite in the church (1:26, "wise . . . influential . . . of noble birth") and applies it to the status of Chris-

sacrifice offered to placate Poseidon in times of great danger (Hanson 1982:214). The term developed a connotation of abuse, since only worthless persons were so sacrificed.

Whether Paul intends some such sacrificial and hence atoning implication in his use here of these words is uncertain, as is the connection to Lamentations 3:45. J. B. Lightfoot notes that Ignatius of Antioch calls himself the "scum" of his Christian friends (*To the Ephesians* 18.1; Lightfoot 1981:50). In the first case the term may convey the idea of substitutionary sacrifice; in the second there may be the sense of "abject, devoted slave of the cross" (Bruce 1971:51). In any event, in the third century the term means little more than "your humble servant" (Hanson 1982:214). Commentators have often noted the similarities in the terms describing the experiences of the founders of the Corinthian church to those describing the experiences of Jesus himself (Mt 5:44; Lk 6:28).

Finally, to conclude this long section on God's view of ministries and the ministry (1 Cor 3:5—4:21), Paul gives the Corinthians a fatherly admonition (4:14-17) and then alerts them that he will soon come and sternly challenge the boastful perpetrators of divisions if they do not repent (4:18-21).

Paul says he has written *this* (v. 14, actually "these things," plural, i.e., Paul and Apollos as coequal stewards of God [3:5—4:7] and his ironic contrasts in 4:8-13) not to *shame* them (though some embarrassment most surely occurred) but to *warn* them (admonish, discipline) as his *dear children*. That is, he wants to see that they are soundly instructed in the content, manner of proclamation and ministry of the gospel. By changing to this image of *father* of the Corinthians, Paul is moving from a description of the ministries of God to his own role and relationship to the Corinthians. Paul planted the church: *in Christ Jesus I became your father through the gospel* (v. 15).

Interestingly, the father-child image functions for Paul in two ways. Not the authority of the father but the life-begetting function surfaces first. Second, the modeling function is emphasized: *I urge you to imi-*

___

tians in Christ, *wise . . . strong . . . honored,* contrasted to the apostles' status in the world's eyes: *fools . . . weak . . . dishonored* (Winter 2002:197-99).

tate me. An earthly father is to be highly respected because of his role in giving life; he is also to be a pattern of life for his children. The Corinthians had spiritual *guardians* (*paidagōgos,* "child supervisors," rather like nannies in modern Western societies), but only Paul is their spiritual father. Therefore they are to *imitate* (emulate) him.

We must understand this, it seems, as pointed irony, otherwise Paul would be contributing to the problem he has so forcefully been refuting: the error of enthusiastically admiring and championing one particular person above others. But Paul wants them to *imitate* (not "follow") *his way* (actually plural, "ways") *of life in Christ Jesus*—and thus to imitate Christ himself (11:1). He calls the high-minded, status-loving Corinthians to imitate his worthless, low-status, suffering way of life (4:10-13). Ironically, Paul's low-status lifestyle was being highlighted by the cultural upper class of Corinth to put him down, not to advocate following his way. Many in the church were emulating their status-conscious interpretations.

The role of Timothy is unique. *For this reason* connects the imitation of Paul (v. 16) with Timothy's mission (v. 17). The Corinthians will learn Paul's *way of life in Christ Jesus* not only from his own teaching about his experiences (4:10-13) but also from the model of Timothy's behavior. Timothy is Paul's spiritual *son* (or child). Timothy has picked up and fleshes out his spiritual father's ways of life in Christ: "I have no one like him, who takes a genuine interest in your welfare. For everyone looks out for his own interests, not those of Jesus Christ. But you know that Timothy has proved himself, because as a son with a father he has served with me in the work of the gospel" (Phil 2:20-22).

For Paul and then for Timothy the community of God's people is their first concern, taking priority over self-interests that cause divisions. Individual preferences must yield to communal concerns through the principle of love (1 Cor 8:2, 7-13) that does not insist on its own point of view (10:33—11:1; 13:5). Paul has taught these ways to all the churches: *I teach everywhere in every church* (cf. Rom 14:1—15:7; Gal 6:1-5; Phil 2:4-5; 1 Thess 5:12-15). There are several more specific examples in this letter of this communal principle. (1) Paul has earned his own living by working with his hands so as not to burden the churches (1 Cor 4:12—9:3-23). (2) He becomes all things to all people to promote their good, not his own interests (10:33). (3) Finally, Paul chooses not to be married in his missionary work (9:5).

The Corinthian church had apparently failed to assimilate Paul's ways. In the Western world, and especially the American church, there is a similar failure to assimilate the ways of Paul that are the ways of Jesus Christ. Doctrine is assimilated, but life change often does not follow. We can learn from Paul that parents and Christian leaders must *model* consistently the ways of Christ and teach the patterns that are illustrated in the specific things they do.

A final warning to *some of you who have become arrogant, as if I were not coming to you* (4:18) ends this part of the letter and the long comment on the problem of boasting and divisions in the church (1:13, "Is Christ divided?" answered in 3:5—4:21). The *arrogant* (inflated) are the same as those in 4:6-7 and elsewhere whose opposition to Paul has been buttressed by their claim that he is too afraid of them to come back to confront them openly. The sending of Timothy instead could be interpreted as supporting their viewpoint. Perhaps the Apollos group was interested in seeing Apollos return, since he was a person more to their liking, an eloquent man well-versed (able) in the Scriptures (Acts 18:24, 28).

Yet Paul will return, and it will be *very soon*. But while returning is his intention, the future is not ultimately determined by him; thus he adds, *if the Lord is willing* (cf. Rom 1:10; Jas 4:15). Paul is the master of his intentions, but the Lord is the determiner of his circumstances. If he comes, he will not be interested in the rhetorical abilities of his opponents but in their spiritual *power.* This is what ultimately matters, for such spiritual power is the essence of the *kingdom of God* (cf. 2:4-5; 6:9,10; 15:24, 50). If the church follows the opposition leaders, Paul, as the father, the apostolic founder of the church, will administer discipline (*whip,* rod), though he would rather come *in love and with a gentle spirit.* The choice is up to them.

The letter could well conclude at this point, but further information may have reached the apostle when Stephanas, Fortunatus and Achaicus arrived from Corinth (16:17) and supplemented the Corinthians' letter to Paul with their own reports concerning the church. Paul first turns to the ethical issues in these reports (chaps. 5-6) before taking up the questions they posed to him in writing (chaps. 7-16). Charles Talbert succinctly summarizes the letter to this point: "1 Cor 1:1—4:21 has a preparatory function. It both establishes Paul's authority and calls on the Corinthians to emulate him and lays a foundation for the content of the answers to be given to many of the issues raised in the letter from the church. With this behind him, the apostle can move to the paraenetic [teaching] section of the letter (chapters 5-16)" (1987:11).

□ Paul and the Moral Issues Reported at Corinth (5:1—6:20)

North American society has seen a sexual revolution occur that began roughly in the 1960s with Hugh Hefner's "playboy philosophy." While the era has probably ended with Hefner's marriage and subsequent divorce and the advent of AIDS, the effects continue. There is still widespread sexual promiscuity in society at large, restrained somewhat recently by the fear of HIV transmission. There is also pressure to revise the church's teaching on sexual ethics. The issue seems to emerge annually in Protestant denominations such as the Presbyterian Church USA. Many see further evidence of this revisionist handling of Scripture in the recent ordination of an actively gay Episcopal priest to the office of Bishop. A notable Christian ethicist, who has carefully analyzed the 1977 Catholic Theological Society's document called "Human Sexuality: New Directions in American Catholic Thought," sees this document in essential agreement with the widespread non-Christian cultural attitude toward sex: namely, insofar as one needs to think about sex at all in moral terms, the primary issue is whether sexual expressions serve "wholesome interpersonal relations." Now the only moral question one needs to think about in sexual behavior is "whether our sexual expressions are or are not expressions of love" (Hauerwas 1991:116).

Paul's view is different. He sees the church as a holy community, a holy temple (1 Cor 3:16-17). Fornication corrupts the holy temple of God's people and must not be tolerated, much less celebrated as an evidence of spiritual freedom in the name of "love." It will take an act of moral courage for those of us who decide to follow Jesus in our sexual expression to teach and practice this biblical view in the democratic and pluralist society in which we live. In fact, adherence to the biblical sexual ethic against the corrosions of modernity may be the main political witness of the church in the beginning of the twenty-first century.

Dealing with reported sins, mainly sexual in nature (*porneia*, "fornication"; 5:1; 6:13, 18), these two chapters form a unit. The key to understanding their content is in the interpretation of two phrases, "Everything is permissible for me" (6:12), and "We know that we all possess knowledge" (8:1). Even if these slogans came originally from Paul, there is a consensus among commentators that they were radically reinterpreted by the Corinthians and applied in a fashion which Paul does not endorse. They had apparently developed a more radical application of Paul's eschatological dualism (already, not yet) than he could allow (Thiselton 1978:515).

It will be instructive for us to trace carefully in chapters 5-6 why Paul could not follow the Corinthians' freedom slogan, "Everything is permissible for me." Some things were not permissible for Paul. How he argues against certain practices and thus restricts the meaning and application of the slogan will provide guidance for us in the complex world of changing sexual values faced by the modern Western Christian.

The Matter of Incest (5:1-13) There are four parts to the first section (chap. 5):

- the actual problem (5:1)
- two appeals for excommunication of the offender (5:2-8)
- Paul's previous letter clarified (5:9-11)
- a final appeal for excommunication (5:12-13)

The Actual Problem (5:1) It is actually (*holōs*, everywhere) *reported that there is sexual immorality* (*porneia*, fornication, prostitution, etc., a term used for any and every type of forbidden sexual intercourse). The type of fornication is identified as a case where *a man has his father's wife* (in all likelihood his stepmother). Whether the man was married to her or living with her as a concubine or whether the father was divorced or dead is unclear. The woman was probably not the man's mother, or Paul would have stated so. Not only do the Mosaic law and the New Testament condemn this kind of union (Lev 18:8; Acts 15:20, 29; 21:25), but Paul indicates that such a *kind . . . does not occur even among pagans* (*ethnesin,* "Gentiles"). Not that he suggests that the pagans have a superior moral standard, but Roman law (not Greek law) prohibited such a union even when the father was dead (Héring 1962:34). It has been suggested that the man was among the upper-class wealthy and that a slave brought the situation to the notice of Paul and his friends.

Two Appeals for Excommunication of the Offender (5:2-8)
While Paul does judge this kind of behavior as sinful (vv. 4, 13), his primary censure relates to the fact that the Christian community seems to be pleased with the whole affair: *you are proud* (inflated). Apparently a significant number of people in the church considered this man's affair a commendable expression of Christian freedom. Perhaps he reasoned in the light of his understanding that he had "already" become a "king" (4:8) that "everything is permissible" (6:12), including incestuous sexual relations. (Today our society and some in church leadership say that what matters morally in sexual activity is a "loving relationship.") The Corinthian congregation was celebrating this bold application of the man's new status, and that was for Paul even a worse offense than the incestuous relationship itself.

Rather, Paul asks, should they not have been *filled with grief* (in the Greek, simply "grieved") that would result in action to *put out of your fellowship the man who did this?* The next three verses describe how this should be done in what is generally called an act of excommunication. Though absent *physically* from the congregation, Paul will actually be present *in spirit,* in the sense that his written word of judgment in this letter will be recalled when the church assembles to excommunicate the man: *I have already passed judgment . . . just as if I were present* (cf. Col 2:5).

However, the expulsion also considers the holiness of the community. Both purposes of discipline (i.e., the individual's reclamation and the purity of the congregation) should be considered, preserving the tension between them. This action calls to mind expulsion texts in Deuteronomy (such as 17:7; 19:19), which likewise call on the commu-

---

5:5 See Thiselton for a complete listing of the various views of "hand . . . over to Satan" (2000:395-400). We should avoid seeing this as a curse formula or as necessarily

nity to remove those who have sinned and thus to preserve the holy character of the community. In the Old Testament this was often done through the death penalty. The church, however, does not assume this authority, nor could it legally carry out such action in most societies. It is hoped that prohibiting offending persons to participate in the worship and fellowship gatherings of the congregation is sufficiently stringent to bring about the repentance of such persons (it apparently worked here; cf. 2 Cor 2:5-8). All church discipline should be remedial and redemptive in purpose (1 Cor 5:5).

When the church meets, Paul says *the power of our Lord Jesus is present* (v. 4). This refers most naturally to the power of Christ present as the church prays in unity about this matter (Héring 1962:35). But how are we to understand, *hand this man over to Satan,* and the especially difficult clause *so that the sinful nature may be destroyed and his spirit saved on the day of the Lord?* These statements have provoked a great deal of discussion among commentators. No view seems free from some theological problems. Let me simply state what I believe is the best explanation and refer readers who wish to explore further to the notes.

First, why would Paul want the Christian man handed over to Satan? Almost everywhere else Satan is to be avoided (1 Pet 5:8-9). He destroys and subverts God's work and is not in the business of reclamation. However, Satan is in one other reference involved in apparent reclamation. In 1 Timothy 1:20 we read that certain persons, Hymenaeus and Alexander, have abandoned conscience and suffered shipwreck in the faith. Paul hands them over to Satan (same wording as in 1 Cor 5:5) so that they may learn "not to blaspheme." Were these also caught up in some doctrinal heresy and behavioral misconduct and excommunicated, as Paul directs here?

Furthermore, what does it mean to suffer the destruction of the *sinful nature* (*sarx,* "flesh," "body," "sinful flesh") and for the man's *spirit* to be *saved on the day of the Lord?* I follow those commentators who understand the delivering to Satan (as "accuser," Job 1:6) for the de-

---

a death consignment. Paul wants the "fleshly" attitude of self-glorying self-satisfaction destroyed in the man as well as perhaps in the community.

struction of the flesh to mean the same thing as when Jesus permitted Peter to be sifted like wheat in a sieve by Satan (Lk 22:31). Also we may relate this to the Corinthians' judging themselves lest they fall under the Lord's judgment and being disciplined so that they will not be condemned with the world (1 Cor 11:29-32). Such unrepentant offenders must learn the folly of the world's snare and have their *sinful nature* destroyed through repentance so that their lives may be saved at the return of Christ. Aquinas observed this and commented:

> In order to overcome their pride, God punishes certain men by allowing them to fall into sins of the flesh, which though they may be less grievous are more evidently shameful. . . . From this indeed the gravity of pride is made manifest. For just as a wise physician, in order to cure a worse disease, allows the patient to contract one that is less dangerous so the sin of pride is shown to be more grievous by the very fact that, as a remedy, God allows men to fall into other sins. (*Summa Theologica* 2.2.q62.6ad3)

A second appeal to expel the incestuous Christian from the fellowship comes through the Passover celebration analogy (5:6-8). Based on Mosaic instruction (Ex 12:15-20) and as practiced to this day in Jewish observances of the Passover, all leaven (yeast) was to be completely removed from Jewish homes, and all bread eaten for seven days was to be unleavened. Originally the unleavened bread symbolized the "bread of affliction," because they came out of Egypt in great distress due to the haste required (Deut 16:3). Later, as in this passage, the leaven also became associated with evil within the community. Hence *let us keep the Festival* (metaphorically speaking, not literally), *not with the old yeast, the yeast of malice and wickedness, but with bread without yeast, the bread of sincerity and truth* (v. 8). In other contexts, leaven may connote that which is good (Mt 13:33).

Christ is *our Passover lamb* (*pascha*, Passover; the Greek omits "lamb," since a goat could also be sacrificed). *Is sacrificed* recalls the analogy the early church found between the lamb of the exodus event

---

5:7 The Geneva version (1557) reads: "For Christ our Easter lamb is offered up for us."

5:11 *Greedy (pleonektēs)* is sometimes a synonym for "thief" *(kleptēs)* or even "vio-

and the death of Jesus: God's delivering his people, the church, from the sin and evil of the world. Since Christ has died, the feast is to be kept by expelling the leaven—the incestuous man—from the fellowship. The popular wisdom saying is true, *a little yeast works through the whole batch of dough* (cf. Gal 5:9). "Souls to souls are like apples, one being rotten rots another" (Thomas Traherne, quoted in Moffatt 1938:57). Paul is concerned that the church, the *new batch,* which is positionally *without yeast* ("evil," "corruption"), should be so in actuality. The church is holy and must be pursuing holiness. The evil person's misdeeds and the boasting about the affair are to stop immediately, because otherwise the whole church could be quickly corrupted (cf. Acts 5:1-11).

Paul's Previous Letter Clarified (5:9-11) *I have written you in my letter* is the first clear reference in the New Testament to an apostolic letter that has not survived in our canonical collection. There were apparently others as well (cf. Col 4:16). This should not be troublesome for us. Not all the apostolic instruction was universal enough in scope to address different congregations' needs, and the Holy Spirit worked providentially to give us those writings in the collection (canon) that would best serve the church in its continuing witness to the gospel of Christ.

Paul's instructions in this former letter were apparently to the effect that the Corinthians should *not associate with* Christian believers who were *sexually immoral (pornos,* fornicator, one who practices sexual acts forbidden in the Scriptures; cf. 1 Cor 6:9; Eph 5:5; 1 Tim 1:10; Heb 13:4). Since Paul goes on to mention other classes of sinners, *greedy . . . idolater . . . slanderer (loidoros,* "abuser," including verbal abuse) . . . *drunkard . . . swindler* (see vv. 10-11), it appears he had meant to use *sexually immoral people* as an example that implied at least these other types of behaviors as well. The Corinthians apparently misunderstood Paul and took him to mean that they should not associate with any evil person of this type, whether in the church or outside in the pagan soci-

---

lent seizure" *(harpax).* Then it means one who uses brute force to enrich himself at the expense of his neighbor. In Ezekiel 22:27 wicked leaders are compared with wolves and are called *pleonektai* (Héring 1962:38).

ety. He states clearly that this was not his intention. If it were, this would practically forbid Christians' having any dealings with the outside society, such as buying and selling, transportation, work, as well as certain common social activities.

But the case is quite different for those who claim to belong to Christ. Paul insists that such behavior, if practiced by those who call themselves Christians, should prompt other Christians to disassociate with that wrongdoer until the behavior is corrected. Avoidance of association would include not only public meals and the table of the Lord in church but also private meals: *do not even eat* together (v. 11). We should remember that this action was redemptive in intent, looking forward to the repentance of the offender and the consequent full restoration to former associations.

Final Appeal for Excommunication of the Offender (5:12-13)
Paul uses the language of *outside/inside* to further clarify the church's responsibility in the matter of the incestuous Christian man. While Paul and others in the New Testament make general assessments of pagan conduct (cf. Rom 1:18-31; 1 Pet 4:3), he does not find that it is his or the Corinthians' responsibility *to judge those outside* (in the sense of handing over for judicial punishment). *God* alone *will judge* sinners *outside* the church. But *inside,* the Corinthians themselves (along with Paul) are given the responsibility to be judges. Therefore, *"expel the wicked man from among you"* (cf. Deut 17:7; 19:19).

The Matter of Litigation (6:1-11) My country, the United States, is a litigious society. For example, a major factor in the American healthcare system crisis is the heavy burden of malpractice lawsuits brought against physicians and the consequent high cost of malpractice insurance. But what is more distressing is the frequent suing of one Christian by another in the public law courts, often over trivial matters. The Christian Legal Society has had no small amount of success in establishing Christian arbitration in lieu of public lawsuits. Are such issues what Paul is talking about? Points of similarity and differences will be

---

6:1 *The ungodly* is *adikoi* and probably should be translated "corrupt judges and juries" (Winter 2001:60-63; Thiselton 2000:424). Another possibility would be *ungodly*

noted in the following discussion.

Paul identifies two main problems (6:1, 7), then in each case makes two arguments against the sinful practice (6:2-4 and 5-6; 6:7 and 8-11). This section on disputes among Christians at Corinth seems at first glance to be somewhat out of place, sandwiched as it is between sections that deal with ethical sexual issues (5:1-13 and 6:12-20). However, there are several factors that show they are related in Paul's mind. The lists of offenses are strikingly similar in 5:10-11 and 6:9-10. Included among them are sexual sins such as fornication and adultery that may have occasioned some of the disputes and the litigation in pagan courts. These disputes over sexual offenses also spill over into the context not only of 6:12-20 but also of chapter 7. Furthermore, the congregation's attitude of indifference to the sin of incest that we saw in 5:1-13 is also one of Paul's concerns regarding the disputes (6:2-5).

The First Problem: Public Lawsuits Between Christians (6:1)
As a further example of the Corinthian's worldly ways (3:3), Paul has received the news that some members of the church were prosecuting others, suing them in pagan courts over such things as legal possessions, breach of contract, damages, fraud and minor injuries, matters of civil rather than criminal law (Winter 2001:65). In Paul's eyes this was shocking: *dare he* (*tolmaō,* "have the audacity"). He indicates that they were bringing these conflicts not *before the saints* (the church) but before *ungodly* judges. The word translated in the NIV as *ungodly* (NRSV "unrighteous") actually means "unjust" in legal contexts. A majority of commentators and translations have attempted to tone down this word, making it simply a synonym for *unbelievers* (v. 6), thereby suggesting that Paul was not making any negative assessment of Roman law proceedings in Corinth. By now, however, there seems to be now good evidence of widespread corruption in legal proceedings throughout the empire (Winter 2001:60-64). Apparently the Corinthian Christians had something (status?) to gain by going to these corrupt courts rather than resolving conflicts within the church.

It is likely, given what is known of the inequities in the judicial sys-

---

(NIV) with no moral judgment as to their fairness (Conzelmann 1975:104n4; Fee 1987:232).

tem, that only upper-class, wealthier members of the Corinthian church were able to bring disputes to the courts, whether the conflict was with others of the upper class or with someone of inferior status. The poor were not able to challenge the wealthy in the courts because of legal privileges that rendered the upper class immune from summons to trial by inferiors. Furthermore, the disputants were not dispassionate before the court. Considerable acrimony and personal attacks were part of the procedure, including advocates' use of vicious language against their client's adversary. All of this belied very publicly the exercise of genuine Christian love among Christ's people (Winter 2001:68).

Two Arguments Against the Practice (6:2-6) The first argument against this practice is from tradition (Paul's earlier teaching?): *Do you not know . . . ?* (vv. 2-3). Here Paul presents his theological bases for addressing the problem. Good theology is essential to right conduct, although good theology alone is not enough to ensure proper behavior. There must be also moral courage to act on the knowledge one has. Courage is a character trait learned through imitation of Jesus and Paul (4:16; 11:1). That *the saints will judge the world* and *angels* provides the theological basis for Paul's argument from the greater to the lesser: if you are qualified to judge the world, including serious and heavy matters involving heavenly angels, why would you think yourselves incompetent to judge *trivial cases* and the ordinary *things of this life?* That there will be a future judgment of the world by God is one of Paul's fundamental beliefs (Rom 2:2-12); that this judgment will involve the saints also judging in some way is confirmed in other biblical writings (Dan 7:22; Lk 22:30; Rev 20:4); the judging of angels is inferred or alluded to in other places in both the canonical Scriptures and noncanonical Jewish writings (Dan 10:13, 20; Jude 6; 1 Enoch 10:12; 12:5-6, etc.).

Is the comment about *those of little account in the church* (1 Cor 6:4) to be understood as describing what the Corinthians were actually doing (NRSV) or as a sarcastic imperative to shock them (NIV)? Further-

---

6:4 *Appoint as judges even men of little account in the church!* (NIV) reflects understanding the verb *kathizete* as an imperative. This would then imply that those *of little account* are Christians who are appointed by the church. Alternatively and preferably, the footnote rendering "do you appoint . . . ?" (NRSV; TNIV, "do you ask

more, are these *of little account* Christians, or is this Paul's way of referring to the outside judges to whom the Christians were entrusting their litigation? Finally, are these people viewed as *of little account* by the Corinthians or by Paul? The commentators are divided. Paul says in the next verse that he has spoken this way to *shame* them (v. 5). This would suggest that he has spoken ironically or sarcastically in the preceding verse. Tentatively, I agree with the NIV translators and believe that Paul is referring sarcastically to the pagan judges as those *of little account;* from Paul's viewpoint they do not have importance in God's kingdom, and the church should view them the same way (not only as *of little account* but as nonstatus persons). He wants to shame them for taking their ordinary disputes before secular judges and juries who for those in Christ have no real importance, no status.

Continuing his irony and sarcasm, Paul further rebukes them for their status seeking and gives them another reason to stop this practice: *Is it possible that there is nobody among you who is wise enough to judge a dispute between believers?* (v. 5). The Sophistic rhetoricians (the "wise") who were prized by many Christian Corinthians, and whom some believed themselves to be, were trained in legal defense and argumentation. Could not one of them be enlisted to judge between believer and believer? The fact that they were going to the civil courts ironically testified to their low view of the "wisdom" possessed by their fellow church members!

The Second Problem: The Litigations Themselves Are Wrong (6:7-11) The existence of legal disputes among them is in itself wrong, so that both accused and accuser, winners and losers, *have been completely defeated already*. In other words, you have lost the case morally and spiritually before even going before a judge. Disputes in themselves, whether taken before pagan judges or before Christians, are an indication of worldliness rather than Christlikeness in the congregation (3:3). Paul has a better way.

His first argument against having any disputes at all is the example

---

for a ruling . . . ?") understands the verb as an indicative question. This would imply that *men of little account* refers to the "unjust judges" in the pagan courts (Winter 2001:69-70; Thiselton 2000:433).

and teaching of Jesus: *Why not rather be wronged?* (The verb means to be treated unjustly; cf. Mt 5:39; 1 Pet 2:23.) *Why not rather be cheated?* (This verb in the passive form means to suffer loss of property, to let oneself be robbed; cf. Mt 5:39-42; Lk 6:30). Paul calls on them to follow Jesus, who suffered injustice and harm and did not seek to retaliate or receive compensation from those who treated him unfairly. While there is disagreement whether this principle of nonretaliation applies to Christians who serve in public government service roles, all affirm that nonretaliation should be the norm for relations between Christians and for Christian personal action toward non-Christians.

But the situation is still worse at Corinth. Not only are the believers seeking redress for wrongs in the courts rather than letting themselves be wronged and cheated, but they are also inflicting wrong and cheating on one another (1 Cor 6:8). They not only failed to resist evil but performed it (Hering 1962:41). Paul warns them that such evil practice is incompatible with the kingdom of God. A moral seam runs throughout God's kingdom, and those who profess to be part of it must heed the serious warning that if you practice evil you will be excluded. *Do not be deceived* is a warning repeated in 1 Corinthians 15:33 and Galatians 6:7. Galatians 5:19-21 has a similar list, called "the works of the flesh," to which is appended also the warning that those who practice such things "will not inherit the kingdom of God" (cf. 1 Tim 1:10).

The evil Paul has in mind is partially identified in the practices of wrongdoing listed here (6:9-10). He has already given a list of evil practices in the previous chapter. The whole list is prefaced with the term *the wicked* ("unrighteous," "unjust," "wicked"; TNIV "wrongdoers"), which in this specific context refers to those who harm or wrong others (v. 8). No doubt some of these offenses were involved in the lawsuits the Corinthians were pursuing. The first three terms in the list are clear. The *sexually immoral* are those who have sexual intercourse

---

6:9 The two terms *male prostitutes (malakoi)* and *homosexual offenders* (*arsenokoitai,* TNIV "practicing homosexuals") have evoked considerable debate. The first term is mistranslated in the NIV (also TNIV); though broader than the second term, it seems in this context to point to playing the female role in sexual intercourse with other males. The latter term here and in 1 Timothy 1:10 is unknown in Greek literature before these references and "literally means 'bedders of males, those [men] who

with others who are not their spouses.

The fourth and fifth terms are more difficult. *Male prostitutes* incorrectly translates the Greek *malakoi* ("soft, effeminate," a term for men and boys who take the more passive role in homosexual relations), while *homosexual offenders* (TNIV "practicing homosexuals") correctly renders the Greek *arsenokoitai*, "those who lie with males" (cf. Rom 1:26-27; 1 Tim 1:10). This latter term refers to men and boys who take the more active role in homosexual relations. Behind Paul's rejection of these practices are Leviticus 18:22 and 20:13, which he sees as still valid for the Christian community.

The other term not included in the chapter 5 list is *thieves* (*leptai*, 1 Cor 6:10). The difference between *leptai* and *harpax* ("swindlers," v. 10, also 5:11) is perhaps related to the violence accompanying the theft. The former refers to stealing in general, while the latter is more like our "armed robbery."

And that is what some of you were (v. 11) anticipates Paul's next remark about their changed life. Not all the Corinthians had been evildoers in these ways. Still, *some* would remind them of the background of sin they all came from; perhaps it suggests also that some black sheep among the flock were affecting the holiness of the congregation. But that they *were* these things suggests that they are no longer. A radical transformation was effected when they were *washed, . . . sanctified, . . . justified.*

Perhaps John Calvin is right that all three terms point to the same reality of the believer's salvation. *Washed* speaks not primarily of baptism but of the deep spiritual cleansing from sin's defilement and guilt that the person of faith experiences when she is brought into Christ (Eph 5:26-27; Tit 3:5; Rev 1:5; 7:14). *Sanctified* refers to the act of God's Holy Spirit setting believers apart (making them holy) from the world and the devil by uniting them to the body of Christ as God's own posses-

---

take [other] males to bed,' 'men who sleep or lie with males'" (for a full discussion of both terms see Gagnon 2001:306; see also 303-39; also Thiselton 2000:447-51).

The Old Testament background of Mosaic ordinances in Deuteronomy 27 and 30 seems evident through this section, and in particular Leviticus 18:22 and 20:13 in verse 9 (Rosner 1994:119-21).

sion, to be used exclusively for his service and worship and thus to reflect his holy and moral character (1 Cor 1:2, 30; 1 Thess 4:3-4, 7). *Justified* expresses Paul's understanding as developed in Galatians and later in Romans: God's act of forgiving, accepting as righteous in advance of the final day of judgment, and empowering with the Holy Spirit on the basis of Christ's death all sinners who believe the proclamation of the gospel (Rom 4:1-8). Three terms overlap in meaning, yet each has a focus that complements the others'. The gift character of God's forgiveness and new status before him should go a long way to correcting the wrong views of earthly status among the Corinthians.

How can the Corinthian Christians be at the same time sinners and washed, sanctified and justified? Is Martin Luther's famous statement true, *simul justus et peccator* ("at the same time justified and sinner")? Yes, but this is not the whole picture. Believers are also *washed* and *sanctified*. Sin in the believer's life is incompatible with this new reality in Christ; there is to be a progressive realization of sanctification in our actual experience. This is elsewhere described as the fruits of righteousness (Rom 6:22; Jas 3:17-18) or the fruit of the Holy Spirit (Gal 5:22-23). While Paul is realistic and knows that sin is present among the Corinthian Christians, he is also insistent that the presence of repeated acts of sin which form the character of a person into a fornicator, or a swindler or homosexual or thief, is incompatible with the kingdom of God. Those who become such evildoers through repeated offenses, even though professing Christian faith, will not share in the kingdom of God.

Washing, sanctification and justification must radically affect the moral life of those who name Christ as Lord. As you are in Christ, so should you be in your life. Failure to yield to the Holy Spirit's ways will destroy the fruits of righteousness (cf. Gal 5:16, 25-26). "The goodness of God—who affords man the greatest imaginable benefit in the world, namely his Spirit as the earnest of redemption—must be stimulant, not for the attempt to acquire merit, but to let God act freely in his will to redeem and sanctify" (Héring 1962:42).

Sex and Saints (6:12-20) One recent commentator aptly titles this section "Keeping the Bedroom Attached to the Rest of the House" (Talbert

1987). Paul here deals with a Christian view of the sexual use of the body. In light of the widespread decline of Christian sexual values in Western cultures in general and even within the theology and practice of the Christian church, we would do well to observe carefully Paul's teaching in this passage. While ancient Corinth was perhaps no more degenerate sexually than some of our own port cities, such as San Francisco or New Orleans, Corinth was widely known for its unrestrained sexual indulgence. The oft-repeated statement that "to corinthianize" had become an equivalent in Greek for "to practice fornication" is probably correct.

Paul's theology of sexuality and its application to concrete issues such as how we can raise a generation of Christian young people free from AIDS is a very pressing and urgent challenge facing the church today. Good sexual theology alone will not solve all our problems of Christian sexual sin, but without it we have little chance of making much progress.

The passage falls into two parts. In the first Paul discusses the freedom of the Christian in respect to sexual uses of the body (6:12-18). In the second Paul continues the thought of the first part, with added emphasis on the sacredness of the individual body of the believer as a temple of the Holy Spirit (6:18-20). In each part there are four parallel emphases. Paul first quotes the Corinthians' slogans or principles, then offers his point of correction followed by the theological bases for his moral principle. Each part concludes with a word of exhortation.

An important key to understanding Paul's teaching here is to recognize and identify the Corinthian slogans or principles that were guiding their moral behavior in sexual matters. There are three in this section (6:12-20). Many translations set them off with quotation marks. We would do well to mark them at the beginning:

- "Everything is permissible for me" (v. 12, twice)
- "Food for the stomach and the stomach for food"—but God will destroy them both (v. 13)
- All other sins a man commits are outside his body (v. 18)

In each instance Paul corrects the misunderstanding. He either qualifies the slogan (as in the first one) or offers a different principle in place of the slogan (as in the last two).

Freedom, the Body, Sex Outside Marriage and the Body of Christ (6:12-18) Everything is permissible (lawful) was the rallying cry of the moral liberals in the church (v. 12; 10:23). Virtually all modern commentators accept this saying as a Corinthian slogan. It could well have originated from a statement of Paul, taken out of its context, in which the apostle was enunciating his view of Christian freedom from the law of Moses (Rom 6:14-15; 1 Cor 9:19-21; Gal 5:1). Some Corinthians thought this meant that they could have sex with whomever they desired. Their first argument went something like this. The sexual desire should be satisfied with the same degree of moral indifference with which we view fulfilling the bodily desire of hunger and food: *food for the stomach and the stomach for food* (v. 13). Furthermore, since natural bodily functions, including sexual desire and its satisfaction, are a part of the present order that will one day be done away (*God will destroy them both,* v. 13), we should live now as if they were morally irrelevant to our spiritual life. Note that this explanation would entail taking the words *God will destroy them both* as part of the Corinthian slogan (*contra* NIV quote ending after *food*).

How does Paul respond? In the first place, he modifies the freedom catchphrase so as not to deny legitimate Christian freedom from the Mosaic law but to qualify that freedom in two ways. Authentic Christian freedom must always be exercised in the context of love that seeks the good of the community: *but not everything is beneficial* (v. 12, to be profitable, good, helpful for someone or some group). Furthermore, undisciplined freedom may become harmful to us personally by fostering addictive or enslaving behavior: *but I will not be mastered by anything* (v. 12, to be made a slave; cf. 7:4). "In all things I may do as I please, but I will not be so false to myself as to let things do as they please with me" (Moffatt 1938:68). Perhaps Augustine captures Paul's emphasis as well: "Love God and do what you please." Since the love of God involves seeking above all else to please him in our behavior, the freedom of the Christian is disciplined by what this love entails.

6:12 *Everything is permissible* seems to be a principle practiced by free people of status: "the wise are permitted to do anything whatsoever they wish" (Dio Chrysostom *Oration* 14.7). At age eighteen the *toga virilis* (adult cloak) was given to the

Second, Paul gives a moral principle: *The body is not meant for sexual immorality (porneia,* fornication or sexual intercourse outside of marriage), *but for the Lord, and the Lord for the body* (v. 13). Our physical bodies, created by God to be the instruments by which we worship and serve him, are very important to God. Far from insignificant or morally irrelevant as the Corinthians claimed, our bodies are not created to be used as agents of fornication. The physical body belongs to and is united to the Lord Jesus; he has a plan for it (including resurrection), and fornication is incompatible with that plan. But why is this so important?

Paul next appeals to three theological realities about our bodies to ground his argument against the Corinthians' viewpoint that the act of intercourse outside of marriage is irrelevant to our moral and spiritual life as Christians. First, he appeals to the future destiny of our bodies. *By his power God raised the Lord from the dead, and he will raise us also* (v. 14; this anticipates chap. 15). A theology of the resurrection of the dead provides for the Christian a strong antidote against present abuse of the body, especially sexual intercourse outside of marriage. God has a future design for and claim on our body. Fornication is incompatible with the future resurrection of the body, because it rejects God's intended purpose for our body: to worship and serve him in obedient love.

Second, Paul appeals to the nature of the church as the body of Christ: *Your bodies are members of Christ himself* (v. 15). Do we ever hear such an appeal in our own day? We do not think of our physical bodies as part of Christ's church. Instead we think of our personalities' or spirits' being united to the one body of the church. But Paul claims that our physical bodies are mystically, by the Holy Spirit, united to Christ (12:12, 27). Our physical bodies, then, participate in Christ. They express his presence in the world. So is it appropriate to take my body that is united to Christ and unite it in sexual intercourse with an illicit sexual partner (prostitute or any illicit sexual partner)? Paul answers

young man, symbolizing freedom to do virtually everything, including reclining at the diners with the *heterae* (prostitutes; Winter 2001:81-82, 86-93).

with his usual strong negative: *Never!* (May it never happen!)

Why should sex outside of marriage be all that bad? Perhaps it is inappropriate, but why is it so sinful? Paul answers by means of a third theological principle: to unite my physical body to an illicit sexual partner is to *become one flesh* with her or him (alternately, *one . . . in body*, v. 16). Paul here alludes to Genesis 2:24, where God institutes marriage saying that the man and woman shall "become one flesh" (Mk 10:7; Eph 5:31). This is generally held to refer especially but not exclusively to the sexual union. The believer is united to Christ and is *one with him in spirit;* to form a sexual union with an illicit partner breaks this "one spirit" union with Christ, since it is impossible to be united at the same time to two bodies (the Lord and the illicit partner).

This is a serious matter in light of Paul's theology of the body. Therefore Paul closes this first part with the exhortation *Flee from sexual immorality* ("fornication"). We naturally think of the moral courage of Joseph, who literally ran away when confronted with a sexual temptation (Gen 39:12; 1 Cor 10:14).

Destruction of Our Inner Life Versus Honoring God (6:18-20)
This brief finale to Paul's instruction regarding the body and fornication is patterned like the earlier part around a Corinthian slogan followed by Paul's moral principle and then the theological basis for it. A final exhortation closes this section. His chief point is that fornication is an abuse of our body because God has purchased it to be used as a sanctuary for the indwelling of his Holy Spirit. Therefore we are to glorify God in our body.

All other sins a man commits are outside his body (v. 18) is a highly problematic statement. The NIV takes this as Paul's own teaching. But for this interpretation the translator must without any evidence add the word *other,* which is not in the Greek text. This would then make the next

---

6:16 *"The two will become one flesh"* does not mean Paul would hold that a man's sexual encounter with a prostitute is a marriage to her. Rather the sexual act unites the two bodies but does not constitute a marriage in the biblical understanding.

6:18 *All [other] sins a man commits are outside his body.* This part of the verse is very difficult. Is this a Corinthian slogan or Paul's own teaching? Arguments for both views seem to be equally convincing. If it is Paul's teaching, it must be asked why sexual sin is a worse sin or more damaging to the body than other sins, such as drug

statement (which everyone believes is Paul's teaching) mean that fornication is the only exception, because it is done inwardly, in the body,
not outside it like other sins. However, for reasons given in the notes, I
believe these words in verse 18 should be taken as another Corinthian
slogan: "'Every sin that a person commits is outside the body.'" I believe
this is part of the Corinthian argument for Christian freedom for all types
of sexual intercourse. They seem to have argued that sin is a matter of
the inward soul and its intentions and motives. Therefore bodily appe-
tites and their satisfaction—whether hunger satisfied by eating food or
sexual desire satisfied by intercourse with a partner other than one's own
spouse—are quite irrelevant to us morally and spiritually. Paul counters
bluntly with his own moral principle: *He who sins sexually* (fornicates)
sins against his own body (v. 18). Far from being harmless, the one who
fornicates harms his or her own body. How or why?

Paul now gives the theological basis for his principle. My individual
body is a sacred member of Christ himself (v. 15), and as such is *a temple
of the Holy Spirit, who is in* me. My body is holy—a place where God's
presence is found, because of the gift of the indwelling Holy Spirit. I must
not abuse my body by defiling it with illicit sexual intercourse (1 Thess
4:3-8). Remember the warning given earlier to those who defile God's
holy temple: *God will destroy* that person (3:17; Heb 13:4).

Furthermore, the Christian's body is no longer his or her own to do
with it as she or he sees fit, because the body now belongs to the Lord
through redemption: *You are not your own: you were bought at a price*
(1 Cor 6:19-20). Our entire physical body with all of its frustrations, including its sexual functioning, has been bought with the price of Christ's
life (7:23; Mk 10:45; Rom 3:24; Eph 1:7; 1 Pet 1:18-19). Our bodies belong to God because of creation (1 Cor 6:13) and also because of redemption. Redemption fulfills God's intended purpose for the creation of

addiction or suicide. In my opinion this part of the verse is a Corinthian slogan, followed by Paul's own rebuttal in the latter part of 6:18, *but he who sins sexually sins
against his own body*. This is true, because in Paul's argument against freedom to
have sex with prostitutes, uniting a body that is owned by the Lord (that is part of
Christ's body) with a foreign body corrupts the integrity of both the individual member and the corporate body of Christ.

the body rather than, as the Corinthians would have it, transcends that purpose so that the body is morally and spiritually irrelevant to our eternal destiny. Since we have been freed from sin's mastery to serve a new master, the living God, we should not allow ourselves to be brought back under slavery to the old master, who would lead us into the bondage of sexual fornication. *Therefore* ("so then," or "don't waste any more time") *honor God with your body* (v. 20). We could paraphrase this exhortation: "Don't waste any more time. Give God the preference in the sexual use of your bodies." There is a strong hint of a trinitarian pattern emerging in this section (Thiselton 2000:459).

So, not because of the fear of pregnancy, or the fear of the deadly AIDS virus, or because of possible future sexual dysfunction, but because our bodies are corporately members of Christ and individually sacred shrines where God dwells, destined for resurrection, we should abstain from all sexual intercourse outside of marriage and use our body to honor God in all its functions.

☐ Marriage, Divorce, Remarriage and Singleness as a Calling (7:1-40)

There is hardly a subject that strikes so close to where most of us live as the one before us in this chapter. In the wider society nearly one marriage in two ends in divorce, and countless thousands of unmarried couples are living together. The subject is just as pertinent in the Christian community, where the divorce rate is only slightly less. An evangelical Christian college reported recently on a study of its first-year students over several years; one finding was that 40-50 percent of these Christian students indicated that they had engaged in sexual intercourse at least once prior to arriving on campus. If true, this is quite alarming.

A host of contemporary questions can be raised about the area of marriage. Should I get married, especially if I want to wholeheartedly serve the Lord, perhaps as a missionary? Can Christians marry non-Christians? Does God approve of divorce under certain circumstances? What are these circumstances? If I divorce for a biblical reason, can I be remarried with God's blessing? Isn't remaining single less than God's best for us? Can I remarry with God's blessing if my spouse has died? If I have been divorced or widowed, would it be better for me to remain unmarried? Most of these questions can be answered from this chapter if we treat Paul's teaching with care.

With the six-times-repeated phrase *now for* (*peri de,* "now about," "now concerning") Paul takes up *the matters* the Corinthians *wrote about* in their official letter. His responses to the questions they raised occupy the remainder of 1 Corinthians. Among these questions are issues with which the modern church also continues to struggle: sex, marriage, divorce, remarriage and singleness (7:1, 25), and spiritual gifts, including miracles and speaking in tongues (12:1). Other questions also vexed the ancient Corinthians which initially seem of less importance to us, such as the eating of food sacrificed to idols (8:1), the relief offering to the poor Christians in Jerusalem (16:1) and the possible visit of Apollos (16:12).

Other issues Paul touches on in these chapters (7-16) are likely answers to other questions they had mentioned, though they are not directly introduced with the same formula (e.g., women's and men's hair attire in worship, 11:2-16; conduct at the Lord's Table, 11:17-34; the doctrine of the bodily resurrection of the dead, 15:1-58). Of course it is also possible that those latter matters were raised in the oral report from Chloe's people (1:11). There were also some matters brought up in the letter that Paul preferred to discuss with the Corinthians personally when he returned to Corinth (11:34), rather than in writing.

Chapters 7-16 of 1 Corinthians probably have been and are turned to more often for guidance on critical issues facing the church than any other section of the New Testament. They are highly instructive, yet their meaning is often controversial. If we desire an apostolic word for guidance in these morally troubled times, it will be important for us to pay close attention to what Paul is actually saying as we seek to call the church to reformation and revival and to follow Paul and ultimately Christ himself in these matters.

Throughout church history and to the present, Paul's remarks on sex and marriage in chapter 7 have been viewed quite differently depending on the commentator or reader. Opinions range all the way from seeing Paul as a great supporter of marriage and sexual relations to viewing him as having quite a negative view of sex and marriage and being an enemy of women. Augustine and other early church fathers, for example, took verse 1 as the basis for rejecting, as a venial sin, sexual intercourse for mutual enjoyment, even within marriage (*Confessions* 2.3). Bertrand Russell called Paul's views on sex and marriage in the chapter a "morbid aberration" (quoted in Phipps 1982:130). Others have seen Paul as advocating a "fire extinguisher" view of marriage.

While not all of the apostle's views in the chapter resonate with modern sympathies, much of the negative attitude toward Paul's views is based on misunderstandings of what he actually said. It is very important then to look at the text carefully in its literary and cultural context and base our modern attitudes and applications of his teaching on the best sense of the text available to us today.

The chapter falls into two main sections, each introduced with the formula *peri de,* "now for" (v. 1), "now about" (v. 25). The first focuses on the questions of ascetic marriages, divorce and remaining in God's calling (vv. 1-24). In the second section the Corinthians' question concerning virgins and marriage is answered (vv. 25-40).

Ascetic Marriages, Singleness, Divorce, Remarriage and Remaining in God's Calling (7:1-24) It may be well to summarize at the outset what I believe to be Paul's views on marriage and singleness. He teaches that marriage with ongoing, full, mutual sexual satisfaction is desirable and good and that singleness is likewise desirable and good. Fornication (sex outside marriage) is bad; burning with passion (frustrated love) and not marrying is likewise bad. Singleness is not better than being married; it is only better than being single and burning with passion. What each of these means will be explained as Paul's statements are examined in detail.

Since differences of opinion abound, it is important to state the fivefold guiding principles I have followed in arriving at the conclusions found in these pages.

1. The thread that runs through the whole chapter is Paul's principle of not changing one's social status for spiritual improvement. Another way to state this principle is that one's social position is irrelevant to authentic Christian existence in the world (7:17-24). This is not the same as a status quo argument. The motives are different. Paul's principle affects many areas of the Christian life, especially marital status. It is

this principle, along with the eschatological principle (see below), that leads Paul to personally prefer singleness over being married (vv. 25-26, 32-35).

2. Paul's instruction is shaped by his belief in a future event that is about to happen (vv. 26, 29). While not described as such here, everywhere else this event is the return of Christ (1:7, 4:5, 11:26, 15:23; 16:22). This pull of the future shapes the present responses of Christians to worldly matters, including marriage. Therefore on the one hand, while some relativizing of and withdrawal from the world are appropriate, on the other, Christians must take fully into account their situation and circumstances in the world (vv. 5, 7, 13, 15, 21, 37) and pursue whatever course of action enables them to serve God with least distraction (vv. 5, 9, 15, 29-35), considering their special gifts from God (v. 7; Thiselton 1978:519).

3. Whatever the source, the backdrop to Paul's responses in this chapter is some type of overly ascetic tendency among some Corinthians. By "ascetic" I mean a withdrawal from the ordinary affairs of this life (sex, marriage, family, foods, drink, socializing, etc.) Ancient Greek and Roman societies were laced with various types of asceticism (Wimbush 1987:2-10). Thus celibacy might be preferable to all, Paul seems to say, if there were no such thing as human nature (vv. 2, 9). "To leave human nature out of account, however, arises *either* from Gnostic ideas which might or might not be present at Corinth, *or* from the combination of a radically realized eschatology and an atmosphere of spiritual enthusiasm" (Thiselton 1978:519). Here Paul must deal with a group at Corinth with these tendencies, a group that is difficult to name. Perhaps we might call them "the those-who-thought-they-were-more-spiritual group," or "the spiritual-sexual ascetics," or "the super-spirituals."

4. We must recognize the occasional nature of Paul's instructions. He is answering real questions about specific cases at Corinth; he is *not* giving a treatise on Christian marriage and singleness. He is dealing with issues on a case-by-case basis, applying one principle here and another there, as well as one principle in one way here and the same principle differently there in a pastoral fashion. "Paul's entire concern in this chapter is to encourage the Corinthians to settle individual cases

on their own merits, in the light of the practical situation of life as it really is, rather than as it is seen by the 'spiritual' theorists. The one practical consideration is 'how to please the Lord' (vv. 32-35) in a given situation" (Thiselton 1978:519).

5. Finally, I believe with others that Paul treats each group or case only once and then moves on to other groups or cases. He doesn't return to give further instructions, as an afterthought, to groups or categories of persons once he has moved on to another case. So verses 2-7 address those getting married after their conversion, verses 8-9 widowers and widows, verses 10-11 those who were already married when they were converted, verses 12-16 those who have an unbelieving spouse, and verses 25-40 the virgins. The only apparent exception is in verses 39-40, where he seemingly gives additional instructions to widows closely paralleling his earlier remarks (vv. 8-9). This, however, may be an additional case specifically mentioned in the Corinthian letter.

Bearing these five principles of interpretation in mind, let us look at the actual content of the chapter.

The Corinthians and Sexual Relations (7:1) It is good for a man not to marry (v. 1; *mē haptomai,* not to touch a woman). The translation must be challenged on several counts. Because Paul immediately qualifies this statement in verse 2 by declaring that men and women should marry to avoid fornication *(immorality),* some have supposed that it should be read as a prohibition of marriage, as in the NIV translation (Grosheide 1953:155). Paul then would be understood to be teaching that it is *good* in a nonmoral, expedient sense, or "better" (in the sense of verse 8 and verses 32-35, Paul's vocational preference for singleness), not to marry (Calvin 1960:135).

In the first place, the expression "not to touch a woman" is not the equivalent of "not to marry." In Hebrew and Greek it is a euphemism for "not to have sexual intercourse with a woman" (Gen 20:6; Prov 6:29). Furthermore, the expression is probably to be taken not as Paul's belief but as another Corinthian slogan, such as we have in other passages (6:12, 13, 18; 8:1, 4; Thiselton 2000:494). Paul's response to this slogan in verses 2-7 is not simply to recommend marriage to avoid fornication but to urge that men and women who marry should continue to have sexual intercourse within the marriage. Thus Paul himself seems to take the rejection of sexual intercourse as the essence of the slogan. Bruce clarifies the matter well:

> In chapter 7 he deals with ascetics who, partly perhaps in reaction against the libertines, argued that sexual relations of every kind were to be deprecated, that Christians who were married should henceforth live as though they were unmarried, and those who were unmarried should remain so, even if they were already engaged to be married. Their outlook was summed up in the sweeping judgment, *It is well for a man not to touch a woman,* which as Origen saw . . . is probably an extract from the Corinthians' letter, and should therefore be placed between quotation marks like "All things are lawful" in 6:12. (1971:66)

Therefore verse 1 is translated correctly in the TNIV, "'It is good for a man not to have sexual relations with a woman,'" indicating the Corinthian slogan by the quotation marks.

When we see that this negative assessment of all types of sexual intercourse, even within marriage, is not Paul's but one he rejects in the following verses, a great deal of misconception that has plagued the church regarding the apostle's negative attitudes toward marriage is dispelled.

It has been suggested that the Corinthians' asceticism may have come in part from Paul himself, not only as he taught the churches to abstain from sexual intercourse outside of marriage (6:12-20; 1 Thess 4:3-4) but from his own example of singleness and sexual abstinence. The zealous ascetics may also have appealed to Jesus' teaching that in the resurrection we will be like the angels in that there will be no marriage (Mt 22:30). Perhaps the "spirituals" at Corinth believed they could go beyond Paul and achieve a higher form of spirituality by rejecting not only fornication but all forms of sexual intercourse, even within marriage, thus showing even more clearly their separation from and superiority over worldly entanglements. We have a twentieth-century religious, albeit not Christian, example of such spiritual-sexual asceticism in Mahatma Gandhi, who refrained from intercourse with his wife for many years as an expression of his longing to go further in his spiritual life.

How does Paul respond? It sounds like a mini marriage seminar!

On Marriage and Sexual Intercourse Within Marriage (7:2-7) Paul's first response is to declare realistically that because of the power of sexual passion and human beings' susceptibility to "sexual offenses" (*immorality;* the NIV's *so much* is not in the Greek), it is easy to fail God in this matter. Therefore, unless we have the gift of controlling our sexual desires (vv. 7, 9), *each man should have his own wife, and each woman her own husband* (v. 2; cf. 1 Thess 4:26-28). This seems to be the first clear command in Scripture for monogamous marriage *(each . . . each).* It has no doubt had a signal influence in the Western world's adoption of this practice. Bigamy and polygamy are no longer acceptable for the people of God, as they were in the days of ancient Israel.

Paul's concern, however, is not merely to affirm monogamous marriage as God's will but to encourage, even command, continued, uninterrupted mutual sexual exchange within the marriage relationship. The Corinthian "spirituals" apparently disdained sexual relations within marriage. They may have even gone a step further and argued that in order for weaker married couples to avoid having sexual relations, they should divorce (vv. 10-11). In any event, Paul makes very clear that the married couple has an obligation to each other sexually (*marital duty,* debt). To refuse to meet one's spouse's sexual desires is to *deprive* (rob, as in 6:8) the spouse of what is their right (v. 5). It is nothing short of amazing for his day to see Paul's egalitarian emphasis *(likewise . . . in the same way)* in intimate sexual relations in marriage.

The wife's body does not belong to her alone but also to her husband (v. 4) is literally "the wife does not have authority [power, right] over her own body, but yields it to her husband" (TNIV). The idea is that the wife (or husband) does not have the freedom to do as she (or he) pleases with her (or his) own body in this matter, because the other has a rightful claim to sexual satisfaction. This requires mutual submission (Eph 5:21). How many marriages might have been saved by this understanding and practice! To be sure, Paul does not deal here with the issue of abuse. However, the principle of mutual submission and *mutual consent* (v. 5) is very important in minimizing abuse. This remarkable passage gives expression to Paul's view of marriage as a profound union that entails a shared body, the two becoming "one flesh" (Eph 5:31).

It is also important to note in this passage that Paul does not justify marriage or sexual relations within marriage by appealing to procreation. Here he separates himself widely not only from the Jewish rabbinical stress on procreation as justification for marriage but also from the same stress in certain Christian traditions. If Paul were giving a complete overview of what marriage entails, we might assume he would have included procreation and family service to others. But here he is responding to the Corinthians' ascetic views, and hence he does not treat these other aspects. However, that love and obligation are complementary sides of Paul's view of marriage is reflected in other places in his writings (cf. Rom 7:4; Eph 5:22-33).

Husband and wife are not to rob each other of their sexual satisfaction except by *mutual consent* (v. 5). There are three conditions for suspending sexual intercourse in marriage: (1) temporary—*for a time* (or season) . . . *then come together again,* (2) by *mutual* agreement, not unilaterally, and (3) for the purpose of devoting *yourselves to prayer* (have time, leisure, for prayer). But even when the reasons are very spiritual, abstinence should not be carried too far, to the point where *self-control* begins to weaken and one is vulnerable to temptation to fornication. The adversary *(Satan)* is roaming about like a lion, seeking someone to devour (1 Pet. 5:8). Let those who think they are strong in this matter be careful, for they too can fall.

However, Paul quickly adds that this temporary period of abstinence from sexual relations for the married is *not . . . a command* but a *concession* (v. 6). He would prefer no interruption, but has yielded this much to the ascetic "spirituals" at Corinth.

His next statement is quite remarkable: *I wish that all men were as I am* (v. 7). In what sense does Paul mean this? He has just presented a strong case for marriage. Does he now reverse himself? Let us look at three possible solutions.

1. If we take *concession, not . . . a command* in verse 6 as referring to marriage itself, then Paul in verse 7 is reiterating the same thought with more specific content. He does not command that all should be married (only those who cannot control their passions, v. 2). Rather, he desires all men (and women) to be single like himself (for reasons given in vv.

26, 32-35). Yet realistically he realizes that God has given different gifts to different people; *each . . . has his own gift from God* (v. 7): *one has this gift* for marriage and family, *another has that* for remaining unmarried (Mt 19:11-12). This makes good sense and does not negate the positive things Paul has said about marriage (Morris 1985:104).

2. We could limit the sense of Paul's *concession* to the issue of abstinence in marital relations and understand *as I am* to refer not to celibacy but to Paul's example of remaining in the state he was in at the time of his conversion. We don't know whether Paul was married earlier in his life, as were most Jewish men, especially rabbis and Sanhedrin members (Acts 26:10), and then was divorced some twenty years before the writing of 1 Corinthians, at the time of his conversion (his wife leaving him). Or perhaps he became a widower or had never married (unlikely). In this view, then, Paul is saying he wishes that all would be like him and not make radical changes in their social status in view of the impending return of Christ. This view solves the difficulty of Paul's apparent ambivalence about marriage. It founders, however, on how the second part of verse 7 fits with the first statement of the verse (Moiser 1983:106).

3. Another explanation takes *I wish that all men were as I am* to be actually another Corinthian slogan, this time using Paul's own words but putting an ascetic twist on them that Paul would not concede. They argued that Paul was himself celibate and that they heard him say he wished all were like him; that must mean Paul sees marriage as morally polluting and celibacy as required. Paul responds by pointing to different gifts in verse 7 and follows with a lengthy exposition of his true views (vv. 8-24). This view, like the previous one, draws its appeal from the way it relieves Paul of saying anything that would disparage marriage or seem contradictory to his remarks in verses 2-6, but it unnecessarily complicates the passage and is unconvincing (Talbert 1987:39).

None of the proposed solutions or variations is completely acceptable. The *concession* seems best understood as a reference to the absti-

---

7:7-8 On Paul's marital status, see the introduction under "Paul, the Author."
7:9 *To burn with passion* is in the Greek simply "to burn" *(pyroō)*. While most interpret this as the NIV does, F. F. Bruce warns against a too hasty elimination of the

nence in verse 5 rather than to marriage itself. On the other hand, he desired to free everyone from unnecessary "distractions" from serving the Lord, in light of his soon return (vv. 32-35). For this reason he wished that all had the gift of celibacy. Verse 7, however, shows that he knew this was not the way God had purposed.

On the Unmarried and Widows (7:8-9) Presumably the Corinthians had brought up the matter of the single person and widows in connection with the broad question raised in verse 1. Once again, Paul's instruction is that *the unmarried* (or "widowers") *and the widows* should stay unmarried, as he has. This advice also must be understood in light of his statement in verses 26-28. In view of the Lord's near return, he wants them not to change their social status in a quest for a more spiritual experience. Yet if they do marry, they have not sinned (v. 28). This agrees with Paul's statement here that if they do not have the gift of sexual self-control, *they should marry.* The undesirable alternative to marrying is to remain single and be frustrated sexually, *to burn* (*pyroō,* be inflamed) *with passion* (not in the Greek). Sexual desire is not a sinful condition if it finds its relief not in fornication but in marriage (6:12-20; 7:2).

Paul, however, actually says "if they are not controlling themselves" (the Greek does not have *cannot*). This understanding could support another view in which "burning" is not a figure for sexual frustration but for hell. A continued lack of sexual control puts one into the category of fornicators, of whom Paul says, "They will not inherit the kingdom of God" (6:9-10).

Either of these views of *burn* is possible. On the first view, *burn* refers not to being oversexed but to being frustrated in love. On the second, *burn* refers to the final punishment of habitual sexual fornication (Heb 13:4).

But who are *the unmarried and widows?* That the first term, *unmarried (agamos),* includes divorced women is clear from verse 11 (*agamos,* unmarried). Later in the chapter an "unmarried woman" is distin-

---

meaning "to burn in hell" (1971:68). At least one modern interpreter believes that this is the correct sense (Snyder 1992:97).

guished from a "virgin," presumably a woman who never married (vv. 32-34). Paul instructs some of the divorced to remarry under the conditions he sets forth in these two verses. Because Paul here distinguishes this group (the unmarried) from *the widows (chērais)*, it is thought by some that *the unmarried* in verse 8 means "widowers," since there is no specific word in Greek for men whose wives have died (Moiser 1983:107). This is not certain. *Widows* may, on the other hand, include widowers on the same grounds (Bruce 1971:68). In any case, the term would surely include divorced persons and may also include single persons, both widowers and the never married, though this is not certain (Paul has already referred to never-married persons in vv. 2-7). Paul includes himself in one or the other of the two categories with his *as I am*. But as indicated earlier, we do not know whether Paul was married before he became a believer. His status therefore could fit within *the unmarried* as a divorced man, a widower or a never-married person.

On the Already Married (7:10-11) *To the married* (those who have been married and still are) Paul now commands that they not divorce but remain together. This anticipates what he says a bit further in the chapter: "Are you married? Do not seek a divorce" (v. 27). Not only were the super-ascetic members of the church apparently advocating abstention from all sexual relations, including between marital partners (vv. 1-6), but some even may have argued that those who were married before their conversion should now divorce in order to more perfectly follow the Lord's will. In response, Paul appeals to a command that the Lord gave concerning married couples: *a wife must not separate from her husband* (v. 10; closest to Mk 10:9, 11-12).

Several things must be observed from the context of chapter 7 about

---

7:10-11 "To separate, to depart" *(chōrizō)* and "to leave" *(aphiēmi)* were equivalent terms in both the Jewish and the Greco-Roman society and meant "to divorce." Men and women had a nearly equal right to initiate a divorce, and remarriage was expected if the divorce was legitimate. Jewish divorces differed only in the matter of a required "divorce certificate" (Instone-Brewer 2002:132, 198-201). If a divorce by separation takes place, Paul commands that everything should be done to reverse the estrangement and bring about reconciliation. Over two hundred papyri documents on marriage and divorce from the fourth century B.C. through the first century A.D. are available online at <www.Instone-Brewer.com>.

Paul's application of this saying of Jesus. First, the word *separate* (*chōrizō,* be separated) probably should be understood here as tantamount to "divorce" (cf. Mt 19:6; Mk 10:9), as it is frequently in Greek papyri and Jewish divorce decrees of the period (Conzelmann 1975:120; Danker 2000:1095; Instone-Brewer 2002:199). The reference to the woman's remaining *unmarried (agamos)* confirms this.

Second, for whatever the ascetic spiritual reason the wife may have had for divorcing her husband (her husband refraining from sexual intercourse with her?), Paul quotes Jesus to the effect that she should not do it. Conversion to Christ ought not to require a change in our marital status. Husbands and wives should remain married. There is no spiritual advantage to be gained by divorcing (v. 27). Marriage in God's purpose is to be lifelong.

Third, "Paul does not mention the exception [to lifelong marriage] Jesus allowed on the grounds of fornication (Matt. 5:32; 19:9). But he is not writing a systematic treatise on divorce. He is answering specific questions" (Morris 1985:106). That Paul is using the teaching of Jesus pastorally (that is, on a case-by-case basis), and not categorically or absolutely, may be seen in the way he makes two further exceptions (beyond Jesus' own exception) in the following verses. He allows remarriage to those whose unbelieving spouses divorce them (vv. 15-16). He also allows remarriage to the widow (vv. 8-9, 39-40) and perhaps also to the divorced, if they are not gifted to control their passions (v. 8).

Finally, we should note how three times in this chapter Paul distinguishes his own advice from the teaching of the Lord: *Not I, but the Lord* (v. 10); *I, not the Lord* (v. 12); *I have no command from the Lord, but I give a judgment* (v. 25). This should alert us that at this very early

---

David Instone-Brewer argues that two additional reasons (beyond desertion) for divorce are alluded to in this chapter: emotional neglect and material neglect (vv. 3-5, 32-34). Thus the New Testament affirms four grounds for divorce: adultery (Mt 19:9), desertion (1 Cor 7:15-16), emotional neglect and material neglect (7:3-5, 32-34). These latter two grounds are derived from Exodus 21:10-11, which states that a husband must give a wife food, clothing and love. "The rabbis and Paul applied these equally to the wife and husband, and they became the basis of the vows in Jewish marriage contracts and in Christian marriage services via the reference to them in Ephesians 5:28-29" (Instone-Brewer 2002:275).

time, the actual authoritative teaching of the historical Jesus was not easily confused with apostolic teaching, not even when an apostle needed an authoritative word (contrary to assertions frequently found in critical scholarship).

On the other hand, there is no warrant for red letter editions of the New Testament, if these imply that we should make a distinction in levels of authority between Jesus and the apostles. What Paul calls his opinion (careful judgment) is just that (vv. 25, 40). What he commands is the command of the Lord, whether or not he has a command from the historical Jesus (vv. 10, 40; cf. 14:37).

But if she does [divorce her husband], she must remain unmarried or else be reconciled to her husband (v. 11). This is Paul's addition to the Lord's command and probably relates to the specific case brought up in the Corinthian letter. *If she does* (NIV) is better translated "If she has indeed divorced" (past tense in Greek). Paul is not sure if in the case he is addressing a divorce mentioned as imminent has already taken place. If it has, the instruction is for the woman to remain unmarried (to anyone else) or to seek reconciliation with her husband (v. 11). In this case Paul recognizes no grounds for the divorce. In any case, his instruction for reconciliation is certainly in keeping with Jesus' teaching that husband and wife should not divorce. His emphasis on the woman's remaining unmarried, if reconciliation does not occur, would be consistent with his theme throughout, remaining unmarried unless passion overrides and indicates remarriage (v. 9).

Appealing to circumstances that might develop, such as when or if the former husband is unwilling to be reconciled, or if he remarries or dies, carries Paul's case beyond its intent; such possibilities are not addressed. Instead Paul adds, *And a husband must not divorce his wife.* What has been said about the woman in the case in point is turned around and applied also to the man. No husband should divorce his wife for his own higher spiritual pursuits without sex or for his wife's refusal to grant sexual intercourse to him as she pursues a so-called

---

7:15 "Yet if a nonbelieving partner has initiated the separation, it is meaningless to say that the believer is free to remain separated. It is also meaningless to say that the believer is free to divorce because if separation has taken place, the couple have already completed the divorce procedure, according to Greco-Roman law. . . . No rite

higher spirituality.

On Mixed Marriages and Pagan Abandonment (7:12-16) *To the rest,* i.e., to couples who were married before the gospel of Christ came to them and only one of the partners became a believer in Christ, *I say this (I, not the Lord)* (see under v. 10). Paul's instructions show a further application of Christ's command to a situation not addressed by the Lord: *he must not divorce her* (v. 12; and *she must not divorce him,* v. 13). The Corinthian problem may have been created by a concern to not be unequally yoked with unbelievers, which would defile not only the believing partner but also any children born and perhaps the church community as well (2 Cor 6:14-18). Paul's answer is straightforward. Don't divorce if the unbelieving partner is willing to live with the believing spouse. This situation and Paul's instruction should not, however, be construed as justification for *contracting* mixed marriages. It applies only to those marriages entered into by non-Christians in which only one spouse subsequently became a believer.

But does not this mixed marriage make impure the relationship? Paul answers, no. The reason this is so sounds strange to the modern Western reader. *The unbelieving husband* (or wife) *has been sanctified through his wife* (or her husband). . . . *Otherwise your children would be unclean, but as it is, they are holy* (v. 14). Rather than the unbeliever defiling the relationship, the believer sanctifies (*hagiazō,* "make holy," "consecrate," "sanctify") the unbeliever (cf. Ex 29:37). If the children are not impure but holy (*hagia;* the Corinthians apparently already believed this), then *both* the parents must be clean or sanctified. The believing partner affects Christianly the unbelieving spouse so the marriage relationship remains pure and does not need to be broken. We must affirm two things regarding this difficult statement. First, whatever the sanctification of the unbelieving partner and children involves, we are confident that it does not mean their salvation, since this comes only as a gift through faith (v. 16). Second, we must admit ignorance up to this point in the history of interpretation as to precisely what

or document was needed to complete the divorce, so there was nothing more that they needed to do to complete a divorce other than separate" (Instone-Brewer 2002:202).

kind of holiness/defilement ideas were present at Corinth that led Paul to respond with the language he uses. To date there is not a really adequate or convincing explanation, though there are some appealing suggestions.

However, the case is different if an unbelieving spouse leaves: *let him [or her] do so* (v. 15). The word *leaves (chōrizō)* is the same word I translated "divorce" in verse 10. If the unbeliever takes the initiative and abandons the believer, the marriage is nullified. The believer *is not bound (douloō,* to be a slave). This seems to imply that the deserted and divorced believer is (almost as in widowhood, v. 39) not only free from any obligation to compel the unbeliever to return but also free to remarry under the conditions set forth in the rest of the chapter (vv. 9, 39-40). "It would be a curious expression to use if Paul meant 'is bound to remain unmarried'" (Morris 1985:107). Could Paul be reflecting here on his own experience (see 7:8)? Luther thought that "what is true of a pagan partner applies also to the case of a bad Christian" (Héring 1962:53).

In any case, Paul makes an exception to the rule given by Jesus that marriage is a lifelong union. The overall guiding principle in such matters is this. *God has called us to live in peace* (v. 15). This applies to the living together of a believer and unbeliever as well as to the situation of desertion by the unbeliever. Such *peace (eirene)* is wholeness of life (Hebrew *shalom*), not only inward but also outward, including justice and social well-being (14:33; 15:11; Rom 12:18; 14:19).

The reason Paul gives for this controlling principle is ambiguous: *How do you know, wife, whether you will save your husband?* (v. 16). An overly ascetic or scrupulous believing wife (or husband) might try to preserve the marriage, despite strife and desertion by the unbelieving husband (or wife), in hopes that the husband (or wife) might become a Christian. Paul would spare them this unnecessary scruple, so he says, "How can you know that he (or she) will eventually be saved?" There is no guarantee.

Alternately, many commentators believe Paul is saying just the opposite. "Do all you can to keep the marriage together, because perhaps you will see your spouse saved, and it will then be worth it all." But this is an unlikely meaning that does not seem to fit the context. Marriage should not be viewed as an evangelistic opportunity, either initially by a believer who marries an unbeliever in hopes of converting him or her, or by a believer who is clinging to a marriage that an unbeliever has determined to end. Therefore the translation should read: "You don't know, do you, wife, whether you will save your husband?"

God's Calling and Our Religious and Social Circumstances (7:17-24) The main import of this section is that when we embrace the gospel call to salvation, we ought not make changes in our religious or social position in the belief that such changes are either required by the Lord or advantageous to us spiritually now that we have become Christians. Of course changes from idolatry or immoral behavior are not in view in this section. Paul wants to emphasize the relative unimportance of religious externals (circumcision or uncircumcision) and social status positions (slave or free) in the Corinthians' calling to follow Christ wherever they find themselves.

When I became a Christian at the age of nineteen, I was between my sophomore and junior years at a state university in southern California. My reaction to all my former life and circumstances led me to leave college and join a Christian group that was seeking to live on a higher spiritual level than other Christians. Had I been aware of Paul's teaching in this passage, I would no doubt have remained at the university, to which I later returned after a loss of some time.

Two great Pauline principles or rules emerge in this section. The first is this: *Each one should remain in the situation which he was in when God called him* (v. 20; also 17, 24). The second guiding principle is that *keeping God's commands is what counts* (v. 19). The import of this latter principle is clearer than the first. In whatever life situation you find yourself (married or unmarried, upper class, lower class, white collar, blue collar, etc.), what is important is the keeping of God's commands, the doing of his revealed moral will. This gives substance to and parallels the three other exhortations in the section ("walk," v. 17; *remain,* v. 20; "remain with God," v. 24). This will result in many different social and cultural styles among Christians who nevertheless will all embody the same obedience to Christ.

The first principle of remaining in one's situation is a bit more difficult to grasp. In the first place, we should note that the "call" of God referred to no fewer than eight times in this section is not a call to a specific job or vocation (the NIV translation in verse 17 notwithstanding) but in each case God's call to salvation (1:26; Eph 4:1). The TNIV is better: "each of you should live [Gk *walk*] as a believer in whatever situation the Lord has assigned to you, just as God has called you." Believers are exhorted: "As God has called you, live up to that calling" (NEB). Second, the exhortation is to *remain* in the situation of life in which we became a Christian (i.e., when God "called" you to salvation). This emphasis seems to be Paul's response to a tendency among the "more spiritual" at Corinth to urge believers to change their social circumstances (including marital) in order to be more spiritual or gain more "status betterment." Paul rejects this. Instead he enjoins them to stay where they are situationally and there serve and obey God. This is his *rule* he lays *down in all the churches* (v. 17; 11:16; 14:33).

Does this mean that a Christian should never change his or her marital status or employment? No. But you should not seek change because you think you could be a better Christian in the new circumstance. God liberates us to be all that he wants us to be in the worldly situation in which his grace finds us. No change is called for. No different situation will add one iota to our salvation (or to our spirituality), which comes to us purely by grace in our worldly place.

I know a businessman who, when he became a Christian, thought he should leave the business world and attend a theological seminary because this would allow him to serve God better. After two years he left the seminary without graduating, and he was quite frustrated. But after a short time he returned to the business world, where he is now an outstanding Christian servant and successful businessman.

Nevertheless (v. 17, if not, otherwise) is strange at this point, since the usual sense is a contrast with what has gone before. The believing man and woman in the previous section had freedom to let an unbelieving spouse leave and sever the marriage bond. Over against this liberty must be set in tension the realistic principle of remaining in *the*

7:17 *Called* is everywhere else in Paul and the New Testament called to salvation (Rom 11:29; 1 Cor 1:26; Eph 1:18; 4:1; Phil 3:14; 2 Thess 1:11; 2 Tim 1:9; Heb 3:1; 2 Pet 1:10). "Calling" as vocation is a later usage than that found in the New Testa-

place in life (circumcised, uncircumcised, slave, free, married, unmarried) *that the Lord assigned* (*merizō,* "give a share in," "portion out"; in regard to gifts, Rom 12:3). God has given gifts of marriage or singleness or permitted circumstances such as slavery to be a part of our life where and when God called us to salvation. Our responsibility is to live (Gk *peripateō,* "to walk," "to order our behavior") in a Christian manner in the situation we are in when God called us to faith in Christ.

The NIV translation of verse 17 is unfortunate. Following Luther and other sixteenth-century reformers who understood "calling" and "called" throughout this passage as vocational or occupational calling, the NIV renders the text as *each one should retain the place in life that the Lord assigned to him to which God has called him.* Better is the TNIV: "each of you should live as a believer in whatever situation the Lord has assigned to you, just as God called you." The primary emphasis is on Christian behavior that is appropriate to our call to faith in Christ in every situation of life in which we may find ourselves when we were called to salvation. On the other hand, that Paul also says *the Lord assigned* [to each] hints that as a secondary matter these life situations may also be thought of as in some sense divinely ordered. The important point is that these circumstances (married, unmarried, widow, widower, celibate, circumcised, uncircumcised, slave, freed, male, female [cf. Gal 3:28]) are irrelevant to serving God. Thiselton captures the sense well: "Paul's thought cannot be far removed from Christology here. The vocation of the Servant is to serve through situations of constraint, in God's freedom, not in spite of constraint in bondage to a grudging spirit" (2000:549-50).

Verse 20 comes closest to Luther's sense of vocational calling although the NIV correctly has a rendering that does not favor this: *Each one should remain in the situation which he was in when God called him.*

In the question *Were you a slave when you were called?* (v. 21) we turn from the religious realm (circumcision vv. 18, 19) to the social. It

---

ment. But doesn't this passage require vocation as the sense? For yes, see Héring 1962:54-55; for no, see Bruce 1971:71; and Thiselton 2000:549.

has been estimated that as much as two-thirds of the population of Corinth consisted of slaves or manumitted (freed) slaves (Bartchy 1973:173). Paul's question in this verse seems to confirm that the "calling" is different from our worldly circumstance (here, being a slave). Paul first speaks reassuringly, *Don't let it trouble you* ("care nothing about it"), because such a state is irrelevant to your service to Christ.

Although if you can gain your freedom, do so raises the possibility of the slave's seeking to be released from the condition of slavery (manumission). But the expression, *although if (ei kai)* can also be translated "even though," and this leads to a different sense when combined with a variation on the next very succinct words of Paul, *do so* (*mallon chrēsai,* rather make use of [it]). What, then, does the "it" refer to? Is the nearest antecedent, *freedom,* the correct connection? The sense then would be that if you, a slave, can gain your freedom, then rather than be a slave, make use of the freedom (get yourself manumitted).

But there is a long tradition in the church, beginning with Chrysostom (d. 407) and including some modern interpreters, that Paul had *slave* in mind as the antecedent. In this case the sense would be: although you can gain your freedom, instead remain a slave (NRSV "make use of your present condition more than ever"). This sounds strange to us, but it fits the context well, where Paul generally argues against change in status (v. 24). It could be argued also that such a translation provides a better explanation of the following verse: *For he who was a slave when he was called by the Lord is the Lord's freedman; similarly, he who was a free man when he was called is Christ's slave* (v. 22).

Nevertheless, the view that Paul urges the slave to choose freedom if it can be obtained (as in the NIV translation) is to be preferred (so Thiselton 2000:559). A freed person *(apeleutheros)* stood in a new relationship to his or her former master, liberated one to benefactor. The Christian slave, while still under the ownership and service of an earthly master, has participated in a far greater emancipation. Such per-

---

7:21 The NIV's translation and the commentary's interpretation of *do so (mallon chrēsai)* are also further confirmed by three recent studies (Harrill 1995:68, 70, 108, 126; Winter 1994:146; Gagnon 2001:446n171). Earlier Scott Bartchy rendered the expression thus: "Were you a slave when you were called? Don't worry about it. But if, indeed, you become manumitted, by all means (as a freedman) live according to

sons have been liberated by Christ himself, and even though they remain slaves, they stand in relation to Christ as freed persons to their benefactor. In other words, don't worry about slave status. On the other hand, if you were freeborn or a freed slave when called to salvation, recognize that you are *Christ's slave* (cf. Rom. 6:15-23).

Paul's point is that service to Christ, not freedom, is the basic foundation of Christian existence in the world. *You were bought with a price* (v. 23; 6:20) reflects the first-century manumission-of-slaves context. Paul of course has in mind the Corinthians' deliverance from sin's mastery and their new service to their liberator, Jesus. Therefore they must have the continual attitude of freed persons who now serve their new master, Christ. Whether slave or free, they must not consider themselves any longer *slaves of men* in any sense, whether socially, legally, psychologically or spiritually. They serve one master, Christ the Lord. This inner freedom is very liberating in many situations, wherever relative bondages or servitudes exist, whether we are dealing with overbearing parents, husband, wife, teacher, employer or manager.

Finally, in verse 24, Paul closes with an exhortation that parallels the one that began this section (v. 17). *Each man, as responsible to God, should remain in the situation God called him to.* The general rule is to remain in the situation you were in "when God called you" (the NIV addition of *to* is misleading here, as in verse 17). But Paul is flexible enough to allow exceptions, such as divorce of an unbelieving deserting spouse (v. 15) and freedom for slaves (v. 21).

On "Virgins" (7:25-38) It is no exaggeration to call this passage one of the most difficult to interpret in all of Paul's letters. Why? First, because there is a great deal of uncertainty as to whom Paul is referring with the term *virgins* (*parthenos,* vv. 25, 28, 34, 36, 37-38). There are five different senses that have been argued for this term, ranging from engaged women or couples to unmarried daughters in verses 36-38,

---

God's calling" (1973:183). "If indeed you can become free, use instead [freedom]" (Harrill 1995:68). "Paul was not just saying 'take the opportunity to become free'; he was exhorting believers to 'use that freedom all the more to serve Christ'" (Gagnon 2001:448).

and from both males and females to females only in verses 25-28.

Second, the context seems to be broader than just female virgins, since Paul includes himself in the group: *I give a judgment* (since he has no direct words of Jesus' teaching on this matter) *as one who by the Lord's mercy is trustworthy* (v. 25). This latter expression probably refers to Paul's trustworthiness not generally as a Christian or even as an apostle, but as one to whom the Lord has given mercy to remain faithful in celibacy (that is, one who has been faithful to the gift of remaining unmarried, vv. 7-8). He can give his opinion on celibacy as one who has personally experienced God's mercy in this lifestyle (Bruce 1971). Furthermore, the advice he gives is directed throughout the section *to men;* therefore the passage is not only about virgin women (vv. 26-28, 36-38).

Finally, the passage is complicated by numerous translation options, and depending on which choice is made, the sense of the passage will vary. Therefore it is important, before looking at the details, to give some overall sense of Paul's exhortations with which most could agree.

Paul's main points are these. He continues emphasizing the goodness of marriage and the desirability of singleness (if one has the gift of self-control). Believers should remain in the social situation they were in when they were called to salvation for three reasons: because of *the present distress* (v. 26), because of the shortness of time before the Lord's return (v. 29) and because the single life, for those so gifted, has potentially fewer temporal distractions from following the Lord (vv. 32-35).

On the other hand, Paul checks the overly zealous "spiritualists" by commanding that those who are married should not divorce (v. 27) and that those who decide to marry should go ahead and marry; such actions are within God's will (vv. 28, 35-38). In other words, Paul relativizes all social institutions, including marriage, in light of the Lord's return (vv. 29-31).

He does see a slight advantage in singleness, given the general principle of not changing our social status and because the nearness of the end calls for certain restraints (vv. 26-28, 32-34, 40). Yet he does not wish to impose this position as a burden on others but to suggest it as a practical expedient for those who can receive it (v. 35).

The first section of Paul's response to the question of *virgins* makes two emphases. First, Paul wants Corinthians who are unmarried not to despise that condition and rush to get married. Nor, on the other hand, does he want those who are married to rush out and get divorced: *I think it is good for you [a man] to remain as you are. Are you married? Do not seek a divorce. Are you unmarried [or divorced]? Do not look for a wife* (vv. 26-27).

Paul cites *the present crisis* (*ananke*, "necessity," "distress," "calamity") as the reason to remain in the social situation one was in when called to Christ. The sense of this expression is not clear. It could refer to some local distress known to the Corinthians but not stated by Paul. A newer version of this view has been argued by Bruce Winter, who believes Paul alludes to pressing famine conditions in Corinth (1989:86-106). While this view is attractive for its possible circumstantial relevance in the immediate Corinthian situation, it does not seem adequate to explain verses 29-31, especially the latter part of verse 31, nor is it in keeping with Paul's emphasis on the return of Christ in the letter (1:7-8; 4:5; 15:23; 16:22). On the other hand, it may refer to the generally predicted increasing tribulation of the last days that heralds the return of Christ (v. 29; Lk 21:23), in the light of which certain constraints would be appropriate, including remaining in one's social situation.

Nevertheless, Paul quickly adds a second emphasis, in order to avoid conceding too much to the ascetic elements at Corinth. *If you do marry* (or "if you have married"), *you have not sinned; and if a virgin marries, she has not sinned* (v. 28). Marriage is good, even if singleness provides certain advantages. Both reflect God's will and model different aspects of God's nature and community. In the one, the bride and groom reflect God's love as a dialectic of similarity and difference, showing the exclusive nature of the divine love, while singleness reflects the love of God in its universal, nonexclusive and expanding nature (Grenz 1990:171-72). It is interesting that Paul addresses male virgins in the second person, while women virgins are referred to indirectly in the third person and the feminine *hē parthenos*. This would explain the use of the feminine form throughout and still allows Paul to include both men and women virgins in the plural (v. 25) and in his instructions throughout the passage.

However, for those who marry there will be additional challenges because they *will face many troubles in this life* (NIV; literally, they will have trouble in the flesh). Paul's reference to "trouble" (*thlipsis*, "trouble," "distress of mind"; NIV's *many* is not in the Greek and is unwarranted) is best explained by his further elaboration of the distractions and stresses married life involves that he would *spare* them (vv. 32-34). For example, "A man who has no wife or children liable to suffer because of his refusal to compromise or deny his faith in face of persecution is in a stronger position than one who must consider what effect his stand will have on his dependents" (Bruce 1971:75).

The next section of Paul's response concerning virgins offers a further reason for them to remain as they are: all social relations are relativized in light of the nearness of the Lord's return, for *the time is short* (vv. 29-31; Mk 13:20; Rom 13:11-14). This section may also be understood as an exposition of *the present crisis* referred to earlier (v. 26). Again F. F. Bruce captures the correct future *and* present emphasis well. "It is not only a question of the impending parousia, in the light of which it is foolish to live as though one had an indefinite tenure on the present course of time; the pressures of the remaining interval will be such that the man or woman of faith must accept the discipline of iron rations and be as free as possible from the ordinary and legitimate distractions of secular life" (1971:75).

The fivefold *as if* or "as though" (*hōs mē*) model for living the Christian life means that we must learn not to abandon appropriate and legitimate involvement in the world and in the common affairs of life. Rather, we are to hold loosely all matters of this present earthly life, including marriage, as being relatively unimportant spiritually in the light of Christ's return and the coming of his kingdom.

Those who have wives should live as if they had none (v. 29) is not a prescription for "spiritual marriages" where normal sexual relations are abandoned, nor does it advocate the neglect of wife and family in pursuit of work or even Christian ministry. Instead it is a call to get our priorities right about what is really of value in this life in view of the future event of the Lord's coming, the resurrection and the kingdom. This is the principle of the eschatological relativizing of all present human values. This word reminds us of our Lord's teaching, "Seek first his kingdom and his righteousness, and all these things will be given to you as well" (Mt 6:33). Christians are called to order their lives according to the values of the coming kingdom, not those of the present secular age. The values of this age are not permanent but fading and relative; those of God's kingdom are enduring (2 Cor 4:17-18).

Those who mourn, as if they did not (v. 30) refers to the relative insignificance of worldly lament and sorrow; *those who are happy, as if they were not* to the fleeting nature of even the most sublime human joy (Lk 6:21) in light of the joys of God's kingdom (1 Pet 1:5-9). *Those who buy something, as if it were not theirs to keep* reflects the inner detachment from material possessions that allows us to be free either to give them away to those in need or to suffer their loss with little care. We do not find our identity in them, and our real possessions are bound up with God's future kingdom, which is indestructible. If we can truly let them go easily, we will seek less to acquire them in the first place. Our well-being does not depend on our success in the world. Likewise, our pleasures are not to be wrapped up in the things of this world: we *use the things of the world,* but *as if not engrossed in them* (v. 31, use to the full).

The reason for this measured renunciation of the world is again not its inherent evil (as the Greeks held) but its temporality in light of the coming of the Lord and his permanent kingdom: *For this world in its present form* (*schēma,* outward appearance, essence; *present* is not in the Greek) *is passing away* like an actor leaving the stage (Héring 1962:59-60). Therefore do not put all your investments (money, time, energies, loyalties) into this world. God has another order coming on stage that relativizes (not abolishes) all our present worldly experiences and relationships. We must as Christians live, as it were, in two worlds at the same time. But the pull toward the future world, where our true destiny lies, relativizes all features of this present life except our keeping the commandments of God (v. 19). The status-hungry Corinthians must take this to heart.

Returning more specifically to the case of the unmarried and virgins and the *troubles* (v. 28) the married will face, Paul expands on his earlier practical preference for singleness by arguing here that singleness allows a more undistracted and single-minded attention to the Lord

(vv. 32-34). A battle mentality is appropriate because there is a present distress (v. 26) and the Lord's coming is near (v. 29). Yet Paul's views are given for their benefit, not to restrict them (v. 35). *Free from concern* means free from "anxious" concern (*amerimnos,* without anxiety) about *the affairs of this world* or family matters (not to be confused with "worldliness" as that term has come to be understood).

Whether this means, as it is often understood, to describe the unencumbered life of certain "specially-called-to-hardship" Christians who would, if married, not be able to carry out such difficult tasks without undue harm to family as well, the text does not itself say. Furthermore, there is no warrant for using this passage to justify a celibate ministry or priesthood. Paul speaks only of individuals who have the "gift" of celibacy (v. 7), who exercise their free choice to remain unmarried.

We should note carefully how Paul, in a gesture of equality, deliberately balances the references to men and women throughout this section (vv. 31-35), as he has done previously (vv. 2-7, 10-11, 12-14). The woman is considered a fully equal and responsible person along with the man in all matters pertaining to marriage and singleness.

These instructions on singleness versus marriage are not intended to be moral but practical in substance (*for your own good*) thus allowing personal judgment and different conclusions in each individual case. Paul did not want to *restrict them* (*brochon epiballein,* "to lay a noose on"). As Héring rightly points out, what the apostle repudiates is celibacy as a pretext for a life of debauchery, or a married life that is not fully lived. What he particularly condemns is "the type of 'married bachelor' who avoids family obligations even for the best of reasons (for example, for the entire devotion of his time to learning or to the Church)" (1962:65).

7:36 *The virgin he is engaged to* is an interpretation of *virgin* favored by most modern commentators (e.g., Fee, Thiselton, Schrage) and translators, especially since 1946 with the publication of the RSV (NIV, NRSV, NLT, ESV, TNIV). Earlier translations favored "virgin daughter." The RSV reads, "his betrothed" (v. 36) and "he who marries his betrothed" (v. 38). The NEB (1970) is exceptional in its rendering "partner in celibacy," apparently reflecting the "spiritual betrothals" view later espoused by Conzelmann (1975:135-136).

The Engaged (7:36-38) The final section of Paul's response to the question concerning virgins occurs in verses 36-38. Exegetically it is a very difficult passage. Scholars have identified at least six possible views regarding whom Paul refers to as *man* (or "anyone") and *virgin* in the section (see notes). If we let the modern translations be our guide, there are only two views taken seriously. I will set out both of these and let you, the reader, discern for yourself.

The first view, the older, traditional explanation—at least since John Chrysostom (d. 401) until the early twentieth century—the view found in the KJV, ASV, NASV and the Jerusalem Bible, is that Paul is referring to a father and his responsibility toward his young virgin daughter. He is ashamed that he is treating his marriageable daughter dishonorably by holding her back from marriage when she may be beyond her prime and has need (sexually) to be married. Let him allow the daughter to marry. He has not sinned. However, Paul himself prefers that the father not give the daughter in marriage, no doubt for the same reasons he has already given for singleness (vv. 32-35).

Objections to this view are several: (1) it is alleged that understanding "his virgin" (vv. 36, 37, 38) as "his virgin daughter" is an unusual interpretation of such terms; (2) the plural "let them marry" would be unintelligible if the father and daughter alone are involved; (3) how could the father sin in withholding marriage from his daughter or giving her in marriage? (4) if the father is in view, he seems to be praised for his determination and self-control while sacrificing nothing himself and not consulting his daughter's desires directly.

Alternately, the *virgin* is understood as "fiancée" (*he is engaged to*, NIV). For the engaged, to marry is not sinful, but it is better, if there is no necessity, to remain single along the lines of Paul's reasons in verses 32-35.

How to render *hyperakmos* (NIV, *she is getting along in years*) is problematic. Thiselton argues that no more can be indicated lexically in the word than "a matter of undue strain." This could be from sexual passion or stress due to the length of the engagement period or even social pressure to marry. Furthermore, there is no way to tell if the woman or the man is the referent (Thiselton 2000:594). Bruce Winter, on the other hand, is convinced that the term refers to the fiancé (man) and that it has a strong sexual passion sense (2001:246-252).

There are problems with this view as well: (1) it is alleged that *virgin* usually means "virgin daughter," rarely to "sweetheart" and never "fiancée"; (2) the word "to give in marriage" (v. 38; NIV *he who marries*) elsewhere in the New Testament (Mt 22:30 and parallels, 24:38 and parallels), and in other first-century and earlier texts, always means "to give in marriage" and not "to marry"; (3) why would Paul need to assure the man that he is not sinning if he marries his fiancée (v. 38)? (4) why is it better to let the engagement go on indefinitely without marrying (vv. 37-38)?

In the light of the problems with the above views, perhaps a slight variation of fiancé-fiancée interpretation is to be preferred. The situation might be described as follows. Paul presupposes the existence of an institution that we might call spiritual marriage: a young man and woman pledge their permanent mutual affection and agree to live together occasionally, but without breaking vows of virginity that they have made.

This dangerous way of living seems to have been known to Hermas (*Similitudes* 9.11), who gave it positive approval. Eventually the church forbade it because of the increasing abuses to which it gave rise (Héring 1962:63). This position, though strange to us, avoids most of the problems associated above with the simple fiancé-fiancée view. Remaining objections are the lack of historical evidence for such a view in the first century and the expression "give in marriage" (v. 38). Both of these can be partially addressed by noting that sources for the practices of the very early church are scant (the best explanation of the later ancient church's practice is this earlier precedent) and the possibility that "give in marriage" (v. 38) is a Greek equivalent for "to get married." The explanation and translation below will follow this viewpoint.

Paul's attitude toward such spiritual engagements is to not condemn them under certain circumstances (v. 37). But he advises in other cases

---

7:38 *Marries the virgin* is *gamizō tēn heautou*. The word *gamizō* presents a problem to the "engaged couple" interpretation. While not a common word, its normal lexical sense in the New Testament is transitive, "to give in marriage" (Mt 22:30; 24:38; cf. Lk 20:34-35), not intransitive, "to marry" (*gameō,* Mt 5:32; 1 Cor 7:9). This objection is usually answered by arguing that the distinction between words ending in *-eō* and *-izō* has all but disappeared in Koine Greek—despite the grammarian Apollonius

for the couple to get married (v. 36). Perhaps the best way to explain this section is by using an expanded paraphrase, since the NIV translation and the alternate in the footnotes there are muddled. *If any (man) thinks he is acting inappropriately (sexually) toward his virgin fiancée, if he is full of passion, and so it must be, let him do what he desires; he does not sin; let them get married* (v. 36). *On the other hand, the relationship may continue without marriage if he stands firm in his heart, not having any (sexual) necessity, but is in control of his (sexual) desire and has in his own heart decided this; to keep his own fiancée (as an unwed virgin), he will do well* (v. 37). *So, he who marries his (spiritual) fiancée does well, and he who does not marry (his spiritual fiancée) does better* (v. 38; "better" in the sense of Paul's argument in vv. 32-35).

Paul's advice is sensible, realistic and practical in the light of human sexual nature. The apostle applies an earlier stated principle to this new situation: "Each man has his own gift from God; one has this gift, another that" (v. 7).

The Remarriage of Widows (7:39-40) While repeating his advice in verses 8-9, Paul may here be addressing a specific case of a wife whose husband has died (*koimaō*, "put to sleep") and who seeks counsel on whether to remain single or to remarry. Christian couples are to remain married until the death of one of them. Death frees the surviving spouse from the marriage commitment, allowing her to marry *anyone she wishes* (that is, she has no Jewish levirate responsibility to marry her former husband's near relative). "Only in the Lord" (NRSV; NIV has *he must belong to the Lord*) means "in the context of the Christian faith," "in keeping with one who is in obedience to the Lord." Thus it is implied but not directly stated that this will also mean marrying a Christian brother.

However, she also has the option of remaining single. Again in Paul's *judgment* (*gnōmē*, "opinion," as in v. 25) this is a *happier (maka-*

Dyscolus's (second century A.D.) assertion that the different verbs *gameō* and *gamizō* are distinguished as active and causative (*Constructione* 3.153). Further, the only known usages of the verb *gamizō* clearly support the transitive (causative) sense, "give in marriage." This sense should not be dismissed here too quickly in order to make way for other views that seem to fit more easily with our modern situation (e.g., engaged couples).

rios, "more blessed") condition because of avoiding potential distractions from a more devoted, focused pursuit of the things of the Lord (vv. 32-35). Again he does not impose this as an apostolic commandment but as an opinion worthy of consideration as one makes one's own decision. He believes that his advice *too* (as well as that of the "spiritual" at Corinth) is motivated by *the Spirit of God.*

□ Eating Idol Food and the Priority of Love over Rights (8:1— 11:1)

Chapters 8-10 form a unit about Christians and food sacrificed to pagan temple deities. It is at once an exciting and a challenging section. If the volume of recent scholarly attention to these chapters is any indication of their contemporary importance, then despite the first appearance, we are approaching material that is highly relevant to our times, but also quite often misunderstood.

Not only are Paul's instructions concerning idol food directly relevant to certain Asian Christians who live in cultures where pagan sacrifices or ancestor worship is still practiced, but the way he resolves the issues is beneficial for all Christians who face similar questions, but different issues, about how to relate to their own pagan cultures, including secularized Western societies.

What precisely was the problem at Corinth, and why did it arise? There has been no small amount of discussion of these questions in recent literature. Here I can only mention highlights of this debate and present my own conclusions with humility, realizing that some of the issues are difficult at present to settle.

As noted in my introduction, archaeological and literary evidence shows that Corinth had temples or sanctuaries devoted to an abundance of gods: Aphrodite (two varieties, Isis and Serapis), Artemis, Dionysus, Poseidon, Apollo, Helius, Pelagrina (mother of the gods), Necessity, Fates, Demeter, Maid, Zeus, Asklepius, Hermes, Athena and Hera Bunaea. Additionally, there were edifices to the mystery religions, such as the Eleusinian mysteries (Yeo 1995:104-5), and to the Roman imperial cult worship (Winter 1995:170).

Sacrifices, initiated by devotees, were daily made to many of these deities. Most of the meat that was not taken by the priests became available for dinners in the temple restaurants or special rooms where the family and invited friends of the one who offered the sacrifice might enjoy a meal marking a birthday, marriage, special healing or another milestone. Some of the meat might also be sold in the marketplace (*makellon,* 10:25).

All the current evidence suggests that these meals in the temple were not for mere social purposes but had a religious significance (Witherington 1993:245). Some invitations to such meals survive, for example: "Herais asks you to dine in the room of Serapheion (Asklepion) at a banquet of the Lord Seraphis tomorrow the 11th from the 9th hour." Another reads, "The god calls you to a banquet being held in the Thoereion tomorrow . . ." (cited by Winter 1990:222).

The poor did not often eat the expensive meat except at a special celebration at a temple to which they had been privileged to receive an invitation. Likewise, only the more well-to-do could afford to purchase meat (offered in the temple sacrifices) in the marketplace.

So what was the Christian problem that the Corinthians wrote to Paul about, introduced with "Now about food sacrificed to idols" (8:1; see at 7:1)? An explanation that is frequent today, the "modern consensus view," sees chapters 8-10 as dealing with a common problem that is stated in 10:25, 28: eating food sold in the market that had been offered in sacrifice in one of the pagan temples. Some Christians can eat this without any scruples of conscience; they know that the gods of the pagan temples are really no gods, since there is only one God. Therefore the food is good and does not defile them morally or spiritually.

Other Christians, however, are condemned by their conscience if they eat this marketplace food; they are "weak" because they cannot dissociate the power of the idol from the meat. Paul's solution is to side with the strong but to urge them to restrict their liberty in the interests of love toward weaker Christians. In this view the matter is very similar to that of Romans 14.

Recently another view has emerged that critiques the above construction and offers an alternate reading of the texts. It is argued that the modern consensus view fails to account for the reference in 8:10 to Christians reclining on meal couches in the pagan temples and for the long section in 10:1-22 on idolatry. Further, that consensus view makes the matter of sacrificial meat purchased in the marketplace (10:25, 28) the main problem of chapters 8-10 rather than, as it seems more likely to those who hold this view, a minor subpoint (so Fee 1987; Witherington 1995; Kim 2003).

This revised modern view reconstructs the situation as follows. Some Corinthian Christians, on the assumptions that (1) "there is no God but one" (8:4), (2) "an idol is nothing at all in the world" (8:4), and (3) "we all possess knowledge" (8:1), have for whatever reason decided to frequent the temple dining rooms and join in certain party celebrations with their friends. Paul explicitly says in 8:10, "For if anyone with a weak conscience sees you who have this knowledge eating in an idol's temple . . ." The religious context is certainly almost always present at such meals. Whether these believers were Gentiles or Jews or both is not clear. Why they were motivated to join in these meals is problematic. Was it their new "knowledge" and the pride that came with it that led them to visibly demonstrate their freedom from the power of the old gods they once worshiped and associated with the sacrificial food? Or was it their desire to "build up" the "weaker" Christians so they too could eat meat at the temple dining rooms (8:10, *oikodomeō*, "emboldened," but in 8:1 "builds up")? But there were problems with the attitudes and behavior of the "know-it-alls," and chapters 8-10 give Paul's response.

He first compares the "know-it-alls" with the attitude of Christian love and finds them lacking (8:1-3). Paul then takes up their arguments about the one God and their irresponsible behavior toward Christians whose awareness could not allow them to frequent the meals at the temples without defiling themselves with a consciousness of worshiping the idols themselves. According to this interpretation, the temple-dining Christians should follow Paul's example and refrain from flaunting their freedom ("rights"), which is causing the destruction of weaker Christians, and instead seek the edification of the whole community (8:4-13).

In this view Paul's example of forgoing rights for the sake of the community good is developed in detail in chapter 9 before he turns to a long

8:1 The only known first-century and earlier references to *eidōlothytos* are 4 Maccabees 5:2; Acts 15:29; 21:25; 1 Corinthians 8:1, 4, 7, 10; 10:19; Revelation 2:14, 20. Fourth Maccabees precedes the Christian era, and it is unlikely to be a Christian

discourse on the perils of idolatry for the people of God (10:1-22). A final exhortation to the know-it-alls concerning what to do about meat sold in the markets and served in private homes, including when someone calls attention to the identity of the meat as temple-sacrificed food (10:23-30), and Paul's great moral principle of seeking in all things the glory of God and not giving offense to the gospel of Christ, closes his response to the question of eating food sacrificed to idols (10:31-33).

The insight about the issue of idolatry that this position has brought to light is most certainly correct. Yet the view is not so much wrong as it is incomplete and therefore inadequate. This revised modern view leaves a number of verses in these chapters (8-10) inadequately explained (e.g., 10:27-30) and stands in dissonance with the rest of the New Testament witness about idol food as well as the consensus among the early apostolic fathers. There is a better view. A defense of the ancient consensus view has been convincingly set forth by Alex Cheung (1999). It is a quite simple explanation that shows that the ancient fathers were on the right track in their understanding and that the modern consensus view and its revised form are doubtful. Cheung's main thesis is simply that the eating of *known* idol food in any context (temple or otherwise) is wrong for *any* Christian in any situation. It is idolatry. This commentary will develop the text in basic sympathy with Cheung's work.

"Enlightenment" and Christian Love (8:1-3) *Food sacrificed to idols (eidōlothytos)* is with one exception a term found only in the New Testament and early Christian writers. Some suggest it was coined at the Jerusalem Council to warn Gentile converts not to attend the pagan temple sacrifices (Acts 15:29; Gardner 1994:15). Ben Witherington states, "*Eidōlothytos* in all its 1st century AD occurrences means an animal sacrificed in the presence of an idol *and eaten in the temple precincts*" (1993:240). This is only partly true. There is no evidence that the use of the word is restricted to the eating of idol food in the temple precincts or in a sacrificial cultic context (Still 2002:233-34). Following Cheung, I will

gloss (contra Witherington 1995; see Cheung 1999:319-22). Furthermore, the "absence of a description of a sacrificial act and the dialogue between Antiochus and Eleazar . . . [lead me to] cautiously take 4 Maccabees 5:2 as evidence for the broader

argue that apostolic teaching forbids the eating of this food *anywhere* if it has been identified as previously sacrificed to an idol. Christian faith, once embraced, requires a clean break with idolatry ("you turned to God from idols to serve the living and true God," 1 Thess 1:9).

It is important at the outset to understand that the issue the Corinthians raised with Paul in their letter, *Now about,* was *both* the issue of Christians' eating in the temples of pagan gods as participants in sacrificial ceremonies *and* the wider practice of eating known sacrificial food in any context. This did damage to "weaker" Christians who could not eat known sacrificial food without consciousness of the idol in whose presence the sacrifice was made. John Chrysostom captures this sense when he explains:

> Many among them, having learnt that (St. Matthew 15:11) "not the things which enter in defile the man, but the things which proceed out," and that idols of wood and stone, and demons, have no power to hurt or help, had made an immoderate use of their perfect knowledge of this to the harm both of others and of themselves. They had both gone in where idols were and had partaken of the tables there, and were producing thereby great and ruinous evil. For, on the one hand, those who still retained the fear of idols and knew not how to contemn them, took part in those meals, because they saw the more perfect sort doing this; and hence they got the greatest injury: since they did not touch what was set before them with the same mind as the others, but as things offered in sacrifice to idols; and the thing was becoming a way to idolatry. On the other hand, these very persons who pretended to be more perfect were injured in no common way, partaking in the tables of demons. ("Homily on 1 Corinthians 8:1")

How did the "enlightened" build their case? First, they argued, *we know that we all possess knowledge.* Their first defense was that all

---

definition of *eidōlothytus*" (Still 2002:230). The New Testament references seem decisive that the word refers to sacrificed food eaten in *any* setting, not merely in the presence of an idol or in the temples (as probably 8:10 and Rev 2:14, 20). The second-century reference in *Didache* 6.3 "refers to a class of food from which abstinence is absolutely required rather than a location in which it is impermissible to eat" (Still 2002:230).

Christians knew that (1) *an idol is nothing at all in the world* (v. 4); (2) *there is no God but one* (v. 4) and this God is indifferent to food (v. 8). Idols and idol food are harmless, since the pagan gods are not real gods with real power; there is only one real God. From this perspective, what is so wrong about participating in the ceremonies and dining at the temples? Christians should show their "knowledge" of this truth by mingling with the local Corinthian citizenry at sacrifices and banquets. They cannot be harmed, because they "know" the *idol is nothing at all in the world.*

Knowledge puffs up, but love builds up. Before Paul directly deals with these distortions of his teaching, he addresses the attitude of the "enlightened" by redirecting their understanding of the boundary marker of a Christian. It is not knowledge (of idols or even of God himself) that distinguishes a Christian. Rather Christ's followers are identified by the love they show toward God (v. 3) and the love that builds up other believers (chap. 13). Humility is the proper attitude of the Christian toward knowledge: *the man who thinks he knows something does not yet know as he ought to know* (v. 2).

Paul defends the weak by calling the "enlightened" to a responsible freedom disciplined by love. True Christian identity is in expression of love to God and love to the neighbor rather than in mere doctrinal correctness. Faith demonstrates its real presence by expressions of love in the community. Yet "getting it right" in certain aspects of our theology does affect our practice, as Paul will argue in the following material in this section. To love God is to be known by God, which is true spirituality (2:9). It is not knowing God but being known by God that marks the Christian as a true lover of God. To be known by God reminds us of God's elective purposes in salvation, reminiscent of Paul's remarks elsewhere: "Now that you know God—or rather are known by God . . ." (Gal 4:9).

In an otherwise fine essay on the importance and legitimacy of the imitation of Christ in 1 Corinthians 8—10, Kim adopts the modern interpretation of idol food as food acceptable for Christians if it does not offend others. Idol food is erroneously (in my opinion) put into the category of Old Testament purity food restrictions that Jesus now gives Christians the freedom to ignore if exercised in love without offense (2003).

Idols and the One God (8:4-6) Now Paul quotes again from the letter of the Corinthian "enlightened" ones defending their position. The first part of their statement is *We know that an idol is nothing at all in the world and that there is no God but one.* The latter part sounds like the Jewish monotheism of the Shema: "Hear, O Israel: The LORD our God, the LORD is one" (Deut 6:4; 32:39). Thus far there is nothing wrong with their point of view, but later I will argue that it is a half-truth that Paul corrects (1 Cor 10:14-22).

For even if there are so-called gods, whether in heaven or on earth (as indeed there are many "gods" and many "lords"). Whether this statement is a continuation of the Corinthian defense or Paul's own words of affirmation or some variation of both is uncertain. In any event, it affirms the reality of pagan religious pluralism in Roman Corinth without any commitment to the reality of their various deities, *so-called gods.*

Yet for us (v. 6) contrasts a Christian view of God as sole Creator *from whom* (source) *all things came,* who is also *Father* in relation to the Son. This latter statement may strike a redemptive note and advance beyond mere monotheism (Yeo 1995:190). Assuming that Paul is not quoting their view here, he presses for a more salvation-communitarian or trinitarian understanding of God that will then allow the apostle to urge the "enlightened" ones to consider out of love their weaker brothers and sisters.

And . . . one Lord, Jesus Christ, completes the parallelism with "many gods" (opposed to one God), "many lords" (opposed to one Lord), *through whom* (agency) *all things came.* The deliberate parallelism of what is ascribed to the Father in creation *(from)* and what is ascribed to Jesus Christ in creation *(through)* is amazing for its high Christology in this early period (A.D. 57), probably before any Gospel was written (see Jn 1:3, "through him all things were made; without him nothing was made that has been made"). *For whom we live . . . through whom*

8:5 We should follow Winter, who argues that there is no distinction between many "gods" and many "lords" (1990:214).

8:7 *Since their conscience is weak, it is defiled* is mostly misread by moderns. *Conscience (syneidēsis)* is better translated here "consciousness." The weak Christians eat the sacrificed food as "food offered to the idol" *(eidōlothytos).* They cannot eat the

we live reflects the new creation effected through redemption. "The Christian lives for God. He lives only to do Him service" (Morris 1958:126).

The Scandalizing of a Christian Brother or Sister (8:7-13) Paul now turns to the actual distressing behavior of the "enlightened" ones. He doesn't actually at this point condemn their frequenting the temple ceremonies; he saves that for a further exhortation (10:1-22). Instead the apostle turns to point out the dire consequences for the weaker-consciousness Christians that the "enlightened" are fostering by their temple visits.

But not everyone knows this (v. 7) corrects the Corinthians' earlier statement ("we all possess knowledge"). There are, Paul says, Christians who do not know that there is only one God and that an idol is nothing, so that they could go into the pagan temples and eat the food sacrificed there without a second thought about it. It is even doubtful in the light of 10:14-22 that Paul himself would claim such knowledge!

Still so accustomed to idols indicates that these Christians were probably Gentile converts who had in their pre-Christian past frequented the temple meals and developed a "consciousness" of eating the sacrificial food in the god's presence in the temple or, as I argue, in other circumstances as well. Now, as Christians, they cannot eat this food in the temple or elsewhere without having the same consciousness of the idol's presence they had before *(they think of it),* despite the reassurances of "enlightened" Christians that such eating is perfectly harmless because God cares nothing about food (v. 8).

Some Christians perhaps experience something similar if they were formerly involved in witchcraft, Satanism and occult practices. One person expressed to me the inability to listen to organ music without witchcraft ceremonies flooding back into their consciousness, because organs were used in worship of Satan. We should not confuse the

---

food without consciousness of the idol. To eat with consciousness of the idol is tantamount to practicing idolatry. This will lead to their (eternal?) destruction (v. 11). Those with *knowledge* eat the same food, but in their minds they allegedly divorce the food from the idol. Later Paul will deny that this is possible (10:20-22).

weak-wavering-in-faith Christians in Rome, who needed to act out of conviction rather than community pressure (Rom 14), with the Corinthian weak, who could not eat sacrificial food except with consciousness of an idol's presence.

However, Paul says that this practice is destructive *since their conscience* (better, "consciousness") *is weak,* not in moral dullness but in its awareness of the power of the idol as a god; it is therefore *defiled* (*molynō,* also in Rev. 3:4; 14:4, both references to idolatry) when food is eaten in the temple or elsewhere as meat offered to a pagan deity. Thus these Christians commit an act of idolatrous worship that results in their sensing themselves condemned and guilty before God. Paul does not offer any word of correction to these "weak-in-consciousness" believers. Instead he continues to address those who are encouraging the weak Christians to defile themselves with idolatrous practices.

But food does not bring us near to God. Some believe verse 8 is another quotation from the Corinthians' argument: what we eat cannot bring us before God in judgment, since food is irrelevant to God. Therefore to eat sacrificial food (*brōma,* "food" in general; but *krea,* "meat" specifically, in v. 13) in the temple and elsewhere (if it known to be idol meat) has no spiritual implications for us in relation to God—*we are no worse if we do not eat, and no better if we do* (Witherington 1995:199). Paul's explicit forbidding of eating at the sacrificial meals in 10:14-22 would otherwise be difficult to explain.

Still, some defend the whole of verse 8 as Paul's own words to the effect that there is no spiritual significance before God in eating, similar to his words in Romans 14, "For the kingdom of God is not a matter of eating and drinking, but of righteousness, peace, and joy in the Holy Spirit. . . . All food is clean" (Rom 14:17, 20). The only condition, they argue, is in eating something that causes a brother or sister to stumble; then it is wrong to eat or drink because of the damage to a fellow Christian. First Corinthians 10:1-22 would then be a warning to not become involved in idolatrous worship in the temples. Yet this view overlooks the clear reference to some Christians who were reclining and eating meals *in an idol's temple* (8:10). Further, as Wendell Willis points

---

8:9 *Freedom (exousia)* is translated "civic right" to attend the Roman dinners, granted

out, Paul is going to considerable length (chap. 8; 10:1-22), "an immense over-kill, if the issue is only why can't we eat sacrificial meat—especially since he will conclude by saying that this is permissible, but be considerate of others' feelings (10:23—11:1)" (1987:9).

It seems best then to conclude that verse 8 is probably the Corinthians' words or a misuse of Paul's teaching about food, applying it wrongly to the temple dining ceremonies (see Fee 1980:191).

The Corinthians' misshaped theology ("knowledge") led immediately to two twin sins, damage to the weak Christians (8:9-13) and idolatry (10:1-22). Paul addresses the first by warning the "enlightened" that by flaunting their knowledge of the one God in appearing and eating at the sacrificial meal *in an idol's temple* (v. 10) they were creating a serious *stumbling block* (*oikodomeō*, "builds up" of v. 1, "edified, strengthened") to eat the sacrificial food as in the presence of the idol (v. 10; see at v. 7). Some edification! Did they really think that they could build up "the consciousness of the weak one" (not *weak conscience* as NIV) by encouraging them to eat in the temples? Love, in contrast, understands the nature of the weakness of some toward idol consciousness and does not try to edify others by boasting in the knowledge that an idol is nothing and that there is nothing harmful in attending banquets in the temples.

But what is this *exercise of your freedom* (v. 9)? The word is actually *exousia*, "authority, freedom of choice. power, right to act" (cf. 9:4-6, 12, 18; 11:10; 15:24). It is not clear whether this "right" or "freedom" that they claimed was a general right to eat in the temples or a civic right for Corinthian citizens to attend dinners celebrating the imperial cult, especially during the Isthmian Games at the invitation of the president of the games (Winter 1994:174). In any event, that Paul does not himself endorse the "right" is evident in his referring to it as *your* right, not necessarily one he shares.

So serious was this *stumbling block* that Paul refers to *the weak*, as a result of their stumbling back into idolatry, as in the process of being *destroyed* (*apollyomai*, perish, ruin, damage). In verse 12 the effect of the action of the "enlightened" is described as *wound their weak con-*

to certain people of status at Corinth (Winter 1994:165-77).

science. *Wound* is *typtō*, "to strike with a blow, beat," and is an especially graphic word for how this brother or sister's weak conscience is given a fatal (?) blow. Bruce, following Calvin and others, comments, "It is not man's eternal perdition, but the stunting of his Christian life and usefulness by the 'wounding' of his conscience when it is weak that Paul has in mind" (1971:82). But can this theology fit the strong language of "perishing" or the problem of idolatry that the passage addresses?

Despite the tension it causes in some theological systems, it seems better to see the problem as serious enough to in some sense impinge on the person's eternal destiny. *By your knowledge*, not by your love, you are doing (eternal?) harm to one *for whom Christ died* (to save them from destruction!). Even the weakest believer in Christ is of infinite value. Such behavior was not only a sin against a family member of Christ's body (TNIV "brothers and sisters") but *against Christ* himself, who contains the whole Christian community in himself (Acts 9:4; 1 Cor 12:12).

Paul concludes with a personal application to himself (v. 12): *Therefore, if what I eat causes my brother to fall into sin* (*skandalizō*, "to set off a trap"; it virtually means the same as stumbling block in v. 9), *I will never* (*ou mē, never, never*) *eat meat again, so that I will not cause him to fall* [*skandalizō*]. Paul makes it an absolute principle for himself that he will eat no food that causes another Christian to stumble or be snared into the sin of idolatry. He forgoes any supposed right to eat in a temple dining hall or to eat known idol food elsewhere for the sake of their eternal salvation (see 9:19-23; 10:23). Christian identity is first of all a sense of being known by God (8:3), then to walk in love both toward God and toward others, with crosscultural sensitivity.

Paul's Example and Defense (9:1-27) At first reading this chapter seems out of place, disconnected from the previous and following discussions of eating in pagan temples. Consequently some have taken the view that, though written by Paul, chapter 9 belongs to another letter. This is held principally because of the lack of any transition into what appears to be a completely new subject before the question of food offered to idols is finished (Héring 1962:75). Yet this conclusion seems unnecessary if we can find connections in chapter 9 with chapters 8 and 10—which we can—and if we can allow Paul a slight digression, though not without pertinence to his overall argument in 8—10 about known sacrificial food eaten in the temple and elsewhere.

But just what is Paul's point in this slight digression? There are two opinions. All agree that Paul is offering himself as an example of how one's "rights" should be viewed when another believer would be harmed by their exercise—an obvious link with the preceding chapter. Some, however, believe Paul is also defending the authority of his apostleship, which has been attacked by certain factions in Corinth (Fee 1980:191-92). For our purposes in this brief commentary, I will assume that the growing consensus favors the first position. Paul's defense (v. 3, *apologia,* reply, response) concerns why he, an apostle with full apostolic "rights," nevertheless made tents (as a leatherworker) to support himself and his colleagues, taking no pay when he brought the gospel to the Corinthians.

Paul will explain that his chief reasons are twofold. He does not want to burden the Corinthian Christians with his support because for some this might present an impediment to accepting the gospel (v. 12). Yet Paul also finds for himself another reason not to take support from the Corinthians. His calling as an apostle carries with it an obligation to preach the gospel to all people. Since this obligation was *given* to Paul, not freely chosen or asked for, he feels he is an unworthy servant doing only what is expected of him. But if he can do his duty while giving up his right to support from those he evangelizes, this is more than expected and will qualify him for a reward from Christ (vv. 16-18).

Just how and why these reasons motivate Paul he will explain in detail in the chapter. The following verses will also offer occasion for bringing up other concerns that may have influenced the apostle's actions.

The Rights of an Apostle (9:1-12) *Am I not free?* seems abrupt. *Eleutheros* ("free," "independent," "not bound") refers to Paul's freedom with regard to indifferent matters *(adiaphora)* such as those he will mention in verses 4-5. In my opinion, contrary to the modern consensus view, this does not include the eating of known sacrificial idol food as discussed in chapter 8 and 10. He will explicitly condemn such a practice in 10:20-21. His point, however, does have relevance to the idol food issue.

Am I not an apostle? Who Paul would have included as "apostles" beyond the original twelve is not clear, but certainly he includes Barnabas in this chapter (v. 6) and James the Lord's brother elsewhere (Gal 1:19; see also *the Lord's brothers,* 1 Cor 9:5), and perhaps Andronicus and Junia (Rom 16:7). In any case, this is a rhetorical question to emphasize that he is indeed an apostle.

Two further similar questions, expecting a "yes" response, emphasize again his apostolic calling. *Have I not seen Jesus Christ our Lord* (cf. Acts 9:1-9; 26:12-18) after his resurrection, like the other apostles such as Peter and James? Paul then reminds the Corinthians of the fruit of his apostolic mission to the Gentiles that they themselves represent: *for you are the seal of my apostleship in the Lord.* Having seen the resurrected Lord and having planted churches authenticate Paul's apostleship.

My defense refers not to his case for being an apostle—this he assumes they accept—but to the argument that follows concerning his apostolic "right" to forgo financial support from the Corinthians, a right that apparently some had questioned *(those who sit in judgment on me).*

As an apostle (part of this group) Paul (and Barnabas) has a *right* (*exousia,* authority, legal entitlement) to support *(food and drink),* to be married and have his spouse accompany him, also with support (*believing wife* is *adelphē gynē,* a sister who is a wife), *as do the other apostles* (notice, no celibacy required of leaders in the early church) *and the Lord's brothers* (James, Judas, Joseph and Simon are mentioned in Mt 13:55; see Jn 7:5) *and Cephas* (Peter; read "and even Cephas"). Are Paul and Barnabas, who are legitimate apostles, to be alone excluded from not working to support themselves (v. 6)? Apparently Paul worked for his own support at Thessalonica (1 Thess 2:9; 2 Thess 3:7-9) and probably elsewhere as well, though he seems to have accepted hospitality, travel aid and perhaps regular gifts from the Philippians (Acts 16:15; Phil 4:10-13).

The rest of the chapter (vv. 7-23) falls into two main sections (vv. 7-

12 and 13-23). Each section argues that Paul has the right to support but gives it up.

The first section (vv. 7-12) presents two arguments for his case. One (v. 7) uses three examples (soldier, farmer, shepherd), put in the form of three rhetorical questions that each expect the answer "No one." Each includes a recompense intrinsically related to the work itself as a "share" in the fruit of the labor. Finally, each analogy is appropriate to the work of the gospel (warfare, seed sowing, shepherding), though Paul might not have intended this connection.

A second argument (vv. 8-12) turns to the Mosaic law for divine approval of Christ's apostles receiving support: *Doesn't the Law say the same thing?* Paul quotes Deuteronomy 25:4 (see 1 Tim 5:18), *"Do not muzzle an ox while it is treading out the grain."* What is curious to us, but nevertheless instructive, is that he emphatically states that God's concern in the command was not the welfare of animals *(Is it about oxen that God is concerned?)* but of humans *(Surely he says this for us, doesn't he? Yes, this was written for us)*. What kind of hermeneutic (principle of interpretation) is this? Certainly the "literal" sense of Deuteronomy refers to the humane treatment of animals. But Paul sees a deeper or broader reference in the command.

First, it says in general to the *plowman* and to the *thresher* that they should be thought worthy of *sharing in the harvest* and thus have *hope*. Second, the text speaks more particularly about the ministry of the gospel (*spiritual seed* is *pneumatika,* things of the Spirit) *for us*. The argument is from the greater (spiritual sowing) to the lesser (*material harvest* is *sarkika,* "fleshly things"). Moses is instructing the Corinthians to give money to apostles like Paul and Barnabas! In fact they have more of a right to this support than others because of their extended labor in founding and nurturing the church (*shouldn't we have it all the more?* cf. 4:15).

The Principle of Forgoing Rights (9:12-23) In verses 12-23 Paul points to the way as an apostle he has denied himself rewards that he might have legitimately enjoyed in order to win men and women for the gospel. He has even given up his privilege to receive pay for his ministry in order to receive a divine reward for his free service that he would otherwise not have obtained because Christ had called and commissioned him directly, personally and specifically to preach the gospel as an apostle (vv. 15-18). Finally, he indicates that he has become a slave to all sorts of persons in order to win them to Christ and thus share in the gospel (vv. 19-23).

Paul and Barnabas do *not use this right* (v. 12); instead they *put up with* all the additional stress of working to support themselves *rather than hinder the gospel of Christ* (v. 12). Why should not working create an obstacle for others to receive and follow the gospel, especially when Christ has said it is all right? Paul has elsewhere indicated that when he preached free of charge he did not covet "anyone's silver or gold or clothing" (Acts 20:33). This may suggest that he feared that if he accepted their regular support, either he might be tempted to greed or others might accuse him of preaching for the material benefits he received—not true, of course. In either case the gospel would be hindered.

Before Paul presses home his case for forgoing his rights, he further draws a parallel with those who serve in the temple and share in the food offered there (1 Cor 9:13). We should not think here of the pagan temple sacrifices at Corinth that Paul will later condemn (10:19-22) but of the Jewish temple that was still standing and operating in Jerusalem when Paul wrote. Temple servants were authorized by Moses to eat from the sacrificial offerings as a part of their reward for service (see 10:18; Lev 6:16, 26; Num 18:8, 31; Deut 18:1-3). Furthermore, and of greatest importance, the Lord Jesus Christ himself authorized his servants of the word to receive a living wage from those who benefit from their service. *Those who preach the gospel should receive their living from the gospel.* Since there was not yet a written Gospel, Paul seems to refer to the written or oral tradition of our Lord's teaching, later recorded in both Matthew and Luke in what scholars call the "Q" tradition, in the words "For the worker is worth his keep" (Mt 10:10; Lk 10:7; also 1 Tim 5:18 NRSV).

Now that the right to receive remuneration is firmly established, Paul can explain why he has *not used any of these rights* (1 Cor 9:15). One reason is his desire to earn a *reward* (vv. 17-18). Since he has been directly and personally commissioned by Christ to preach the gospel as an apostle, he views the discharge of this office as a duty to be fulfilled joyfully but not as something he has freely chosen on his own initiative. Therefore no special recognition is to be given to him beyond faithful service to this calling. But to forgo his right to be paid is not required of him to fulfill his apostolic calling. This gives him the opportunity to offer to Christ an extra measure of loving service that he believes will be recognized in the future by his Lord (vv. 15-18). This reward should not be understood in terms of earning his salvation but in the sense of chapter 3, building on the foundation of Christ with gold, silver and precious stones.

To this example of using his freedom to forgo the right of receiving pay Paul now adds that though he is *free* from obligation to any person, he nevertheless has made himself *a slave to everyone, to win as many as possible* (v. 19). Christ freed Paul by making him his servant (7:22). Now he puts himself at the disposal of Jews, Gentiles and the weak in order to win for Christ as many from these groups as possible. In other words, Paul sees his freedom not as an excuse to live free from obligation to others but as freedom *for* service to others. This is the social dimension of his freedom that Luther captures in his opening words of *Liberty of a Christian Man:* "A Christian man is a most free lord of all, subject to none. A Christian man is a most dutiful servant of all, subject to all" (quoted by Bruce 1971:86).

Paul adopts the cultural customs of those to whom he preaches so that nothing will hinder people's embracing the gospel of Christ. To the Jews Paul adopts Jewish ways *like a Jew* (see Acts 21:20-26). *To those under the law* he follows the 613 commandments of Torah *like one under the law,* yet he is not himself *under the law,* since through Christ and the Spirit he has been freed from the obligations of the Mosaic law as a covenant system of righteousness (Rom 6:14-15). This should put to rest the modern view that Paul did not see his fellow Jews in need of the gospel of Christ or that he had no evangelistic mission to them.

Among *those not having the law,* or "outside the law" (NRSV), that is, Gentiles, Paul adopts Gentile cultural ways (1 Cor 9:21). But to avoid being misunderstood as an advocate of unrestrained moral freedom, Paul adds that he is *not free from God's law* (not lawless with respect to God) *but . . . under Christ's law.* There is incidentally a hint here of Paul's Christology at a very early period (A.D. 53!). To be under *Christ's* law is at the same time to be under *God's* law (translate "governed according to Christ's law"). To practice true Christian liberty does not mean to live without divine restraint but rather to live under the cross, to follow Christ in humble service to the other's best interests. Paul adopts Gentile ways to be a servant to the Gentiles to win them for Christ.

To the weak . . . to gain the weak (v. 22): who are the weak? In 8:7-13 "the weak" are possibly those believers at Corinth who were conditioned to eating sacrificial food as "idol food," conscious of the demons' presence (cf. 10:20-21). However, this identity of the weak runs into the problem that Paul is here talking about his missionary activity to non-Christians, not about his behavior with weak-in-consciousness Christians. Therefore it is better to see *the weak* here as in 1:27, as those who are sociopolitically vulnerable within the society compared to the influential—landowners, employers, patrons (Thiselton 2000:706). This seems to mean that Paul adopted the customs and lifestyle of those of low social standing. Earlier he had referred to such in the words, "We are weak, but you are strong! You are honored, we are dishonored! To this very hour we go hungry and thirsty, we are in rags, we are brutally treated, we are homeless. We work hard with our own hands" (4:10-12). Again this manifests the cruciform lifestyle that Paul follows.

In conclusion he states a broad principle that governs his missionary life: *I have become all things to all men.* A better translation here is "To them all I have become everything in turn through every possible means" (Thiselton 2000:706). This does not mean that Paul observed no theological or moral limits to this principle (cf. Gal 2:1-14). As Anthony Thiselton remarks, "he does not say that he became an idolater to idolaters or an adulterer to adulterers. But in matters that he did not see as ethically or theologically essential or implied by the gospel, Paul believed in flexibility" (1995:213). In this style of ministry Paul follows the kenotic (self-emptying) example of Christ (Rom 15:1-3; Phil 2:4-8). This example of self-identification service does not end with Paul but extends as well to the congregations at Corinth, who are to identify themselves with those they hope to see saved. *For the sake of the gospel* (v. 23) defines the reason behind Paul's flexibility. It is not to promote his own popularity or even to serve a larger sociopolitical end but totally to effect the saving purposes of Christ's gospel.

The exact sense of the words *that I might share in its blessings* is debatable. Literally the Greek is "that I might be a partner of it." But does Paul mean a partner in the *blessings* of the gospel (NIV, NRSV), a partner in the work of the gospel or a partner in the nature of the gospel, "to instantiate what the gospel is and how it operates" (Thiselton 2000:707)? I think that this latter is the correct sense. The gospel is to be proclaimed not in word only but also in lifestyle. The Corinthians, and we as well, need to imitate Paul as he had imitated Christ's self-emptying (11:1). "Is it not paradoxical that in shying away from this idea, Christians have looked for other models for ministry—and those models have tended to be about status and authority, instead of about kenosis? Paul, I think, would claim that when that happens, men and women have misunderstood, not simply Christian ministry, but the gospel itself" (Hooker 1996:100).

Running to Win the Race (9:24-27) Finally Paul uses an example drawn from the Greco-Roman Isthmian Games, whose administration was given back to Corinth in 2 B.C. and which were held in A.D. 57, when Paul was no doubt in Corinth and wrote the epistle to the Romans. Second only to the Olympic Games and held biennially in the spring, it involved athletic events of various sorts that included both men and women, such as foot races, boxing and war-chariot races. Such an event could not have escaped Paul's personal experience when he arrived in Corinth the first time in the spring of 50 and probably did not leave until the middle of the year in 51 (Acts 18:12-18; Furnish 1988:20).

We, of course, are reminded of the modern Olympic Games, viewed by millions around the entire globe by satellite TV. I have had the privilege of knowing two Olympic athletes personally, one a medal winner and the other a four-time competitor. I can testify to their unending, grueling training, deliberate abstinence from the normal life we all live, and focused determination when their event was under way.

What is Paul's point in drawing from this athletic event? Just this. If athletes can expend focused effort and practice sustained, deliberate abstinence from whatever dulls the physical body's performance, including mental concentration, in order to win the prize—a paltry, perishable vegetable crown (celery) and its fleeting glory—then how much more we Christians, who have at stake our eternal victor's crown (2 Tim 4:8; Jas 1:12; 1 Pet 5:4; Rev 2:10), should we be willing to give up rights, lifestyles, habits of self-indulgence. We should make the necessary effort because we have the goal clearly in mind: to win people to Christ by such cruciform identification with them (1 Cor 9:19-23).

This is real Christian freedom. Paul is living his life this way. He wants the Corinthians to imitate him. This will include his sensitivity to the "weak-in-consciousness-of-idols" Christians, who may stumble back into idolatry by following the example of so-called enlightened progressives who were in the name of Christian freedom eating food known to be sacrificed to the gods, as well as the categories of people he elaborates in 9:19-22. Paul fears that when all is over and he stands before the Judge of all, he will fail the test of subordinating everything to the gospel passion of his life (v. 23).

Surely this word of Paul is urgently needed in the affluent, convenience-oriented church in America. Luther's "Let goods and kindred go, this mortal life also" sounds quaint and excessive to most of our ears.

While the translation *in a race* (v. 24) is correct, the Greek is literally "in a stadium." No actual stadium existed in Roman Corinth, but other cities nearby such as Isthmia did have athletic event stadiums to which Paul could be referring. In Corinth the games were held in the temple of Poseidon. "In a stadium" could also refer to one of the races, the two-hundred-meter sprint (Kent 1966:29).

Run in such a way as to get the prize (v. 24). This requires focus. Christians are, each one, to run the Christian-life race intent on winning the prize of Jesus Christ himself and his approbation, "Well done, good and faithful servant." This is not an exhortation to only a special group of called-to-ministry persons or missionaries. It is addressed to all Christians as a model for their life. In preparation for the race, two things are required for winning. One is determined effort to train the body for the event, and the other is abstinence (*enkrateuomai*, NIV's *strict training*, NRSV's "self control") from even good things that distract from either the focused goal or the training needed to achieve the prize.

As for Paul himself, he is so running the race with "his eye clearly on the goal" (NIV *not . . . running aimlessly*) and not as one who "shadow boxes into empty air" (v. 26; Thiselton 2000:715). He has shown the "enlightened" ones at Corinth, who prided themselves in their knowledge and self-indulgent freedom, that the Christian way is marked by love and disciplined restraint out of consideration for those who are "weak" in consciousness of idols.

I beat my body and make it my slave (v. 27) has been difficult to understand. Paul could hardly be advocating a form of physical masochism. Both words (*beat,* Lk 18:5, and *body,* 1 Cor 6:19-20) are used frequently in the New Testament metaphorically rather than literally. It may be best to so understand them here. Paul would then be saying, "My day-to-day life as a whole I treat roughly, and make it strictly serve my purposes" (Thiselton 2000:708, 715-16). The purpose for strict discipline in his day-to-day life, according to the NIV, continuing with the boxing metaphor of verse 26, is so that *I myself will not be disqualified for the prize.* While this is a possible interpretation, it is better to see the boxing metaphor dropped and to translate this as "I will not stand the test." Paul expresses the irony that without this strict discipline, when all is said and done and the secrets of his heart are brought into the light of God's judgment (4:4-5), he himself, the teacher, might fail the final test of complete faithfulness to Christ ("in all things," 9:25, NRSV). This should not be seen as a loss of salvation but a loss of Christ's commendation, as in 3:12-15 (Rom 14:10-12; 2 Cor 5:9-10).

To sum up chapter 9 briefly: Paul has addressed the misuse of Christian knowledge and freedom undisciplined by Christian love by placing his own lifestyle as a model to follow. Though he has all the rights of a legitimate apostle of Christ, he has no reluctance in setting aside some or all of these freedoms when they do not serve the higher purpose of the gospel of Christ. For him this has meant that he has worked for his living rather than be paid by the churches. And rather than freeing himself from others' needs, he has become a servant of all types of people in order to win them to Christ and share in the essence of the gospel. Finally, he has treated his freedom as a strict discipline, like the athlete who strives for the perishable vegetable crown. The Corinthians who were abusing their freedom and damaging other believers by eating food known to be sacrificed to idols were to follow Paul's example of using freedom—and the "kenosis" model of Jesus. who freely gave up his own privileges and rights and out of love took up our interests and made them his own (Phil 2:3-11).

> But do not, with a vile crown of
>   fraile boyes,
> Reward my muses white sincerity,
> But what thy thorny crown gain'd, that
>   Give me,
> A crown of glory, which doth flower always.
>
> JOHN DONNE, *"La Corona"*

"Your thoughts, finances, and time—and your physical, sexual, marital, and ministerial lives—need continuous maintenance. Spiritual power seeps out through unguarded personal gates. Think about the end of the race. Run in such a way that you may win (1 Cor 9:24). The willingness to forgo immediate pleasure in order to obtain the ultimate prize lies at the core of victory" (Hendricks 2001).

Paul's Final Word About Food Offered to Idols (10:1—11:1) We should see this chapter as Paul's final word on the matter of food offered to idols, which he has addressed from different aspects in both chapters 8 and 9. In chapter 8 he has pleaded with the "enlightened" to not destroy weak-because-of-idol-consciousness Christians by boldly eating known sacrificial food. In chapter 9 he has called them to follow the model of the cruciform life, illustrated by Paul's forgoing of apostolic rights for the sake of the salvation of others and by the strict discipline that keeps his use of freedom limited to this kind of service.

Paul argued in chapter 8 that eating food sacrificed to idols was potentially destructive to Christians who could not eat it without consciousness of the idol to which it was sacrificed (8:10-11). He condemns this behavior on the part of the "enlightened" and closes the chapter by appealing to his own approach of not eating any food that causes another Christian to stumble (into idolatry). Yet he stops short in chapter 8 of actually connecting idol food to idolatry or of specifically commanding Christians not to eat idol food at all. Now in chapter 10:1-22 Paul turns directly to the issue of idolatry and advances a command that implies a stinging condemnation: *Flee from idolatry* (v. 14). I will argue, with Cheung (1999), that this prohibition refers to the practice of eating *known* idol food in any circumstance, whether in the temple precincts or elsewhere. This view at the moment goes against all but a few modern scholars, but it is in complete agreement with the early church fathers, and I believe with Paul as well.

To address the deeper issue of the danger of idolatry among Christians at Corinth, Paul now turns to the examples of the Israelites who departed from Egypt under Moses' leadership. In his mind there must be a series of close parallels or correspondences between the cited incidents of Israel in its wilderness wanderings and the dangers facing the Corinthian community. So the NIV rightly includes the connective particle *gar,* translated *For* (unfortunately left untranslated in RSV and NRSV), and links chapter 10 to chapters 8 and 9, and especially to 9, where Paul has just given examples from his disciplined self-control, which enables him to remain true to the Christian faith and in the end not to be disapproved.

The contents of the chapter fall into four sections. In the first (10:1-13) Paul turns to the Israelite generation that left Egypt under Moses to demonstrate that although they all shared in the sacraments of redemption and participated in the redeemed community of God's people, God was displeased with most of them. They rebelled against God and contended with his representative, Moses, on numerous occasions. Paul's purpose is to warn the Corinthians not to follow the evil cravings which led them to be destructive examples of idolatry (v. 7), sexual immorality (v. 8), rebellious quarreling against God (v. 10) and presumptive testing of God's love and grace (vv. 9, 12-13).

In the second section (10:14-22) Paul directly appeals to the Corinthians to run away from the worship of idols; this presumably is connected with the eating of food sacrificed to idols (v. 18), discussed initially in chapter 8. To be joined to the Lord in the Lord's Table is absolutely contradictory to also being joined to an idol by eating food sacrificed to demons (10:20). This will invite the strong judgment of God on Christians involved in this practice (v. 22).

This leads Paul in the third section (10:23-30) to deal with the case of idol food that is bought in public markets or served in a dinner at a non-Christian home. Paul permits freedom in the eating of such food as long as the origin of the food is unknown. Christians are not required to inquire about the origin of the food, but if without their asking are informed that the food has been sacrificed to idols, they are to refuse to eat it.

Finally, Paul sums up the whole section from 8:1 to 10:30 by urging Christians to eat and drink in the manner that will avoid sinning and thus bring glory to God in their body and not create stumbling blocks for any cultural group's reception of Christ's gospel. This way will be Paul-like and ultimately Christlike (10:31—11:1).

The Formative Warning: Models of the Exodus Israelites, the Corinthians and the Modern Church (10:1-13) *Brothers (adelphoi)* should be "brothers and sisters," as in TNIV. *Our forefathers* raises several interesting features of Paul's next defense of his position on Christian freedom and idol food. First, it needs to be emphasized in passing that Paul has no hesitancy in turning to the Old Testament for Christian moral guidance. There is, then, continuity with the Hebrew Bible and Christianity. This has been the position of the Christian church since the first century, but not without exception. For example, the second-century Christian Marcion (d. 160), a wealthy shipowner, son of a bishop, taught that Christianity was wholly a "gospel of love" to the absolute exclusion of law. This law and grace contrast led him to reject the Old Testament and all of the New Testament except the epistles of Paul and a modified version of Luke's Gospel.

While Marcion's extreme views have seldom been repeated, there continues to be a vigorous discussion in the church surrounding different approaches to the use of the Old Testament in Christian ethics. Recently there has been renewed attention to the New Testament's practical use of the Old in terms of biblical law (Rosner 1994; Tomson 1990; Fowl 1998; Bockmuehl 2000). It is clear in the chapter and this section in particular that Paul sees explicit authoritative ethical instructions to the Corinthian Christians in the events of biblical Israel in the desert. *Now these things occurred as examples to keep us from setting our hearts on evil things as they did. . . . These things happened to them as examples and were written down as warnings for us, on whom the fulfillment of the ages has come* (vv. 6, 11).

Furthermore, Paul states that the "rock" that the Israelites drank from in the wilderness not only was *spiritual* (divinely provided) but *was Christ* (v. 4), thus directly linking the Christian community with the biblical Jewish community under Moses. At this point we cannot look at the whole question of the Christian's relation to the Old Testament, but it is sufficient to say that no adequate view could be formulated that ignored or deemphasized the authoritative use of the Old Testament in both Christian theology and ethics. Just how the proper balance is maintained between continuity with the old and discontinuity because of the new that has come with Christ is the subject of a much longer discussion than space allows here.

Great initial spiritual blessings are no guarantee of continuing divine favor (10:1-6). Paul will now cite the experience of the exodus Israelites, who all had a common baptism into the leadership of Moses in the cloud and through the sea, and all shared in the spiritual drink and food that God miraculously provided in the wilderness (notice *all,* five instances in Greek). *Nevertheless, God was not pleased with most of them* (or "many of them," v. 5). All of the adults died in the wilderness except Joshua and Caleb, many of them perishing under the hand of God's judgment (Deut 1:34-40; 2:14). Some particulars of their failures are cited by Paul in 10:7-11, but his focus there is on sexual immorality and idolatry.

How could this have happened to a people who participated in such rich blessings of God's grace and presence? Paul does not answer this question directly, but could a part of the reason lie in the people's failure to discipline their lives in the way Paul advocates in 9:24-27? In any event Paul sees sufficient parallels in what happened to the Israelites to issue a warning to the Corinthians in verse 6 that these incidents have become authoritative ethical models, so that they may not crave evil things as their ancestors did and suffer a like fate under God's judgment.

Our forefathers is an expression that links the Jewish and Gentile believers in Corinth to the elect people of God in the exodus period. For Gentiles this could only be true in the sense that Paul elaborates in other places where union with Christ through faith makes them spiritually part of the great family of Abraham, "the father of us all" (Rom

4:16; cf. Rom 4:11-12; 3:28-29).

All under the cloud and . . . all passed through the sea . . . all baptized into Moses in the cloud and in the sea (1 Cor 10:1-2) brings us into the narrative of the Egyptian exodus of Israel and prepares the reader for the events Paul will mention later in connection with the wilderness journey. We have here (vv. 1-6) and in the following section (vv. 7-13) a Pauline Christian midrash (an exposition or homily on Scripture) based mainly on Exodus 13:21-22; 14:22-29; 40:34-38; Numbers 9:15-22; 14:14; and Psalm 78:14. The import of the cloud by day and the fire by night seems to include ideas of God's protective and saving presence, his faithfulness and mercy (Neh 9:19), and the glory of God (Is 4:5).

However, Paul's emphasis is on the total participation of all the people in this marvelous experience connected to their redemption. *They were all baptized into Moses* (v. 2) strikes a note of parallelism between Christian baptism "into Christ" (Rom 6:3; Gal 3:27), which, like the baptism of the Israelites "into Moses," is a shorthand for being baptized into (or with reference to) the name of Jesus Christ, or brought into identification with Christ's death and resurrection (Rom 6:3-11) and into the following of Jesus Christ. While the Israelites *all* were baptized (or "had themselves baptized") into the name of Moses, and *all* enjoyed God's salvation and protective presence in the wilderness, some (most) of them rebelled against God and suffered his judgment because of it. Initial stupendous blessings are no guarantee of continued obedient response to God.

They all ate the same spiritual food and . . . spiritual drink (vv. 3-4) again refers to the participation of *all* the Israelites in the Spirit's divinely given (*spiritual* is *pneumatika,* of the Spirit) manna and springs of water (Ex 16—17), further blessings and signs of their incorporation into Christ and his community. The parallels to the Christian participation in the food and drink of the sacrament of the Lord's Table seem quite strong, especially in view of the explicit reference to the Lord's Supper in verses 16-21.

The spiritual rock that accompanied them (literally "followed"), *and that rock was Christ* (v. 4) clearly makes their experience directly connected to the Corinthians' Christian experience. Paul's pointed identification of the accompanying rock in the wilderness that gushed forth water (Ex 17; Num 20) with Christ has raised questions about both its source and its meaning. Studies have examined rabbinic traditions that mention a movable, rock-shaped well that rolled along with the Israelites in their journeying (Thiselton 2000:728).

However, two factors suggest that Paul was not alluding to this legend. It is probable that the first-century texts speak of an accompanying stream of water, not the rock itself (Ellis 1957:68). Furthermore, it is often overlooked in Paul's own text that even though he says the Israelites received both spiritual food and drink (vv. 3-4), when he states why the food and drink were gifts of the Spirit, he mentions only their drinking of the rock that was Christ (v. 4). Could it be that Paul understood the rock to be the source of both the Israelites' food and drink? If this is the case, then Paul is following a different tradition from that found in the rabbinic sources (Bandstra 1971:11-12).

But in what sense does Paul refer to the rock as Christ—allegory, analogy, metaphor, type or preexistence? Whether Paul alludes to the Jewish idea of the identity of the rock with the preexistent "wisdom of God" we cannot be sure (cf. 1:30). More likely is the connection between rock and the name of God in Deuteronomy 32:4, 15, 18, 30, 31, a passage that seems to be uppermost in Paul's mind throughout the whole of this chapter. I will say more about this shortly. *Rock* is a frequent name for Yahweh elsewhere in the Old Testament (Ps 18:2, 31; 19:14; 28:1; 62:2; 78:35; 89:26; 144:1; Is 8:14; 26:4; 28:16), and the New Testament writers do not hesitate to use the name or figure in reference to Christ (Mt 7:24-25; Rom 9:33, 1 Pet 2:8; but probably not Mt 16:18, where it means Peter).

Combining this with the frequent mention of the "angel of God" who accompanied Israel in the wilderness (Ex 14:19; 23:20-23; 32:34; 33:2, 14; cf. Acts 7:30, 38) and even perhaps references to the Lord (*Kyrios* in the Septuagint), who provided healing, guidance and protection to Israel throughout the wilderness, seems to go "far beyond the conception of the Messiah as a second Moses, supplying his people with bread and water (cf. Jn 6:14; 7:37-41a)" (Bruce 1971:91). Witherington is certainly right to say Paul is asserting not that Christ is now the equivalent of what the rock was then but that the "rock *was* Christ.

The tense of the verb is crucial" (1995:221). Paul means that the Christ himself, the preexistent Christ, was present with the Israelites in their wilderness journey (Bandstra 1971:14). We may then confidently see both a divine wisdom (Prov 8) and a preexistence Christology in the rock reference.

Nevertheless, God was not pleased with most of them (v. 5) signals the point Paul is driving at: great experiences of God's grace and blessings in community are no guarantee of continued divine blessings and favor. Paul develops just what caused this colossal failure in verses 6-13. Jude has his own read on the same happening: "the Lord delivered his people out of Egypt, but later destroyed those who did not believe" (Jude 5). In this view the cause of their destruction was unbelief in God. We will among other matters explore whether Paul also sees their failure as ultimately rooted in their unbelief.

Examples (v. 6) is *typoi* (*typikos,* v. 11) and is perhaps stronger than the NIV *examples*. Something like "moral models" or, more academically, "paradigmatic models" or "formative models" (Thiselton 2000:731) seems closer to the sense. Paul turns to these Old Testament incidents as negative or bad models to warn Christians at Corinth "so that we may not crave for evil things as they craved" (NIV's *to keep us from setting our hearts on evil things* is a loose paraphrase). This would be no doubt a reference to Numbers 11:4, where we are told that the "mixed crowd" craved fish, remembering the abundant fish in Egypt.

Most commentators take this "craving" as the first in the list of five bad-model incidents (craving, idolatry, sexual immorality, testing the Lord and grumbling). However it seems better to see "craving for evil things" as the root cause of the following four incidents of sin (Thiselton 2000:733). Craving or misdirected desire was identified by Augustine as closely linked to the essence of human sin. I do not want to follow Augustine's identification of sexual desire as the original sin and root of all other sinful desires. But the close connection of misdirected desire to sin in Augustine seems right from Paul's perspective. In Romans 6:12 Paul uses the same Greek word *(epithymia)* to connect sin to desire for evil things: "Therefore do not let sin reign in your mortal body so that you obey its evil desires" (cf. 1 Pet 2:11).

The ancient theologian also refers to Catiline, an ambitious Roman revolutionary in the first century B.C., who committed murder. Augustine asks, why? He answers he did it so that "after he had seized Rome, he might obtain honors, commands, and riches and, in his poverty and guilty knowledge of his own evil deeds, might be freed from all fear of the law and all financial difficulties. Even Catiline, therefore, did not love his own crimes; what he loved was something else, for the sake of which he committed them" (*Confessions* 2.5). G. G. Findlay calls our attention to the similarity between "craving" the fish of Egypt and "the attraction of the Corinthian idol feasts" (cited in Thiselton 2000:732).

Augustine also links the essence of sin with "pride" or "absolute self-willing," and one commentator reminds us that all the sins in 1 Corinthians spring from the self-will that puts self in the center and uses everything else as a means to the self as an end (Thiselton 2000:734). On this prideful overconfidence, see comments on verses 12-13 below. *Their bodies were scattered over the desert* refers to the large number of those who craved the meat who died as a result of God's judgment (Num 11:33-34).

Paul now applies four warning models to the Corinthians (10:7-13). The first (v. 7) involves idolatry, a central concern in the whole section (chaps. 8-10). Paul cites the incident of the people's melting earrings to make an image of a young bull, associated with the Canaanite Baal cult (Cole 1973:214) while Moses was on the mountain receiving the law (Ex 32). Interestingly, Paul quotes directly only the part of the account where *the people sat down to eat and drink and got up to indulge in pagan revelry* (*paizein,* to dance, to play, to mock, to play with another sexually), from Exodus 32:6 (LXX).

"The golden calf episode was the classic instance of Israel's idolatry" (Meeks 1982:69). Rabbi Eliezer ben Jacob is reported to have said, "For their iniquity there is enough to punish Israel from now until the dead are resurrected" (quoted in Meeks 1982:69). While the NIV paraphrases the sense of *paizein* as *to indulge in pagan revelry,* this hardly gets at the strong overtones of religious sexual orgy. "In view of the bull-cult there is probably an orgiastic undertone" (Cole 1973:214).

There is also the possibility that the whole structure of 10:1-22 may be recapitulated in the quotation from Exodus: *The people sat down to eat and drink*—that is, they ate the *spiritual food* and drank the *spiritual drink* (of the young bull idol)—*and rose up to play*—that is, to commit the four sins following (suggested by Meeks 1982:69). This would certainly strike to the heart of the issue of whether the Corinthian Christians should eat food *known* to be sacrificed to idols in any circumstance whether at pagan banquets in the temples or in pagan homes. To do such is to flirt with idolatry and its disastrous consequences in breaking the covenant relation with God.

In the second warning-model incident of a failed test, *sexual immorality* (v. 8) is referred to in the context of idolatrous worship of Baal Peor, narrated in Numbers 25, where the women of Moab had sexual relations with the men of Israel and invited them to the "sacrifices to their gods. The people ate [food sacrificed to idols] and bowed down before these gods. So Israel joined in worshiping the Baal of Peor. And the LORD's anger burned against them" (Num 25:2-3).

In one day twenty-three thousand . . . died. Paul's number is not the same as that given in Numbers 25:9, twenty-four thousand. While various attempts have been made to harmonize this discrepancy, such as that Paul's emphatic *in one day* leaves the possibility that another thousand were killed before the plague was over, no satisfactory solution has been agreed upon. Perhaps Paul was drawing on his memory of the account and simply missed the number slightly. In any case, the point he is making is in no way affected by the precise number. "The occurrence however should warn us against positing a view of the inspiration of Scripture which does not take account of such discrepancies as found here" (Bandstra 1971:18).

Consider also another apropos comment on this verse: "As we have noted, the competitiveness and status-seeking at Corinth suggests parallels with [the tendency of] early twentieth-first-century modern/postmodern cultures . . . to dispense with moral restraint and to tolerate everything except any transcontextual truth claim which might interfere with an individual's 'right' to instant gratification. All of this resonates

---

10:9 The reading *Christon* (Christ), now confirmed by the early witness of p[46], is al-

with a postmodern ethic that is founded only on 'where society is' at the beginning of the twenty-first century" (Thiselton 2000:739).

The third warning model involves putting the Lord to the test (v. 9). While the NIV reads *not test the Lord,* we should see the form of the verb used here *(ekpeirazō)* as stronger than merely "test." Something like "put . . . to the test" (NRSV) is preferable. Further, there is good textual support for reading "Christ" here in place of *the Lord.* The Corinthians were actually in the process of putting Christ to the test by their brazen eating of known idol food. If this is the correct reading, then we have another direct reference to Christ's being present to the Israelites in the desert, paralleling the earlier reference to Christ as the rock (v. 4).

The incident Paul draws on is recounted in Numbers 21:5: the people "spoke against God and against Moses, and said, 'Why have you brought us up out of Egypt to die in the desert? There is no bread! There is no water! And we detest this miserable food!'" There is impatience with God, no fear or trust in God's provision and goodness. Further, there are rebellion, envy and factions within God's people. In Psalm 106 the psalmist has given us an assessment similar to Paul's: "In the desert they gave in to their craving; in the wasteland they put God to the test. So he gave them what they asked for, but sent a wasting disease upon them" (Ps 106:14-15; see also Ps 95:8-11). Most of the references Paul cites are also found in this great psalm of lament. *And were killed by snakes* is perhaps better translated "they were destroyed by snakes." The verb and tense Paul uses *(apollymi,* destroy) is a dramatic imperfect and vividly portrays them as suffering ruin (see 1 Cor 10:10).

What does it mean to "put Christ to the test"? The Israelites *"presumed* to force God's hand to preserve them by putting his love and salvation to the utmost test. . . . Presumption is the premature self-willed anticipation of what we hope from God; despair is the premature arbitrary anticipation of non-fulfillment" (Thiselton 2000:741-42). The Corinthians presumed they were immune to the danger of idols when they knowingly ate food sacrificed to idols either in temples or in pagan homes. They thus put God to the test, assuming that he would preserve and protect

---

most unanimously accepted as the best reading over against *kyrion* (Thiselton 2000:740).

them in these situations. On the other hand, they despaired that God would meet their needs if they did not participate in eating idolatrous food and all the social occasions associated with this practice.

The Israelites' grumbling is the final warning model Paul parallels with the Corinthian situation: *and do not grumble [gongyzō], as some of them did* (v. 10). The exact incident he has in mind is not clear, since there were numerous times when the people of Israel murmured against God, Moses and Aaron (Ex 15:24; 16:2; 17:3; Num 11:1; 14:2; 16:11, 41; Deut 1:27; Ps 106:25). In light of these many cases, we should see Paul's reference more as a summary of numerous occasions. More important is the sense of the grumbling. This was not a mere impatience with life's circumstances but a deliberate challenge to God's authority and purposes for his people and to his appointed leaders, Moses and Aaron. Not content with their new freedom from slavery, the provision of manna, and God's guidance and protection in the cloud and fire, they exchanged their blessed redeemed condition for self-pity and ingratitude, seeing themselves as victims rather than victors. *Were killed by the destroying angel* (NIV) is not a very accurate rendering of the Greek *(apōlonto hypo tou olothreutou).* "They suffered ruin by the destroyer" (not identified; but see Ex 12:23 LXX; Heb 11:28) may be more accurate textually and theologically.

Paul now reaches a conclusion and issues a summary warning in verses 11-13. His conclusion parallels verse 6 in mentioning again the warning models *(typikos,* NIV *examples),* incidents in the lives of the Israelites that *were written down . . . for us* (v. 11). They were written so they would not be forgotten, and written especially *for us,* that is, "for our instruction" (NIV *warnings)* or "admonition." Again, the Old Testament's continuing authoritative spiritual instruction for Christians is evident in Paul's mind (see Rom 4:23-24; 15:4).

In whom the fulfillment of the ages has come (literally, "unto whom the ends [*telos,* "end," "goal"] of the ages [double plurals] has arrived") occurs only here and has been quite difficult for commentators to clearly identify. Certainly Paul has in mind some significant eschatological sense that he attaches to the people of God who now live in the days of the Christ event and the giving of the Holy Spirit. Perhaps the sense is similar to other New Testament writers' use of expressions like "in these last times" (1 Pet 1:20; 2 Pet 3:3; Jude 18), "this is the last hour" (1 Jn 2:18), "in the last days" (2 Tim 3:1) and "the end of all things is near" (1 Pet 4:7). Since the coming of Christ we have been living in the last days or the last hour. Some would connect the expression to Paul's "the fullness of time" (so NRSV paraphrases Gal 4:4), which would again emphasize that the consummation of all the ages—the redemptive promise of all previous ages—has arrived in the Christ event.

We stand in an unparalleled point in God's historical purposes, then, and in light of this must be warned by the previous models not to be overconfident in our freedom and knowledge in relation to the matter of idol food. For we—like the Israelites, who had great privileges under Moses—are capable of falling into sin and disobedience to Christ. *If you think you are standing firm, be careful that you don't fall!* (1 Cor 10:12). "Their confidence rests in their own theology rather than on a day-by-day re-appropriation of divine grace" (Thiselton 2000:747). Paul rebukes such an approach to life before God.

Temptation (v. 13, *peirasmos*, "testing," "trial," "temptation") is probably the best translation in this context, since the four previous cases involved wilderness situations that tempted the people to let go of trust and obedience to God and led to their failure and God's judgment on them. It was not the temptation itself but the craving for sinful things that led them into disobedience. Also, living an undisciplined life may unnecessarily put us into the way of temptation. The temptations the Corinthians faced to compromise loyalty to Christ by eating idol food (known to be such) is not so unusual; it is in fact *common to man* (*anthrōpinos*, "human").

This is not an encouragement but a mild rebuke to those who may have been justifying their eating of cultic food offered to idols in Corinthian social life by saying, "What else can we do? It's part of the game we must play to have social and political access to the goods of the culture. How can it hurt, since an idol is nothing and idol food is harmless?" (v. 19; 8:4).

Nevertheless, those who are tempted need to know that God will not allow them to be *tempted beyond what [they] can bear.* God, who knows all things including our inner strengths and weaknesses, will not allow any temptation we face to be too much for us to handle. Instead in his faithfulness *he will also provide a way out* (*ekbasis*, "issue," "end," "escape," "way through"). This may be deliverance out of the temptation or a way through it without yielding to it. But if the Corinthians (or we) "deliberately put themselves in the way of temptations to idolatry and its associated evils, they were ignoring the preferred 'way of escape' and need not be surprised if they 'fell'" (Bruce 1971:94).

The Incompatibility of the Table of the Lord with the Table of Demons (10:14-22) In this section Paul will argue directly against participation under any circumstances in the eating of *known* sacrificial idol food. Eating it is tantamount to violating the new covenant with Christ and the unity of the people of God, the reality behind believing communities' participation in the Eucharist. To do so is to become idolaters and incur God's judgment as the exodus generation of Israelites did.

Flee from idolatry (v. 14) parallels 6:18, "Flee from sexual immorality" (cf. also the parallel in 2 Cor 6:11—7:1). "Participation in 'Christ,' i.e., the messianic community, precludes participation in idolatry and unchastity" (Tomson 1990:70). This is a strong, direct, urgent appeal to the Corinthians to avoid this spiritually destructive practice. The figure "flee" is found in the New Testament only in Paul, in moral exhortations (cf. 1 Tim 6:11; 2 Tim 2:22).

Paul's teaching is clearly to the point for Christians in parts of the world where idols are still worshiped or leaders are divinized, such as in some Asian and South American areas. But does it apply, as has sometimes been argued, to Christians living in Hindu countries such as India, with reference to whether Christians should eat beef (or pork in Israel or in Muslim countries that may present a similar situation)? The argument goes like this: Since Paul argues that Christians living in Corinth should not use their freedom to eat all foods including idol food if it offends a weaker Christian or a pagan host, loving Christians will be sensitive to the food they eat that is offensive to another Christian who may be weak in conscience or to a pagan neighbor who cannot eat such food due to their religious convictions (such as Hindus who do not eat beef or Jews and Muslims who do not eat pork). In such cases Christians will limit their freedom out of love (Rom 14). Indeed, this is a problem in these cultural contexts, and the offensive issues should be handled sensitively and lovingly by Christians.

But contrary to much modern opinion, as I have argued, this is *not* the problem facing the Christians at Corinth in the matter of idol food. However, Paul's direct linkage elsewhere of idolatry to *greed* would make the command have equal force in materialistically oriented societies in the Western world in particular (Eph 5:5; Col 3:5; see also Mt 6:24). Additionally, the growing presence of Hindu religions in the Western world where actual food that has been offered to idols (gods) in the temples is then eaten at meals may present a more direct parallel to the Corinthian situation and call for Christians to refuse to eat any known sacrificial food whether in Hindu temples or in Hindu homes.

Sensible people (v. 15) may echo the prophets' appeals to the people of Israel to think about how foolish it is to worship something made by human hands that cannot speak or see or hear and must be carried about (Is 40:18-20; 44:9-20; Jer 10:1-15). Yet Paul wants the Corinthians to think with him about the incompatibility of eating food sacrificed to idols and eating the food of Christ's table. There are two different communities with different objects of worship.

God, the Father of the Lord Jesus Christ, and those who participate in him by eating the bread and drinking the wine of the New Covenant form one community. The other community is made up of all those who participate in various idols by eating and drinking the food associated with their altars. Biblical religion throughout history can never legitimately be syncretized with any other worship. The God of both Old and New Covenants is a holy, jealous God who cannot be worshiped alongside any other deity or object of worship. "Hear, O Israel: the LORD our God, the LORD is one" (Deut 6:4). "Do not make any gods to be alongside me" (Ex 20:23). "For us there is but one God" (1 Cor 8:6).

Paul's point in this section is not to give instruction concerning the Eucharist (Lord's Supper)—he will say something about that later (11:17)—but to argue that eating food sacrificed to idols involves one in the community of those who participate in sacrifices made to pagan gods and consequently in the worship of these deities (called *demons*, 10:20). Again, Deuteronomy 32 and Psalm 106 are in Paul's mind; he quotes Deuteronomy 32:17 directly in verse 20, and there seems to be a clear allusion in verse 22 to Deuteronomy 32:21.

The cup of thanksgiving (*eulogios,* "blessing," "consecration," "praise," v. 16) designates the cup of wine that was blessed before the sabbath meal in Jewish homes (Moore 1962:2:36). While the cup of the Lord's Supper is not so designated elsewhere in the New Testament, this reference shows the original connection with the Jewish Passover cup (the third or fourth cup) in the upper room. In the Passover ceremony it is *God* who is blessed (praised), not the cup (Lk 22:14-20). Paul's point is that this cup is a *participation* (*koinōnia,* "sharing," "communal participation") in *the blood of Christ.* Covenant overtones are not far away in such language (cf. Lk 22:20). "This cup . . . is the new covenant in my blood."

This communal participation is further stressed by the *bread that we break a participation in the body of Christ . . . one loaf . . . one body, for we all partake of the one loaf* (vv. 16-17). The main reality that binds Christians to Christ and, in him, to each other is the communal eating and drinking of *the Lord's table* (v. 21). Here *participation [koinōnia] in the body of Christ* is not participation in the church as the body of Christ (chap. 12) (although *one body* and *one loaf* (v. 17) do refer to the church community) but to participation in Christ's body in the same sense as the parallel "participation in the blood of Christ" (v. 16).

The language of *participation* in both cases seems to suggest the Lord's Table has a meaning stronger than mere symbolic "remembrance" (as Ulrich Zwingli taught). However, based on this passage it is not possible to argue persuasively for or against either the real presence of Christ (Luther) or the sign that points to Christ and also unites us with Christ in some mysterious way (Calvin; see Cunliff-Jones 1978:398). There is no indication from this passage that any grace is "given" or "communicated" by our participation (as Anglican theology teaches). *The bread that we break* (v. 16) is best understood to refer to both the broken body of Christ given for us (Lk 22:19-20) and the sharing of the one community in that redemptive event.

Consider the people of Israel (*kata sarx,* "according to the flesh," v. 18). Does Paul refer to current Jewish practices in the Jerusalem temple, where sacrifices were being made daily (cf. Heb 13:10), or to the

Israelites of old (10:1-6) who became involved in sacrifices at pagan altars? The expression occurs only here in the New Testament. Paul's use of the present tense might argue for the former, while the context of Deuteronomy 32 (quoted in v. 20) would argue for the latter.

However, the reference to Israel "according to the flesh" suggests an Israel "according to the Spirit" of true believers (Gal 6:16; Phil 3:3). This together with the context of 1 Corinthians 10:16-18, where Paul's point is to argue that eating the bread and drinking the cup of the Lord identifies us with Christ and the community that worships the one God through him, would argue for the present, nonbelieving Jewish community. This is true of the earthly Israel as a community that continues to eat and drink sacrifices in the temple and thus to share in the altar of worship.

That a sacrifice offered to an idol (*eidōlothyton,* "idol food") *is anything, or that an idol is anything* (v. 19): having argued that participating in the communal meal of the cup and bread of the Lord binds us not only to Christ but also to the one body of Christ's redeemed people (vv. 16-18), Paul now draws out the point he is trying to make more specifically. First, is he saying that idol food and the idol actually are spiritual or religious realities? Didn't he already agree with the "enlightened" on this matter (8:4-6)? Yes, the idol food and the idol are not real, but there is another side to the issue. Using the argument of Deuteronomy 32 and other parts of the Old Testament, Paul appeals to the "not real yet real" dialectic found in these texts: "They sacrificed to demons, which are not God—gods they had not known, gods recently appeared, gods your fathers did not fear. . . . They made me jealous by what is no god and angered me with their worthless idols" (Deut 32:17, 21). "For all the gods of the nations are idols, but the LORD made the heavens" (Ps 96:4; see Gal 4:8).

While the idol (and its sacrificial food) has no reality as a god or divine being, since there is only one true God, the Father of Jesus Christ (1 Cor 8:6), nevertheless idols (and their food) have power over their worshipers: *No, but the sacrifices of pagans are offered to demons, not to God* (v. 20). *Demons* were viewed in pagan circles as lesser deities or spirits that were either good or harmful in influence. Some connected them with departed ancestors. In Jewish thought they are evil powers opposed to God and destructive of human well-being. No connection is made with the departed dead. The New Testament usage follows that of the Old Testament and Jewish tradition (Foerster 1964:2:1). Paul believes in the reality of these entities, connected to the power of the idol. Because of the "consciousness" of the demon associated with the idol, it is not simply a harmless nonentity. Paul tells the Corinthians directly that he does *not want [them] to be participants with demons* by partaking of food known to have been offered to idol-demons; such sacrifices are not offered *to God* (v. 20). To further clarify his command, he opposes the *cup of the Lord* to the *cup of demons,* the *Lord's table* to the *table of demons* (v. 21).

These two participations are basically incompatible for Christians. They cannot do both either logically, empirically (something will be destroyed) or institutionally (and still be counted as Christian). They cannot simultaneously participate in Christ and his redemptive community of the Holy Spirit and God's love and "participate in the seductive, assertive, manipulative powers of evil which inspire idolatry by substituting themselves in place of God" (Thiselton 2000:776).

Furthermore, and most important, they will incur judgment from God. Are *we trying to arouse the Lord's jealousy? Are we stronger than he?* (v. 22). Forget about whether this is a warning directed to the "strong" at Corinth ("strong"/"weak" terms are not used in these chapters!): *we* includes the whole Christian community, which was in jeopardy over the eating of idol food and of stirring up the Lord's jealousy, which would lead him to destroy the disobedient among the congregation. Reflecting again on Deuteronomy 32, Paul sees the Lord's strength arising against all false gods and his own people who have provoked him to jealousy by leaving him and his covenant love in exchange for idols. Paradoxically, when Israel was "fat" or strong, they wandered from their Rock and sought worthless idols (*so, if you think you are standing firm*—10:12). "Thus in the teaching of 1 Corinthians, verse 22b of chapter 10 should be placed alongside 5:13b and 11:29-32, and recognized as a text which deals with the discipline of the church in the 'strongest' terms" (Rosner 1994:203).

Charles Wesley's hymn ties in wonderfully with Paul's sentiments at this point and our need for weakness before the Lord and his strength:

Oh! Give me, Lord, the tender heart
That trembles at the approach of sin;
A godly fear of sin impart,
Implant, and root it deep within,
That I may dread Thy gracious power,
And never dare offend Thee more.

It would be a mistake to limit the problem of idol food to the eating of sacrificed food *only* or primarily in the pagan temple precincts (8:10), as argued by some commentators (Fee 1980:178-79; 1987:359-60; Witherington 1993:254). The following section shows that idol food could also be a problem in marketplaces and in pagan homes where Christians were guests from time to time.

Marketplace Food and Pagan Dinner Invitations (10:23-30)

Two quite practical matters remain for Paul to address in his long treatise on idol food. What should Christians do when buying meat in the market? Should they ask the shop proprietor whether he knows which meat has been sacrificed in pagan temples and which has not? And then what about when they are invited into pagan homes for meals? Should they go? If they do, should they inquire before they eat whether the food has come from temple sacrifices? What if someone at the pagan home informs them voluntarily that the food has been offered to an idol? Should they eat it? Paul's instruction is quite surprising and in a place or two also quite challenging to understand.

Let me begin with an incident that was shared with me by an anthropologist colleague. He has given me permission to use this story. My friend was doing field research in the state of Yucatán, Mexico, on the "Day of the Dead" ritual, which roughly corresponds to the Christian All Saints' Day. He was invited into a Yucatec Maya home to observe and share in the October 31 ritual. In Yucatán the rituals are more than commemorations to honor the memory of dead ancestors. The people believe that the spirits of dead relatives actually return to the house and visit the family. The visitors must be fed, given drink and honored with ritual meals on October 31 (the day of dead children) and November 1 (the day of dead adults).

In a ceremony involving an altar-table where some sweets, fruit and food were put in bowls for the dead children, the family waited for the visit of the departed ancestors. Later the food was served in a meal. My colleague participated in the whole ritual and was permitted to take pictures. He also ate the offerings in the meal that followed. He reports that at the time he experienced no uneasiness. But was he right to eat the food that he knew was a part of offerings to the dead in the light of Paul's teaching in this chapter? We will return to this question shortly.

"Everything is permissible" (*exestin,* "permissible," "proper," "possible") is rightly (as in 6:12) set off in quotation marks as a Corinthian slogan to express the liberation/freedom side of the gospel as Paul preached it. The saying appears only here and in 6:12 in the canonical Bible, but the sentiment of Paul's response *(but not everything is beneficial)* is reflected in the apocryphal book of Ecclesiasticus: "Not all things are helpful for all, nor do all souls prefer all foods" (37:28, quoted in Tomson 1990:204). There it appears in a wisdom context as a saying advocating temperance in eating. Evidence exists that an attitude of no restraint was considered by some in Greco-Roman society as the mark of those who had social status, were free (not slaves), wise and powerful. In other words, it was an expression of the elite (Winter 2001:81-82).

At Corinth some were using the freedom slogan to justify the eating of known sacrificial food along with anything else they desired. Paul, on the other hand, limits the use of his freedom to things that benefit or build up the Christian community. This is the moral principle that we found Paul arguing for in 9:19-23. Our behavior is to be modeled on the Messiah's earthly ministry, that is, characterized by other-centeredness, not self-centeredness (Winter 1990:225). Eating known sacrificial food in any context is not acceptable; it would damage the community of Christ and lead individuals and the community into idolatry.

Instead, the moral norm for the Christian is that each believer should not seek his own good but *the good of others* (10:24). Paul had already advocated this principle in the previous discussions (8:13; 9:19-

---

10:25 *Meat market* (*makellon,* possibly a loanword from Latin *macellum,* only here in the New Testament) is referred to in two Latin inscriptions found at Corinth in 1898, but no structure has yet been found (Gill 1992:389-93). The discovery in one shop of whole sheep skeletons at the macellum at Pompeii strongly suggests that animals were slaughtered here and sold as well as sacrificed meat brought from nearby

23). In effect, he is telling us what love does. Love freely takes and furthers the interests (good) of the other and makes them one's own interests (Brümmer 1993:164). This is the proper use of Christian freedom: to build up the Christian community in love. But how does this relate to sacrificial food sold in open markets and to food served in pagan homes where Christians are guests?

Eat anything sold in the meat market without raising questions of conscience (10:25) seems, at first sight, contradictory to the ban on all idol food that I believe Paul is teaching. A greater or lesser portion (there is a debate) of the food sold in the local markets likely came from the pagan temple sacrifices a short distance southward down the Lychaeum road. The most popular modern solution (e.g., Fee and Witherington) is built on the assumption that Paul in 1 Corinthians 8—10 is forbidding the eating of sacrificial food only in the temple precincts, in connection with pagan worship sacrifices or when such eating tempts "weaker" brothers or sisters to eat idol food as truly sacrificial idol food.

On this reading Paul's wide-open permission to eat all that is sold in the meat market indicates that he had no problem with consuming idol food as long as it was not eaten in connection with pagan worship practices or celebrations. Yet this view cannot adequately answer why Paul would command the Corinthians not to inquire about the food's origin for the sake of *conscience* (*syneidēsis,* better translated here and in vv. 27-29 as "consciousness" or "self-awareness"). If all idol food was fair game for Christians as long as one was not eating as a participant in temple worship, why prohibit asking questions about the food?

Further, this view "underestimates the weight of the idolatry prohibition not only in ancient Judaism but also in Christianity" (Tomson 1990:206). Appealing to either the "weak" or the "strong" as the recipients of Paul's instruction here fails, since Paul does not use weak-versus-strong terminology anywhere in chapters 8-10. Tomson is correct in

---

temples. Fish, fruit and bread were also sold (Cadbury 1934:140-41). How much nonsacrificed meat was available? The question is irrelevant for Christians, for Paul says they may buy *everything* sold in the macellum as long as they do not know it is sacrificed food. This would mean that at least some of the food was not sacrificed (Winter 2001:293-95; Cheung 1999:154-55).

stating: "In the last unit of his section on idolatry [10:23-30] Paul gives practical instruction on what to do in doubtful cases, where food of uncertain nature is found in a pagan setting" (1990:208).

Paul allows freedom to eat all foods, provided they are not identified with sacrifices. There is no inherent demonization of the food itself even if it has been sacrificed to demons. All food is created by God and is fit to eat if it is received with thanksgiving: *For, "the earth is the Lord's, and everything in it"* (v. 26). Paul quotes Psalm 24:1, used in Jewish prayers to bless God for good things (cf. 1 Tim 4:3-4). If there is no known connection of the food with idolatry in the "consciousness" of the believer, then there is no problem with eating it. So don't ask! Obviously, if the Christian knows it came from the temple or a celebration, she will not eat it because of its idolatrous associations in her consciousness *(conscience),* and also because it may signal to another Christian or even a pagan that Christians eat idol food with impunity as well as eating the bread and cup of the Lord Jesus. "Augustine likewise relates an example of a hungry traveler who finds food in front of a statue or altar with nobody around. The fact, Augustine explains, that it is left where it is indicates that it is intended as an offering and therefore it is prohibited. But if there is no such indication, it is not prohibited" (Tomson 1990:209).

But what should a Christian do when invited to a pagan home for a meal (vv. 27-30)? Earlier I quoted two invitations surviving from Corinth. For example: "Herais asks you to dine in the room of the Serapheion (i.e., Asclepion) at a banquet of the Lord Seraphis tomorrow the 11th from the 9th hour" (quoted in Murphy-O'Connor 1983:101). What would or should a Christian do if they received such an invitation? Other invitations may have been to a home setting where no connection to idol food was evident. Paul's instruction is consistent with his previous meat market rule: *eat whatever is set before you without raising questions of conscience* ("consciousness," v. 27). As long as

_____

10:27-30 "A virtually exhaustive survey of early Christian writings turns up no evidence that any early Christian writer had any inkling of what would become the traditional understanding of Paul's approach [i.e., idol food was neutral and should only be avoided if it caused offense to the 'weak']. . . . Paul stands firmly together with other Jews and Christians in seeing the conscious consumption of idol food as

the nature of the food is unknown, there is no problem.

But if anyone says to you, "This has been offered in sacrifice," then do not eat it (v. 28). The word used here for *offered in sacrifice* is not Paul's word elsewhere in chapters 8-10 (nor of other New Testament writers) for idol food *(eidōlothyton)*. It is *hierothyton*, a word used frequently for "sacrificial offerings" in pagan literature. This and other factors suggest that the interlocutor is probably a pagan, perhaps the host, rather than another Christian who is present (Conzelmann 1975:178, contra Kim 2003). We cannot be sure.

But the reasons given for refraining from eating when the nature of the food is disclosed have raised interpretive problems: don't eat *both for the sake of the man who told you and for conscience'* (consciousness's) *sake* (v. 28). Cheung's analysis is helpful at this point:

> *syneidēsis* is one's consciousness and knowledge with regard to the nature of food with moral implications for the rightness or wrongness of the act of eating. In the pagan consciousness, the food is religiously significant and the moral implication is that it is wrong for the Christian to eat it. Lying behind the non-Christian informer's remark is the assumption that Christians have nothing to do with pagan gods and are not supposed to eat their sacrificed food. This may indicate that abstention from idol food had already become a fairly standard early Christian practice by the time Paul wrote 1 Corinthians. (1999:159)

The Second Helvetic Confession (1566), discussing things indifferent to faith versus things not indifferent, rightly comments: "Paul does show that it is lawful for a man to eat flesh if no man do admonish him that it was offered to idols (1 Cor x.27, 28); for then it is unlawful, because he that eats it does seem to approve idolatry by eating of it (1 Cor viii.10)" (chap. 27; quoted in Leith 1973:187).

But, it might be objected, doesn't Paul say that the "consciousness" of idol food is not that of the Christian but of the pagan who disclosed

---

a denial of their allegiance to their Lord" (Cheung 1999:298-99). Still agrees with Cheung on the broader definition of idol food but disagrees with him on whether Paul saw that the enlightened at Corinth had a right to eat the food, even in the temples. Nevertheless (in agreement with Cheung), according to Still Paul exhorted all Christians to abandon the practice of eating *known* idol food (2002:233-34).

the nature of the food: *the other man's conscience, I mean, not yours* (v. 29)? It will not do to say that the person who made this disclosure was a "weak" Christian unable to distinguish between God's good creation and sacrificial food. The discloser is (probably) a pagan who shows his intention regarding the religious significance of the food set before his guest. While the Christian was under no moral obligation to abstain from the food as long as it was of uncertain origin, as soon as the idolatrous intention or connection is revealed the Christian must refrain from eating. Otherwise the believer is participating in the religious significance of the food and thus supporting idolatry. "If the [Christian] Corinthians eat the food regardless, they will compromise their confession of the One God and abandon the basic Christian (and Jewish) critique of pagan gods. As Conzelmann put it, the unbeliever would not only be strengthened in his [idolatrous] conviction, but the Christian would objectify the power of the gods, and thereby '"preach" faith in them'" (Cheung 1999:159-160). Paul articulates his missionary attitude in 10:33: *For I am not seeking my own good but the good of many, so that they may be saved.*

For why should my freedom be judged by another's conscience? (v. 29). This question and the one in the following verse are considered by almost all commentators to be the *crux interpretum* (the difficult or unsolved problem) of the whole extended passage (chaps. 8-10). Is this Paul's view (so Tomson 1990:216-21) or a Corinthian objector to Paul's view who is arguing that one's freedom in grace is hindered if we stop eating because of another person's conscience (so Witherington 1995:228)? If, as it seems, this is Paul's view, to whom is it addressed and just what is its sense? And does this statement belong with the beginning of verse 29 or go back to verse 27, making verses 28-29 parenthetical? What does Paul mean by his *freedom?*

Many assume the reference is to Paul's own freedom to eat known idol food with impunity, providing he is not injuring another's weak conscience. However, as I have already argued, Paul does not eat food known to have been sacrificed to pagan gods under any circumstance, nor does he permit other Christians to do so. Therefore another sense of *my freedom* is required. It is his *freedom* to eat all foods of unknown origin without inquiring into their nature—and to refuse to eat when he learns of another person's intention or consciousness associating the food with idolatry.

Be judged by another's conscience ("consciousness," "intention"): it is not clear why the other person has acted to call attention to the sacrificial, religious nature of the food. Some believe the pagan neighbor wants out of kindness to protect the Christian from violating the known Christian practice of refusing to eat sacrificial food, even if they misunderstood the Christian position (Clarke and Winter 1991:134). It is, however, unlikely that a pagan would be concerned about the sensitivities to sacrificial food of an unrecognized religion. Again I must stress that the word *conscience (syneidēsis)* should not be understood in the moral sense (though there may be moral implications). It is better translated throughout as "consciousness": "consciousness, I say, not yours but the other person's" (v. 29).

It is the other person's consciousness of the idolatrous association of the food that causes Paul to change his behavior and not eat the food. He then explains that otherwise he has freedom by grace to eat food of uncertain origin that he receives with a prayer of thanksgiving (*with thankfulness,* v. 30; see also v. 26). However, he limits his freedom in this case, to avoid a pagan's unnecessary criticism that Paul eats sacrificed food that Christians are not supposed to eat.

Ambrosiaster (fourth century) captures the point well: "Paul is saying that an idolater can have it both ways. On the one hand, he can glory in his idols, and on the other hand he can attack the apostle for eating what has been sacrificed to them, even if the latter does so after giving thanks to God. Such a person has an excuse for remaining in his error and sets a bad example to the brethren" (in Bray 1999:101). Of course the pagan discloser does not understand the concept of freedom that Paul teaches and espouses. Unfortunately many modern Christians likewise misunderstand. Again Paul shows sensitivity to his pagan host and guests and at the same time avoids offense and criticism by refraining from eating sacrificed food.

Now to return to the case of my anthropologist colleague. How should we judge the situation in the light of Paul's teaching in chapter 10? The Yucatec Maya custom of feeding dead spirits seems to be a clear case of participating in pagan idolatrous rituals, which Paul would have condemned regardless of the research motives.

In fact the professor himself came to this conclusion after having an unusually vivid experience the same night he had participated in the ceremonies and meal. He recalls that about 3:00 a.m. he had a dream of being in a chapel of a Latin American church. "As I walked down the center aisle I saw Franciscans praying to the Lord. Turning to go through the narthex to the main sanctuary I encountered difficulty due to dancing figures in white. When I reached the main church a great sense of evil descended upon me." Turning to leave, he again had trouble getting through the crowd of white-robed dancers and heard a woman singing, "Come thou Almighty King. Help us Thy name to sing. Help us to pray . . ." The sense of evil began to lift, but it descended again when she stopped singing. "I cried out, 'Don't let her stop!' Then I realized my dilemma and cried out, 'Jesus, help me!'" He woke up and began shuddering and crying. His wife took him in her arms and said three times, "Jesus is in control." He asked forgiveness for what he had witnessed and taken part in, and then experienced the "power of the Holy Spirit rushing over me, giving me confidence and peace."

My colleague had planned on taking his two teenage daughters the next day to ceremonies honoring dead adults. He interpreted his dream as a warning that he should not go or take the girls. "Needless to say, 'the Spirit forbade me to go' and I did not go." My friend's final reflection on the incident from his journal is worth quoting: "I had never had an experience anything like that before and it gives my understanding of the ethics of research for the Christian a whole new (and seemingly irrational) twist: investigating the spirit world—even by naiveté or innocence—may be dangerous (even forbidden) for the Christian social scientist, although not expressly forbidden by the Scripture. The words of 2 Corinthians 6:16—7:1 have new meaning for me. . . . 'Therefore come out from among them and be separate, says the Lord . . . touch no unclean thing. . . . Let us purify ourselves from everything that contaminates body and spirit, perfecting holiness out of reverence for God.'" This is Paul's teaching lived out today.

Conclusion and Paul's Formative Model (10:31—11:1) Commentators generally agree that this concluding section refers back to the whole of chapters 8-10 on the question of Christian behavior and idol food. The three major themes of these chapters appear: avoiding offense of any major religious-cultural group *(Jews, Greeks, church of God)* for the sake of the gospel's effectiveness (chap. 8), seeking the good of others, not one's own, after the cruciform pattern of Jesus (chap. 9) and bringing glory to God by avoiding idolatry and by exalting Christ (chap. 10).

Do it all for the glory of God (v. 31) is often taken as a general principle governing the Christian's conduct, and this may well be Paul's intent. However, more specifically it may be related to how believers handle the issue of idol food discussed in these chapters: to avoid sinning in eating or drinking that which is known to be offered to idols. "Just as glorifying God in one's body means abstaining from *porneia* ['fornication,' 6:20], eating and drinking to God's glory means avoiding *eidōlothyta* ['idol food']" (Cheung 1999:162). Paul himself does this, and he links his style of living to that of Christ (11:1). He wants the Corinthians to imitate him and in turn Christ, not in every aspect of their lives but in the aspect of his saving work expounded in Philippians 2:6-11—in his humility, self-denial, self-giving, in love taking up the interests of others and making them his interests in order that life might be brought to them.

☐ The Dispute over Head Attire for Men and Women in Worship (11:2-16)

Here we enter into a section of Paul's letter that touches on controversy about gender differences and male-female role relations. Along with 1 Corinthians 14:33-36, Ephesians 5:21-33 and 1 Timothy 2:11-15, this passage has generated a mountain of contemporary literature addressing in detail almost every possible nuance of these verses. Admittedly it is a difficult section. But why all this attention to 11:2-16 at this moment in history? Among other reasons, it is no doubt due to the renewed women's movement arising in the 1960s. We are perhaps in the third wave of a continuing effort on the part of women (and many men) to effect a practical equality with men in the society and the church.

What many see as a largely positive development is viewed by others as cause for concern and even alarm. To trace and evaluate the larger movement for women's equality in our day is well beyond the constraints of a modest commentary such as this. What is of immediate interest here, however, is the way that commentaries in the last century have modified their views on 1 Corinthians 11:2-16 at key points affecting the ministry of women in the churches.

For example, in Calvin's sixteenth-century commentary on 1 Corinthians 11:2-16, when there was no women's equality movement, he could argue for the inferiority of women *by nature* to men and conclude that women's subordination logically followed. Furthermore, "praying and prophesying" were identified as public leadership roles that *men* exercised in the church. Today it would be difficult to find even a conservative commentator who would hold to either of these two views of Calvin. But it was not until around 1908 that any commentator took issue with Calvin! About this time Marcus Dods wrote a commentary making reference to a "Corinthian women's liberation movement," and G. G. Findlay produced another which made apparently the first recognition that *women* were also "praying and prophesying" publicly. Archibald Robertson and Alfred Plummer (1929) follow Calvin in both of these points but concede that in "rare circumstances" women might pray or prophesy in public meetings of the church. The changes reflected the first and second waves of the women's movement in society. As women began to be more involved in public life, including speaking publicly, biblical interpreters apparently began to loosen some of the restrictions on women in the churches. They also departed from Calvin's view that only leaders could pray and prophesy in church (since women were also now seen as praying and prophesying publicly in Corinth). Now women could generally pray and speak publicly if they were regulated by male leaders.

Interestingly, the churches for the most part ended up adopting the previous era's gender-related social changes, but only after resistance and strong reactions to the new roles women were seeking. For example, in most churches women no longer wear hats to church or refrain from cutting their hair or are prohibited from offering public prayers (Mercadante 1979:22-23).

Reactions from some conservative male church leaders to the women's movement in contemporary society continue, as do the role divisions between males and females that Calvin accepted—except that women's nature is no longer seen as inferior; in that sense they are now "equal" to men. A "spiritual" equality between the sexes is now recognized in conservative Christian churches, but not a practical equality of function, since gender role distinctions give the male or husband authoritative leadership rights and responsibilities that are not given to the woman, who is to be subordinate.

On the other hand, since the 1960s there has arisen a group of conservative evangelical scholars and commentators who have challenged the traditional male-authority viewpoint with its restrictive subordinate roles for women in the church. Each of these two groups has given themselves a name to enhance their position vis-à-vis the other's position. Both have also given the other viewpoint names that are sometimes pejorative. Zealous advocates of both positions have at times used overstatement, exaggeration, unsupported generalizations, and guilt by association and displayed a lack of Christian humility and kindness toward those who differ. While I do not believe we can be completely objective when exegeting these passages—the interpreter's overall theological commitments clearly influence the handling of the details of the text—we can attempt to be fair with the evidence, whether it fits our overall view or not, and fair to state the views of others in a manner they would accept. Such will be my attempt in what follows.

Personally, my overall theological commitments in this area have been influenced by several factors. My strong evangelical roots have given me a deep theological commitment to the absolute authority and integrity of Scripture as the revealed Word of God. My early theological training was in a context where women were guests and observers, not full participants; these theological classes were male dominated, male taught, and aimed at male ministries of preaching and teaching. Women could not even audit a class. The current wave of the women's movement was just beginning to appear. Following seminary education, my family arrived in the Chicago area and visited a conservative Bible church, where much to my surprise a popular woman teacher taught the main adult Sunday School class. I told my wife that we would not attend this church because they allowed a woman to teach Scripture in a mixed male and female class, which violated the Bible's teaching. So we joined another church where all the adult classes were taught by males.

At this time new policies in the public schools began to give more equal emphasis in athletics to girls and boys. My four daughters began asking me why women were not full participants in Sunday worship services. Why were only men speaking, praying, reading Scripture, serving Communion, leading and even ushering? Why not women? My response was something like this: "Well, this is the way God wanted it. It was his creation plan that men lead the worship, and women do other things like serve meals, prepare Communion cups, meet with other women for prayer and Bible study, teach children, make quilts for missionaries and the like. There are plenty of things for women to do in the church other than teach men or pray and preach publicly or serve Communion." They had trouble accepting this, and frankly my own reasons were rather sketchy, dogmatic and increasingly unpersuasive to myself or to my wife.

In the early 1970s my academic associations brought me into contact with other conservative theologians whom I deeply respected— such as Berkeley and Alvera Mickelsen, Nancy Hardesty, Gordon Fee, Gilbert Bilezikian, Patricia and Stan Gundry, Roberta Hestenes, Gretchen Gaebelein Hull, Walt Kaiser, Ken Kantzer—who had come to a different reading of these same texts and had found them not to teach the severely restrictive view of women's roles I had always identified with biblical teaching. I began to change my mind and position. I found that without any Scripture twisting I could now without reservation support and advocate the full participation of women in all aspects of the gospel ministry, including the highest leadership positions in the church. Needless to say, my earlier experience of rejecting a woman's teaching of an adult Bible class now seems quite unbelievable.

This brief preamble is necessary to alert the reader that as much as one tries to be fair with the evidence of the text, one's prior theological formulations will affect judgments, especially in textual areas that are hotly contested, such as 1 Corinthians 11:2-16, where broader theological conclusions and vested interests will weight the judgment of the commentator one way or another.

Whatever else may characterize this text, its multiple exegetical problems seem unparalleled. One careful analyst has identified no fewer than twenty-two crucial debatable issues related to the meaning of the passage, including the meaning of "head" (v. 3), whether the entire passage is talking about men and women in general or wives and husbands, whether verses 4 and following refer to a veil or to long hair, and if a veil, what kind of veil is it, whether the veil reflects the Jewish, Greek or Roman cultural pattern, the meaning of *exousia* (authority) in verse 10, why Paul mentions "the angels" (v. 10), and the nature of the overall problem in Corinth that Paul addresses in the passage (Hull 1987:251-57). Each of these and others will be discussed as we look at the passage.

The Context and Problem Paul Addresses in 11:2-16 In the previous chapters (8-10) Paul has addressed the concerns related to the eating of idol food and idolatry. He emphasized the responsible use of Christian freedom governed by the principles of self-effacing, loving concern for the good of Christian brothers and sisters; deliberate self-discipline; and concern for nonoffense to protect the church's mission to the non-Christian culture. All three of these themes can be understood as carrying over into this section. Additionally, it has been pointed out that in 11:2—14:40 Paul deals with three actual cases of factionalism in the congregation: proper and improper decorum for men and women in worship (11:2-16), abuse of the Lord's Supper (11:17-34) and irregularities in the use of spiritual gifts (chaps. 12-14; Mitchell 1991:261). In any event, the two incidents noted in chapter 11 are introduced by "I praise you" (11:2) and "I have no praise for you" (11:17).

But what is the chief problem Paul addresses in 11:2-16? After a thorough examination of discussions of the passage in ancient as well as modern literature, my honest conclusion is that not only is there no consensus on Paul's main point but there is no consensus on a number of the details. Yet having said this, I have a slight preference for the recent analysis of the passage offered by Judith Gundry-Volf (1997a, b, c; 1999). She makes a careful exegetical case that Paul's chief concern was to correct a practice in Corinthian worship that incurred serious social shame not only on certain male and female individuals but on the church as a whole. This shame-producing activity involved boundary-transgressing hairstyles that blurred gender distinctions between males and females during worship.

Both men and women were involved in this practice, which Paul saw as harmful not only to the individuals and their respective "heads" but also to the missionary witness to nonbelievers who might enter the church. Paul wants a nonoffensive worship practice with respect to hairstyles that socially symbolize both respect and clear gender identity. In order to support his position, Paul first turns to the creation accounts in Genesis 1 and 2 and argues for both a gender differentiation and a gender hierarchy in terms of honor or preeminence. Thus for Gundry-Volf, Paul supports identical roles for men and women in worship while maintaining gender identities with some patriarchal distinctions (i.e., hairstyle or head covering).

But Paul also gives us a second reading of creation in 1 Corinthians 11:11-12, based on redemption in Christ or the eschatological new creation. There is now through creation an interdependence of male and female "in the Lord," based not on distinct (and unequal) gender roles (as some interpreters have claimed) but on the interdependence of those who are different sexually but equal in Christ. Both men and women are by creation the source of the other's existence. "They are thus interdependent as equals from the perspective of creation" (Gundry-Volf 1999:283).

How did Paul come to this reading of creation? It occurred because of his worship of God through the gifts of the Spirit. As the community functions as a body in the Holy Spirit (male and female), gender distinctions are maintained but are relativized socially (and not merely spiritually), resulting in an egalitarian community patterned according to the redeemed creation, or new creation relationships, rather than according to fallen cultural norms. Paul's ethical approach is to make the new creation in Christ present as a liberating and transforming agency within the old creation order (enculturation). On the one hand Paul supports aspects of the gender hierarchy and the shame-honor pattern, including woman's inferiority, as assumed in Mediterranean cultures of the first century. This is to read the creation story through Paul's patriarchal culture. But in contrast to this reading, he gives also a fully egalitarian, redemptive reading of creation where male and female are mutually and equally dependent on one another.

Thus there is a clear tension between 11:2-10 and 11:11-16. But why would Paul do this? Gundry-Volf's answer is, because of the church's mission to the world. By allowing women to pray and prophesy publicly with covered heads, and males to alternate with them in praying and prophesying with uncovered heads, not only does the church respect the outward patriarchal social pattern of sexual distinction in its worship, but alternating male and female submission and leadership are fostered within the congregation. Thus their public worship maintained social respectability but also allowed for the expression of a new social equality "in the Lord" (1997a:169).

Paul's method, then, of addressing the issue at Corinth involves three mutually interactive points of reference: (1) culture, (2) eschatological life in Christ and the Spirit, and (3) creation. While not a perfect explanation of all the details, this insightful study advances the stalemated discussion beyond mere traditional hierarchical (role complementarian) and mere egalitarian (nonhierarchical complementarian) readings of the passage. It is a viewpoint adopted in the exhaustive commentary on 1 Corinthians by Anthony Thiselton (2000). Points at which I may differ with Gundry-Volf will be noted in the discussion of the passage that follows.

Overview of 11:2-16 After praising the Corinthians for following the traditions he had given them, Paul notes three pairs of persons and identifies the "head" person in each pair: Christ-everyman; man/husband-woman/wife; God-Christ (vv. 2-3). Then, using the ancient shame-honor motif, he states that a man (or husband) who prays or prophesies in worship with something on his head puts to shame his head, that is, Christ (v. 4). On the other hand, a woman who prays or prophesies without something on her head puts to shame her head, that is, the man (or husband; v. 5). The effect would be the same as if the woman had shaved her hair or clipped it short (v. 6). Appealing to the creation accounts, Paul again decries the man or husband's covering his head, for he is the image and glory of God, while the woman or wife is the glory of the man or husband (v. 7). The woman (wife) derives her existence from the man (husband) and was created for the man (husband), not the other way around (v. 9).

So far the argument is directed toward maintaining outward or public distinctions between males and females who pray and prophesy by wearing of appropriate symbolic sexual-identity markers (whether cover or coiffure). Christian men who are covered (or who coiffure their hair) bring dishonor on themselves and consequently on Christ, their "head," while a Christian woman who does not coiffure her hair (or cover it) brings shame on herself and consequently on her husband, her "head," whose honor is effaced.

The correct social honoring and avoidance of shame behavior between males and females is supported by Paul from a particular reading of the Genesis accounts of the chronological order and purpose of man's and woman's creation. This reading of the accounts, along with Paul's use of "head," assumes a gender hierarchy of sorts that serves his purpose of correcting socially shameful failures to give proper social honor to one's corresponding "head," whether male or female. In keeping with first-century patriarchal cultural norms, the proper hair display would signal visibly and clearly not only the distinction between male and female in worship but also the role relationship of honor and shame socially expected in the culture of the day.

What about the transitional verse 10, with its references to "authority" and to "angels"? Admittedly, it is on all accounts a *crux interpretum*. I think that despite the difficulties with the reference to the angels, Paul intends to clearly indicate that women who appropriately and respectfully use the customary hairstyle have authority to pray and prophesy as leaders alternately with males in the congregation's worship.

But the previous argument based on the preeminence of Christ with respect to the man, and of the man/husband with respect to the woman/wife, rooted in the shame-honor cultural context and a certain patriarchal reading of the creation narratives (vv. 3-9), is not the whole story. Paul can also argue with equal force that as seen through redemption ("in the Lord"), creation gives priority not only to the man but also to the woman, through whom every man has come into the world and to whom every man owes his existence, and thus both find their existence in God (vv. 11-12).

There is then a tension between what he has just taught and what he now is asserting. At least this is a statement of a *qualified* patriarchalism, at best it is an *egalitarian* perspective that nevertheless maintains distinctions between male and female. This is the eschatological viewpoint Paul brings to bear on practical, moral and social (not merely spiritual) relations in the congregation at Corinth. In verses 11-16 he breaks with the patriarchal subordination of females to male authority. Women have freedom to *lead* in worship and to prophesy apart from male supervision. Yet they must do so without abandoning the sexual identity markers that are customary in their culture.

Since customary feminine hairstyles might be misinterpreted by the Corinthians as indicating female inferiority (as they were in the culture at large), Paul argues in this section from his redemptive reading of the creation texts that the primacy of males, since Adam, is relativized by the primacy of a woman in every male's birth, "man is born of [*ek,* from] woman" (vv. 11-12).

Yet Paul wants to retain the clear sexual identity of males and females as they lead the worship service. Why? We cannot be sure, but there seems to be a twofold reason. Because of his Jewish background, as well as the views of other cultures around him, Paul thinks in patriarchal terms, yet it is a modified patriarchy because of his understanding of what it means for women as well as for men to be "in Christ" and equal members of the body of Christ (1 Cor 12).

Women are joint heirs of the salvation in Christ, baptized (circumcision was only for males in the Old Covenant), joint participants in the Lord's Table, jointly gifted by the Holy Spirit, jointly involved with males in leading and prophesying, and all of the above without male supervision over them. Yet in the Corinthian situation women must still observe social honor-shame requirements with respect to husbands and other males, just as men must not dishonor their head, Christ, with hairstyles that blur their male identity.

Additionally, we should note well that Paul is *not* concerned about whether uncovered women will be a sexual temptation for males, or to press for the subordination of women to males, or that female uncovering will obscure God's glory in the male. Instead his concern throughout these chapters is in the church's gospel mission. He wants the Corinthian Christians to maintain social respectability with the outside culture in gender-related shame-honor practices. Why? Because Paul does not want morally indifferent cultural practices to hinder the gospel mission by causing unnecessary offense (cf. 9:19-23; 10:33; 14:23), especially within an ingrained patriarchal culture. At the same time, he wants to promote and encourage the mutual submission and mutual leadership of females and males.

Paul's final two arguments for the Corinthians not to abandon conventional male and female hairstyles in the church are given in 11:13-16. The first (vv. 13-15) is a sociocultural argument based on the Corinthians' judgment whether it is appropriate for women to pray to God (in church gatherings) without the proper cultural hairstyle. He answers his own question by referring to the natural-cultural observation that men's hair is relatively shorter than women's and that long hair on a man creates shame while long hair on a woman is her honor. Her hair, when modestly coiffured, provides the culturally necessary female identity marker instead of a veil (which has numerous cultural meanings and is sometimes worn or not in local settings).

Is there a corresponding marker of female or male identity today in the Western world? Is there an expected honor deference to men in our culture? Or are we moving more and more to mutual respect and honor, with sexual difference relativized in terms of honor and shame categories?

Finally, Paul appeals to the practice of the other churches. They all follow the practice of women praying and prophesying along with males and of women having their longer hair coiffured on top of their heads and men having shorter hair without any coiffure adornment (v. 16).

The Shame-Honor Culture I have already alluded to the shame-honor motif in first-century Mediterranean cultures and its importance for this chapter. A few further remarks may be helpful. Unlike modern Western cultures, especially in North America (and more like Asian cultures such as China and Japan), the ancient Mediterranean world had in place an elaborate honor-shame code governing the public and private behavior of men and women.

In Jewish settings women, especially wives, were generally secluded at home and kept separate from males except to shop at the markets, where they were not to speak to any man (Ilan 1995:129). Similarly, women in ancient Greek tradition were to be secluded at home and to practice the virtues of chastity, silence and obedience, in subordination to their husbands (Torjesen 1993:122). In Roman societies the practice was less strict. Males, on the other hand, were to excel in the public sphere and develop the virtues of courage, justice and self-mastery, the latter being evidenced by becoming a noble warrior and an active participant in the Greek city.

A woman's honor, in distinction to the male's, was her *shame,* in the sense that her honor was her good reputation and chastity, which required her to have a sensitive consciousness of her sexual vulnerability. She was to excel in the practice of sexual modesty, being discreet, shy, restrained, timid and subordinate to male authority. While boys were socialized to be sexually aggressive, girls were to be passive and "feminine," their sexuality surrounded with a sense of shame. A woman's avoidance of all appearance of sexual indiscretion was her honor and also the honor of her husband (Torjesen 1993:138).

Males competed for honor with other males. When women entered the public arena (e.g., teaching) they were seen as competing as males for male honor (using the male virtues cited above). Therefore most attacks on women leaders or teachers in the early church were to impugn their private, "feminine" virtues of chastity, silence and obedience (Torjesen 1993:145-46).

Gender identity differences in social roles were coded to hairstyles. By reversing hairstyles, the Corinthians were changing the social boundaries between the sexes and acting against nature (that is, culture). This brought "shame" on individuals and their corresponding "head." The problem Paul is addressing is the incurring of social shame through boundary-transgressing hairstyles (Gundry-Volf 1997a:154). Such social shame in the church would damage the missionary outreach to outsiders, who would be offended by the Christian women's lack of proper social respect (honor, glory) for their husbands or other men and the husbands' disrespect for their wives or other women when they adopted women's hairstyles (e.g., letting their hair grow long, v. 14).

The Metaphorical Meaning of "Head" (kephalē) Another discussion—often hotly debated—is the correct sense and translation of the Greek word *kephalē* when it is used as a metaphor. A brief summary of the discussion to date (2003) is in order. I will here draw from and add to an excellent summary by one of the leading commentators on 1 Corinthians (Thiselton 2000:812-22). Three viewpoints have emerged: *kephalē* means (1) "authority over" (Fitzmyer 1989, 1993; Grudem 1985; 1990; 2001), (2) "source, origin, temporal priority" (Bedale 1954; Bruce 1971; Murphy-O'Connor 1979; Bilezikian 1985; Fee 1987; Schrage 1995), and (3) "preeminent, foremost, representative," the part representing the whole (Cervin 1989; Perriman 1994; Thiselton 2000).

While the debate continues, several points can be made safely. First, the evidence the proponents of each view cite for its support is shrinking, though it is difficult for each position to concede this. Second, some in each view now acknowledge that the word may in fact have a usage or two that fits better in another viewpoint. In fact, today it would be difficult to maintain that any one of these views fits the evidence to the exclusion of others. It should be evident now that to base one's position on which meaning of the three is allegedly more "frequent" or "well attested" is to skate on thin ice. Actually, some are beginning to argue that the paucity of clear metaphorical usage for the word in nonbiblical sources may throw us back on its actual New Testament uses as the best evidence for its meaning.

In this connection it *may* be possible to argue (1) that in its metaphorical uses the sense may be different in different contexts and (2) Paul could be himself creating a *new* live metaphorical sense for the word in certain contexts (Dawes 1998:127, 133). Therefore, in the following comments on 11:3-16 I will attempt to let the text itself determine as much as possible in what sense *kephalē* is being used metaphorically.

Hairstyle or Head Covering? The earliest English translations read "having something on the head" for males (v. 4, Tyndale 1525; Geneva 1565; KJV 1611) and "bareheaded" for women (v. 5). This continued until the Revised Version (1881) rendered these expressions as "head covered" (v. 4) and "head unveiled" (v. 5). This translation wording has continued in the RSV (1946) and NRSV (1989) and a few other versions. The NIV uses simply "covered" or "uncovered" throughout the passage.

Where is current research pointing in this matter of what Paul is referring to in the language of covering and uncovering? We may distinguish two basic views. There are, on the one hand, a number of commentators who hold that Paul's language (*kata kephalē*, v. 4; *akataka lyptos*, vv. 5, 13; *katakalyptomai*, vv. 6-7) refers to some type of external *clothing* worn on the head. Whether this is a veil, snood, cloak or shawl will vary between commentators. The reasons given for adopting this view are partly from literary evidence and partly from Greco-Roman statues, reliefs and other archaeological artifacts (Belleville:2003). Gordon Fee also argues that if Paul is not referring to some type of covering, what would it mean for the men to be "covered" or "uncovered" (vv. 4, 7; 1987:496)?

On the other hand a quite convincing case can also be made that Paul, rather than referring to some external cloth covering on the head, is actually referring to the way the hair was worn or coiffured, differentiating in this manner males from females in worship leadership. The case for this view relies heavily on an abundance of archaeological evidence from the Mediterranean world of Paul's day. It is argued that the words Paul uses do not actually mention any cloth covering or veil (whether covering the face or over the head). Instead this sense is read into the texts.

The abundant archaeological evidence shows totally nonuniform practices of veiling and not veiling. Men could be veiled in worship, and the practice varies geographically and according to time period as well as social class of the person involved, whether Jewish or pagan, Greek or Roman cultural context, and whether in religious worship or public places. This leads one student of the "veiling" evidence to conclude, "We therefore have a variety of evidence for women wearing head coverings in antiquity, but so far little that sheds light on the nature of the conflict about head coverings in the Corinthian church" (Keener 1992:28).

In the light of this wide evidence of divergent head-covering practices, it is argued that what Paul was actually talking about was the short and noncoiffured hair of men and the long but coiffured hair of women, pinned up on the top of their heads. This practice not only was nearly universal in the Roman culture as far back as the second-third century B.C. but was the *normative* way males and females were distinguished when they were in public or in worship (Blattenberger 1997:53, 61). Furthermore, this view has the benefit of providing a natural explanation and direct connection to Paul's later statements about men having by nature short hair and women long hair, the latter being given to her as (or instead of) an external covering (11:14-15).

While the matter is not totally certain, and while it is not impossible that Paul was trying to establish a different Christian practice of veiling in the churches from that existing in the Roman world (Morris 1958:152; Ryrie 1958:73-74; Witherington 1995:235-36), the ample literary and sculptural evidence now available renders these views more difficult to maintain. On the other hand, the view that Paul is advocating that the churches maintain the clear cultural markers that distinguish male and female, as in the general Roman society—the different lengths and styles of hair—is in my judgment the better position (so Blattenberger 1997; Padgett 1984; Hurley 1981; Horsley 1998).

Paul's Commendation and the Three "Headships" (11:2-3) *I praise you* (v. 2) is to be contrasted with "I have no praise for you" (v. 17) and probably refers to the authoritative apostolic traditions or *teachings* that Paul gave to the churches concerning the "eschatological inclusion of men and women as active participants in prayer and prophetic speech in contrast to the issue of clothing [or hairstyle], which Paul believes must still generate signals of gender distinctiveness on the basis of the order of creation, which still holds sway even in the gospel era" (Thiselton 2000:811).

With the words *the head of every man is Christ* (v. 3) Paul begins his teaching to correct the problematic blurring of sexual identity in worship and the social respect (honor) due to the corresponding *head* (*kephalē*) of each of the three pairs of persons (Christ, man, God). While there is no implication in the verse that Christ ever dishonored or shamed his *head* (God), the men have in Paul's view shamed their

---

11:3 *The head of the woman is man.* There is a good possibility that Paul is using "head" language in this section as a live metaphor that he himself has coined. If true, then no lexical study can reveal his sense; only the context can decide the meaning.

head (Christ) as the women also have dishonored their *head* (the man-husband). While there is still some uncertainty, it seems best here and in the rest of the passage to understand *every man* to refer to every redeemed man in Christ, including husbands, and *the woman* to refer to every redeemed woman in Christ, including wives.

When allowing the context to determine the metaphorical sense of *head* in this verse, the "authority over" sense seems less likely, since there is no reference to submission *(hypotassō)* in the passage and no strict hierarchy of order is proposed, such as beginning with God, then Christ, then man, then woman. Rather there is an honor order of pairs: man honors Christ, woman honors man, and Christ honors God. The *head* then in each case is the honored member, the archetype of the other, or we could say the "honored source" of the pair in each case. This would point in the direction of combining views two and three, listed above, regarding the meaning of *head* in this context. If there are any patriarchal overtones in Paul's honored person pairs, it is muted and does not figure significantly in the passage in any specific way.

Cyril of Alexandria's (d. 444) comments on the passage are interesting: "Thus we say that the *kephalē* of every man is Christ, because he was *excellently made through him.* And the *kephalē* of woman is man, because she was taken *from his flesh.* Likewise, the *kephalē* of Christ is God, because He is *from Him according to nature*" (*Ad Arcadiam* 1.1.5.5(2).63).

Similarly, Cyril in another context explicitly says, "Head means beginning *(archē),*" and as in the preceding quote he links "head" to what seems to be the sense of "archetypal nature" or "source having the same nature." Thus he can argue that just as every redeemed man has the incarnate humanity of Christ as its pattern, substance and source of being (not Adam), so the woman has the redeemed man as her pattern, substance and source of being. Therefore, and this is Cyril's real point in context, Christ has God the Father himself as his pattern, substance and source of being as the incarnate Word of God (see *Ad Pul-*

Furthermore, the same word can have a plurality of live metaphorical meanings, each depending on its own context (Dawes 1998:65-78, 122-49).

cheriam 2.3.268).

While one may read into 11:3 the idea of "authority over" in the use of head, there is nothing explicit in the whole passage that suggests or requires this (contra Wire 1990:121). Yet historically and in the present, numerous commentators have read "authority over" ideas into not only verse 3 but the whole passage (11:3-16). However, the idea (as in Cyril) of "pattern, substance and source of being" admirably fits the context and especially the later language, "for man did not come from woman, but woman from man" (vv. 8, 12). Thus the headship of the man in this passage is a preeminence as honored source of the woman and not one of "authority over" and "submission." These ideas are not present in the context and would add nothing to the understanding of the problem at Corinth (Gundry-Volf 1997a:158-59).

The Problem of Hair at Corinth (11:4-10) The problem of displaying dishonoring or disrespectful hairstyles (or less likely, coverings) involved both men and women at Corinth. Paul begins with the man who *prays or prophesies* (better: "utters prophetic speech"). This should be understood as the offering of public prayers and prophetic speech of a serious, sustained and instructive nature and may include "*applied theological teaching, encouragement, and exhortation to build the church,* not merely (if at all) *ad hoc* cries . . . delivered as 'spontaneous' mini-messages" (Thiselton 2000:826; see 12:10, 28-29; 14:1-5; 24-39).

With his head covered (kata kephalēs echōn, literally "having down head") is a unique expression found only here in Scripture. Elsewhere in Greek literature the expression is, unlike here, combined with a reference to the object or cloth that is upon the head (e.g., toga or cloak pulled up over the head or to a person being hit over the head with a walking stick). Is the reason Paul does not specify any object on the head (here or elsewhere in the passage) that he is talking about the man's long hair arranged on his head (v. 14, contra Witherington

---

11:4 Attempts have been made by David Gill (1990:245-60) and Bruce Winter (2001:121-33) to link Paul's criticisms to certain contentious males who wore Roman toga coverings to express their social status and to some contentious wives who abandoned their marriage veils in the presence of their husbands (now reflected in the ESV rendering, "every wife who is uncovered"). While these attempts to place

1995:233)?

Dishonors ("disrespects," "shames") *his head* refers to the religious implications in a shame-honor culture of a man's leading the congregation in worship with the symbolic hair signs belonging to women in the culture. By doing this the man *dishonors* or shows disrespect to Christ, his head, his archetypal source, and as well, to his own person.

On the other hand, a woman leading the congregation in prayer or prophetic speech (instruction, comfort, exhortation) likewise *dishonors her head,* the man (or husband), as well as her own person, if she has *her head uncovered (akatalyptos),* that is, not pinned up on her head as was the manner of all decent women in that culture when in public, but hanging loose (v. 5). Such disrespect for cultural sexual-identity markers would place such women in the same category as women who had their heads *shaved* (v. 5).

It is suggested that a woman's shaved head could denote either humility or a forced humbling and disgrace imposed on an adulterous woman or prostitute (Gill 1990:256). This may be reading too much into Paul's comparison. He may simply want to indicate that loose hair on a woman suggests a public social incongruity that violated the shame-honor order in the culture.

Paul presses the point home by asking whether it is a *disgrace (aischron,* "shame") *for a woman to have her hair cut* (literally "clipped short") *or shaved off;* if so, then let her *cover her head* (v. 6; that is, pin her long hair up on her head).

Again, I am convinced that the problem was not that the Corinthians blurred natural differences between the sexes, giving the impression of homosexuality or sexual immodesty, in their worship practices (contra Murphy-O'Connor, Thiselton, Keener, Hooker, Fitzmyer, Belleville). Nor was it excesses of a Corinthian woman's liberation movement that Paul must restrict (contra Wire). And the problem was not that the uncovered female was manifesting in worship the glory of her head, the

---

the problem in the cultural context are worthy, the specific solutions offered are less satisfactory in light of the exegesis of the passage. I tend to think that David Blattenberger's thesis is closer to the evidence: the issue is not status "coverings" but male-female distinctions that were signified by hairstyles (Blattenberger 1997:62-68).

male, thus diverting attention from God's glory (contra Hooker, Wire, Belleville).

Rather Paul's explicit purpose is to avoid causing shame (vv. 4-6), and correspondingly that each bring honor to their head (vv. 7-9). "This purpose should guide our interpretation of the passage" (Gundry-Volf 1997a:155).

In verses 7-9 Paul turns to creational material (Gen 1-2) to root out practices that are actually causing social shame in the Corinthians' public worship, given how men and women are relating to each other within the cultural system of the Mediterranean world. "Creation provides him the motif of glory which he uses to define gender identity and roles, and also with notions of gender difference and hierarchy, which are key components in the definition of shame and honor in the ancient Mediterranean world. Gender differences and hierarchy, however, are not themselves the goals" (Gundry-Volf 1997a:157). We must remember that early Christian worship gatherings were most often held in homes in a space that was only semi-private, at best (see at 11:17).

A man . . . is the image and glory of God (v. 7) alludes to Genesis 1:27 as read through Genesis 2. This allows Paul to speak only of *man* as *image and glory of God;* he adds the word *glory* and drops the word *image* when talking of the *woman.* This interpretation of Genesis 1—2 follows known Jewish rabbinic exegesis, which disallowed the divine image to Eve (Hooker 1963-1964:415), though such an understanding ignores the statement in Genesis 1:27, "So God created man *[ʾadam]* in his own image, in the image of God he created him; male and female he created them" (see 1 Cor 5:1-2). Both male and female are in the image of God, as evidenced by their both having ruling functions over the creation (Gen 1:28). Paul seems to use the rabbinic view, however, to get at the glory that the man ought to bring to God, as opposed to the shaming of his "head" by an nonmasculine hairstyle.

On the other hand, *the woman is the glory of the man* (v. 7) and should not wear her hair in a manner that disrespects and shames the man (or husband) according to cultural norms. Each by creation is the "glory" of another, but since the other is different, they must use different means to avoid shaming their respective "heads." This need not be taken as a denial of woman's creation in the image of God. Rather,

Paul may intentionally omit this in order to stress that women are the "glory" of men; in the cultural social order the woman "owed" honor to the man because she was the "glory" of the man by creation (Gundry-Volf 1997a:156).

That the woman is the "glory" of the man is grounded in both her creation *from man* (v. 8) and her creation *for man* (not vice versa), that is, to be man's "helper as his partner" (Gen 2:18 NRSV), so that he might have a companion to overcome his loneliness. Therefore the woman has the responsibility to not shame the man (or husband). She avoids this shame by being a woman and not rejecting the cultural symbol code that signals this—her long hair pinned up on her head.

While some patriarchal connotations remain (the preeminence of the man), "the view that 11:3 announces the themes of authority and subordination which are then taken up in 11:7-9 can thus be set aside on the basis of contextual considerations" (Gundry-Volf 1997a:159).

Finally, Paul utters a quite obscure sentence: *For this reason, and* (there is no "and" in the Greek) *because of the angels, the woman ought to have a sign of* (the Greek has no "a sign of") *authority on her head* (v. 10). By all accounts this is one of the most difficult texts to interpret in the book. Let me briefly sketch the possibilities.

Earlier interpretations took the expression *to have . . . authority on her head* as a conclusion to Paul's (alleged) case in 11:7-9 for male authority over women. The *sign of authority* (RV, NEB, NIV) was a reference to the head covering on the woman (RSV "veil on her head") and to the subordination of the woman to the male's authority. This interpretation is now discredited on lexical grounds (Hooker 1990).

Authority over (exousia epi) occurs a number of times in the New Testament, never with the passive sense, always active; it is best translated "authority over [or control over] her head" (see Lk 9:1; Rev 2:26; 6:8; 13:7; 14:18; 16:9). It is the *woman* who has the "authority" or "control," not the man. But authority over what? Some believe it is over her own hairstyle (Padgett 1984:71-72; Hays 1997:187-88; Keener 1992:38); others, over her metaphorical "head," the man (McGinn 1996:97-98). Some argue for "to retain control over" her head, in the sense of retaining the determination of how she will fix her hair to express the semiotic cultural code that distinguishes male from female. By thus controlling her head she will have the "authority" also of leading in worship prayers and uttering prophetic speech (Thiselton 2000:839).

Because of the angels seems to connect to *For this reason* in the earlier part of the verse. The reason women should have control or authority over their heads is *the angels*. But what is the connection? Earlier interpreters thought the angels were priests or bishops (Ambrosiaster), or "fallen lusting angels" (Tertullian), or "holy angels" who are present and participate in worship (Augustine), or "guardian angels" (Theodoret).

More modern views continue the above or, curiously, see *the angels* as "government informers" (as messengers; Winter 2001:136-37), or "observers of the created order" (Witherington 1990:170), or the evil principalities and powers whom women will judge (1 Cor 6:3). If women will by their authority "judge angels," then they can control their head appearance to avoid shame on their male counterparts (Keener 1992:42). Others see *the angels* as mediators of revelation from God (McGinn 1996:98; Gundry-Volf 1997a:164) or as female messengers such as Phoebe (Padgett 1984:81).

Two possible solutions—none seem satisfying—are in my opinion more likely. One is to follow those who combine the "guardian angels of order" and "participants in the worship of the church" (Thiselton 2000:841). In this view women are to exercise their freedom and authority in worship in a manner that will show control of their head, by respecting the honor-shame social system with its appropriate male-female markers, because the holy angels are present and join in the church's worship (see 1 Tim 5:21). The other is to follow Sheila McGinn and see the angels as mediators of divine revelation; verse 10 would then read, "Owing to all these things, the woman has authority over the 'head' [the man] through [or 'by'] the angels." In 11:2-16 Paul is concerned not with the speech of women but with their dress and to support the authority of prophetic women *as women*. "Thus verse 10 is the key verse of the passage. Once chosen by the Spirit for a prophetic task, a woman's range of authority now includes even power over 'her head' (i.e., men, even her husband). . . . Women have access to the Spirit, just as do men and, when they are gifted by the Spirit, women have the same divine authority as do prophetic men. . . . The head covering unmistakably proclaims their redeemed 'femaleness' to all observers" (McGinn 1996:99-100). In any event it is clear that the text does not support the idea of male authority over the woman actually or symbolically.

Re-creation and Gender (11:11-16) At this point Paul wants to go in a different direction, so he uses a strong adverb, *however* (*plēn*, "but," "in any case," breaking off a discussion and emphasizing what is important; Danker 2000:826; see Lk 10:20; 11:41; 12:31; Eph 5:33). There is, then, something else to be said about gender that in some sense contrasts with what he has said in verses 7-9.

This contrast is indicated by both content and form. In form, instead of contrasts (e.g., "man is not . . . but woman is"), there are comparisons and parallels ("neither woman . . . nor man"; "just as woman . . . so also man"). In content, the priority of man is now replaced with "not man without woman" and "man is through the woman."

Further, Paul locates this different interpretation of gender with his frequent term for the new redeemed reality, *in the Lord* (or "among the Lord's people"). This is a Paulinism (forty-seven times in Paul and only one time elsewhere) and virtually synonymous with his other frequent expression "in Christ" (seventy-three times). "Whereas the creation order entails a differentiation that may also embody a hint of priority, at least in terms of the Genesis narrative, Paul adds that in the gospel, differentiation is determined more explicitly by a principle of mutuality and reciprocity" (Thiselton 2000:842).

Thus, Paul says, *woman is not independent* (*chōris*, "without," "apart," "from") *of man, nor is man independent of woman*. This is more than merely an argument from procreation, since the statement is linked inseparably to *in the Lord*. "Paul is not claiming here that man needs woman as his subordinate and woman needs man as her 'head,' nor even simply that they are essential to each other according to God's design, but that since neither exists without the other, neither has exclusive priority over the other and therefore gender does not determine priority in their relationship 'in the Lord'" (Gundry-Volf 1997a:163).

For (v. 12) gives us the reason woman and man in the Lord are not without the other; *as woman came from [ek] man* reflects directly back on verse 8, where Paul used the Genesis 2 account to argue for Adam's (male) priority over Eve's (female) derived nature. Here Paul is taking up the issue of origins again, but he is giving the discussion two new features. First, the original historical creation of man and woman (woman from man) is compared with the creation order of how human life is produced: *man is born* (not in the Greek) *of (dia, "through") woman*. This comparison qualifies what Paul has previously stated. That woman has priority over man in the created order must at least balance the previous male priority argument (vv. 7-9) and may stand in tension with it.

"The assertion, 'just as the woman is from the man, so also the man is through the woman,' thus abolishes man's *exclusive* priority in creation and gives women equal status. Both are origins of the other, though in different ways, which respects their creational difference" (Gundry-Volf 1997a:163). This seems to point in the direction of Paul's actually inverting the hierarchical relationship between the sexes and breaking out of the strictly patriarchal system for constructing gender identity and roles.

Second, the closing statement in 11:12, *But everything comes from God,* relativizes male privilege by asserting that *everything* is directly dependent on God, including both male and female. In the context of Christian worship, gender roles are relativized "in the Lord," and leadership in worship (prayers and prophetic utterances) is given by both men and women while the distinction between the sexes remains. This seems to be the same teaching that we find in Galatians 3:28.

In verse 13 Paul appeals yet again to the Corinthians to *judge* (or "decide") *for themselves* whether it is *proper* (better: "appropriate") *for a woman to pray* (or conduct public prayers) *to God with her head uncovered* (with her hair not bound up over her head). What is asked is not a merely instinctual decision, but one based on due reflection on

---

11:14-15 *The very nature of things,* while difficult, is understandable. One of the best short discussions is in Keener 1992:42-45. *Long hair* is komē or komaō in these verses and occurs only here in the New Testament. It is not clear from a number of uses of the noun in the LXX (twelve) that the word means "long hair" rather than simply "hair of the head." Classical Greek likewise uses the word as "hair of the head" (with one possible exception in Josephus's *Antiquities of the Jews* 14.45). Gagnon

Paul's argument and the virtues of the Christian faith applied in the Corinthians' social context (see Phil 4:8).

Finally Paul appeals to *nature (physis)*. Thiselton's comment is helpful: "Depending upon the context of thought Paul may use *phusis* sometimes to denote the very 'grain' of the created order as a whole, or at other times (as here) to denote 'how things are' in more situational or societal terms" (2000:845). The NIV translation here reflects the former: *the very nature of things*. But this is not a necessary translation and may lead to moral judgments that in every culture or situation women *ought* to have long hair and men short.

It is better to take *nature* to refer to the generally observed fact that women's hair tends to be longer than men's and to the cultural custom of attaching *glory* or honor to the *long hair* of women (when properly pinned up on the head) and of viewing long hair on a man as *a disgrace* (so Fee, Thiselton, Tomson, Thompson, Keener—with different views on the head "covering"). Augustine seems puzzled as to why some Christian men in his day wore long hair, contrary to the precept of the apostle. "I refrain from saying more concerning this habit [of men wearing long hair], because of certain long-haired brothers whom, in almost all other respects, we hold in high esteem. But in proportion as we love them the more in Christ, to that degree do we advise them the more earnestly" (in Bray 1999:109). Augustine seems, unlike Paul, not to appeal to the cultural way men were wearing their hair, but to the cultural way men wore their hair in Roman Corinth as a transcultural principle for all times and cultures. We believe this interpretation can be questioned as argued above.

But what should we make of Paul's last remark about women's long hair being *given to her as* (*anti*, "as" or "instead of") *a covering (peribolaion,* "covering," "shawl," "robe," "cloak"—a different Greek word from those used previously)? Many commentators believe that Paul is

---

proposes that Paul's "natural" argument is about men's propensity toward baldness, whereas women tend to keep their hair as a covering (Gagnon 2001:373-77). My suggestion would be that *komē* is related to a certain kind of coiffure that is appropriate for the woman's gender identification but inappropriate for the man in that cultural context. Alan Padgett's suggestion that the two questions should be read instead as statements is to be taken seriously even if not accepted ultimately (1984).

here giving an analogy: just as a woman's long hair naturally provides a covering for her head, so she should wear a cloth covering. Leon Morris says, "This fact [the longer hair of the woman] points to nature as giving in symbol the need for a woman to have her head covered on appropriate occasions" (1958:155-56). But this strains the actual wording. The woman's long hair itself is her covering when it is appropriately placed up on her head!

Finally, Paul appeals to the custom or *practice* (*synētheian,* "custom") of *the churches of God* (v. 16). *Contentious* (*philoneikos,* "argumentative") refers to those who put self-interest above the congregation's growth in grace and the church's gospel witness to outsiders by promoting behavior that dishonors the opposite sex. Paul's instruction that men and women should both lead in worship and at the same time maintain gender distinctions with symbolic markers appropriate in the shame-honor culture is the *practice* all the churches follow. Those who oppose *this practice* are the *contentious* ones.

How does this long and difficult discussion relate to our present life in the churches? We should begin with honesty and never pretend to understand more than we do. This might involve both admitting we don't understand it all or accept it all (e.g., equal male and female leadership of worship or a hierarchical ordering of male and female in worship). Second, we must not dismiss the text as "culturally conditioned." For as Richard Hays points out, "all texts are culturally conditioned" (1997:190).

Among others, three areas of special application may be considered. First, how do men and women cause social shame to the opposite sex in our culture? How might we cause shame today to the opposite sex in the ways men and women participate or perhaps are restricted from participating in worship? How does our practice affect the church's mission to outsiders? Does an all-male preaching staff turn some outsiders away? Could a woman preaching reach some non-Christians?

Our dress and outward appearance should reflect our sexual identity in the church. At the same time, based on the previous exegesis, men and women *both* should be leading in worship as equals, as joint heirs of the grace of God and stewards of the gospel ministry according to their gifts from the Holy Spirit (chaps. 12-14). We agree with

Hays, "Anyone who appeals to this passage to silence women or to deny them leadership roles in the church is flagrantly misusing the text" (1997:191).

"What roles do women play in our churches? Do they take up only traditional female roles, or are they also students of theology, teachers, proclaimers, missionaries, Spirit-filled speakers of the Word of God? Is the way made hard for these women to pursue callings not traditionally open to women, or is their willingness and determination met with *appreciation* and *encouragement?* Are there attempts to *remove the obstacles* that stand in the way of women's full participation in the ministries of the church, such as lack of theological education, or do we stand by and let these obstacles continue to serve as justifications for women's exclusion?" (Gundry-Volf 1997b:49-50).

Finally, we must acknowledge that there is some sort of patriarchal ordering in Paul's argument in verses 7-9. While this is not the whole story (vv. 11-12 take a different tack), the tension must be faced and handled honestly. In the end we may not be able to fully embrace either the subordinationist or the egalitarian reading of the passage.

☐ The Problems in the Corinthians' Practice of the Lord's Supper (11:17-34)

Prompted by oral reports (v. 18) rather than the Corinthians' letter questions, Paul addresses elements of their practice of the Lord's Supper that he obviously is displeased about: *I have no praise for you, for your meetings do more harm than good* (v. 17). But what was wrong? In answering this question we are aided today by both archaeology and ancient literary texts describing the architecture and the practices of communal as well as private meals in the Roman world of Paul's day. Additionally, linguistic studies raise new possibilities for difficult statements in the passage. Nevertheless, the exact reconstruction of the problem(s) is not completely certain.

Since the 1980s commentators have pointed to the architecture of Roman homes of the period in places such as Ostia (outside Rome) and Anaploga (near the Corinthian site) as well as the social customs of the day. Early Roman homes were designed to reinforce social status and difference, especially between slaves and owners and between dinner guests and kitchen staff (Osiek and Balch 1997:199, 215).

Apparently in some locales the church met upstairs in modest homes *(insula)* of artisans like Priscilla and Aquila, similar to our apartments located over stores at street level. On the other hand, a few wealthy Christians could host larger gatherings in a more spacious home *(domus* or "villa"), like those of Philemon of Colossae or Stephanas and Gaius of Corinth (1 Cor 1:15-16; 16:15-16; Rom 16:23).

"Roman domestic architecture is obsessively concerned with distinctions of social rank, and the distinctions involved are not merely between one house and another . . . but within the social space of the house" (Osiek and Balch 1997:29). The wealthier the household, the more status was recognized in the partitioning of space within the home. This was especially the case when meals were served. The better food and service came to the guests of greater status, who occupied the large triclinium dining room, while those who counted less were served in the nearby atrium with scraps of food.

The first-century Roman governor of Bithynia and letter writer Pliny the Younger complains about how some were treated at the home of a wealthy man: "I happened to be dining with a man, though no particular friend of his, whose elegant economy, as he called it, seemed to me a sort of stingy extravagance. The best dishes were set in front of himself and a select few, and cheap scraps of food before the rest of the company. He had even put the wine into tiny little flasks, divided into three categories, not with the idea of giving his guests the opportunity of choosing, but to make it impossible for them to refuse what they were given. One lot was intended for himself and for us, another for his lesser friends (all his friends were graded), and the third for his and our freedmen" *(Letters* 2.6, quoted by Murphy-O'Connor 1983:159-60). This secular practice seems to have crept into the Corinthian church gathering and in some manner into the Lord's Supper observance, with disastrous consequences.

Two slightly different scenarios of the specific problem are possible. If the temporal force of the verb in verse 21 is stressed, as in the NIV and NRSV *(goes ahead),* and the sense of the verb in verse 33 is given as *wait for* (NIV, NRSV), the problem would be the following. Certain upper-class friends of the host would arrive early with their larger portions of fine food and wine and would dine in the special areas for honored guests. They would gorge themselves and have plenty of wine (*gets drunk*, v. 21). The working-class church members would come later and be required to occupy the overflow (atrium) area. The food that was left over or that they could afford to bring was not enough to satisfy their hunger (*hungry*, v. 21). They perhaps tried to satisfy their hunger pangs by eating the bread and wine as part of their meal, failing thus to distinguish their meal from the "Lord's meal" in the Eucharist. Both the leisured and the poorer working class were guilty of abusing the intended purpose of the Lord's Supper through selfish greed and discrimination based on Corinthian social status. Therefore the leisured who arrived and ate earlier were to *wait for* the late arrivers, and all were to eat together a shared meal or only the Communion elements.

A somewhat different scenario develops if we see the verb in verse 21 as simply meaning "to devour" and the verb in verse 33 as "to welcome, receive" one another (in loving hospitality). The problem Paul addresses, then, would be the greed of the few who brought private meals and gorged themselves with fine food and wine as the poor were neglected and remained hungry as the Lord's Supper took place.

This was *not* the Lord's Supper as patterned originally after the Jewish Passover meal, providing equal and free access of all to the meal (11:20). Therefore the remedy was to restore the original Lord's Supper emphasis on sharing in his death through the elements and for each to "receive" the other "in the sense of sharing food and drink" (Winter 2001:151).

At least one modern translation picks up elements of this second view. Eugene Peterson's *The Message* renders verse 21 as follows: "And then I find that you bring your divisions to worship—you come together, and instead of eating the Lord's Supper, you bring in a lot of food from the outside and make pigs of yourselves. Some are left out, and go home hungry. Others have to be carried out, too drunk to walk." Yet verse 33 is rendered, "If you're so hungry that you can't wait to be served, go home and get a sandwich." This follows more the common sense of the verb as emphasized in the first view.

In the exposition I will argue for the first view while recognizing some valid elements of the second. While evidence does exist to support the second view's readings of the verbs in verses 21 and 33, these are not the common meaning of these words in Paul's writings or elsewhere in the New Testament. Furthermore, Paul does use a slightly different word when he wants to emphasize "welcoming or receiving" others in fellowship (cf. Rom 15:7, *proslambanō*).

In both views the problem is twofold. There has been an incursion of sinful secular social divisions into the practice of the observance of the Lord's Supper, together with drunken gluttony on the part of some. This has also caused the poor in the church to be shamed. Both of these outrageous practices broke the unity and equality of the body of Christ, which are central to the significance of the Lord's meal.

The Problems (11:17-22) Before Paul offers corrective exhortations, he identifies why he cannot *praise* the Corinthians and why their *meetings do more harm than good. When you come together as a church* may emphasize larger gatherings of the "whole church" (Rom 16:23) in distinction to smaller gatherings in apartments. This would help explain why there are *divisions (schismata)* and *differences (haireseis)*. Individual church groups in the city may have developed different social habits in their gatherings. When they came together, these differences were incompatible with their unity and equality as the body of Christ, and thus the Lord's Supper was being nullified.

These differences, divisions or splits are not likely the ones mentioned earlier in 1:10-12, where a "party" spirit was in evidence. Paul's strong condemnation of the Corinthians' socially discriminating practices would argue against interpretations of *to some extent I believe it* that would suggest Paul's sources were not quite clear at this point. Either a stronger rendering, "I am convinced of a certain report" (Winter 2001:159), or a more judicious pastoral caution, as in the NIV, is probably closer to Paul's intent.

11:21 *Each of you goes ahead without waiting* basically translates the one word *prolambanō* that usually would bear the sense of the NIV. However, Winter has argued that in eating contexts the word loses its temporal sense and should be translated simply as "takes" or "devours" (2001:144-48). This would change the sense of the whole passage, so the problem Paul was addressing becomes selfish gorging by

No doubt there have to be differences presents more of an interpretive challenge. Some have suggested that Paul speaks with irony here to shame the Corinthians' behavior. In effect, then Paul would be saying, "You Christians must have your social divisions so that the truly distinguished ones among you may be identified." Alternately, if Paul has some eschatological (prophetic) saying in mind, such as "Dissensions are unavoidable" (2 Tim 3:8-9), then he may be simply stating that conflict is inevitable in a mixed Christian group as "the end" approaches (Bruce, Hays, Schrage, Fee, et al).

The problem with this explanation is that it seems to suggest that Paul endorses the very divisions that he insists are sinful. However, if the Corinthian troublemakers are themselves the proponents of the saying—if they have anticipated criticism of divisions within the assembly by arguing that these divisions are necessary to distinguish the truly tested and approved from the false—a more acceptable sense may be possible (Thiselton 2000:858).

It is not the Lord's Supper states Paul's negative assessment of their discriminating behavior in the strongest language possible. Whatever their excuses for eating as they were doing, their practices had nullified "the Lord's meal." *The Lord's Supper,* based on the Jewish Passover meal, included all, and all participated equally (see at v. 23). The gravity of the situation is captured by F. F. Bruce: "It was no more possible for the Lord's Supper to be eaten in an atmosphere of social discrimination than it was for the same people to 'partake of the table of the Lord and the table of demons' (10:21). The Eucharist could be profaned by faction as certainly as by idolatry" (1971:110).

Rather than a shared meal in which all participated equally (similar to our potluck dinners) and during which the Eucharist was taken, the gathering was being treated by some Corinthians as a private meal. Some separated themselves and gathered in the more honored triclinium dining area, where they reclined and consumed their own

---

some while others had little or nothing to eat. It also requires adopting a questionable meaning of the verb "wait for" (as "receive") in verse 33 (q.v. note). Winter's view is apparently based on only one inscription usage and should be cautiously tested against the other evidence that points to the temporal sense (Mk 14:8; Gal 6:1; Wisdom 17:16).

food with as much to drink as they desired (*another gets drunk,* v. 20). Others were standing in the adjoining atrium with little to eat and drink (*one remains hungry)* beyond the bread and wine served in the eucharistic ceremony. It was apparently during the Communion service that "the haves" were enjoying a sumptuous meal that excluded "the have-nots" and left them hungry. Such lack of sharing with the poor not only violates fundamental aspects of the meaning of Christ's sacrificial death for us and for our salvation but also is actually to *despise the church of God and humiliate those who have nothing* (the poor, v. 22).

Archaeological evidence indicates that there was a famine in the Corinthian area during the time Paul was writing this epistle (Gill 1993:333). This would intensify the shamefulness of holding a dinner without providing food for all to share. If the Corinthian Christians want to eat this way, Paul wants them to do it in their own *homes.* Their unchristian behavior could bring nothing from him but sharp censure.

The Tradition (11:23-26) Paul now presents the tradition (*I received . . . I also passed on;* see 11:2; 15:3) concerning the eucharistic meal that originated *from the Lord.* This latter expression could mean "received directly from the Lord by revelation" (cf. Gal 1:11-12), but more likely Paul is indicating that these words originated with the Lord and were handed on orally or perhaps in written form in the Christian tradition. There is a similar Jewish formula ("received . . . passed on") for the transmission of sacred traditions (Witherington 1997:249). This material in 11:23-26 is the earliest historical reference to the institution of the Lord's Supper.

It seems virtually certain that the context for interpreting the Lord's Supper correctly is the Jewish Passover meal (Lk 22:15; Thiselton 2000:874; Routledge 2002:203-21). *The Lord Jesus, on the night he was betrayed* (*paradidomi,* "betrayed" or "handed over," i.e., to death) reminds us of the historic night before the crucifixion when Jesus presided over

---

11:24-25 *For you* is the best textual reading, rather than "broken for you," but in Luke 22:19 the text is "given for you." Paul departs from Luke 22:20 in omitting

the Passover meal (Lk 22:7-20). In Paul's account there are six actions that encompass the ceremony: (1) *took bread,* (2) gave *thanks* to God, (3) *broke* the bread, (4) spoke the words *"This is my body,"* (5) *took the cup,* and (6) made reference to his *blood* and the *new covenant.*

The complete Passover celebration involved a longer and more detailed ritual (Seder). We can find elements of this longer ceremony in the Gospel accounts of the Last Supper. For example, Luke records not one but two cups (Lk 22:17, 20), and two of the Gospels record a hymn at the conclusion of the ceremony, which is still sung today in Jewish Passover celebrations (the Hallel, Psalms 113—18; cf. Mt 26:30; Mk 14:26). The Jewish ceremony actually includes four cups. Probably the third cup was the one Jesus referred to as his "blood of the new covenant."

The purpose of the Seder was to bring the Jewish participants into a personal, existential experience of the first Passover, when the Israelites were liberated from Egyptian servitude, as told in the exodus story *(haggadah).* Every Jew, then, in every generation is expected to "look on himself as if *he* came forth out of Egypt" (Glatzer 1969:5). If Jesus had this in mind when he said, *"Do this in remembrance of me,"* then he is in effect calling each of us to personally go back to the night of the Last Supper, as if we reclined at the Passover table as Jesus broke bread and gave it to us! Above all, it is a living actualization of the past in light of the future return of Christ (v. 26). The African American spiritual comes close to this: "Were you there when they crucified my Lord? Were you there when they nailed him to the tree?"

Jesus *broke* the bread or loaf. This must first of all have reference to the communal or fellowship sharing (10:16) in which all were to participate equally. There may be a secondary sense that the action of breaking the bread may point to the broken body of Jesus in death, which the words *for you* may signify.

This is my body is at once unique and highly controversial in the history of the church. This study cannot survey the extensive literature representing different understandings of the Lord's words. However,

---

"which is poured out for you" (found in all three Synoptic Gospels) and adds in verses 24-25 the words not found in the Gospels: *do this in remembrance of me.*

following the Passover setting that Paul repeats in this passage we may safely emphasize that the words *"This is my body . . . for you"* introduce a surprise identification of the bread in the ceremony.

In the ancient ceremony after the blessing of the first cup of wine, there follows the eating of raw vegetables (hors d'oeuvres) dipped in saltwater, a narration of the Haggadah (the redemption of Israel from Egypt), benedictions on the unleavened bread *(matzah)*, the drinking of a second cup of wine, eating of the main meal of roasted lamb and more bread, the drinking of a third cup of wine following blessings of God and Scripture recitations, and a final cup of wine accompanied with the singing of the Hallel psalms (esp. 136) and closing songs (Glatzer 1969:6-10). Jesus, though not necessarily the disciples, apparently abstained from the fourth cup, which is a cup of praise and "looks forward to God's victory over his enemies and the final vindication and future blessing of his people. Jesus knew that that time was not yet; before it could come he had another cup which he must drink first: the cup of suffering and death (Mt 26:38-39; see also Mk 14:35-36; Lk 22:42)" (Routledge 2002:219-20). That Jesus abstained is indicated by his words after having shared the third cup, "I will not drink again of the fruit of the vine until that day when I drink it anew in the kingdom of God" (Mk 14:24; cf. Mt 26:29).

The benediction on the unleavened bread is likely the point in the ceremony when Jesus surprisingly identifies the bread as "my body for you." In the Passover ritual the bread is identified thus: "This is the bread of poverty which our forefathers ate in the land of Egypt. Let all who are hungry enter and eat; let all who are needy come to our Passover feast." But now Jesus identifies the bread with his own body given for us *(for you)*. Just as the bread represented or signified but was not in actuality the bread the Israelites ate in poverty in the land of Egypt, so it is difficult to see Jesus making more than such a "remembrance" or representative reference to his own body. Yet we must keep in mind that the Hebrew idea of remembrance in the Passover celebration goes beyond thinking about or recollecting the event; in some sense it involves a *participation* in the event remembered (1 Cor 10:16).

After supper suggests not only the original Passover meal setting but also the continued meal context for the early church's observance of the Lord's Supper (11:21, 33). *This cup is the new covenant [kainē diathēkē] in my blood* refers to the third cup in the Passover ceremony, which came after the meal and the words "Blessed are you, O Lord our God, king of the universe, creator of the fruit of the vine." Again surprisingly, Jesus identifies the cup with his own death as establishing *the new covenant* (Lk 22:20; simply "covenant" in Mt 26:28; Mk 14:24).

Outside the book of Hebrews, where it is central to the fulfillment of Jeremiah 31:31-34 in Jesus, "new covenant" language is not frequently used to describe the work of Christ (2 Cor 3:6), though it may be thought of as undergirding the whole significance of his death. Forgiveness of sins is the special gift that the new covenant secures (Heb 8:12; 9:15).

Whenever is best rendered "as many times as" (Thiselton). *You proclaim* (or "preach") *the Lord's death* perhaps in the Passover meal context means "You make a *haggadah* [long story] of the death of Jesus." In the Supper of the Lord we participate in and appropriate the redemptive benefit of the cross and also the lifestyle that reflects this participation. Yet only when *he comes* (1 Cor 1:7) will the meal be fulfilled as we dine with him in the "wedding supper of the Lamb" (Rev 19:9). So the table not only calls us to the past event of the cross but also recalls Jesus' words of promise and points forward to our destiny in the manifestation of the kingdom of God: "For I tell you I will not drink again of the fruit of the vine until the kingdom of God comes" (Lk 22:18; 1 Cor 16:22).

> Feast after feast thus comes and passes by,
>> Yet, passing, points to the glad feast above,
> Giving sweet foretaste of the festal joy,
>> The Lamb's great bridal feast of bliss and love.

HORATIUS BONAR, (1808-1889) (untitled hymn #323, *Church Hymnody,* rev. ed., 1927)

The Two Solutions (11:27-34) Paul now appeals to the Corinthians to correct their malpractice of the Lord's Supper by first *recognizing the body* (v. 29) and then *wait[ing] for each other* and if hungry *eat[ing] at home* (vv. 33-34).

Looking at this first section (vv. 29-32), I am reminded of something a friend who serves among African Christians in Nairobi told me. Many believers, he said, leave the worship service before Communion begins, for they fear that because of sin in their life they will get sick or die if they partake of the elements. Is this what Paul is saying?

To eat and drink *in an unworthy manner* (v. 27) suggests that the way the Corinthians were eating and drinking was not appropriate to the message nor to the solemnity the occasion demanded. We will probably want to connect this with the expression *without recognizing [discerning] the body* (*of the Lord* is not in the Greek; v. 29). But the latter expression is ambiguous.

Does *body* refer to Christ's physical or spiritual body mystically present in the consecrated elements of the Supper? Or alternately, are we to understand *the body* to refer to the body of Christians, the church? Or is there a third option? The first understanding argues that the previous uses of *body* in the passage refer to Christ, not the church (vv. 24, 27). This reading can lead to a mystical sense of the bodily presence of Christ in the elements of the bread and wine or to the Roman Catholic view that in the Eucharist, ordinary bread is transformed into the actual body of Jesus. Nothing in the text requires either of these understandings.

Others argue that *the body* refers to the church as the body of Christ. This would mean Paul's concern was that the Corinthians' conduct was "without any consideration for the most elementary implications of their fellowship in Christ. Such conduct was as serious a profanation of the holy supper as was the table segregation between Jewish and Gentile Christians in Syrian Antioch, which Paul condemns in Gal 2:11ff; it was not surprising that those guilty of it should incur divine judgment" (Bruce 1971:115).

While a number of modern interpreters (mostly but not exclusively evangelical) follow Bruce here (Fee, Witherington, Hays, Blomberg), I believe that the primary emphasis is on the Lord's own physical body, not as mystically present in the bread but in the saving significance of his death and the consequent social behavior required of all who are identified with him (v. 24). Recognition of the grace of Christ and his

---

11:29 *The body of the Lord* reflects one set of manuscripts; another set omits "of the

death for all leads to social transformation: all social rankings and separations among believers are relativized when they gather for the Lord's meal.

As John Chrysostom rightly sensed, the problem at Corinth was that "the Corinthians were disgracing themselves by turning the Lord's Supper into a private meal and thus depriving it of its greatest prerogative. The Lord's Supper ought to be common to all, because it is the Master's, whose property does not belong to one servant or to another but ought to be shared by all together" (in Bray 1999:111).

To recognize the body is to be mindful of the uniqueness of Christ, who stands apart from all for his gift of himself for others in sheer grace. The Lord's Supper, by underlining participation in and identification with the cruciform Christ, generates the social transformation that is Paul's second concern. His first concern is the "proclamation of the cross (1:18-25) as the ground of identity transformation, and it is of the very essence of the Lord's Supper (and of baptism) to keep this anchorage in grace and in the cross in sharp focus" (Thiselton 2000:893).

To eat *in an unworthy manner* is to not take the Lord's Supper seriously. We do this by not focusing on Christ and the cross whereby he gave himself in grace for our salvation. Such disregard for the meaning of his death for all makes us *guilty of* (*sinning against* is not in the Greek) *the body and blood of the Lord* (v. 27). The sin is not against the elements of the Lord's Supper but against Christ, with whom presumably the Corinthians identified while at the same time using the meal for social honor and status enhancement. They thus denied its essential meaning as a participation of all equally in the saving death of Christ. Such actions and attitudes were serious violations of Christ's intention for the meal and led to *judgment* from the Lord on them (v. 29).

Paul cites evidence of the divine judgment: *weak and sick, and a number of you have fallen asleep* ("have died"). Are these naturally caused diseases and fatalities related to their eating excesses (*drunk*, v. 21) and/or special divine judgments unaccounted for by mere natural causes? In either case, Paul read certain of their afflictions as the chastening (*disciplined*, v. 32) hand of the Lord (cf. Heb 12:5-11; 1 Pet

Lord." The two manuscript traditions in this case are equally divided in strength.

4:17). Such judgment is *so that we will not be condemned with the world*. God's grace forgives our sin but also requires the transformation of our behavior (Rom 8:1-4). God's painful discipline of his children aims to vindicate his righteous judgment on sin and at the same time, through repentance, to turn us away from continuing in the sin.

To avoid this judgment, the Corinthians should do two things. They should judge themselves (v. 31) and *examine* themselves (v. 28). To judge ourselves is to recognize as sin the eating and drinking of the Lord's Supper in a manner that denies the essential saving significance proclaimed in the meal and the consequent behavior appropriate to the meal. The Lord's Table is not our own private meal but the *Lord's* meal, to be shared equally with all who have gathered. Repenting (turning from) wrong attitudes and practices will turn away the Lord's judgment from us.

To *examine* ("test for genuineness") is not, as often understood, to become either retrospective or introspective concerning our sinfulness, however needed that might be from time to time, but "to confirm that [our] understanding, attitude, and conduct are *genuine* in sharing . . . in all that the body and blood of Christ proclaims, both in redemptive and in social terms" (Thiselton 2000:891). We must recognize our part in the crucified-Christ-for-us before we eat the bread and drink the cup.

When you come together to eat, wait [ekdechomai] for each other (v. 33) suggests that in the Corinthian setting the Lord's Supper was observed in the context of a meal. This should be a common meal in which all participate, with equal sharing of food. If some arrive early (for whatever reason), they must not go ahead and eat their own meals before the others arrive. This would contribute to sinful class distinctions within the congregation—apparently such was already happening at Corinth. The first comers must *wait* for all to arrive before the meal begins. Those who arrive early should not come hungry; they should

---

11:33 *Wait* is the normal lexical sense of the verb *ekdechomai* in the New Testament (Jn 5:3; Acts 17:16; 1 Cor 16:11; Heb 10:13; 11:10; Jas 5:7). The classical usage may include "take" or "receive," but "in our lit. to remain in a place or state and await an event or the arrival of someone, *expect, wait*" (Danker 2000:300). See note at 11:21. This meaning is opposed by a number of modern commentators (Fee, Hays, Hors-

eat at home beforehand, so that all may eat together when the Lord's Supper is observed (v. 34).

When I come I will give further directions (v. 34) should not be read as indicating that Paul will create an oral tradition for the church that will exist authoritatively alongside the written Scriptures, but simply that he can attend to (set in order) other related matters better in person than through further remarks in this letter.

How then should we observe the Lord's Supper in the contemporary church? Several points can be suggested. First, the celebration should be open to all confessing believers in Jesus Christ equally, without discrimination based on age, sex, social class, race, political party, church affiliation, baptism (infant, immersed or none); it should include the divorced, the remarried, gays and lesbians, patriots and nonpatriots: "This is my body for all." The practice of a "closed" Communion open only to members of a particular denomination or sect—such as the Roman Catholic and Orthodox exclusion of believers outside their communions—is a shameful contemporary practice that violates the very essence of the *Lord's* Table.

Second, believers should approach the remembrance with due solemnity and sobriety, not only calling to mind the events of the first Supper with Christ and his disciples but seeing ourselves as involved in a living actualization and participation in all that Christ's death for us means. We should keep Christ's grace and cross uppermost in our partaking of the bread and cup. This is how we should judge our genuineness as we approach the celebration.

Third, as we so participate in the events that form the narrative core of our salvation in Christ, accompanied with due "remembrance" of the great future event of Christ's return, we also open ourselves to the important but secondary emphasis of the Supper, the transformation of our attitudes and behavior toward others in the community as well as outsiders. The cruciform life is an inseparable consequence of authen-

ley, Winter) but accepted by others (Murphy-O'Connor, Schrage, Thiselton) and almost all modern translations. Unwisely, in my opinion, two modern versions follow classical rather than New Testament usage: "make everyone equally welcome" (TNIV); "be reverent and courteous with one another" *(The Message).*

tic participation in the Lord's meal as Paul conceives it.

□ The Spirit's Manifestations in Worship (12:1—14:40)

In our day perhaps no other section of Paul's letter has received as much prolonged attention and debate as these chapters on the ministries of the Spirit (12-14). Historically, since the apostolic age there have been three or four periods of intense interest in "manifestations of the Spirit." In the later part of the second century the prophecies of Montanus and his associates, though later condemned as heresy, captivated even the great apologist Tertullian. Luther, Calvin and Zwingli all opposed the "new revelations" and "prophecies" of a radical wing of the sixteenth-century Anabaptists known as the Munzerites.

Though there were certain eighteenth-century manifestations such as the Irvingites in England, the Shakers in America, and certain Spirit expressions in the revivals under John Wesley, George Whitefield and Jonathan Edwards, the great renewal of the Spirit's manifestations has come largely in the twentieth century. Today every major segment and tradition of the church worldwide has been involved in this renewed emphasis on the Holy Spirit and his manifestations. Additionally, since the beginning of the twentieth century tens of thousands of new Pentecostal charismatic denominations have been formed (Synan 2001:388-91). As one contemporary theologian has put it, "In former times the Holy Spirit has been the Cinderella of the Trinity. The other sisters went to the ball but Cinderella was left behind. Now all that has changed" (McGrath 1997:279). But not without controversy.

Some strongly oppose manifestations of the full range of Spirit's ministries referred to in these chapters; they argue for a historic cessation of certain of these workings of the Spirit (see at 13:8-12). Others enthusiastically embrace the manifestations and make them central to their personal and church life. Still others find no scriptural or historical reason for the cessation of these ministries of the Spirit and welcome those who worship in an enthusiastic manner within Paul's strictures, but they do not themselves practice these ministries in their private life or corporate worship.

Wherever we find ourselves on this spectrum, a fresh look at the primary teaching of Paul on this subject can not but help us to be more discerning about this important, widespread and controversial area in the modern church worldwide. Paul's teaching can and should be a mirror to hold up to our own churches' life and practices today.

Regardless of our position, the fact remains that the modern church has felt the impact of the Pentecostal and charismatic wave that has swept through the entire Christian church beginning in the early twentieth century and continuing into the new millennium. Professor Thomas F. Torrance of Edinburgh has aptly caught the significance of this renewal for the church:

> As I understand it, the astonishing movement of the Spirit is, on its negative side, a mighty protest against the deterministic forms of the Church's existence in the world which continually arise as the Church yields to the temptation to institutionalize its service of the divine mercy and to build up power-structures of its own both through ecclesiastical success and prestige among the people and through socio-political instruments, by means of which it exerts pressure to attain its ends and impart to its service the kind of efficient power which can recognizably compete with the other power-structures of organized society in the world . . . to substitute worldly power for the power of the Holy Spirit, or, if you like, to generate its own "holy ghost." It is against all this that the widespread resurgence of downright belief in the Holy Spirit is a mighty protest in the name of the living God. . . . Constructively . . . it represents a recovery of belief in *God,* not some remote inactive deity, but the mighty living God who acts, and who interacts with the world he has made. (Torrance 1975:290-91)

One early desert father of the church reminds us that we should not fail to experience the Spirit as we study and reflect on these chapters of 1 Corinthians: "It is one thing to give descriptive accounts with a certain head knowledge and correct notions, and another in substance and reality, in full experience, and in the inward man and in the mind, to possess the treasure and the grace and the task and the effectual working of the Holy Ghost" (Pseudo-Macarius).

What Was the Problem at Corinth? Before we proceed into the text itself, it may be helpful to inquire as to what issue(s) in Corinth may have prompted Paul to write at such length (three chapters). From the content of the chapters themselves we may gather that the Corinthians had some concerns about manifestations of the Spirit, especially the experiences of tongues (the whole of chap. 14), in their worship services.

Further, as elsewhere in the epistle, there are problems of spiritual status discrimination, lack of unity and disrespect for others, especially those whose contribution to the church was considered of less value, the "less presentable" parts of the body (12:23). The Corinthians had failed to perceive the nature of their salvation through the self-giving cross of Christ and to nurture love that cares for others without discrimination. Their distorted understanding of the Spirit's concrete manifestations or showings led them to value some of these ministries above others because of the status they brought. Paul "is seeking to bring the disorderly and self-centered worship practices of the Corinthians under control so that the church as a whole may be built up (14:5, 12, 26, 40)" (Hays 1997:206). How does he do this?

Summary of Chapters 12—14 After laying down a christological criterion (12:2-3), Paul describes the concrete varieties of these ministries as all coming from the same source, the triune God, who distributes them as he wills for the benefit of all (12:4-11). Paul stresses both diversity of ministries and unity of source, based not on the personal abilities or the spiritual status of individuals who manifest these Spirit expressions, but on God the Spirit.

Taking up the body metaphor, Paul continues the theme by emphasizing the necessary diversity among the parts and at the same time their unity in the one body, which is the corporate Christ. There is no place for feelings of either inferiority or superiority, because the body needs all its diverse parts to be a body. God has appointed the individual parts as he has willed, with no thought of superior or inferior status. Furthermore, God has himself so constructed the relationship between the parts that they are mutually interdependent and each receives equal honor, respect and care from the others, so that there is no status competition among them (12:12-26).

Finally, Paul states directly that the Corinthians are the body of Christ and they each have God-appointed public ministries (or parts) in the church, the body of Christ, beginning with apostles, prophets and teachers, then a variety of other public manifestations. He emphasizes once again that the variety or differences among ministries is absolutely necessary for the church to function as Christ's body. Not all are apostles, not all are prophets, not all speak in tongues. Yet they are to be enthusiastic for the greater Spirit expressions that Paul will explain in chapter 14, the ministries, such as prophecy, that edify the whole church (12:27-31).

In an unforgettable excursus, Paul interjects an appeal for a most excellent and superior way of relating to one another in the body: through Christian love. The whole purpose of the Spirit's concrete manifestations is to express the love of God in Christ Jesus our Lord and to thus build the believers into a community of love. Without love, the Spirit's manifestations will not effect God's purposes for his church (chap. 13).

Finally, to conclude the whole section Paul turns to the most prominent element of the Corinthians' "spiritual problem," the emphasis on tongues manifestations. Tongues are legitimate expressions of the Spirit, but they are mainly to be kept for private, personal edification, since they are unintelligible speech (unless interpreted). Prophecy is to be preferred because of its intelligibility and serviceability both for the evangelism of outsiders and the building up of the Christian community (14:1-25). Worship services should be conducted in an orderly fashion, not forbidding the expression of tongues, if interpreted, and allowing all the prophets to speak one by one. Wives are to remain silent in the churches, because to speak will bring disgrace on them and their husbands. The church will be edified as the apostles' commands are followed (14:26-40).

Underlying Paul's discussion of the Spirit's expressions is his apparent concern for an undercurrent of self-seeking and status seeking in Corinth. Whenever certain Spirit manifestations were being sought above others because they were judged to bring higher status, the church was not being built up into the image of Christ, who humbled himself and served others in love.

The Nature and Christological Test of the Spirit's Expressions (12:1-3) *Now about* signals that Paul is taking up further questions contained in the Corinthian letter to him (7:1, 25; 8:1). *Spiritual gifts* in the Greek is simply *pneumatikōs,* either "spiritual persons" (14:37) or more likely here either "matters of the Spirit" or "manifestations of the Spirit" (12:7; 14:1). The idea of "gifts" is added, supposing the identity of this term with a different word used in verse 4 (*charismata,* also 1:7; 12:31) which is usually translated "gifts" (see Rom 12:6). Whether Paul's preferred word was *charismata* and the Corinthians' *pneumatika* is not important.

More significant is the nature of these Spirit gifts or manifestations. It must be said at once that they do not refer to abilities that believers are given but to ministries of the Spirit, manifestations of God's many-faceted, many-colored, diversified grace (1 Pet 4:10). Translating this as "gifts" is not so much wrong as misleading if it leads us to think of some special abilities God has given to us rather than of the concrete way God expresses his grace through us in ministries directed and energized by the Spirit (Berding 2000:51).

With a reference to the Corinthians' former pagan practices, when they were *led astray to mute idols,* Paul distinguishes Spirit-inspired speech from non-Spirit-inspired speech. Just why Paul refers to their pagan experiences of "repeatedly being led [captive] before speechless idols" (more literal rendering; cf. Ps 115:7; Jer 10:14; Hab 2:18) is not clear. If frenzied or ecstatic experiences are in view, the text itself does not say this directly. Some believe Paul is drawing a comparison with pagan experiences of glossolalia to devalue the Corinthians' overemphasis on this phenomenon in their Christian worship (Bassler 1982).

Paul does, however, make it clear that utterances "in" (NIV *by*) the *Spirit of God* confess that *Jesus is Lord (Kyrios,* Rom 10:9; Eph 4:5; Phil 2:11). More than verbal agreement is intended by this baptismal confession. Jesus, the speaker confesses, is the One who now owns me as his purchased slave and is responsible for my care (Thistelton 2001:926). Contrariwise, those utterances that say, *Jesus be* (better "is") *cursed [anathema]* cannot arise out of the inspiration of the Holy Spirit.

12:3 *"Jesus be cursed" (anathema Iēsous)* has generated no fewer than twelve different interpretations. Most recently it has been explained as "Jesus grants a curse" against one's Christian enemy in the manner of the pagan curse formulas. This would enhance the status of the Christian by punishing rivals (Winter 2001:177-83).

While there is much discussion regarding this expression, I believe that the parallelism with the expression *Jesus is Lord* is most convincing and therefore it was a real expression, perhaps related to some Jewish appraisals of Jesus' death on a "tree" as evidence that he was cursed by God (cf. 2 Cor 5:16; Gal 3:13).

This christological test is absolutely necessary for today's church to remember in connection to any ministries of the Holy Spirit. "Those who affirm and continue to affirm in the Spirit that 'Jesus is Lord' are those to whom the Spirit distributes the gifts. The focus of the community is not the Spirit but the exalted Lord. A truly charismatic community, therefore, is not Spirit-centered but Christ-centered" (Williams 1990:328). Jesus is Lord, then, is the preeminent sign of the presence and authentic ministries of the Spirit.

The One Source of Variegated Manifestations of Grace (12:4-11)

Paul now turns to enumerating the multiple concrete manifestations of the Spirit, but in such a way that their source is shown emphatically to be the triune God himself. There is an interesting literary way the apostle does this. Three times in verses 4-6 he refers to the workings of the Spirit under three different words (*gifts, charisma; service, diakonia* [plural]; *working, energēma* [plural]). In each case the concrete ministry is attributed to a different Person of the Trinity (*Spirit, Lord* [Jesus], *God* [Father]), and finally to the one God, who *works all of them in all men.*

A minor question has to do with the precise sense of Paul's word translated in the NIV as *different kinds (diairesis;* v. 11). The NIV gives one sense of the word: diversity. The other sense of the word, however, may be preferable here: "division or distribution . . . apportionment" (Danker 2000:229). This would mean that Paul's emphasis is not on the diversity of the gifts (though he abundantly attests this) but on their source, unity and distribution in the one God's activity. Though the gifts' diversity is not Paul's main concern here, today a

---

While one should take seriously this suggestion, the parallelism with *Jesus is Lord* and its christological centrality would lead us to expect in the contrasting statement not a rebuke for status seeking but a denial of this lordship of Jesus (cf. 2 Cor 5:16).

greater emphasis on the multiplicity and diversity of the Spirit's ministry is needed in many churches, where the congregation's role in worship has been severely reduced to being spectators to the "dance of the clergy."

Continuing his emphasis on God's sovereign work as the source of these ministries, Paul indicates that Spirit manifestations are given to all the people of God *(to each one) for the common good (sympheron;* v. 7). More precisely the apostle states that every believer is given the *manifestation (phanerōsis)* or public display or "showing" of the Spirit. Perhaps we should not think of gifts as a permanent ability or capacity but of specific, public acts of the Spirit, which may be either spontaneous or prepared with previous reflection and which are energized by the Spirit on a particular occasion. Some manifestations, however, may lend themselves to repeated expressions that are more permanent characteristics of certain members of the church, such as apostles and teachers.

These showings of the Spirit are not to bring personal benefit or status to the individual but advantage to the whole community (the context indicates this, not the mere sense of the Greek word, which simply means "benefit" or "advantage"; 6:12; 7:33, 35). This advantage is the building up of the church community into the image of Christ (10:22-23; 14:3-4, 17). Here is Paul's second test (see 12:3) of the genuineness of the Spirit's activity among them, "where the *public manifestation* serves the *common advantage* of others, and not merely self-affirmation, self-fulfillment, or individual status" (Thiselton 2001:936).

In verses 8-11 he enumerates nine different specific manifestations of the Spirit, given to different individuals but all sovereignly distributed, originated and produced by the one Spirit. Each manifestation is merely mentioned, not explained or illustrated. Three additional ministries of the Spirit are mentioned later in the chapter (v. 28, apostle, helping, guidance). Only tongues and prophecy receive further discussion in chapter 14.

In addition to the twelve "gifts" listed here, there are four or five other ministries mentioned in Romans 12:6-8 (exhortation, giving, mercy, ruling, serving) and one more in Ephesians 4:11 (evangelist), making a total of possibly sixteen or seventeen different specific identifications in Paul. The fluidity of these lists may suggest that these manifestations are merely representative of a number of others.

The message (or "utterance") *of wisdom* most likely refers to the revelation of the wisdom of God centered in the cross of Christ, in contrast to the human "wisdom" of the Corinthians (1:17-22; 2:1-5; 3:19).

The message (or "utterance") *of knowledge* is difficult to distinguish from the message or utterance of wisdom. *Knowledge* was another watchword of the Corinthians (8:1). It may prove fruitless to try to identify this manifestation with any certainty, beyond pointing in the direction of knowledge about God's saving purposes in Jesus Christ and the gospel.

Faith (v. 9) cannot be "saving" faith, since all exercise this, but rather the faith that can "move mountains" (Mt 17:20). The phrase to *another* here should be read, "to a *different (heteros)* person." The Greek may suggest that Paul is contrasting this special faith manifestation to more ordinary expressions of faith manifested in all of God's people. It is tempting to see it as an attendant manifestation related to the ministries of wisdom and knowledge and to those that follow, healings and miracles; but this is conjecture. Closer perhaps is the idea that this faith is a special enablement of God in certain circumstances to have an "indomitable assurance that God can overcome any difficulties and meet any emergencies" (James Moffatt, quoted in Thiselton 2000:947).

Often—and appropriately—the nineteenth-century George Müller of Bristol, England, is cited as a person who manifested this ministry. Müller founded a large orphanage, where he fed, housed and otherwise cared for over two thousand orphans with no guaranteed income from any source. He trusted God daily for the milk, food and funds to care for the children.

Mrs. Charles Cowman wrote the following revealing story about Müller:

> I went to America some years ago with the captain of a steamer, who was a very devoted Christian. When off the coast of Newfoundland he said to me, "The last time I crossed here, five weeks ago, something happened which revolutionized the whole

of my Christian life. We had George Mueller of Bristol on board. I had been on the bridge twenty-four hours and never left it. George Mueller came to me, and said, 'Captain, I have come to tell you that I must be in Quebec Saturday afternoon.' 'It is impossible,' I said. 'Very well, if your ship cannot take me, God will find some other way. I have never broken an engagement for fifty-seven years. Let us go down into the chart-room and pray.'

"I looked at that man of God, and thought to myself, what lunatic asylum can that man have come from? I never heard of such a thing as this. 'Mr. Mueller,' I said, 'do you know how dense this fog is?' 'No,' he replied. 'My eye is not on the density of the fog, but on the living God, who controls every circumstance of my life.'

"He knelt down and prayed one of the most simple prayers, and when he had finished I was going to pray; but he put his hand on my shoulder, and told me not to pray. 'First, you do not believe He will answer; and second I believe He has, and there is no need whatever for you to pray about it.'

"I looked at him, and he said, 'Captain, I have known my Lord for fifty-seven years, and there has never been a single day that I have failed to get an audience with the King. Get up, Captain, and open the door, and you will find the fog gone.' I got up, and the fog was indeed gone. On Saturday afternoon, George Mueller was in Quebec for his engagement." (Cowman 1925:241-242)

Such a Spirit manifestation of faith encourages all of us by showing us God's work and also by providing a model to help our own trust in God to grow. Thus this gift ministers to the edification of the whole body of Christ.

That *gifts of healing* (v. 9) are mentioned also in verses 28 and 30 may indicate that either Paul or the Corinthians put emphasis on this evidence of grace. This is the only manifestation for which he uses the word *gifts (charismata)* to describe, perhaps to stress, the occasional, unexpected, undeserved nature of this working of the Spirit. The plural denotes "various kinds of healing, such as 'sudden' 'gradual' 'physical' 'mental' 'with medication' 'by direct sole divine agency'" (Thiselton 2001:948).

Three things should be noted. First, the indefinite plural indicates that "the gifts of healing are sovereignly bestowed upon some believers commensurate with the illnesses present, either in number or kind," and thus "denies the notion of elevation to the status of a singular healer for all illnesses" (Schatzmann 1987:37). Second, these gifts are for the benefit of the church community, and they are not to be demonstrations of power that raise the status of the individual through whom the Spirit ministers healing. Third, Scripture does not teach that healing is *now* included in the death of Christ, as are forgiveness and reconciliation. These latter benefits of the cross are universally accessible to every believer, while healing is not promised to all. Yet God does give us occasional, sovereignly bestowed gifts of healing in anticipation of the eventual redemption of the body and healing of all our illnesses included in Christ's saving work on the cross (Mt 8:17 [Is 53:4]; Rom 8:23; Rev 22:2).

We may expect God to heal in the above-mentioned ways as he sovereignly wills on certain occasions, but we have no promise or claim of universal healing now, regardless of the size of our faith. Our most fervent prayers for healing are not always granted. Even Paul left Trophimus sick at Miletus (2 Tim 4:20), and his own eye malady was not healed through prayer (2 Cor 12:8-9; Gal 4:13-15).

The term *miraculous powers* (v. 10) is better rendered as "effective acts of power" (*energēmata dynameōn*). The exact expression occurs only here (*dynameis* alone in v. 29), but similar combinations occur elsewhere referring to the workings of divine power: "I became a servant of this gospel by the gift of God's grace given me through the working [*energeian*] of his power [*dynamis*]" (Eph 3:7; cf. Eph 3:20). *Power (dynamis)* is frequently a manifestation of God's power, often referred to as a "miracle" (Mt 14:2, with "signs" and "wonders"; Rom 15:19; 2 Cor 12:12; Heb 2:4), yet not the same as "gifts of healings."

But what is a miracle? Is it any more a divine working than the other gifts or ministries of the Spirit? Are miracles workings of God after the pattern of Jesus' miracles—healings of the body, exorcisms of demon spirits, and nature miracles? We certainly should not use the word *miraculous* to elevate such divine acts over other, less spectacular forms of divine action.

The position of this Spirit manifestation, fifth in a list of nine, suggests it should not be given any special significance over and above the Spirit's less visible workings. "Deeds of power" can equally be signs of the cross, expressions of a cruciform life of self-sacrificing ministry to others. Unusual workings of power that impress us signally with the divine presence should not blind us to his everyday powerful and effective workings in less unusual ways. To what degree we can expect God's unusually visible workings of power in our midst today is debated among various Christian traditions (see further at 13:8-12).

Defining *prophecy* (12:10) presents an even greater challenge. Within the present context (chaps. 12-14), the claim that prophecy is the most important of the Spirit's manifestations is no overstatement. In chapter 14 this is because of its communicability and power of building up the Christian community. James D. G. Dunn comments on its indispensability: "Without it the community cannot exist as the body of Christ; it has been abandoned by God" (quoted by Schatzmann 1987:22). Almost all commentators agree that this operation of the Spirit is not ecstatic but rational and communicative speech. The noun "prophet" occurs some 144 times in the New Testament, fourteen times in Paul, five of which are in 1 Corinthians. The verb form "to prophesy" occurs twenty-five times in the New Testament, ten times in Paul (all in 1 Corinthians).

But there are three questions in dispute about this kind of communicative speech. (1) Is it spontaneous or a planned sermonlike message? (2) Do New Testament prophets foretell the future as well as bring words of warning, exhortation and hope, as the Old Testament prophets did? (3) What distinguishes *prophecy* speech in the New Testament from other forms of speech such as the sermon?

In the first place, there is a division among scholars as to whether prophecy speech is "spontaneous" (Schatzmann, Fee 1987, Turner, Dunn) or "pastoral teaching and preaching" (Hill, Thiselton). Siegfried Schatzmann says, "Prophecy refers to the function of communicating revelations from God as spontaneous utterance" (1987:21-22). On the other hand, quoting agreeably from Gerhard Friedrich in the *Theological Dictionary of the New Testament,* Thiselton concludes, "The prophet is a Spirit-endowed person 'whose preaching contains admonition and comfort, the call for repentance and promise' and who also counsels, as a pastor, and 'blames and praises.' That, we submit, may be legitimately called a ministry of pastoral teaching and instruction. . . . Christian prophets exercised a teaching ministry in the Church which included pastoral preaching" (2000:960).

In my opinion there is evidence supporting both of these views. While 1 Corinthians 14:29-31 seems to lean more in the direction of spontaneous "revelations" occurring during the service itself, 14:3 and 31 seem to recognize a teaching and doctrine function of the prophets. While all apostles are prophets as well, not all prophets are apostles. Paul was both—and "teacher" as well (Acts 13:1). Apostles, such as Paul, have authority over the prophets and teachers (14:37-38). Prophecy and teaching seem to overlap somewhat in function, since they both serve to instruct and edify the congregation, but they are not totally identical. Perhaps prophecy tends to occur in the present moment with exhortation, comfort, hope, rebuke and call for repentance, while teaching involves more explanation, in-depth understanding and clarification of the faith.

Second, does prophecy in the New Testament include foretelling as well as forthtelling or exhortation? Old Testament prophets seemed to do both. While some New Testament "prophets," such as Agabus, predicted events that would occur in the near future (Acts 21:10-14), and apostles addressed and warned of future apostasy (Acts 20:29; 2 Tim 3:1-5) as well as the Lord's return and future judgment (1 Thess 4:13—5:3), their chief focus seems to have been exhortation, teaching, warnings and hope.

Finally, in my judgment there seems to be no separate *form* of prophetic speech (such as ecstatic speech—uncontrolled emotional experience, rapture or trance) that would distinguish it from teaching or a sermon (so Aune, Grudem 1982, Thiselton). Content alone seems to distinguish prophecy from other forms of Spirit-inspired speech. There is no indication that Spirit-inspired prophecy in the New Testament comes in the speech form of God's speaking in the first person ("I") through the prophet; the book of Revelation seems to be the one exception. Contemporary so-called prophets who speak in the first person as if God were speaking, then, are highly questionable.

Distinguishing between spirits, placed between *prophecy* and *speak-*

ing in . . . tongues, is also difficult to identify. Two major interpretations have been advanced. First, some would see this ministry as one of distinguishing between good and bad spirits (Origen, Grudem 1982, Schatzmann) or between angelic and demonic spirits (Ellis 1978). The chief problem with this interpretation is that while some other New Testament authors do this (Mt 8:16; Acts 16:16; 1 Jn 4:1), Paul nowhere else uses the term *spirit* for evil spirits, with only one exception (1 Tim 4:1, "deceiving spirits and things taught by demons"). He uses "spirits" for human spirits (1 Cor 14:32; Gal 6:18), not for evil spirits.

Therefore, the more probable sense is distinguishing between manifestations of the divine Spirit and of merely human spirits. One who exercises this ministry discerns how the Spirit is working, whether certain manifestations promote the lived-out lordship of Christ as self-effacing, loving service, rather than self-serving status seeking or deceptive uses of Scripture "that would distort or imperil the heart of the gospel and God's strategy for mission" (Thiselton 2000:969). James's crucial discernment at the Jerusalem Council seems to exemplify such Spirit-directed discernment between the Judaizers' mistaken understanding and that of Barnabas and Paul (Acts 15:13-21). How the churches today need this Spirit-given ministry!

Speaking in different kinds of tongues . . . interpretation of tongues (1 Cor 12:10). Paul will say much more about these Spirit manifestations in chapter 14. Discussion here will focus primarily on the nature of "tongues" speech. There are at least five different plausible interpretations of this kind of speech.

1. Foreign languages unknown to the speaker (Bruce, Turner, Forbes, Gundry, also Cyril of Alexandria, Aquinas, Luther, Calvin). *Different kinds* (*genē,* "species"), then, would refer to a variety of languages that would require translation as the corresponding gift.

While this is a common view often based on the Pentecost phenomena of Acts 2:8—"How is it that each of us hears them in his own native language?"—the position fails to account for Paul's repeated emphasis in chapter 14 on the unintelligibility of tongues utterances

---

12:10 Some commentators have opted to explain *tongues* as the "language of angels," as in 13:1 (Fee 1987:598; also Barrett, Conzelmann [1975], Witherington [1995],

(14:2, 9, 16, 23). Acts 2 can easily be understood as a miracle of hearing rather than of speaking. If foreign languages were meant, why don't we find any missionary use of this gift reported in the New Testament documents or from the early post-New Testament church? It is possible that Acts 2 records a different phenomenon from tongues speaking elsewhere in Acts and in 1 Corinthians 12-14. Could this difference be included in the *different kinds of tongues (genē)* to which Paul refers here?

Extensive worldwide investigation of modern "tongues" phenomena has yielded no verifiable case of xenoglossolalia, tongues as unlearned foreign language. Additionally, this research has found no discernible structural language pattern in any of the hundreds of cases of "tongues" that were taped and analyzed (Samarin 1972). Critics would argue that such judgments of modern-day alleged expressions of "tongues," however, may not relate to the phenomena of Paul's day.

I heard the following story directly from the Rev. Ruolneikhum (Kuhma) Pakhuongte, president of the Free Churches of India. Once he was asked to preach the gospel to a small, unevangelized village in the Assam province of eastern India. When he arrived, he discovered that the local residents spoke only in a language that he did not know. There was no interpreter. Rather than return home, he was led by the Holy Spirit to preach to them for two hours in his own language. At the close of his message, he asked them to turn to Christ for salvation. To his amazement, the entire village responded to his invitation to receive Jesus as their Lord. Later he learned that they had all heard him speak in their own language during those two hours. Could this be a modern-day parallel to Acts 2, if we understand the Pentecost phenomenon as a miracle not of speech but of hearing? Incidentally, Kuhma said this has never happened in his ministry before or since.

2. Audible sounds, languagelike but not structured language (Samarin, Thiselton). This position holds that "tongues" expression in 1 Corinthians involved audible but inarticulate, unintelligible (until interpreted) Spirit-inspired utterances, arising from the depths of the heart

---

Ellis [1978], Dunn). If true, then for angels' speech to pass away at the parousia (13:8) would seem curious (Thiselton 2000:972-73).

and expressed evocatively but not in a frenzy or ecstatic trance. *Interpretation,* then, would be better rendered "to bring to articulate expression or *to put into words*" (Thiselton 2000:978). From a lexicographical and contextual standpoint, this view has much to commend it.

3. Liturgical, archaic or rhythmic phrases (D. Martin). This explanation sees "tongues" as poetic phrases, musical cadencies, quasi-dance motions, endlessly repeated words or phrases from ancient liturgical language (e.g., "hallelujah"). Such expressions could be status indicators that the more educated and socially elite could integrate in their expressions of joy and praise. While this could account for some forms of tongues at Corinth (as well as modern Pentecostal expression), it doesn't seem to fit 14:8-13, 21-25. Different forms *(kinds)* of tongues may have occurred.

4. Ecstatic speech (Tertullian, Morris 1985, H. W. House 1983, Boring 1992, L. T. Johnson 1992). "Ecstatic" means without understanding, out of one's mind, in a trance. If this interpretation involves trances where one loses all control, then such an expression cannot be what Paul has in mind, since he indicates that all genuine manifestations of the Spirit are subject to the control of the person through whom they are expressed (14:32).

5. Language of the unconscious released in "groans that words cannot express" (Rom 8:26; Theissen, Stendahl, Thiselton). "The specific work of the Holy Spirit in actualizing inarticulate yearnings directed toward God from the depths of the heart [the unconscious] of the believer in Romans 8:26-27 forms a retrospective summary from Paul's point of view of the phenomenon which occupies many verses in 1 Cor 12:10-14:40 but very few elsewhere in the NT" (Thiselton 2000:985). Tongues in this view, then, are audible expressions of the deep wells of the heart originated and articulated by the Spirit, and when interpreted by the same Spirit, they may become intelligible language to oneself and others.

This manifestation, as well as all the others in these chapters, are gender inclusive, as the ancient theologian Theodoret (d. 488) states: "These gifts were given to women as well as men, as the Acts of the Apostles makes plain" (in Bray 1999:122).

To sum up, tongues may take different forms and should not be restricted to only one form or type of audible expression. However, views 1 and 4 above have problems; the other options are preferable and probably within Paul's range of meaning. All seem to agree that (1) tongues edify only the speaker unless interpreted, and (2) were being used at Corinth as status symbols in their various "species."

Tongues in public (uninterpreted) can be divisive: since not all speak in tongues (12:3), they can become a badge of membership for a subgroup within the church. Paul's strategy, then, is to play them down (14:5) and to privatize them to the home (14:18-19), while not forbidding them in church if there is an interpreter (14:5, 39). He also prioritizes the manifestations of prophecy, teaching and the like on the basis of whether the ministry benefits others, in the pattern of Christ's self-sacrificial love (12:25-26; 13:1-13).

The *interpretation of tongues* (v. 10) means either translation of foreign languages or the articulation in human language of the Spirit's audible but inarticulate sighings from deep within the believer's heart (see above). I believe the evidence favors the latter understanding. The ideal interpreter would be the same person who utters tongues sounds (14:13). Alternately, another may bring to cognitive expression (or explain) what was uttered inarticulately, so that all (including the tongues speaker) may understand the utterance and be built up in their faith (14:5).

All these (v. 11) begins a summary of 12:4-10 that again emphasizes the One source, the Spirit, and his sovereign choice of what ministries are exercised and through whom (cf. v. 18). This divinely created diversity-unity dialectic ensures the significance of *each one* and at the same time the essential interdependence of each with all others. To this emphasis Paul now turns more specifically.

The Body of Christ Metaphor: The Functional Purpose of Gifts (12:12-31) Once before in this letter Paul clearly used the metaphor of the *body* to refer to the Christian community (10:17, "we who are many are one body"; possibly 6:15 also). Some two years later he used the same image briefly when writing to the Romans from Corinth (Rom 12:4-5). Later the body of Christ metaphor reappears in Ephesians

(1:23; 4:4, 12; 5:23, 30) and Colossians (1:18; 2:17; 3:15). The image does not appear elsewhere in Paul or the rest of the New Testament; it is apparently limited to Paul and thus could be understood as his own live metaphor for the Christian community. While we cannot be sure, his metaphor may have derived from his Damascus Road experience, when his persecution of Christians was described by the risen Lord quite amazingly:

"Saul, Saul, why do you persecute me?"

"Who are you, Lord?" Saul asked.

"I am Jesus, whom you are persecuting," he replied. (Acts 9:4-5)

By persecuting believers, Paul was persecuting Jesus.

Metaphorical use of the body and its limbs for political communities was not, however, unique to Paul. Plutarch and Epictetus (late first century) speak of the harmony, mutual interdependence, and mutual benefit of the eyes, ears, hands, and feet of the body (cf. 1 Cor 12:15-17; Thiselton 2000:992). Yet in these secular writings the political body is viewed as hierarchically constituted, with different stereotyped roles assigned by nature to different members. For example, the limbs (workers) are to remain active (no strikes!) so the belly (ruling class) can be fed, otherwise the whole body will die. Such use of the body image for high-status conservative ideological purposes is not Paul's point. What is the difference?

The Many-Parts-One-Body (12:12-27) First, Paul identifies the whole body with Christ: *so it is with Christ* (v. 12). Later he will identify the believers as *the body of Christ* (v. 27). Curiously, he does not call Christ the "head" of the body in this chapter (but see Eph 1:22-23; 4:15-16; 5:23; Col 2:19). This may alert us that Paul is here (1 Cor 12:12-30) using the body metaphor differently than in Ephesians and Colossians. Here the point is not the head-body metaphor but that many parts form one body.

In Paul's mind there is some sense in which the divinely constructed union (v. 13) of the many diverse parts—organically interrelated, interdependently, harmoniously and functionally one body—constitutes now through the Holy Spirit the reality of Christ's visible presence and activity in the world. It is important to note that it is the historical, empirical church of Christ in the world, not some ideal, invisible, heavenly model, that is the real *body of Christ* (vv. 12, 27).

As united to Christ in his incarnate reality the Church constitutes the sanctified community within which we may draw near to the Father through the Son and in the Spirit and share in the eternal life, light and love of God himself. That was surely the primary truth embedded in the mind and worship of the Catholic Church in the fourth century, and was rightly given precedence over all questions of external form, organization and structure. It was as they believed, the empirical Church that had been incorporated into Christ as his Body, then the real structure of the Church as lodged in Christ himself, and had to be lived out in space and time through union and communion with the risen, exalted and advent Lord whose kingdom will have no end. (Torrance 1995:153)

So the metaphor points to an ontological reality that Paul describes in the next verse.

Baptized by one Spirit so as to form *one body* (v. 13). Just what is this Spirit baptism? Early Pentecostal writers held that subsequent to salvation, the believer can experience the baptism of the Holy Spirit, and speaking in tongues as evidence of it, in a similar manner as the original apostles on the day of Pentecost (Acts 2). More recent Pentecostal scholars see this verse as referring to our receiving the Spirit when we become Christians (Fee 1987:605), and speaking in tongues may be one evidence among others (e.g., fruit of love, joy, peace) of this special baptism of the Spirit.

In response I would argue that baptism of the Spirit is the common experience of all Christians at the time that they receive Christ as Savior (Rom 8:9). First Corinthians 12:13 supports that conclusion by emphasizing that the total body of Christ experiences immersing (baptizing) in and infusion (drinking) of the Holy Spirit.

Jews or Greeks, slave or free shows that Paul is emphasizing a unity that is not merely a unity of diversity of gifts but is social and political in nature (cf. Gal 3:28). On the other hand, Pentecostal interpreters are correct to emphasize, in distinction to traditional interpretations, that in these images of immersing (baptism) and infusion (drinking) there is a strong suggestion of personal experience with God the Spirit. Many traditional interpretations of the passage gloss over this implication of the vivid imagery.

Clement of Alexandria (third century) captures the force of the divine activity and purpose of the Spirit's creative work in forming the church body: "You are all one in Christ Jesus. It is not that some are enlightened gnostics and others less perfect spirituals. Everyone, putting aside all carnal desires, is equal and spiritual before the Lord" (in Bray 1999:125). The next section expands this thought.

The theme in 1 Corinthians 12:14-27 is the many-parts-one-body idea. As noted above, in first-century pagan society the body image was used to quell political factions (Mitchell 1991:556-76; D. Martin 1995:39): as each person or group performed the hierarchically assigned roles given by nature (often class determined), then and only then would the whole body politic be preserved from chaos. This is not Paul's use of the metaphor in this section. Instead he reverses the standard use and argues that there is no hierarchy of important or elite versus unimportant persons in the body that is Christ's. All are important and necessary to the realization and functioning of the one body that God has put together, giving *greater honor to the parts that lacked it* (v. 24).

Schatzmann helpfully suggests that two basic principles crucial to the harmonious functioning of the body are set forth in verses 15-27 (1987:46-47). First, there is no room for inferiority complexes (vv. 15-20). Those who may feel that their contribution to the body is minor or negligible—*if the foot should say, "Because I am not a hand, I do not belong to the body"*—Paul quickly counters by reminding them that *it would not for that reason cease to be part of the body* (v. 15; see also vv. 16-20).

Just as it is absurd to think that the body is made up of only the more prominent parts, so is it to think that the body could function without its less prominent parts. Don't underestimate the importance of your grace ministry to the vitality and wholeness of the body of Christ! You are equal in importance to the body, even if you are not equal in prominence to some other members.

Second, there is no room for superiority complexes (vv. 21-26). *The eye cannot say to the hand, "I don't need you!"* Paul may well have addressed this to the tongues speakers, workers of mighty deeds and ministers of healings, who were tempted to view themselves as the really essential parts of the body, not needing the supposed lesser, unspectacular parts. They were wrong. They failed to recognize that the alleged *weaker* members were in reality *indispensable,* essential to the health of the whole body. Their attitude betrayed their misunderstanding of the sovereign grace source of their own ministries (v. 24), as well as their dependence on the other "parts" for their well-being.

A number of years ago I was invited to a special educator's Colorado Outward Bound rafting experience. Beginning at Steamboat Springs, Colorado, we traveled for ten days down the Green River for ninety miles in a six-person raft to the Dinosaur National Park in Utah. As we approached rapid after rapid, we rotated positions to see where we functioned best to help the whole raft make it through the rapids without spilling us all out into the cold mountain water. I thought I would be best as the steersman or captain in the rear directing the others. Quickly I found out that another raftmate, a not too obviously bright person, was the best at guiding us through the rapids. I ended up in the power-turning position in the front right side of the raft. When we were all paddling in our best positions we found we could handle even the scariest of the rapids without being overturned. What a valuable lesson I learned about functioning in the body of Christ according to God's plan.

The *weaker* (read "less endowed with power or status"), the *less honorable* (read "less presentable"), the . . . *unpresentable* (read "unpresentable private parts") in our bodies are *indispensable,* worthy of *special honor* and *treated with special modesty* (by covering, vv. 22-23). These verses can be obscure unless we realize Paul is referring to the bodily parts that have to do with procreation (male organ and female vagina) and nurture (female breasts). These parts, though treated with modesty and covered, are in reality *indispensable,* while the more dispensable parts of the body (such as limbs and hands) we often display openly.

Jürgen Moltmann even suggests that physically and mentally challenged persons present "a gift of the Spirit" to the church through their offering of "weakness":

> [Paul] expects that in the community of Christ there will be strong
> and weak, educated and uneducated, people who are good to
> look at and the plain. No one is useless and of no value. No one

can be dispensed with. So the weak, uneducated and ugly have their own special charisma in the community of Christ's people. Why? *All* will be made like in form to the crucified Christ, because the crucified Christ has assumed not just humanity but also the misery of humanity, in order to heal it. . . . For that reason there is no good charitable ministry by the non-disabled to the disabled unless this first of all recognizes and accepts the charitable ministry of the disabled to the non-disabled. Congregations without disabled members are—to put it bluntly—disabled congregations. (1997:67-68)

Those whom the church likes to put 'on display' as our 'best' people (whether because of their supposed wisdom and knowledge, or more visible gifts of the Spirit such as tongues or 'mighty works') are far from being the essence of the church. . . . *On the contrary* [v. 22] . . . is expounded by means of an unexpected twist in the standard political rhetoric of the body. (Thiselton 2000:1009)

Contemporary churches and Christian organizations and institutions need to pay close attention to this teaching of Paul. Often the tendency is to showcase the most "successful" Christians who have won achievement awards, excelled in gaining wealth, or risen to prominent positions in government, entertainment or book publishing. These members often are appointed as church leaders or college trustees. Instead, without ignoring these "parts," we should look for those who have less visibility yet have displayed unusual faithfulness, especially through suffering and loss, who have given away great wealth, are self-effacing, have showed restraint in material possessions, exhibited downward mobility in seeking to serve Christ, and are filled with the fruit of the Spirit despite relative obscurity. These and others like them should be our main showcase examples in the church.

"For Paul, therefore, the unity of the body was only guaranteed when members acknowledged the need for diversity of function, expressed in interdependence. . . . Oscar Cullmann has noted this aspect and reasoned: 'Where the Holy Spirit is at work, there exists no unity without multiplicity and no multiplicity without unity . . . ; he maintains their individuality while creating this unity—this is the paradox of the Holy Spirit in the New Testament'" (Schatzmann 1987:47, citing Cullman 1972:812).

With this marked twist in his use of the conventional political-body metaphor, Paul has prepared us for a further penetrating insight into the nature of the church, Christ's body. In verses 24-26 he again appeals to the work of God himself, who has put the body together (*synkerannymi*, "blend," "unite," "compose"), having given *greater honor to the parts that lacked it* for the purpose *that there should be no division* (or split; see 1:10), *but that its parts should have equal concern for each other.* God has likewise fashioned, blended, composed his own Son's body, the church, so that the various persons (parts) with their Spirit ministries each receive the concerned attention needed, first by God himself and then by other members, so that there will be no splits in the church body caused by an obsession with competitive groups or status seeking.

This purposed attention or equal care for one another is further explained as *If one part suffers, every part suffers with it; if one part is honored, every part rejoices with it* (v. 26). Our natural bodily parts are so blended that when part suffers pain, the whole body suffers with it.

Recently I suffered a gouge in the knuckle of my pinkie finger on the right hand. It seemed as if everything I tried to do after involved my hitting this sore knuckle, which sent pain through my whole body. When it finally healed, I was very happy. I had not realized how important that little finger was until it was hurt. Likewise to give honor to, say, the legs of a runner or the hands of a surgeon brings praise to the whole person. When the ministries of the Spirit are used as God intended, the whole church rejoices, and when one member misuses their gift for selfish ends, the whole church suffers. The more obvious sense of empathy and congratulation is also likely in Paul's meaning, as Augustine exhorts, "Far be it from us to refuse to hear what is bitter and sad to those whom we love. It is not possible for one member to suffer without the other members suffering with it" (in Bray 1999:128).

Now you are the body of Christ, and each of you is a part of it (v. 27) seems to wonderfully summarize the preceding section (vv. 12-26), although it often is taken as the introductory statement of the final section on the body metaphor for the church (vv. 28-30).

Paul's Prioritized List of the Ministries of the Spirit (12:28-30) Thiselton calls this section "an exegetical and lexical minefield." *God has placed in the church first of all apostles, second prophets, third teachers* (v. 28). Does *first . . . second . . . third* mean first, second, third in order of importance (at least for the first three), or is this simply a list with no attempt to rank the ministries? Charles Talbert espouses the second view: "If Paul were ranking gifts here, he would be involved in the very problem he is seeking to combat in the Corinthians' behavior. He would be saying that he, because of his apostleship, out-ranked them because they were not apostles. This kind of one-upmanship is the very thing that Paul wants to avoid" (1987:85; also Fee 1987:619; Hays 1997:217; Witherington 1995:261).

On the other hand there are those who argue that Paul is establishing a hierarchy of ministries beginning with the highly important "proclamation gifts" of apostle, prophet and teacher and ending up with tongues as the least important (Thiselton 2000:1015; Bruce 1971:122; Chrysostom in Bray 1999:129). What should we say?

There seems to be truth in both positions. The numbering does give the first three some historical priority in the founding of the local churches: apostles bring the message of the gospel, prophets and teachers establish and build up the congregation (Fee 1987:620). By mentioning the apostles first, Paul may be suggesting his authority over the local Corinthian prophets (see 14:37). There is no warrant for seeing these three ministries as "offices" in the church with some kind of ecclesial authority, while the other ministries are lay services. Beyond the first three, however, there does not seem to be any specific order of importance. Tongues are mentioned last because this was the problem in the Corinthian church, not because of their lesser importance, as long as they were interpreted (14:5; Fee 1987:619).

In this list Paul mentions several ministries of the Spirit not covered in 12:8-10. For the other gifts mentioned in verses 28-30, see comment on 12:4-11.

Apostles (v. 28) means "those who are sent forth"; the word refers to a narrow group, but wider than merely the original Twelve, who witnessed Jesus' death and resurrection and carried the message of Christ out from Jerusalem, establishing and teaching new churches in the

Christian faith (1:1; 9:5; 15:7; Acts 14:14; Rom 16:7; Gal 1:17, 19; Phil 2:25). These witnesses also participated in Christ's weakness and the transforming power of his resurrection (Thiselton 2000:66). In the New Testament the original apostles of Jesus, plus Paul (perhaps also the brothers of the Lord; 1 Cor 9:5), seem to have an authority derived directly from Christ to command and to teach the gospel that other apostles do not share (1 Cor 9:1; 14:37; 2 Pet 3:2). Further, this authority does not seem to be transmitted to others—even to those who were their close associates, such as Barnabas.

Do we have apostles today? Certainly not in the sense of the original Twelve and Paul. They laid the foundation of the church once for all, with Christ as the chief cornerstone (Eph 2:20). But in the broader sense, today there are apostles, charismatically empowered by the Spirit to witness the message of Christ and to live out an identification with the weaknesses of Christ before peoples who formerly had not heard. This may take many forms, including, but not limited to, missionary and church-planting efforts.

However, there is nothing here or elsewhere in the New Testament that would justify the elaborate structure of apostolic succession, including the accompanying "sacrament of holy orders," found in some Christian faith traditions. These were later developments in church polity and must be judged as to whether they are compatible with or contradictory to the patterns found in the New Testament itself.

Teachers (v. 28): who or what ministry do these have, and how does this expression of the Spirit differ from prophecy and apostleship? Further, does teaching involve spontaneity or reasoned reflection or both? It is not difficult to find defenders on both sides of the second question (spontaneous or reasoned). Perhaps it is safe to include both types of teaching as valid expressions of the Spirit's ministry.

But how do we distinguish a prophet from an apostle from a teacher? Most of the attempted explanations fail ultimately for lack of evidence. Perhaps the best suggestion to date is that of Thiselton, who utilizes the speech-act theory of J. L. Austin and John Searle. After stating that the difference between a prophet and a teacher is not spontaneous speech (prophet) versus speech that is the result of reflection (teacher), Thiselton says, "Prophets *perform speech-acts of announcement, proclama-*

tion, judgment, challenge, comfort, support, encouragement, whereas Teachers *perform speech-acts of transmission, communicative explanation, interpretation of texts, establishment of creeds, exposition of meaning and implication, and, more cognitive, less temporally applied communicative acts.*" The ministry of the teacher forms the foundation on which "*the pastoral and situational* speech-acts of prophets can have their effect" (2000:1017). This explanation is attractive as long as it does not force a spontaneous versus reason/reflection type of speech onto either the prophet or the teacher ministries.

Helping (v. 28) is *antilēmpsis* (plural) and means "help, assistance, reciprocity"; it occurs only here in the New Testament but numerous times in the Greek Old Testament (and Apocrypha), with the frequent sense of "divine aid or assistance." This ministry of the Spirit should neither be limited to nor exclude official administrative aid to a church or organization. Rendering help to individuals in the believing community is also likely in view. If 13:1-3 is any guide to the gifts in 12, then the gift of *helping* "may be dramatized in two actions, rendering oneself destitute to help another, or the acceptance of a supremely painful death in a great cause" (Murphy-O'Connor 1979:124). How encouraging it is to see brothers and sisters who have substance, knowledge and skills step up and quietly come alongside with help for those who have various needs.

Gifts of administration (v. 28) is *kybernēsis* (also plural), a term for "shipmaster, captain, steersman, pilot, guidance" (Acts 27:11; Rev 18:17; LXX of Prov 1:5; 11:14; 24:6). Interestingly, the NIV rendered this ministry administration, but the TNIV altered it to "guidance." Thiselton argues for "ability to formulate strategies," especially "through the choppy waters of strife and status seeking within and potential persecutions without" (2000:1022). This work of the Spirit through individuals who can steer the ship of the church through troubled waters is sorely needed in today's church.

Finally, Paul returns to his emphasis on the body as made up of not a few prominent parts but a multiplicity of parts (1 Cor 12:29-30). In a series of seven rhetorical questions, each in the Greek expecting a negative answer, Paul indicates that not only are the gifts diverse but not all Christians are recipients of all the Spirit's ministries. *Are all apostles?*

No. *Are all prophets?* No. *Are all teachers?* No. *Do all work miracles?* No. *Do all have gifts of healing?* No. *Do all speak in tongues?* No. *Do all interpret?* No. This should settle any claim that any one of these Spirit manifestations is required evidence of Christian spirituality for all Spirit-filled (or baptized) believers.

But eagerly desire the greater gifts (v. 31) is a transitional sentence that raises one or two questions. The grammatical form Paul uses can mean either an imperative command, as in the NIV, or an indicative statement, "Now you are eagerly desiring the greater gifts." Only the context can help us decide between the two readings. Those who support the indicative (Talbert 1987:85-86) argue that Paul would not exhort the Corinthians to strive for love as the higher gift in the following verses (13:1-13). Love is not a gift of the Spirit but a fruit of the Spirit. Second, in chapter 12 Paul has been arguing against their coveting of the so-called higher gifts. Now he is simply stating the sad state of affairs at Corinth as a mild rebuke. This could be paraphrased as "But you are eagerly desiring the greater gifts of tongues and miracles."

On the other hand, those who argue that the imperative is what Paul intended (Thiselton 2000:1024-25; Carson 1987:56-57) point to 14:1, where he uses the very same expression; therefore, they say, it must be understood as an imperative. Further, the word for *eagerly desire (zeloō)* need not mean "to strive," and *greater gifts* is redefined by Paul to be prophecy (14:1), not the Corinthians' tongues.

The most excellent way (12:31, or "a far better way," Danker 2000:1032): yes, there is even a greater way than enthuasiasm over the most excellent gifts of the Spirit. Paul will expound on that way before he continues with his case against the unwarranted prominence the Corinthians have given to tongues speaking in their meetings (chap. 14). That "way beyond measure" (Williams 1990:343) is not intended to exclude the manifestations of the Spirit (chap. 12), even tongues speaking (cf. 14:39); it is the superlative and indispensable way in which all the gifts are to be ministered.

The Greatest of These Is Love (13:1-13) This chapter has been called the "greatest, strongest, deepest thing Paul ever wrote" (Adolf von Harnack 1908:I.148). Ralph P. Martin suggests that it is "in a class by itself in Pauline literature. Chapter 13 is poetic in its style and carries all the marks of a lyrical composition . . . a 'hymn of love,' or better, an *aretology* (i.e., poetic rhapsody composed in praise of a deity or some attribute regarded as divine) dedicated to *agape*" (1984:42-43). It has been perceptively noted that here the apostle is "hardly writing as an apostle. He is scarcely teaching or preaching at this point. He sings" (Ruler 1958:7). The language of 1 Corinthians 13 has found a way into the church's marriage liturgy, sermons, hymns and every Christian's heart as the most profound description of the kind of love expressed through Jesus Christ toward us as well in the life of his servant, Paul. I can myself recall numerous times when a bride and groom asked to have verses 4-8 read or recited at their wedding ceremony.

But in the larger secular culture as well, persons without any Christian commitment often claim that the only thing that really counts in life is to show love to others. Lyrics from the popular musical *Showboat* say,

Fish gotta swim, birds gotta fly,

I've got to love one man till I die.

Can't help lovin' that man of mine.

John Stott has asked, "What are we made for?" He answers, "As fish are made for water, humans are made for love." In the words of a sixteenth-century Catholic poet, "Not when I breathe but when I love, I live."

This general use of the chapter to point to love as the very essence of life should not obscure, as it mostly has, the more particular application of this "hymn of love" to specific problems facing the Corinthian church. Recent studies of the passage have not only shown the authenticity and integrity of the poem as Paul's own work but have also persuasively demonstrated its appropriateness to the Corinthian problems addressed throughout the epistle, and in particular to issues of the gifts of the Spirit, including tongues (see Thiselton 2000:1027-30).

Love, distinctly Christian love, is inseparable from the revelation and acts of the triune God, centered in the coming, life, sufferings, teachings, ministry, death, resurrection and ascension of Jesus Christ. Christian love, then, takes on the shape of the Christ story and becomes the *sine qua non* of authentic Christian existence in the world. It is therefore christological, cruciform (cross-shaped) and communal in nature.

The preeminent sign that the Spirit of God is present and freely operating is love within the Christian community and through it to the world (Rom 5:5; Gal 5:22). This love is above all else zealously concerned with the interests and welfare of the other. Going beyond mere concern, this love identifies with the other, taking up the interests and the concerns of the neighbor and making them one's own. This is precisely what God's love expressed through Jesus Christ to us has modeled (see Eph 5:25-27; Phil 2:5). Paul's great hymn of love calls for this very understanding of the importance, characteristics and function of love in the Christian community.

Authentic love is gravely needed today as Christians relate to and seek to respect those of different Christian faith traditions. While not ignoring differences, and while in appropriate contexts debating those differences, this love finds ways to show the actions mentioned in verses 4-7, both avoiding wrong expressions (eight negatives) and doing positive deeds, especially toward those who differ from us most (Catholic and Orthodox toward Protestants, evangelicals to Catholics and Orthodox as well as other evangelicals who are more progressive or more conservative).

While it is important to have as much of our theology "right" as we can, it is more important to consistently show the love that this chapter describes.

Today we evangelicals face a crisis of love. Issues of who are the true conservatives, who is more faithful to Scripture's authority, who has capitulated more to cultural trends, who has the right view of God, and so on, appear on every front. Some individuals and organizations have taken it upon themselves to proclaim for other evangelicals the "right" view on a wide variety of issues with scarcely a trace of authentic Christian love—love as Paul describes in detail in this chapter—being expressed toward those who differ.

What has gone wrong? Surely Paul lays bare the soul of genuine Christianity for the Corinthians in this song of divine love. For Paul, the moral issue—love—must always take precedence over Christians' correctness and superiority of knowledge or skills. In what is probably the greatest of all expositions on this chapter, Jonathan Edwards in 1765 urges, "Be exhorted, then, as the great thing, to cherish sincere love or

Christian charity in the heart. It is that which you must have; and there is nothing that will help your case without it. Without it, all will, in some respect, but tend to deepen your condemnation, and to sink you to but lower depths in the world of despair. . . . Charity or Christian love, which is here spoken of, is the summary of the Christian spirit" (Edwards 1989:184).

We do well, especially at this moment in the history of Christianity, to return often to and drink deeply from this well of God's heart. Nothing less than the credibility of Christian existence is at stake. Not just the means, love is also the end of all Christian living now and in the life to come.

The structure of the poem is tripartite. Part one (13:1-3) contains three highly personal conditional assertions in the pattern, "If I speak [have] . . . but do not have love, I am . . ." In each case there is an allusion to one or more of the manifestations of the Spirit mentioned in chapter 12 (Murphy-O'Connor 1979:123). The content has been summarized as "the preeminence of love" or "the superiority of love." While true, these do not go quite far enough. Paul is really asserting the greatness and indispensability of Christian love to authentic human existence in community.

Part two (13:4-7) of Paul's song in praise of love tells us what this love does and what it does not do, with terms describing virtuous kinds of actions (acts kindly, shows patience, is not angered, etc.) rather than specific deeds. Love is known by what it does, not by abstractions. Jesus' own actions hold up a mirror to test the authenticity of our love (R. Martin 1984:46). Each action/quality can be related back to the Corinthians' factionalism and the issues related to the Spirit's manifestations (chaps. 12 and 14). Love, not "knowledge" (8:1), creates an authentic, harmonious Christian community that promotes the upbuilding of each part of Christ's body.

Part three (13:8-13) turns to the permanence of love. The present age of the Spirit's manifestations of knowledge and mysteries is contrasted with the age to come, when these incomplete understandings will be replaced with full knowledge. Paul uses three illustrations from his own life to bring home this contrast between the incomplete experiences of the present and the fullness of the age to come: childhood versus adulthood (v. 11), seeing in a mirror versus face-to-face seeing, and knowing bits and parts of something versus knowing completely and fully, as God now knows us (v. 12).

The chapter ends on an unexpected note as Paul compares three great present Christian realities—faith, hope and love—and concludes that the greatest of them is love. This trilogy of Christian virtues appears elsewhere in Paul's writings, perhaps indicating that it is part of the Christian tradition that he strongly espouses:

> We continually remember before our God and Father your work produced by faith, your labor prompted by love, and your endurance inspired by hope in our Lord Jesus Christ. (1 Thess 1:3)

> But since we belong to the day, let us be sober, putting on faith and love as a breastplate, and the hope of salvation as a helmet. (1 Thess 5:8)

> We always thank God, the Father of our Lord Jesus Christ, when we pray for you, because we have heard of your faith in Christ Jesus and of the love you have for all the saints—the faith and love that spring from the hope that is stored up for you in heaven. (Col 1:3)

Yet love exceeds the other two, because love binds all else together and remains into eternity, whereas faith and hope will be turned into sight at the resurrection (Rom 8:24-25; 2 Cor 5:7).

The Greatness and Absolute Necessity of Love (13:1-3) I remember the first time I tried to bake a cake. I carefully measured and then blended the recipe's stated ingredients, poured the mix into the right size pan, set the oven temperature and timer, and placed the pan in the oven to bake for forty-five minutes. Afterward I took it out and the cake looked like a pancake! Why? I had forgotten to put the baking powder into the flour. Without baking powder, no cake. Without the practice of Christian love, Christianity fails.

Paul's first conditional thesis, *If I speak in the tongues of men and of angels* (v. 1), alludes to the manifestation of tongues inspired by the Spirit (12:10; 14:1-40). "Tongues of angels" may be the Corinthians' term for some kinds of tongues manifestations, but that does not seem to be Paul's view. In any case this obscure reference should not be made the focus of any theory or practice about "tongues," as did Edward Irving in the early nineteenth century. Irving's theory was that foreign language tongues that were unknown to the speaker were the "tongues of men," while those utterances that could not be paralleled in any known human language were the "tongues of angels" (Knox 1950:552-53). That tongues were a highly prized Spirit manifestation among the Corinthians is clearly evidenced by the lengthy attention Paul gives to correcting their abuses in chapter 14. Yet not even this highly prized gift, if it is not manifested with Christian love, can produce authentic Christlike character.

A resounding gong or a clanging cymbal: the identification of these musical instruments is generally not understood. The first term is *chalkos ēchōn;* actually there is no "gong'" in the phrase. The older KJV is closer to the correct translation, "sounding brass." Paul may be thinking of the resonating jars lined up on a stage to project the voices of actors and music (Thiselton 2000:1036, citing W. W. Kline 1986). The image is of endlessly reverberating resonance that has no musical pitch.

Clanging cymbal (kymbalon alalazon) is better translated "loud sounding crotol." This instrument is not a cymbal as we use the term but a thick metal plate, hit directly or struck with a mallet and having a distinct musical pitch. The crotol is thousands of years old, while the modern cymbal is of Turkish origin. The two images do not suggest a majestic sound but intrusive, invasive, self-important noises that disturb rather than please the senses. Without love (concern for the other), great eloquence (see 1:17; 2:1-5) produces only prideful cacophony in the body rather than edification.

Paul's second conditional thesis (v. 2) relates to achievement or status through exercise of *the gift of prophecy,* understanding of *all mysteries* (through tongues, 14:2?) and *knowledge* (8:1) or the manifestation of unusual *faith* (12:9). *That can move mountains* is a Jewish proverb for something that is impossible (R. Martin 1984:44; cf. Mt 17:20; Mk 11:22-25) or merely difficult (Thiselton 2000:1041, citing Morna Hooker). Even great achievements of eloquent speech, intellectual brilliance and amazing displays of spiritual faith, if unaccompanied with *love* (identification with other's needs), render us inauthentic, merely professing Christians—not simply "useless" but *nothing* (literally "nothing I am") or "nonexistent."

Christian being is constituted in love for others, and without love there is no authentic Christian being. Jonathan Edwards again strikes the correct sense: "All the fruit of the Spirit, upon which we are to lay weight as evidential of grace, is summed up in charity or Christian love, because this is the sum of all grace" (Jonathan Edwards 1989:169). It is not that the gifts are unimportant, but they bear fruit only where love attends them and is their driving force.

The final conditional thesis (v. 3) is actually twofold and takes us into the areas of philanthropy and self-sacrifice. Paul's thesis is that there may be great performances of outward philanthropic expression toward the poor that, lacking deep sincere love, result in no benefit (growth). *If I give all I possess* is literally "If I distribute bit by bit (like pieces of food) everything I own." Paul commends the gift of "helping" (12:28) and here dramatizes it with the act of making oneself destitute for the sake of the poor. Yet "the ideal of Christian charity is not to treat others *as if* they were one's best friends, but to *be* to them as life-giving as God is to us in Christ" (Murphy-O'Connor 1979:124). Motive seems central here (cf. Acts 5:1-11; 1 Jn 3:17-18). The early disciples left all to follow Jesus and commended others who did so (Acts 4:36-37; Gal 2:10). Yet Paul stresses that "nothing we can do can make up for the want of that which is the sum of all that God requires" (Edwards 1989:180).

Surrender my body to the flames presents us with an exegetical and textual problem. The traditional rendering (RSV, NIV, ESV) "to be burned" follows one textual tradition that reads the verb as *kauthēsomai* ("burn"). Some recent translations, however, have followed earlier Greek manuscripts that read *kauchēsōmai* ("exult," "boast," "take pride in," "glory"; NRSV, NLT). The TNIV reads "give over my body to hardship, that I may boast." Modern commentators are divided as to whether they prefer the reading "burn" (Bruce, Barrett, Snyder) or "boast" (Thiselton, Fee).

The lack of any historical evidence that immolation was a form of either punishment or protest in the Greco-Roman world (though it was earlier in Babylon, Dan 3:28) could lean us slightly toward the NRSV and TNIV rendering. But we would need to understand *boast* not to have the negative sense of the word but the positive use, "to exult, to glory" (cf. 2 Cor 10:13, 18, 21; 12:10). On the other hand, the reading "to boast" "reflects a later period when pride in martyrdom might have occurred" (Snyder 1991:175). The reader will need to decide which of these alternatives best fits the context and the way Paul is arguing. In any event, the emphasis is on extreme acts of self-denial in hardships and sufferings. Without love even these great accomplishments of self-expending suffering add nothing to our growth in Christian being or holiness!

Close to the time I wrote this, the whole world waited to learn of the fate of two American missionaries to the Philippines, Gracia and Martin Burnham, who were taken hostage by a radical Muslim group while they were on a holiday celebrating their eighteenth wedding anniversary. After a fifteen-year-old Filipina who was with the Burnhams was released, she recounted how she would have never survived without the loving support of Gracia, who treated her as a daughter. The girl also reported that over time Gracia had also befriended her captors, who later killed her husband.

With the examples of verses 1-3, Paul makes his point very clear. No quantity of rhetorical (speaking) skills or spiritual expressions, even of deep mysteries and divine revelations, or spectacular philanthropy or heroic acts of bodily deprivation, hardship, and expenditure of life, as good as these things may be, have any value before God unless Christian love is their motivation, accompaniment and goal. Love is what must take center stage in the Christian community. If it does not, which is often the case, nothing else matters! But just how do we distinguish authentic Christian love from other types of love in human relations? Paul now turns to this question in his poem of love.

Recognizing Authentic Christian Love (13:4-7) How often I have worked to clean a window until I thought it was pretty clean, only to discover multiple streaks across it when direct sunlight streamed through. Paul's description of the kind of Christian love he has in mind is like the direct light of the sun (and the Son) shining

13:4 Some of the classic biblical and theological treatments of Christian love include Augustine, Jonathan Edwards (1989), Anders Nygren (1969), C. S. Lewis (1988),

through our social relations, exposing the streaks of our imperfect attempts to follow the One who said, "This is my body for you."

Because Paul uses the word *agapē* ("love") throughout, many have tried to argue that this Greek word has a particular theological content as opposed to other such words for love, such as, *eros, philia* and *storgē*. These discussions, while not without value, are misleading, because authentic Christian love may be referred to by any of these words. The theological meaning of a word is not intrinsic to the word itself but attributed through its use in different contexts.

Agapē is used elsewhere in the New Testament to describe the love crooks have for one another—hardly the same kind of love that Paul is here commending to the Corinthians (cf. Mt 5:46; Lk 6:32). A compound of *philia* is used by Peter to denote the proper kind of love among Christians, along with *agapē* (1 Pet 1:22). Actually the noun *agapē* is relatively rare outside the New Testament; the verb *(agapaō)* is more frequent, especially in the LXX (cf. 2 Sam 13:15). In building a theological understanding of love in the New Testament, what we want to do is to derive the meaning and content of the word from its specific usage here and elsewhere and then combine these senses with the meaning of the other Greek words for love.

The picture we see emerging is that authentic Christian love represents the power of the new age stamping us with the life of heaven that has come into our world preeminently in the incarnation, life, sufferings, death, resurrection and ascension of Christ, together with the Holy Spirit's mission. Christian love is God's love as it is embodied in the story of Jesus and the Spirit. This love shows itself in habitual acts of concern, caring and respect for the welfare of others, causing us to identify with the other by making their interests our own interests (Brümmer 1993:165). This love is unapologetically christological and cruciform. "It is love alone that triumphs" (Barth 1958:824).

Paul will tell us seven things that Christian love chooses to do and eight things that it refuses to do, in the pattern two positives, eight negatives, five positives (vv. 4-7). Paul chooses to use *verbs* to describe

Lewis Smedes (1978), Vincent Brümmer (1993) and Gene Outka (1972).

these positive and negative character-actions, though the translations often obscure this (literal renderings would read "exercises patience," "shows kindness," etc.). The emphasis is not so much that love is the static quality of kindness or patience but that Christian love repeatedly *exercises* kindness and patience. These habitual practices form the Christian character or virtues that in turn transform us into persons and communities that embody Christian love as their fundamental disposition, attitude and expression.

Love is patient (*makrothymei,* literally "far from wrath and anger," or "long temper") is the first of two things that love does habitually. The two qualities are joined together (in noun form) as part of the "fruit of the Spirit" (Gal 5:22). Love waits patiently on others and circumstances rather than getting angry and acting prematurely without due regard for the interests of others. Love expressed in patience calms quarrels among believers at Corinth and promotes unity rather than factions (Prov 15:18; Eph 4:2-3). "Warn those who are idle and disruptive, encourage the disheartened, help the weak, be patient with everyone" (1 Thess 5:14 TNIV).

Patience is exercised toward us by God (Rom 2:4; 1 Pet 3:20; 2 Pet 3:9, 15). He is "slow to anger" (Num 14:18; Ps 25:6-10) in his dealings with his people (cf. Jas 5:7-11). Love inspires and constrains us to be patient with others as we remember how patient God must repeatedly be with us.

Love is kind (*chrēsteuetai,* "shows undeserved generosity"). Like patience, this expression of love is shown toward us in Christ by God (Eph 2:7; Tit 3:4). This action-virtue is a natural partner, offering a positive counterpart to patience by actively seeking the good of those who may be irritants to us and the community. Thus it is linked to compassion and forgiveness of others in Ephesians 4:32, "Be kind and compassionate to one another, forgiving each other, just as in Christ God has forgiven you." This kindness is also to be extended to those who have made themselves our enemies, after the pattern of God's kindness to ungrateful and wicked enemies (Lk 6:35).

Kindness can break cycles of passion, resentment, anger, violence and vengeful retaliation. The practice of showing kindness even to the wicked and the ungrateful should not be thought to be limited to interpersonal relations. Groups and national entities, through their leaders, can also act in kindness to break destructive, fruitless cycles of violence.

It [love] does not envy begins the list of eight actions that are incompatible with this kind of love. Envy or jealousy reflects zeal for one's self-advancement rather than the community's growth. The word *(zēloō)* includes the idea of burning or boiling with jealousy. Paul's earlier connection of jealousy with "quarreling" and with factions following certain preachers above others is evidence of the seepage into the church of the non-Christian culture (3:1-4; Gal 5:20), showing how much genuine love had eluded them.

Envy is also associated with resentment toward others (perhaps first toward God?) for what they are or have that we are not or have not attained or been given. Envy always involves the comparative *-er,* better, brighter, prettier, richer, stronger, wiser, or the adverb *more*—more skilled, more competent, more successful, more disciplined, more mature, more cultured, more spiritual.

It [love] does not boast, it is not proud names the second and third actions incompatible with love. At first sight these two types of action seem to be the same or at least similar. The first *(perpereuetai)* is a bragging action ("I don't need you!" 12:21). The second *(physioutai)* involves having inflated thoughts of one's self-importance and seeking attention in the manner of children who, untouched by life's sufferings, lack humility (cf. 4:6-13; 5:1-2). "The opposite of love is the thoughtlessness of 'all things are permissible'" (Thiselton 2000:1049, quoting Ceslas Spicq).

It [love] is not rude (v. 5; TNIV "does not dishonor others") describes the fourth action opposite to love. The verb is *aschēmonē,* "to act ill mannered, to display improper or rude conduct" (contrary to requirements of propriety and good order). The verb occurs only here and in 7:36; the adjective in 12:23. Its opposite *(euschēmonōs)* occurs in 14:40; compare "presentable parts" *(euschēmōn)* in 12:24.

Often (if not always) the word has sexual connotations (Winter 1998:78-80). Some translations capture this; the KJV has "does not behave indecently." Love is not insensitive to improper sexual overtones of our words and actions as we relate to others in the Christian community. Standards of propriety may vary from one culture to another, but the moral requirement that love imposes, to respect what is sexually appropriate, is constant.

It [love] is not self-seeking (literally "seeks not her own things") points to the fifth negative action that nullifies authentic Christian love. This is one of my own most pressing, repeated impediments to acting lovingly. My immediate intentions and dispositions, trained altogether too much by the surrounding secular culture, push me to consider not the other's but my own interests first. After reflection I see my failure, but the action has already been done.

When my children were younger, I regularly took them to the bowling alley on Saturday afternoons. One day soon after arriving we were looking for bowling balls to use from the racks. One of my daughters had selected a ball and was about to place it on the ball return pedestal, when another young girl came up to her and said, "That's *my* ball you have." As I was near and overheard the conversation, instead of staying out of it as a good father would have done, I intervened and told the little girl that my daughter had gotten this ball from the common bowling racks and that *she* should go get her own ball to use. Half in tears, she turned and left us.

Afterward the Lord said to me, "Is this the way you show love to this girl and model the kindness of Jesus to her and to your own children?" I had responded according to the standards of the world. I was right from the culture's standard of self-interest first, but I was wrong on the basis of Christian love first.

Though I still do not always respond first with love, I now know that my own long-term best interests in God's kingdom are served well when I identify with the other person, making their interests my own. Instead of insisting on my own way, I am challenged to follow Christ's way of love, as Paul so clearly describes it in that great hymn of God's unrelenting love in the event of Christ's coming, Philippians 2:6-8.

Self-seeking, or failure to lovingly take the needs of others into consideration, has expressed itself in the Corinthians' factionalism (1:10-12), lawsuits (6:1-11), "everything is permissible for me" slogan (6:12; 10:23), eating of idol food (8-10), hairstyles (11:1-16), eating the Lord's Supper before others' arrival (11:17-34), and rudeness in worship practices (14:29-33).

It [love] is not easily angered. This is difficult both exegetically and behaviorally. It is Paul's sixth action incompatible with love. The verb occurs only once elsewhere in the New Testament, in Acts 17:16 to describe the emotion Paul felt in Athens: "he was greatly distressed *[paroxynetai]* to see that the city was full of idols." Perhaps "angered" or "provoked" gets at the sense better. The noun form occurs in Acts 15:39's account of the altercation Paul and Barnabas had over taking John Mark with them to revisit previously evangelized areas: "They had such a sharp disagreement *[paroxysmos]* that they parted company."

Did Paul himself fail to exercise the aspect of love he is now exhorting the Corinthians to have? Perhaps, but its close connection with envy in 1 Corinthians suggests that love is "not provoked to anger" by resentment of others' gifts and ministries ("as in the case of Korah in Num 16:30 LXX, *paroxynein,* an attitude that is joined in Num 17:6 with grumbling, *gongyzein,* a verb associated with the Corinthians' disaffection according to 1 Cor 10:10"; R. Martin 1984:50). The word means "to incite" and can also be used positively, as in Hebrews 10:24, "Let us consider how to spur *[paroxysmon]* one another on to love and good deeds." In 1 Corinthians 13:5, then, it does not mean to be *easily* angered (NIV). It means to be incited to anger by resentment.

It [love] keeps no record of wrongs is Paul's seventh action incompatible with love. The word used is generally associated with grace and justification (Rom 3:28; 4:3-12, 22-25; Gal 3:6) and may carry allusions to this Christian truth. In this context the word *(logizomai)* means "to take [evil] into account" so that the offender can be repaid in kind, or to "count something against someone, punish the person for it" (2 Cor 5:19). "Love keeps no score of wrongs"; it does not "give careful thought . . . think about, ponder, be obsessed with" injuries (Danker 2000:597-98). Love does not condone the wrong or harm done but names it as evil; then, however, shows willingness to forgive the wrong by not keeping an account of each harm with a view to future retaliation.

Love does not delight in evil is the eighth and final action that love does not do. "Not being glad when others go wrong" is James Moffatt's translation (cited by R. Martin 1984:50). *Evil (adikia)* is "unrighteousness, injustice or harm" and could refer to the evil or harm of suing other Christians (6:1-11). Or it may refer to the failures of others that we may "maliciously joy or gloat over" (Bruce 1971:127), taking pleasure in saying "I told you so" and lecturing them. Love may also refuse to be drawn into evil and instead hold back from a censorious attitude (cf. Phil 1:15-18).

Rejoices with the truth is the positive, loving action that is juxtaposed to taking pleasure or delight in evil. *Rejoices (synchairei)* here is a more intensive form than *delight in* in the earlier part of verse 6 and means "rejoices together, applauds, joyfully celebrates" *the truth*. But what *truth* is meant? Is it the truth of the gospel (Fee) or "this or that truth of a matter" that may be the issue before us (Thiselton)? In any event, love is exceedingly glad when the truth of a matter prevails.

Finally, Paul points to the limitless quality of authentic Christian love (v. 7). In North America today, the culture encourages us to push against and challenge the limits in all areas of life, physical, social, sexual, spiritual and economic. One advertisement begins with the claim "Today there are no limits!" and illustrates with bungee-jumping, parasailing and wake-boarding adventures. Perhaps we have missed the most important purpose for a higher education. With all our learning we should learn, contrary to the secular culture, that life has limits. But there is one activity in life that has no limits. It is Christian love.

In four two-word affirmations, each beginning with "all" *(panta)*— and in the original each verb has the same rhythm-producing ending *(-ei)*—Paul produces a memorable cadence that sets forth what love does continually and without limit. Thiselton argues that the sense is best conveyed by using four negatives: "Love never tires of support, never loses faith, never exhausts hope, never gives up" (2000:1058).

[Love] always protects. The word is difficult. NRSV has "bears all things," Moffatt "slow to expose," Barrett "supports all things," Conzelmann "covers [with silence] all things." The verb occurs in 1 Corinthians only here and in 9:12, "we put up with anything." That seems to emphasize endurance. It occurs elsewhere in Paul in 1 Thessalonians 3:1, 5 with the sense "stand it no longer"; again a sense of perseverance is uppermost. Others believe the same sense (but not the same

word) is given by 1 Peter 4:8 and James 5:20: "love covers over a multitude of sins" instead of "exposing them or blazing them abroad" (Bruce 1971:127). Then the action would be discretion, opposed to cowardly unconcern (R. Martin 1984:51). Paul through love limits his freedom in the interim age between the now and the then of the final age (cf. 1 Cor 4:8; 6:12).

Always trusts (pisteuō, "believes," "trusts") is less difficult; it means "never loses faith" by seeking to give the most favorable interpretation the truth will allow, or "believing the best" (Augustine), or "is not unduly suspicious." Love always *hopes* even against probabilities, *always perseveres* and never gives up on people or circumstances, even those of Corinth. This last action is also referred to elsewhere as the fruit of the Spirit (Gal 5:22).

The Permanence of Love (13:8-13) In this third and last movement of the poem, Paul compares the transient and imperfect nature of the Spirit's present manifestations (gifts) with the permanence and superiority of Christian love. Most of this section is nonproblematic, except for the identification of "completeness" and its relationship to the question of the cessation of certain spiritual gifts (v. 10).

Love never fails introduces the section and establishes the main theme of love's permanence. *Fails (piptō)* means "to become invalid, come to an end, fail" (Danker 2000:815). On the other hand, *prophecies, tongues, knowledge* will all *pass away* because their imperfectness (incompleteness, *in part*) will be replaced with perfectness (completeness). The connection of chapter 13 with the previous and following chapters is once again (as in vv. 1-3) quite evident.

The transitory nature of all gifts of the Spirit because of their incompleteness is in contrast to love, which never comes to an end (or is never invalidated). This should lead the Corinthians (and us) to deemphasize Spirit manifestations compared to the practice of love. The gifts are from God and should be part of the church's public worship (except uninterpreted tongues), but these Spirit manifestations must not take priority over or be exercised except in the context of the practice of authentic Christian love.

When perfection comes is more difficult to identify. The word is *teleion,* variously translated "complete, mature, perfect," here with the article, "the complete" or "the mature." Paul used the word earlier with the idea of maturity of believers (2:6). Everyone agrees that this completeness is in the future from Paul's time of writing; it is at this time that the gifts mentioned in verse 8 will cease. This seems clear from the twice repeated *now . . . then* comparison in verse 13.

But docs *perfection* refer to some future development of the Corinthians as they individually and corporately mature in love (Talbert, Murphy-O'Connor, Mitchell, Snyder), or to some future eschatological event associated with the parousia of Christ (R. Martin, Carson, Grudem, Ruthven, Schatzmann, Hemphill, Thiselton, Bruce, Witherington, Fee, Turner), or to the completion of the New Testament canon (Augustine, Aquinas, Calvin, Edwards, Warfield, Walvoord, Geisler, MacArthur, Gaffin)?

I side with the consensus in identifying *perfection* with the coming of Christ (1 Cor 1:8; 4:5; 15:50-58). This conclusion alone, however, does not settle the question whether all the Spirit's manifestations that were present at Corinth are still present today. It simply removes 1 Corinthians 13:8-12 as a text supporting cessation of certain gifts. Whether such gifts are present today will depend on other factors, such as the witness of postbiblical history, larger theological issues and the parallels of modern phenomena with biblical descriptions.

The three illustrations, child versus adult, mirror versus direct vision, partial versus full knowledge (vv. 11-12), further highlight the contrast between partial divine revelation now and the full, complete, future knowledge that God will disclose at the coming of Christ and all that that event will change *(now . . . then)*.

When I was a child . . . when I became a man does not focus on the slow maturation process (contra Murphy-O'Connor, Snyder) but highlights the two stages, childhood and adulthood. The comparison therefore is not to emphasize the Corinthians' self-centered immaturity and lack of love (contra Thiselton) but to correct the mistaken realized eschatology that had led them to emphasize spectacular and revelatory ministries of the Spirit as evidence that the fullness of the kingdom had

---

13:10 A quite helpful bibliography on all three views can be found in Ruthven

already come at Corinth (4:8).

What they failed to realize was that the whole present age is, in comparison to the age to come, a mere passing, incomplete, partial revelation and knowledge stage, like the time of childhood. Not now but in the coming age there will be fullness of knowledge (adult); *now* (child) our best understanding is like kindergarten understanding. Therefore what are required now are humility and love, two character qualities lacking in the Corinthians' tendency toward pride in revealed knowledge and status-seeking in Spirit expressions without seeking the benefit of the community above all else.

Now we see but a poor reflection as in a mirror; then we shall see face to face (v. 12). Corinth was known for its highly polished bronze mirrors, which, while lacking the sharp images given by our coated glass mirrors, could provide a fair reflected image. In this second illustration Paul compares the indirect, imperfect image we see in the mirror (our present experience in this age) with the direct, complete, clear knowledge of God and his truth *(face to face)* that we will experience at the resurrection and beyond.

Face to face may reflect Numbers 12:8, which contrasts the indirect manner the Lord uses to revealing himself to most prophets (visions, dreams) to God's revelation to Moses: "With him [Moses] I speak face to face, clearly and not in riddles; he sees the form of the LORD." The hymnwriter reflects this encounter:

Face to face! O blissful moment!

Face to face—to see and know;

Face to face with my Redeemer,

Jesus Christ Who loves me so.

Face to face I shall behold Him,

Far beyond the starry sky;

Face to face in all His Glory,

I shall see Him by and by!

CARRIE BRECK, 1855-1934

Now I know in part. Again, in this third illustration Paul states that

---

1993:138. On the lack of historical evidence for the alleged cessation of prophecy, see Shogren 1997.

his best knowledge of God *now* is partial. We do have true truth now, but it is incomplete. We do not have the full picture yet. We know enough now to unconditionally trust God, to follow him faithfully, and to have hope kindled brightly in us, based on God's promises. But we need humility given the limited knowledge God has revealed and our only partial grasp of it. Even Paul admitted to his partial understanding (4:3-5). How much more should I disclaim that my understanding or my group's knowledge of God is the truth of his revelation, the norm to which others should conform? "Knowledge puffs up while love builds up. Those who think they know something do not yet know as they ought to know. But whoever loves God is known by God" (8:1-3 TNIV). This latter thought is picked up by Paul in the second part of 13:12.

Then I shall know fully, even as I am fully known. This refers to the glorious future event of Christ's return, the judgment of the world, the resurrection and the inauguration of God's eternal kingdom. Again, in this third illustration, partial knowledge now (this age) is superseded by complete, full knowledge. The comparison focuses on God's elective, personal and full knowledge of us as his children now as the norm for our understanding of God in the future eschaton. Those who love God are his elect (Rom 8:28; 1 Cor 8:3). They are known fully, savingly, personally and everlastingly by God.

Our focus now should be on God's knowledge of us, not on our knowledge of him (as important as that is in its proper context). To know that we are known by God, personally, savingly, completely, is the greatest knowledge, surpassing all other knowledge as the light of our sun surpasses all other lights. "Because the sun rises, all lights go out" (Karl Barth, quoted in 1993:147).

And now these three remain: faith, hope and love. In what sense do these three great Christian action-virtues *remain?* Does *now* carry a temporal meaning, "now in the present age," or is it merely connective, summative, meaning "in conclusion"? The "nows" *(arti)* in the previous verse are clearly temporal, but Paul uses a different word in verse 13 *(nyn)*. Does this signal a shift to the resumptive, logical "now"? Is Paul saying that *now* in the present age faith, hope and love remain and im-plying that in the age to come only love will remain (Ruthven, Calvin)?

Or does he mean that faith, hope and love will all remain on into eternity (Barrett, Carson, Thiselton)?

A major objection to the latter interpretation is that faith and hope seem to be tied to our present trust in unseen realities, realities that will in the eschaton become visible (see Rom 8:24-25; 2 Cor 5:7; Heb 11:1). One way of countering this objection is to argue that all three remain on into eternity (faith, hope and love), but only love will not undergo transformation, whereas, faith and hope will be modified by the realities of the new age (Thiselton 2000:1074). This leads to the conclusion that love is greater because unchanged in eternity. This latter view would not nullify Paul's point in the previous verses and may be adopted even though the majority of commentators favor Calvin's view (above).

But the greatest of these is love. Why is love greater than faith and hope, as well as all the gifts of the Spirit? Several answers may be given.

1. Love, if it never ends but always remains (vv. 8, 13), must be superior to those Christian qualities that are fulfilled at the eschaton. Love, after all, is the nature of God (1 Jn 4:8); faith and hope are merely human Christian character traits.

2. All the manifestations of the Spirit need love to have any Christian value (Gal 5:22). Faith and hope are important features of our life too, but they do not touch everything else the way Christian love does (Col 3:14).

3. Love binds the community together and therefore will continue into the new age and into eternity as the church itself continues forever (Eph 3:14-21).

4. One further possibility is presented by a contemporary commentator. *Faith, hope and love* are repeated a number of times in Paul's writings, so the phrase may be seen as a tradition, a preformed triad of theological virtues in the early church (Rom 5:3; Col 1:3; 1 Thess 1:3; 5:8; etc.). The adjective *meizōn (greatest)* is a comparative ("greater") that is normally rendered as a superlative ("greatest"). But if we retain the comparative sense and take *these* as a genitive of comparison, then the sense is "Faith, hope, and love remain [the Christian triad], but the greater than these [human virtues] is the love [of God as seen in Jesus

Christ]." This would be a "note of unexpected climax" as Paul appeals to what has no doubt been at the center of his thought throughout the passage, God's unimaginable love for us through Christ (R. Martin 1984:55).

While Paul could probably heartily agree with the theology of this fourth view, it seems to be a stretch to see the love at the end of the poem to be different from the Christian love presented throughout.

Thus love is the greatest because all the Christian virtues and ministries of the Spirit depend on it for their validity, it lasts for eternity, it binds the Christian community together now and eternally, and it is the nature of God as revealed in Jesus Christ.

So what is this Christian love? James Denney quotes a source that seems to get to the very heart of the issue by saying that this love "is the identification of ourselves with God's interests in others" (James Denney 1911:161). Love is what God in Christ has shown and done for "others" in their hopeless plight as sinners (R. Martin 1984:56). Love makes God's interests in the other our own interests.

This chapter could well stand as the center of Paul's theology, as it is a splendid blend of Christology, soteriology (salvation) and Christian ethics. Our churches can face no greater challenge nor find any more perfect model to live out than what Paul has given us in this unparalleled poem of love.

Pastoral Correction of Tongues and Prophetic Speech (14:1-40)
Paul's final chapter on the Spirit's manifestations in worship (the section 12:1—14:40) continues his pastoral and corrective emphasis with focus on the intelligibility and order of the worship service. While for us this is a quite difficult chapter in some places, it gives us perhaps the only detailed historical example of early Christian worship. This alone would be enough to make the chapter indispensable for careful study. Beyond this, however, the material is highly instructive, touching as it does on important phenomena in the modern worldwide church, tongues speaking and prophecy.

You may have experienced, as have I, a worship service that was unintelligible due to many people's speaking at the same time or in a language you did not understand. I was left uninvolved, alienated and feeling like a total outsider when my wife and I sat through an Anglican worship service in Ramallah, Israel, that was totally in Arabic. After the service we learned that there had been an English-language service the previous hour!

Paul's approach to the problem at Corinth in this regard is politically sensitive and actually quite simple. The major problem is not the practice of tongues speaking or prophetic speech or even the Corinthians' zeal for the manifestations of the Spirit. Paul commends their zeal (vv. 1, 12, 39) and censures any prohibition of these gifts in the public worship services of the church (v. 40). However, at Corinth both practices have been abused. Prolific, simultaneous, uninterpreted tongues speech and prophetic speech (vv. 26-31) produced a disordered, unintelligible worship service that virtually prevented the growth of the congregation into Christian maturity and the evangelistic witness of the gathered group (vv. 12, 20, 22-25).

Why this was happening is a matter of speculation. Perhaps the types of gifts emphasized at Corinth, though legitimate manifestations of the Holy Spirit, were status markers for certain church members, viewed competitively as advancing one's personal recognition and value in the church. In any event Paul sees what is happening as counter to the true nature of God and of the Christian church.

While carefully not negating these gifts, he deftly argues first for the diminution of tongues speech by showing the superiority of prophetic speech, then concedes the use of tongues speech when interpreted into intelligent language. Finally, he urges the ordering and control of all speech gifts to serve the purpose of intelligibility and thereby to edify the whole congregation.

I say the solution is simple because throughout Paul has one overarching fundamental goal for congregational worship with its varied expressions of the manifestations of the Spirit. He says, "All of this must be done for the strengthening of the church" (v. 26). Upbuilding the whole congregation is to be the benchmark goal of all that is done in the worship service (vv. 4, 12, 17, 19, 26, 33, 40). For Paul everything is tested by this single purpose. Edification or building up (*oikodomeō*) is further defined as to instruct others (vv. 17, 31), to promote *peace* (wholeness, harmony, well-being, v. 33), and to strengthen, encourage and comfort others (vv. 3, 31).

In the Corinthian church the obscuring of this great overarching principle of the edification of the congregation calls forth *two important principles* to correct this failure. First, edifying, transformative congregational worship must emphasize intelligent communicative speech in contrast to nonintelligent vocal expressions (tongues). Edification is inseparably tied to understandable speech.

Second, strengthening, encouragement, comfort, learning are also not possible if the manner in which the service is conducted produces cacophony (many competing voices) or a failure to "hear" what is being said even when the speech is intelligent speech. Thus, the principle of order, fittingness, peace that is characteristic of the nature of God (v. 33) becomes essential to achieving the overarching goal of the edification of the church (vv. 27, 29). Speech in the service must be controlled speech for it to be upbuilding.

Tongues Speech Contrasted with Prophetic Speech (14:1-5)

In this first section Paul encourages the Corinthians to *follow the way of love* that he has expounded unforgettably in chapter 13. *Follow* (NIV) is not quite strong enough for Paul's word *(diōkō)*. To "pursue" (or "chase after" as hunters chase their prey) love without neglecting the manifestations of the Spirit provides the proper balance in the church. But in Corinth, where tongues have become dominant, prophetic speech is to be preferred: *especially* (or "rather") *the gifts of prophecy.* Having already discussed both the gift of tongues and of prophecy (see at 12:10), I will supplement that discussion here with additional point. On the questions of the cessation of these gifts, see comment at 13:8-12.

Paul makes three comparisons between those who speak in tongues and those who speak in prophetic speech:

I would like every one of you to speak in tongues is not a reversal of Paul's wish to lessen the use of tongues in the worship service; it is hyperbole that expresses his pastoral encouragement of this gift for private edification (v. 28). Thus he immediately adds, *But I would rather have you prophesy. He who prophesies is greater than one who speaks in tongues,* only in the sense that prophetic speech is intellig-

Prophecy	Tongues
speaks to members of the congregation (v. 3)	speaks to God (v. 2)
intelligent speech for *strengthening, encouragement and comfort* (v. 3; Acts 15:31-32)	no one understands him; he utters mysteries with his spirit (v. 2)
edifies the church (v. 4)	*edifies himself* (v. 4)

ible and therefore edifies the congregation. If tongues are put into intelligible speech, then they are as valuable as prophetic speech to the congregation.

Public Uselessness of Unintelligible Sounds (14:6-12) In three illustrations Paul again shows the unfruitfulness of speaking in tongues for the congregation's upbuilding. If even Paul himself visits the Corinthians and speaks in tongues, they will not benefit. Instead he will come with some intelligible *revelation or knowledge or prophecy or word of instruction.*

Revelation (apokalypsis, "uncovering," "disclosure") seems to be an immediate divine disclosure of some truth or divine directive or leading (Rom 16:25; Gal 1:12; 2:2). Since individuals in the congregation may also speak revelatory words (1 Cor 14:26), these *revelations* may be limited to local situations, without universal authority in all the churches.

As noted, Paul argues from three illustrations. (1) Musical instruments (*lifeless things,* v. 7, better "inanimate things") such as a *flute or harp* must be played with an intelligible *distinction in the notes,* or else no one can recognize and benefit from the music. (2) A *trumpet* sound (v. 8) that is not a clear call-to-arms melody fails as a signal of an impending battle. (3) *I am a foreigner to the speaker, and he is a foreigner to me* (vv. 10-11) draws from the human experience of alienation from those who speak a language that one does not know.

In each case, lack of communication makes the sounds worthless, and in the latter example it even distances us from the one who is speaking. Such is the case of uninterpreted tongues speech in the congregation (v. 9). Since the believers *are eager to have spiritual gifts* (*pneumatōn,* manifestations of the Spirit), they should *excel in gifts that build up the church* (v. 12), that is, in verbal expressions that are intelligible to all.

Why Tongues Speech in the Church Must Be Put into Intelligible Words (14:13-21) *Should pray that they may interpret what they say* (v. 13): in comment on 12:10 I argued that tongues speaking is not unlearned foreign languages but wonder, praise, thanksgiving and deep desires that well up and overflow, generated by the Holy Spirit in our innermost being and expressed vocally in nonintelligible sounds (Rom 8:26-27). Anyone who speaks in tongues in the assembly of believers should do so only if God grants them the accompanying ability to put what they have uttered into understandable words. Otherwise they should remain silent (1 Cor 14:28).

To speak in a tongue is to pray, praise, sing or give thanksgiving *with my spirit* ("in my innermost spiritual being," Thiselton 2000:1110), Paul says (v. 14). But his *mind* ("understanding") *is unfruitful* (better: "my mind produces no fruit from it"). The Holy Spirit controls both our innermost spiritual depths and our mind. Therefore Paul recommends that in the church there must be an alternation between unintelligible sounds of the tongue and a corresponding putting into words that are understood by the worshipers (vv. 15-16).

Otherwise *how can one who finds himself among those who do not understand say "Amen" to your thanksgiving* (v. 16)? To not understand uninterpreted tongues speech puts other believers in the position of feeling like outsiders in the church. The word is *idiōtēs* (see vv. 23-24) and means a novice, layperson or amateur in any field of learning (e.g., medicine, military, politics; Danker 2000:468). Today we speak of "seekers" in distinction to baptized, committed church members. Unintelligible tongues place a baptized church member into the same position as the seeker.

Therefore Paul does not want to speak in tongues in the church, even though he boasts that outside the church *I speak in tongues more than all of you.* Tongues speech in public does not produce

---

14:16-23 *Those who do not understand . . . some who do not understand* is *idiōtēs,* "uninitiated, unlearned, inexperienced," and may relate either to what we would call

edifying instruction to others (vv. 18-19). It is not clear whether this means the Corinthians must interpret their tongues before they come to the meeting and then bring only this intelligible speech to the congregation (so Thiselton 2000:1118-19), or whether the tongues are uttered first in the meeting followed by the interpretation. In the first instance Paul would be arguing that there should be no tongues at all in congregational meetings. Yet it is difficult to see how this view can be compatible with Paul's earlier treatment of tongues as a gift of the Spirit to be manifested in the congregation, interpreted for its edification.

To not understand this is to engage in *thinking like children* rather than *adults* (v. 20). Note well that Paul does not say that tongues speaking is infantile. The childish thinking is the failure to recognize that tongues speech in public worship without interpretation does not benefit the congregation. It is the self-centered, childish love of display and attention seeking that Paul deplores. "Children love anything that shines or moves or makes noise. . . . Many modern Christians have the same mentality. . . . They would rather be made to feel than to think . . . fall too easily under the spell of virtuosi . . . anyone with charm. . . . It shows lack of maturity in the things of the Spirit" (Deluz, quoted in Thiselton 2000:1120). It is proper to be innocent, even infantile—uninvolved and inexperienced—with *regard to evil*. Verse 20 seems to fit best as a conclusion to verses 13-20 rather than a preface to the next section (vv. 21-25).

Why Untranslated Tongues Speech in the Services Hinders Evangelism (14:21-25) The general sense of these verses is clear even though verses 21 and 22 present a classic interpretive crux. In general Paul is continuing his argument against use of unintelligible tongues speech (uninterpreted) by pointing to an additional problem it causes. He has already indicated that uninterpreted and uncontrolled tongues speech in worship is unprofitable for the congregation and leads to the alienation of believers who hear it (vv. 16-17). But such uncontrolled tongues speaking—*everyone speaks in tongues*

"seekers" or to Christians who are unlearned or unexperienced in tongues speaking in the eyes of the Corinthian tongue speakers (Thiselton 2000:1114-15).

(v. 23)—also confuses "seekers" *(idiōtēs)* and nonbelievers who are present in the church gatherings. They conclude that this is just another pagan cult meeting where all are overwhelmed with ecstatic-frenzied experiences and are *out of [their] mind* (v. 23; not "insane"). They will leave without hearing the message of God's redemptive love in Christ.

On the other hand, if *everyone is prophesying* in clear and intelligible words and seekers or unbelievers come into the meeting, they will hear God's message of salvation, comfort and hope. As a consequence they will be convicted *(elenchō)* of sin and brought under judgment *by all* (as the Spirit uses their words, v. 24), as the secrets of their hearts are *laid bare*. As a result they will *fall down* on their faces *and worship God, exclaiming, "God is really among you!"* (v. 25). Prophetic speech is evangelistically effective to bring about genuine Christian conversion; tongues speech is not.

Recently I heard of a young Jewish woman from South Africa who was living temporarily in London, England. She went to an evangelical Anglican worship service near the apartment where she was living. As people were speaking and testifying, she was "overpowered" by a sense of God's presence that she had never before experienced. This was the event that led to her turning to God through Jesus, the Messiah. Today she lives in Jerusalem.

But how are we to understand verses 21-22 and their connection to the rather clear teaching of verses 23-25? Why did Paul even have to mention this confusing comparison? He begins with a somewhat modified quotation from Isaiah 28:11-12 (cf. Deut 28:49) that he introduces with *in the Law* (meaning the Old Testament as a whole, cf. Rom 3:19). The quotation follows strictly neither the Hebrew nor the Greek Septuagint; instead Paul appears to quote the text partially and to apply it partially to the Corinthian situation.

In Isaiah the words most likely refer to the invasion of Israel by the Assyrians, a people whose native language would not be understood by the northern kingdom Israelites. Since the Israelites had despised the word of God spoken to them in intelligible prophetic speech through Isaiah, God would speak to them through the invaders in unintelligible words. And even then the rebellious Israelites would *not lis-*

ten to (or "not obey") God (v. 21). Now it gets much more difficult.

From this quotation Paul concludes *(then)* that *tongues* (unintelligible sounds) *are a sign [sēmeion], not for believers but for unbelievers* (v. 22). But a *sign* pointing to what? In the light of verse 23, it cannot be a sign of grace or of the cross or of God's power that would lead an unbeliever to God through Christ. Paul teaches just the opposite in verses 23-25. In the Isaiah passage the unintelligible public speech of the Assyrian invaders was a sign to the unbelieving Israelites that God's judgment was coming upon them in the form of the Assyrian conqueror.

But how does this relate to the Corinthian church? Perhaps Paul intends it as a negative warning sign of impending judgment, much like the "sign of Jonah" (Lk 11:29-30). *Not for believers* is much clearer in the context where Paul has repeatedly argued against tongues speech in public meetings (unless interpreted) as alienating and unfruitful (vv. 6, 16-17, 20). But tongues speech is also a gift of the Spirit to believers and is therefore not a negative sign of judgment for them.

Prophecy, however, is . . . not for unbelievers (v. 22) seems to contradict Paul's argument in verses 24-25, where the *unbeliever* and seeker *(idiōtēs)* are benefited by prophecy and come to God through this ministry of the Spirit. One explanation would be to understand *unbelievers* here as pointing to the attitude of unbelieving Israelites who rejected Isaiah's intelligible prophetic speech (v. 21). It is true that prophetic speech is *for believers,* to warn, exhort, teach, comfort those who already believe. In this sense prophetic speech is not directly intended in the worship service of the church to address *unbelievers.*

However, compared to unintelligible tongues speech (uninterpreted), intelligible prophetic speech may indeed lead to the conviction and turning to God of a seeker (inquirer) or unbeliever as a secondary effect. Sensitivity to outsiders and how they would respond to unintelligible speech in contrast to intelligible was especially needed in larger Christian meetings in spacious homes (villas), where outsiders often flowed in and out of the more public areas (Snyder 1985:67-82, 248-49).

Good Worship Order and the Nature of God (14:26-40) Several years ago we visited a church attended by one of our daughters. What struck my wife and me was the almost total lack of any structured order in the service. We could not tell when the actual worship service began, for a long list of announcements was made that transitioned into stories about what people were doing during the week. A brief message of sorts was given much later, but there was no congregational singing or other participation. Finally the leader sat down, and everyone else got up and started to talk before leaving the sanctuary. There was very little Scripture, little prayer, one choir piece, no congregational singing, and no invocation or benediction. Thankfully, a short time later our daughter and family found another church with a much different service.

At Corinth there was a problem of a different sort. These verses (vv. 26-33) give a rare picture of a Christian church service in the Gentile world in these early years (c. 54-55). We find no leaders, no reading of the Law, no set order and no single sermon (different from Jewish synagogue worship). Instead we find a quite democratically functioning group, with one offering a Christian song (*psalmos,* "psalm," "hymn," "Christian song"), then another giving *a word of instruction,* another bringing *a revelation* (cf. v. 6), still another speaking in *a tongue* and then giving *an interpretation* (or another giving an interpretation, v. 26).

Are all of these spontaneous, or are they thought about beforehand and presented in the meeting, or a combination of both? We cannot be sure. *Words of instruction* seem to require prior reflection for genuine edification. *A revelation* or "prophecy" may be spontaneous (v. 30), yet there is no reason this gift would necessarily exclude a previous revelation that was reflected upon before being presented to the congregation (Thiselton 2000:1135). The Holy Spirit and human reasoning processes are not incompatible. Both spontaneity and reflection are part of a God-ordered worship service. Perhaps "ordered spontaneity" captures the essence of this balance.

Again, what is important is that *everything must be done for the strengthening of the church* (v. 26). There does not seem to be any-

---

14:29 The *Didache* (A.D. 117-130) reads: "You shall not test or examine any prophet who is speaking in the Spirit," since blasphemy against the Spirit "will not be forgiven" (11.7). But eventually some testing had to be done, and the theological crite-

thing comparable in Judaism to this democratization of worship found in 1 Corinthians 14 (Snyder 1991:187). But this freedom of the Spirit has limitations, and what had developed at Corinth bordered on disorder and unintelligibility that undermined Paul's great goal of building up the church.

Therefore he lays down a few basic rules to control a situation that was moving in the direction of unprofitable disorder. Tongues are permitted, if interpreted, but only *two—or at most three . . . one at a time* (v. 27). Does this mean two or three in the whole service, or two or three and then an interpretation? The same limitations are put on prophetic speech (v. 29), yet with the added words *you can all prophesy in turn* (v. 31), which may apply to tongues as well.

In any event, tongues speech (with interpretation) or prophetic speech must be heard one at a time to ensure intelligibility, an absolute requirement for edification, the supreme goal of all that is done in the Christian worship service. Thus if tongues speakers cannot put their own sounds into intelligible words (and another cannot either), they *should keep quiet* (in contrast to "stop speaking") *in the church and speak to himself* (in contrast to *in the church*) *and God* (in contrast to people; v. 28).

Prophetic speech likewise (*two or three,* one at a time, vv. 30-31) is controlled; the rule indicates that this gift also was being abused. *Others should weigh carefully* (*diakrinō*, to differentiate, sift, distinguish between; Danker 2000:231) *what is said* (v. 29). The *others* are best understood not as other prophets or apostles or leaders, but in keeping with the whole democratic emphasis in the passage, the whole congregation (Thiselton 2000:1140-41; cf. 1 Thess 5:21; 1 Jn 4:1-6).

This suggests that modern-day authority figures who claim to prophesy in the name of the Lord in the first person ("The Lord says, 'I . . .'") and seek to control the congregation without any sifting of the content of their speech or who establish ecclesiastical structures of authority that override the truth of prophetic speech place themselves

---

rion of Paul is replaced in the same document with a lifestyle criterion, "But not everyone who speaks in the Spirit [in the guise of] is a prophet, unless such a one exhibits the life-style of the Lord" (11:8, quoted by Thiselton 2001:1141).

outside the tradition established by Paul. Prophets may be self-centered, self-deceived, erroneous in part or in whole, and thus the congregation as a whole sifts the content of the speech—not the lifestyle of the speaker. A late first- or early second-century church document argues just the opposite: "Do not test or examine [*diakrineite*] any prophet who is speaking in the spirit, 'for every sin shall be forgiven, but this sin shall not be forgiven'" (*Didache* 11.7).

Presumably all who are gifted with prophetic speech may speak *in turn* (v. 31). This may suggest a possibility but not settle the question raised above concerning "two or three" (vv. 27, 29). A series of two or three prophets spoke, then there was discussion, followed by another series of two or three prophets and then discussion, until all the prophets had spoken. The goal of controlled worship is that *everyone may be instructed and encouraged* (v. 31).

The spirits of prophets are subject to the control of prophets (v. 32). *Spirits* has been variously understood. Is it the "prophetic Spirit" in each of the prophets, or is it the human spirit of each prophet? It is clear from the context that control of speech is from the Holy Spirit as much as the content of a speech. Yet the speaker as the agent of the Spirit's speech is responsible to be sensitive to the Spirit's leading in the service. This is evidenced by Paul's command to yield to another who is sitting but indicates that the Spirit has given them a revelation (v. 30). Therefore the prophetic Spirit's manifestation is subject (*hypotassō*) to the prophet's own will and can, unlike pagan prophetic speech, be controlled by the prophet. Prophets (and tongue speakers) can speak, keep quiet or stop speaking at will.

Chrysostom (d. 407) captures the sense well: "For that the man might not strive nor be factious, he signifies that the gift itself was under subjection. For by 'spirit' here, he means its actual working. But if the spirit be subject, much more thou its possessor canst not justly be contentious" (John Chrysostom, *Homilies on 1 Corinthians* 36.6).

For God is not a God of disorder but of peace (v. 33). Here Paul appeals to the ultimate ground for an ordered service of worship: order and *peace* are part of the very nature of God. Paul's word for *disorder* (*akatastasia*) means "disturbance," "tumult" (2 Cor 6:5, probably of mob action), "unruliness, disorder" (Jas 3:16; 2 Cor 12:20 with "factions" and "slander"; Danker 2000:35). "If disorder appears in the Corinthian assembly, it has been caused by some agent other than God" (Barrett 1968:329).

Chrysostom compares his own church with the Corinthian assembly and wishes for a more rigorous order that he knows exists in other churches of his day:

> But here great is the tumult, great the confusion, and our assemblies differ in nothing from a vintner's shop, so loud is the laughter, so great the disturbance; as in baths, as in markets, the cry and tumult is universal. And these things are here only: since elsewhere it is not permitted even to address one's neighbor in the church, not even if one have received back a long absent friend, but these things are done without, and very properly. For the church is no barber's or perfumer's shop, nor any other merchant's warehouse in the market-place, but a place of angels, a place of archangels, a palace of God, heaven itself. As therefore if one had parted the heaven and brought thee in thither, though thou shouldest see thy father or thy brother, thou wouldest not venture to speak; so neither here ought one to utter any other sound but these which are spiritual. For, in truth, the things in this place are also a heaven. (*Homilies on 1 Corinthians* 36.8)

Thiselton helpfully comments: "Paul's larger point is that this *order* in the nature of God who acts coherently, faithfully, and without self-contradiction should be reflected in the lifestyle and worship of the people of God" (2000:1145).

As in all the congregations of the saints (v. 33): whether this clause goes with the first part of verse 33 or with verse 34 following is debatable. Some versions make it the beginning of the next verse and begin a new section on women's speech: *As in all the congregations of the saints, women should remain silent* (NIV, NRSV, ESV, JB, NEB). However, the TNIV reads, "not a God of disorder but of peace—as in all the congregations of the people of God." This sense is also followed by ancient as well as modern translations (KJV, AV, RV, NASB, NLT).

Many modern commentators believe that the clause belongs to the next section (Witherington, Collins, Thiselton, Carson), while others argue for its connection to the general principle in the first part of verse

33 (Hays, Fee, Keener). If this latter view represents the correct attachment of the phrase, the sense would be that all the churches elsewhere (churches founded by Paul?) follow the rule of order and peace Paul has advocated in verses 26-32. If the proper connection is with what follows (vv. 34-35), then Paul is appealing to the practice of all the churches in keeping women/wives silent in the services.

While the conclusion does not affect significantly the exegesis of verses 34-35, my own view is that the clause, however awkward it may appear, belongs with the general principle in verse 33 (as in TNIV) for the following reasons. First, in other instances in the epistle an appeal to the churches' practice comes after Paul's discussion of a particular issue, not before (4:17; 7:17; 11:16). Second, when verses 34-35 are displaced to follow verse 40 in some manuscripts and versions, the last part of verse 33 does not go with the section on women/wives. Third, there does not seem to be a clear instance in biblical Greek literature (New Testament and LXX) of *hōs* ("as") beginning a sentence with a verbless dependent clause, which would be the case if the last part of verse 33 were attached to 34.

While not conclusive, these factors lean me in the direction of the earlier translations and commentators on this issue (cf. Chrysostom *Homilies on 1 Corinthians* 36.7: "For God is not a God of confusion, but of peace, as [I teach] in all the churches of the saints").

Far out of proportion to the length of verses 34-35 is the multiplicity of the problems one encounters in ascertaining its sense. Bruce perceptibly begins his discussion by noting, "After the recognition in 11:5ff of women's 'authority' to pray and prophesy, the imposition of silence on them here is strange. We must, of course, beware of accommodating Paul's views to ours, but here the difficulty lies in accommodating the views expressed in these two verses to Paul's clear teaching earlier in this letter" (1971:135). So does Paul take back here what he gave in 11:5-16? Ways of resolving this tension or contradiction abound. A study by D. A. Carson identified eleven views, including his own (1987:121-36). Frankly, it is much easier to cite views and dismiss them

---

14:34-35 These verses are transposed to follow verse 40 in several Greek manuscripts, and some argue that this indicates that the verses are an interpolation in the

for various reasons than to offer a completely satisfying alternative. In the space allowed I can only sketch some of the views, offer an objection or two for each, and suggest a conclusion.

A growing number of modern scholars believe verses 34-35 (36?) are a later interpolation (gloss) added at an early stage in the manuscript transmission (Conzelmann, Fee, Murphy-O'Connor, Schrage, Snyder, Payne, Hays). This would mean that the two verses are not authentic. This certainly takes care of the problem. But what supports this view? The abrupt rule for women upsets the context, interrupts the theme of prophecy and spoils the flow of thought. In content, it outright contradicts 11:5-16, where women's speaking and praying in the church are presupposed. There are peculiarities in linguistic usage and thought, such as *Law* without a citation and *subjection* without a referent. The flow of the passage (vv. 33-40) reads perfectly well without verses 34-35. Certain manuscripts transpose verses 34-35 to the end of verse 40, an indication that the scribes who copied the text did not have these verses in their manuscript. These are formidable objections to verses 34-35 as Paul's own.

On the other hand, a not insignificant number of respected scholars have concluded that the verses are authentically Paul's and must be explained without recourse to interpolation theories (Dunn, Thiselton, Carson, Witherington, Martin, Mitchell, Wire, Keener) for the following reasons. There are a large number of contextual word links in verses 34-35: "speak" (*laleō*, vv. 27, 23, 28, 29), "silence" (*sigaō*, vv. 28, 30), "in church" (vv. 19, 29, 33), "subject" (*hypotassō*, v. 32), and more distant, but relevant, "shame" (honor; 11:4-6).

But the strongest argument for the authenticity of the verses is the manuscript evidence. No Greek text or version omits the verses altogether. The few Western texts that reposition the verses after verse 40 can be reduced to one major witness. Were it not for the content of the verses, it is difficult to imagine anyone arguing against their authenticity on textual grounds—though admittedly I would welcome this as the solution if it were appropriate.

chapter (Fee 1987:699; Payne 1995). This view has not gained wide support and is effectively answered by Niccum 1997 and Thiselton 2000:1148-50.

Others argue that verses 34-35 are a Corinthian slogan, a view that the apostle sharply rebukes in verse 36 as being contrary to his own views (Odell-Scott, Bilezikian, Flanagan and Snyder, Talbert). This technique, it is claimed, has been used previously by Paul (6:12; 7:1; 10:23; perhaps 8:1-6).

The best refutation of this view is given by Ben Witherington, who argues that the previous quotes of Corinthian views in the letter were actually stated and then refuted or circumstantially modified by Paul. The apostle does not engage in mere sarcastic remarks. In fact Paul was probably anticipating the kind of response he was going to get (see v. 36). More telling against this view is the large number of words in verses 34-35 that resonate with the immediate context (Witherington 1988:90-91).

There are other views that are less probable for various reasons, such as that chapter 11 is a concession by Paul while chapter 14 is his real position (Calvin); chapter 11 applies to private gatherings, chapter 14 deals with the public assembly of the church; women were segregated and were involved in loud "chattering"; single women are being addressed in chapter 11, married women only in chapter 14. Most of these lack evidence or raise additional and unnecessary problems.

There are two additional views that are held more widely and deserve some comment. Both agree that women are permitted to prophesy and pray publicly in the worship services of the church according to chapter 11. Both argue that in the context Paul is dealing with order in the use of the speech gifts of tongues and prophecy. The immediate context concerns the congregation's responsibility to evaluate or sift prophetic speech (male or female; vv. 29-33).

The first view (view A) further argues that women cannot be involved in this oral weighing or sifting of the content of prophetic speech, for that is not permitted in any of the churches. Paul's appeal to *the Law* is less likely to Genesis 3:16 and more probably to the creation texts of Genesis 2:20-24, to which he already has appealed in 11:8-9 (cf. 1 Tim 2:13). Man's being created first, woman second, establishes a pattern regarding the roles they play. Women are to be in subjection to men (or at least the wife to the husband).

In the context of the Corinthian sifting of prophecies, says view A, women/wives were involved in evaluating all the husband-prophets who spoke, including possibly their own husbands. All the women/wives needed to stop this practice and remain silent. Otherwise they would not be in subjection to men/husbands: they would be exercising authority over them by teaching them to distinguish truth from imagination or error.

Further, this view says that in all the churches Paul "refused to permit any woman to enjoy a church-recognized teaching authority over men (1 Tim 2:11ff) and careful weighing of prophecies falls under that magisterial function" (Carson 1987:129-30; also Hurley, Knight, Grudem, Thrall). In other words, this is an authority issue of men over women. Presumably what broke up the edifying and peaceful order of the service was not some disruptive speech practice as such but wives/women who were not subject to husbands/men. The issue, then, is not disorder in the flow of the worship service but disorder in family relations.

Sometimes this view of male-female roles is extended to society as well as church and home. Alfred Lord Tennyson captures this sentiment well in the lines from a famous poem:

Man for the field and woman for the hearth;

Man for the word and for the needle she;

Man with the head, and woman with the heart;

Man to command, and woman to obey;

All else confusion. (*The Princess,* lines 437-41)

If women can prophesy, why must they be excluded from evaluating other prophets? The response of view A is that New Testament prophecy (unlike that of the Old Testament) is not absolutely authoritative and requires evaluation in light of the apostolic teaching. Since only males can teach apostolic doctrine and apply it to prophecies, all females are de facto disqualified.

This is not the place for an extended critique of view A, but a few observations may be appropriate. There is nothing directly in the text about a male authority issue between women/wives and men/husbands. Such an issue must be imported from a particular interpretation of Genesis 3:16 or at least Genesis 2:20-24 with 1 Timothy 2:11-15. *Law* has no citation attached to it and could just as well refer to Job 29:2, which speaks of the silence of someone who is a learner (Witherington 1990:177).

Likewise, the reference to *submission (hypotassō)* is in the absolute form without a personal object. It could refer to wives' submitting to their husbands, but this is an assumption. It could as well refer to women's submitting to the principle of order in the worship service, the principle of silence and respect while another is speaking (v. 30). Further, if the issue is simply women/wives' sifting of male prophets' messages, then why wouldn't Paul permit women to sift the messages of women prophets and restrict them only from evaluating male prophets?

View B offers, in my opinion, a helpful alternative to position A. It is as follows. The problem Paul addresses in verses 34-35 is not a creation order or family order issue but a matter of church worship order. Certain women/wives were interrupting the service by asking questions during prophetic speech. These questions may have been legitimate learning inquiries, but the manner in which they were being asked was in some way inappropriate and disruptive. From the standpoint of the great principle of Paul for judging the practices of the gathered church, everything must be done so that the church may be built up (v. 26) and that all may learn (*manthanō,* v. 31). The women's behavior was keeping this from happening. All else is speculation.

Paul's remedy is for these women to keep quiet, that is, to desist from this disruptive practice. Yet Paul wants them to learn, to have answers to their questions (quite progressive for his day and culture!). He therefore instructs them to ask these questions of their husbands in another setting (at home), where their speech (*laleō,* their questions) will not disrupt the learning of all in the congregation (Witherington 1988:103-4; Thiselton 2000:1156-58).

Why were women/wives, then, doing this and not the men/husbands? We don't know, but perhaps Craig Keener is right that those asking questions were not as well educated as the men. He quotes the Roman philosopher Plutarch from the same period: "And for your wife you must collect from every source what is useful, as do the bees, and carrying it within your own self impart it to her, and then discuss it with her, and make the best of these doctrines her favorite and familiar themes" (Plutarch *Bride* 48; *Moralia* 145B, LCL, cited by Keener 1992:84-85).

Thus in view B the issue is circumstantial (not cultural, as in chap. 11) and not universal (as it is in view A), as Keener observes: "It is doubtful that this particular problem obtained in most other churches in the Mediterranean world. Indeed, if this is the point on which Paul appeals to the custom of the other churches (14:33) . . . he may do so because women were not interrupting other churches' services" (1992:81). This view, now supported by a number of evangelical exegetes (Witherington, Thiselton, Keener), seems in my opinion to deal best with the text and its tensions with chapter 11. The following brief textual comments will try to complement what has already been said.

Women (*gynaikes,* "wives" or "women"; v. 34) presents the same problem of translation as in 11:2-15. Generally when "woman" is used in the same context with "man" *(aner),* "wife" is the correct translation (1 Cor 7:14; Eph 5:22; 1 Tim 3:2; 1 Pet 3:1). On the other hand, there are places such as in this context where "woman" and "man" may be more appropriate (Acts 5:14; 8:12; 22:4; 1 Cor 11:11-12). However, the construction in verse 35, *their own husbands (idios aner),* occurs a number of other times in the New Testament always with the sense "one's own husband" (1 Cor 7:2; Eph 5:22; Tit 2:5; 1 Pet 3:1); this leans me heavily toward that sense in 14:34-35 as well.

To speak, if taken to mean all forms of speech, with no qualification, not only would eliminate the prophetic and prayer speech of women Paul already certainly approved in 11:5-16, but, if universalized, would impose a childlike silence on all women in church services, prohibiting singing, praying aloud or giving a public testimony. *To speak (laleō)* should not be restricted to prophetic speech or tongues speech, however, but may legitimately refer to any speaking (not "chatter") that disrupts the service. In this context, as argued above, it specifically refers to the uninspired raising of questions in a manner that disrupted the service. "If you can't learn it in church except *the way you're doing* it, you need to ask your husbands at home" (Keener 1992:72).

Must be in submission (hypotassō, v. 34) lacks any object. It is too readily assumed that the object is "their husbands." In verse 32 the same word is used for prophets' being self-controlled in their prophetic speech. Witherington argues that the sense here requires the translation "Let them keep their ordered place," because "women are not being commanded to submit to their husbands, but to the principle of order" (1988:102-3). Galatians 3:28 shows that their "ordered place" was not submission to men. Paul's concern is not to disempower women but to (1) reflect in life and worship a dialectic between creativity and order, in keeping with God's own nature; (2) keep the missionary vision in view, considering how outsiders will view what is done (cf. 9:19-23; 14:23-25); and (3) to avoid localized, autocratic, arrogant self-sufficiency in relation to other churches (Thiselton 2000:1158-59).

As the Law says (v. 34): first, to refer *law (nomos)* here to either rabbinic or Gentile laws prohibiting women from speaking in public (Liefeld 1986:149), or to Paul's own apostolic rule (R. Martin 1984:87), may raise more questions than it answers. Since there is no citation, it has often been assumed that Paul has in mind Genesis 3:16, "Your desire will be for your husband, and he will rule over you" (so Chrysostom and others). Yet "this is unlikely, since in the MT and LXX Gen. 3:16 speaks of the woman's instinctive inclination or passionate desire (Hebrew *tesuqah,* Gk *apostrophē)* towards her husband, of which he takes advantage so as to dominate her" (Bruce 1971:136).

Others incline toward the creation narratives, especially Genesis 2:20-24, because Paul has previously used this text (11:8-9). But if this is the background, is it necessary to connect the text to 1 Timothy 2:13 as some do? This seems to read more into the ambiguous reference to *the Law* than is warranted, and the two texts are not sufficiently close.

On the other hand, some suggest not the creation texts but Job 29:21, which involves "the silence of respect for a teacher, the silence of someone who is a learner" (Witherington 1988:102). Finally, *the Law* could mean the whole Old Testament's repeated emphasis (especially in the Pentateuch) on the principle of order and differentiation whereby God turns chaos into order (Thiselton 2000:1153-54).

To inquire (v. 35) should be translated "to learn" *(manthanō).* The word always has the sense of learning attached to it (Danker 2000:615; see 1 Cor 4:6; 14:31; etc.). Though the women wanted to learn, their manner of interrogation was disrespectful.

For it is disgraceful [aischron, shame] for a woman [wife] to speak in church (v. 35) seems to be Paul's final, albeit secondary, reason why this kind of wives-speaking-in-church (v. 34) is shameful rather than honorable: Community standards of propriety—outside and inside the church—were being violated by the women's behavior (see Tit 1:11-13, where leaders in the church are similarly rebuked). "The importance of the honor-shame universe of discourse for first century Corinth (in contrast to the purity-guilt contrast of the post-Augustinian West) stands in the foreground here" (Thiselton 2000:1160).

Or did the Word of God originate with you? (v. 36). The Corinthians' attitude about the need for order in church worship (vv. 26-35), including the localized issue of disruption of prophetic speech by disrespectful wives/women (vv. 34-35), is now sharply rebuked by Paul with a rhetorical question.

The very first word (*ē,* "or," "either . . . or," or the interjection "what!") should not be seen as introducing a statement rejecting the previous two verses, as if they were an aberrant Corinthian viewpoint, but as Paul's anticipation that his rules to control speech practices at Corinth would anger the Corinthians. As Gordon Fee correctly points out, "Has God given them [the Corinthians] a special word that allows them both to reject Paul's instructions . . . and to be so out of touch with the churches?" (1987:710). "It appears the Corinthians were trying to make up their own rules, and perhaps thinking their own word is sufficient or authoritative or even the word of God for themselves" (cf. v. 36; Witherington 1988:98). See also the *all* and "only you" contrast between verse 33 and verse 36.

Word of God occurs numerous times in the New Testament, almost always as a reference to the gospel message about Christ (Acts 4:31; 8:14; 11:1; 13:5, 7, 44, 46, 48; 2 Cor 2:17; 4:2; Phil 1:14). Perhaps the closest parallel to our text here is the contrast mentioned in 1 Thessalonians 2:13: "When you received the word of God, which you heard from us, you accepted it not as the word of men, but as it actually is, the word of God, which is at work in you who believe."

Or are you the only people it has reached, so that you can set up your own practices and ignore the common order of all the churches? Prophets and others gifted by the Spirit (*pneumatikos,* "of the Spirit") should recognize that Paul's words throughout this section are *the*

Lord's command, not merely his opinion. *If anybody . . . ignores this [claim of Paul], he himself will be ignored* (as a prophet or "of the Spirit"). This seems to highlight the difference between mere prophetic speech authority and the apostolic authority that judges all other truth claims. A person of the Spirit, now as then, is in submission to the apostolic writings (Carson 1987:133).

In verses 39-40 Paul hammers home his central thesis of at least verses 26-38, and probably the whole chapter. *Be eager to prophesy* (because it builds up the church), and *do not forbid speaking in tongues* (in public *if interpreted,* in private if not, v. 28); *but everything should be done in a fitting and orderly way* (vv. 26-38), because this is God's nature (v. 33). *Fitting (euschēmonōs)* may carry, along with "propriety and decorum," overtones of sexually appropriate behavior.

What practical instruction can this chapter provide for modern-day churches?

1. There is a great need for churches today to be balanced between the spontaneous creativity of the Spirit and the ordered, fitting flow of the service. Order in this context does not involve a hierarchy of gifts, status, gender or office. Along with order, intelligent speech (exhortations, songs, prayers) must prevail, so that everything that is done promotes the building up, the learning, comfort, warning and exhortation of the congregation. This applies to Latin or any other language used in church liturgies that is not understandable by the congregation, as well as tongues speech.

Tongues speech should not be presented in public worship unless it is interpreted, not because it is a lesser gift of the Spirit but because intelligible speech edifies the whole church. If uninterpreted tongues speech occurs, it should not be opposed. Tongues speech is not a mark of higher spirituality or of being baptized or filled with the Spirit.

2. Churches should examine their public services to see if they include practices that unnecessarily confuse or offend "seekers" or nonbelievers who visit. Sensitivity to mission is necessary in a church seeking to be faithful to the tradition Paul taught.

Churches (and denominations) should avoid idiosyncratic practices and brazenly unilateral, authoritarian self-regulation that nourishes a sense of self-sufficiency, "a church taken up with itself exclusively, to the neglect of others" (Calvin 1960:469).

On the other hand, do churches of more recent origin need to reflect every customary practice of older churches? Calvin answers, "Paul here [14:36] does not employ an argument of universal application, but one that was specially applicable to the Corinthians, as is frequently the case. . . . Hence it does not necessarily follow, that churches that are of later origin must be bound to observe, in every point, the institutions of the earlier ones, inasmuch as Paul himself did not bind himself by this rule, so as to obtrude upon other churches the customs that were in use at Jerusalem" (Calvin 1960:470). This distinction between particularity and universality of practices requires careful and wise attention in modern churches.

Building community through the participation of each member so that all may learn and all may be encouraged is the model Paul presents to us. We must ask ourselves how our present styles of worship gatherings actually serve to teach, encourage, warn and exhort the community of faith. "Few churches can read 1 Corinthians 14 seriously without finding themselves invited to discover more broadly participatory styles of worship" (Hays 1997:250).

3. In worship services in churches established and mentored by Paul, women prophets spoke the Word of God also alongside men prophets (chap. 11). There appears to be no gender hierarchy, only a gift hierarchy based on the criterion of edification (Witherington 1995:290). Untaught women who disrupted the service with inappropriate questions were to desist from this practice and get answers from home instead. Men who are in control of evangelical churches today should learn to move over and invite Spirit-gifted women to share the pulpits with them and work as partners in the leadership ministries of the church. The Spirit shows no gender discrimination in the giving of his gifts to the people of God (chaps. 12-14).

☐ Corinth and the Resurrection of the Dead (15:1-58)

Recently I attended a funeral service for a well-known Christian man who had been my personal friend. He was eulogized extensively and quite appropriately for his dedication, selfless service, determination and rugged individualism. Several participants, including the pastor in his sermon, referred to the deceased as having "gone into the presence of the Lord" and "entered into glory," as "enjoying the splendors of heaven" and so on, but no mention was made of the resurrection of dead as the great Christian hope. This experience has been repeated numerous times in Christian funeral services I have attended over the past several years. It is almost as if we believed these persons were fulfilled, complete, at rest, glorified right now without any need for the resurrection.

For many years I have asked my evangelical theology students whether they believe in the resurrection of Jesus from the dead. Almost all unhesitatingly put up their hands. But then when I ask if they believe that Jesus is 100 percent human right now as well as divine, almost no hands go up. What has happened? I believe they cannot conceive of Jesus as now existing in a new human form (body); instead they think of him as some sort of disembodied spirit, even after the resurrection.

While these current tendencies do not fit exactly the Corinthians' beliefs, they do, I think, show that faulty thinking about the resurrection has invaded the modern mainstream church, even among evangelicals. "Although opinion polls tell us that most Americans believe in heaven, it is clear that the resurrection of the body is a doctrine that causes acute embarrassment, even in mainstream Christianity" (Bynum 1995:14).

The third longest chapter in the New Testament (the very longest are Lk 1 and 22), 1 Corinthians 15 is the resurrection chapter of the whole Bible. "The most positive subject that can be imagined, [it] forms the very peak and crown of this essentially critical and polemically negative Epistle. . . . We have to do here with the doctrine of the 'end,' which is at the same time the beginning, of the last things, which are, at the same time, the first" (Barth 1933:107, 113). In an important sense, chapter 15 anchors the whole book (Hays 1997:252).

The resurrection of Christ and the resurrection of believers were early in the church recognized as absolutely essential matters of Christian belief. In early "rules of faith" and in both of the great creeds, Nicaea-Constantinople (381) and the Apostles' (fifth to seventh century) these beliefs were affirmed. "He rose on the third day according to the Scriptures. . . . We look forward to the resurrection of the dead . . ." (Nicene). "On the third day [Jesus Christ] rose again from the dead. . . . We believe in the resurrection of the body" (Apostles'). Every major creed since has affirmed these twin doctrines.

Once the problem is clearly identified, the main contents and form of the chapter fall easily in place. The overall point of the chapter is to set forth and argue for God's ultimate victory over death in the resurrection of the dead (vv. 26, 54, 57). Genesis 1—3 forms a subtext for the whole chapter (Wright 2003:313). The doctrine is developed here by mean of two main emphases. First, Paul takes great pains to establish the essential connection of the future resurrection of all those who are in Christ to the gospel message and the Corinthians' experience of salvation (1 Cor 15:1-34). Then he argues that the resurrection body will be a new creation, a body that has been radically transformed from our present earthly body yet is in some sense continuous with our present life. This transformation will happen instantaneously when Christ comes. Our future mode of existence will be adapted fully to the Spirit (vv. 35-57). Such assured hope should lead us to stand firmly without wavering for the gospel and to serve God faithfully throughout our life (v. 58).

The following brief outline may be helpful in keeping these themes clearly before us:

A. The reality of the future resurrection of the dead (vv. 1-34)

    1. The gospel proclaims the event of the resurrection of Christ from the dead (vv. 1-11)

    2. Denial of the resurrection of the dead negates the gospel (vv. 12-19)

    3. Because Christ has been raised, all who belong to him will also be raised (vv. 20-34)

    4. Otherwise, hope, suffering and faithful service would be pointless (vv. 29-34)

B. Resurrection means a new creation of the body (vv. 35-58)

    1. The possibility and conceivability of the resurrection body (vv. 35-49)

    2. A mystery revealed: Both the dead and the living will be changed at the coming of Christ (vv. 50-57)

    3. Therefore stand firm, for our labor is not in vain (v. 58)

The Future Resurrection of the Dead (15:1-34) Paul is deeply concerned about what he has heard (orally or in writing): some in Corinth are saying *that there is no resurrection of the dead (anastasis nekrōn,* v. 12). Considerable discussion has surrounded the exact sense of this denial. To begin with, it should be recognized that Paul is not trying to argue the truth claims of Christianity to a pagan audience but to correct Christians in wrong beliefs (Witherington 1995:291). The basic views regarding the Corinthian problem can be summarized briefly in three main categories (Thiselton 2000:1172-75).

1. A group unable to believe in any form of life after death (Epicurean). Verse 29 is seen as decisive against this view, since whatever its exact sense, it presupposes that the Corinthians did hold some sort of belief in an afterlife. Paul's language seems to imply that they denied not some continuation of an immortal soul but rather *the resurrection of the dead.*

2. A group that held that the resurrection already occurred some time ago, like Hymenaeus and Philetus mentioned in 2 Timothy 2:17-18. Chrysostom and Luther seem to have proposed this view. "If Christian believers have already been raised with Christ to a new mode of life, all that happens at death is the dissolution of the physical body, while the already existing 'pneumatic' or 'spiritual' nature continues its existence without the husk of the body" (Thiselton 2000:1173).

This view of the problem is often connected to a suggestion that the Corinthians were involved in an "overrealized eschatology" (4:8; Thiselton 1978 but not 2000) or an early Gnostic-like interpretation (R. Martin 1984; Bruce 1980; Barrett 1968; D. Martin 1995). Yet Paul does not oppose his view of a future resurrection to a Corinthian notion of a present resurrection. They were denying any resurrection, not simply a future resurrection; that is, "there is *no longer* any resurrection" (Witherington 1995:301-2; Wright 2003:279).

3. A group unable to accept the resurrection of *the body* from the dead (Chrysostom; Murphy-O'Connor 1979; D. Martin 1995; Thiselton 2000; Holleman 1996). This view rests heavily on Paul's extensive elaboration in verses 35-49 on the nature of the resurrection body. Such a Corinthian view would have involved a dualistic anthropology holding that there are two different classes of people, nonspiritual and spiritual.

The spiritual person (inspired by the transcendental spirit) transcends all bodily matters. The body is nothing more than a house in which the immortal soul lives. The final separation of the spiritualized soul from the body occurs at death. Not only is a resurrection of the body impossible, it is unnecessary because immortality is reached by receiving the Spirit (Holleman 1996:37).

Perhaps this view of many at Corinth is represented in *Eumenides,* written by Aeschylus (fifth century B.C.), which says that when the Areopagus court was founded in Athens, the god Apollo said, *"Andros d' epeidan haim' anaspasē konis hapax thanontos, outis est' anastasis:* 'When the blood of a dead man is once and for all dust, there is no resurrection'" (Bruce 1990:387).

Paul's antidote is to emphasize a final end-time (eschatological) resurrection of the dead in Christ at his coming. The present, perishable nature body will be replaced with a new, imperishable "Spirit" body of God's own creation.

It was, then, the bodily character of the resurrection that a Corinthian group opposed on the basis of a dualistic anthropology. This view seems to best fit the evidence of the text and what is known about Greek philosophical ideas of body-soul dualism (even if these were modified somewhat at Corinth), and fewer problems are associated with it. The exposition that follows assumes the basic correctness of this identification of the problem of *no resurrection of the dead* (*anastasis nekrōn,* v. 12).

The Gospel Proclaims the Resurrection of Christ (15:1-11) In this section Paul rehearses things the Corinthians had received and believed about the gospel. This provides a basis for his linking the resurrection of Christ to the gospel they had believed and to the resurrection of the dead in the future (vv. 12-34). This section provides us with the clearest, earliest (A.D. 53) summation of the apostolic gospel that we possess.

Gospel (*euangelion,* "good news") is apparently a word usage coined by Paul (sixty of seventy-six times in the New Testament are his) for his proclamation of the saving message about Christ. *To the word* (v. 2) is better translated as "to that word," the substance of the gospel that Paul had proclaimed to the Corinthians. This conditional clause beginning with *if* both alerts them that he will deal further with the essential contents of the message (vv. 3-8) and at the same time presents them a warning to examine their faith lest they *have believed in vain* (v. 2).

In verses 3-8 Paul succinctly sets forth the essential matters that are *of first importance* ("foremost" or "top priority") that he himself *received* and *passed on* to the Corinthians. This is the earliest creedal formulation the church possesses (A.D. 53). Since it has been *received* by Paul, it is shared not just by Paul and the Corinthians but by all Christians. This Christian confessional statement contains four historical events: (1) *Christ died for our sins according to the Scriptures*, (2) *he was buried*, (3) *he was raised on the third day according to the Scriptures*, and (4) *he appeared to Peter*. All of these are historical events in time and space, and they are linked as if in a golden chain. In this chapter Paul is concerned with the resurrection link to anchor the church's preaching in the risen Lord, but each of the other moments is equally important in God's purposes through Christ.

Christ died (v. 3) is quite striking from the Jewish perspective. The early church, following Jesus' self-revelation, redefined the Messiah, contrary to Jewish expectations, as a *crucified* Messiah. This was part of the "offense" of the gospel (1:23; Jn 12:7, 24, 32-34; Gal 2:20). *Christ died* is the event; *for our sins* is the divine significance of his death as given to the disciples by Christ himself and proclaimed by the church (Mt 26:28; Mk 10:45; cf. Lk 24:25-27, 44-46). *For* (*hyper*, "in behalf of" or "instead of") *our sins* in the sense not only of forgiveness of our guilt for violations of God's law but also of our release from sin's power.

That this death of the Messiah and its significance was predicted in the Old Testament is affirmed in the phrase *according to the Scriptures*. The reference is quite general and no doubt refers to many strands of messianic predictions, such as sacrifice (e.g., the Passover lamb; 1 Cor 5:7) and covenant (e.g., Jer 31:31-34; Heb 1:3; 9:25-28; 10:12-18), as seen through Jesus, who interprets the Scriptures about himself (Lk 24:25-28, 44-46). However, specific texts also could be in mind, such as Isaiah 53:5, "He was pierced for our transgressions, he was crushed for our iniquities; the punishment that brought us peace was upon him, and by his wounds we are healed" (cf. 1 Cor 15:6, 8, 10, 12; see Dan 7:21-22).

That Christ *died* a real death and did not merely become unconscious is affirmed by the statement *He was buried* (v. 4). This emphasis on burial is generally taken to counter an emerging Gnostic-like teaching that played down the real body of Jesus and his real death. Perhaps, but because of parallels with baptism texts that stress codeath and coburial with Christ (Rom 6:3-4; Col 2:12), Paul may be instead emphasizing death to the old age and to sin's dominion over Christ and us and the beginning of the new people of God. "People of the old age (law, tradition, dependence, works of law) go to the tomb, face their own death, and find the tomb empty" (Snyder 1991:192). The burial's direct connection to the resurrection strongly suggests the Gospels' emphasis on the empty tomb (Witherington 1995:299-300). The resurrection is central to the whole of Christian faith and its message of good news. The twin themes of vindication and promise surround the event.

He was raised by God—a divine passive—forms the third moment of the gospel proclamation. There is no indication that Paul understood this affirmation to be of a different historical genre from the first two. As the Messiah's death and burial occur in time and space as historical events, the resurrection has the same historical eventness claimed for it. That historians cannot study the event itself, since no person directly witnessed it, does not invalidate the truth claim that the event occurred—something happened! Furthermore, "'resurrection' does not refer to some part or aspect of the human being *not* dying but instead going on into a continuing life in a new mode; it refers to something that *does* die and is then given a *new* life. . . . When Paul said 'resurrection,' he meant 'bodily resurrection'" (Wright 2003:314).

Not only will Paul offer testimony of his own experience of seeing the risen, alive Jesus, but he will cite numerous other living witnesses who report the same (vv. 5-8). The resurrection is the beginning of the new age. The resurrection is the new creation, the future-in-the-present. The whole future consummation of God's purposes in redemption is wrapped up in the resurrection of Christ.

On the third day again emphasizes the public nature of the event and the empty tomb motif, an event in our world and time. The expression also occurs in Jesus' predictions of his death and resurrection

(Mt 16:21; 17:23; Lk 9:22; etc.). *According to the Scriptures* once again points more generally to promise and fulfillment. The resurrection of the Messiah is the divine, sovereign act of God vindicating his redemptive work in Christ's death on the cross. Perhaps texts such as Isaiah 53:11-12, Hosea 6:2 (LXX uses the word "resurrection") and Psalms 16:10 (cf. Acts 2:27-28) may be in the background.

He appeared to Peter begins Paul's fourth and final emphasis on the gospel content, where he will cite a number of historical appearances to individuals and groups in the day after Jesus' resurrection (vv. 5-8). *Appeared to* (objective manifestation) is not "was seen by" (subjective experience). Why is Peter mentioned first? Perhaps because he was identified as the rallying figure of one faction in Corinth (1:12) or because he seems to have been prominent among the apostles, usually named first in the Gospel lists of the Twelve (Mt 10:2; Lk 6:14) and in other settings (Lk 24:34; Jn 21:7-19; Acts 1:15; 15:6).

Why are no women mentioned by name in Paul's list? They may be included indirectly in the five hundred brothers and sisters (v. 6) and *all the apostles* (v. 8). Perhaps in the culture their testimony was not deemed to be a legal witness in the courts. *The Twelve* is something of a technical term used repeatedly for the original Jerusalem apostles, who may have symbolically represented the new Israel (Lk 22:30).

Five hundred of the brothers ("and sisters," TNIV) *at the same time* is referred to only here in the New Testament; this may indicate that there were other appearances also not recorded. That Jesus appeared to groups of people (the Twelve, five hundred, all the apostles) is strong evidence against the claim that individuals were simply hallucinating or having private visions or dreams. Groups do not have hallucinations. Some of these five hundred have died *(fallen asleep),* but *most of [them] are still living,* Paul says, indicating that some twenty years later (assuming the resurrection occurred in A.D. 34) eyewitnesses of this resurrection appearance could still be contacted personally.

15:7 An ossuary owned by an antiquities collector in Jerusalem, dated in the first century (A.D. 62?) and bearing the inscription "James son of Joseph brother of Jesus" in Aramaic, surfaced for the first time in public display in November 2002 in Toronto, Canada. If it is authentic (some claim it is a forgery), it is either the actual burial box of James's bones or part of a memorial to him. In any event, it would be

James (v. 7) is not James the son of Zebedee, brother of John, who was put to death by Herod (Acts 12:2), but James the brother of Jesus, who may have remained an unbeliever until this appearance of the resurrected Jesus to him (Jn 7:5). He was a principal leader of the early Jerusalem church (Acts 12:17; 15:13; 21:18; Gal 1:19; 2:9, 12; Jas 1:1). *All the apostles* seems to be a wider group than just the Twelve (v. 5) and may have included James the Lord's brother, Barnabas (9:6), Andronicus, Junia and others (Rom 16:7).

Last of all he appeared to me also begins Paul's short report of Christ's appearance to him (see Acts 9:1-9; 22:1-21; 25:9-18). *Last of all* because Paul is the *least of the apostles,* as he views himself, because he *persecuted the church of God.* Perhaps *last* also refers to a chronological end of these special appearances to called apostles such as the Twelve and Paul.

But why does he call himself *abnormally born?* The word he uses *(ektrōmati)* refers to an "aborted foetus" or "miscarriage" (Danker 2000:311). In the context (vv. 9-10) this is best related not to his defense of his apostleship but to his sense of incompetence to be an apostle. His former life before he knew Christ was like an aborted fetus until he was reborn through the resurrection appearance of Christ to him (Thiselton 2000:1209-10).

By the grace of God emphasizes Paul's sense of the awesome generosity of all God's dealings with him though he is totally undeserving. This grace, however, was not wasted on Paul but became effectual to energize his labors and sufferings beyond the other apostles (2 Cor 11:22-29). *Yet not I, but the grace of God* shows a needed delicate balance and insight concerning our own intents, purposes, will and labors with absolute reliance on God's supply of grace for all that we do (cf. Phil 2:12-13).

Paul would certainly have been able to sing with deep feeling Robert Robinson's (1735-1790) beautiful hymn of God's grace:

the earliest known evidence for the existence of not only the New Testament James but also Jesus. The Web has numerous articles both pro and con, including a recent charge of forgery brought by the Israeli Antiquities Department in Jerusalem (search by "James ossuary").

> Come, Thou Fount of every blessing,
> Tune my heart to sing Thy grace!
> Streams of mercy, never ceasing,
> Call for songs of loudest praise. . . .
> Jesus sought me when a stranger,
> Wandering from the fold of God;
> He, to rescue me from danger,
> Interposed His precious blood.
> O to grace how great a debtor
> Daily I'm constrained to be!
> Let that grace now, like a fetter,
> Bind my wandering heart to Thee.

Finally Paul returns to his main point by appealing to the wider apostolic preaching *(they . . . we)* of the gospel that is based on the resurrection of Christ from the dead. This gospel, Paul reminds them, the Corinthians have *believed* (v. 11).

Denial of the Resurrection of the Dead Negates the Gospel (15:12-19) Now Paul is ready to get directly to the issue at hand: *some of you say that there is no resurrection of the dead* (v. 12). His argument in a nutshell is this. There is a divinely purposed unity between three elements in the gospel that the Corinthians have received and in which they stand (15:1). To break or deny any one of these three links is to destroy the whole chain of God's saving purposes in Christ. The three links are the future resurrection of the dead, the present experience of the forgiveness of our sins through faith, and the resurrection of Jesus from the dead. To deny or eliminate any of these three is like trying to sew a fabric without a knot in the thread (Brunner 1947:563).

If there is no resurrection of the dead [in the future], then not even Christ has been raised (v. 13) clearly shows this linkage. Paul has already rehearsed in detail the evidence for the resurrection of Christ from the dead (vv. 4-8), which presumably the Corinthians (or at least most) did accept when they first believed Paul's preaching. If they deny this, then that which is preached is void and so is their faith (v. 14). Furthermore, the apostles *(we)* are found to be *false witnesses* because they preached that *God . . . raised Christ from the dead* (v. 15).

Now Paul's point again is that there is a unity between the future resurrection of the dead and the resurrection of Christ. If the dead are not raised, then Christ is not raised; if Christ is not raised, then the dead will not be raised, and salvation by faith is destroyed, together with the forgiveness of our sins (vv. 16-17).

Furthermore, all hopes for those who have died (*fallen asleep,* or better "laid to sleep," in hope of being *raised*) *are lost* (v. 18, *apollymi,* perish, destroy). For Paul it is not a continuation of the life of the soul that gives hope for those who have died, but the resurrection of the dead. This hope of resurrection is grounded in and inseparable from not a spiritual resurrection or the soul's presence with God, but the resurrection of Christ from the dead.

If only for this life (v. 19) may grammatically be translated also as "If in this life our hope is only in Christ [or, in Christ alone] [and in *his* resurrection but not in our future resurrection—exactly the point disputed, according to v. 12], then we are most to be pitied" (R. Martin 1984:104). In the NIV rendering the emphasis is on *this life* only (not in a future life), while the second possible translation focuses on *hope in Christ* alone (and his resurrection). The latter seems preferable, since in the Greek "alone" occurs at the end of the clause and modifies the whole.

With this sense, then, Paul would be saying, *We are to be pitied more than all men* because without the future resurrection of the dead, all the negative consequences of verses 13-18 would then be true (Christ is not raised, preaching is useless, faith void, there is no forgiveness of sins, and the dead are lost forever). This is of course precisely what Paul does not believe, and he will now turn to the positive and its consequences.

Because Christ Has Been Raised, All Who Belong to Him Will Be Raised (15:20-28) In this section Paul argues two basic points. First, Jesus' resurrection is not merely a paradigm of the future resurrection but is actually the beginning of the future resurrection itself. Second, people will be raised from the dead because they participate in and are identified now with Christ, and they will share his final victory over the last enemy, death, when he comes.

My wife's first experience of meeting Christians who had this hope was as a nurse working in hospital wards where some believers and some nonbelievers were dying every day. "There was such a peace with some patients, I wanted to know why." Her first interest in the Bible came as a result of this experience.

Firstfruits (*aparchē*, vv. 20, 23) is a metaphor drawn from Old Testament harvests. A small portion of the anticipated grain harvest was offered up symbolically, dedicating the whole future harvest to God. The "firstfruits" came first and contained in them the whole rest of the grain harvest to come (Ex 23:16, 19; Deut 26:1-11; cf. Rom 11:16). Similarly, Christ's resurrection is part and parcel of the future resurrection of all who belong to him at his coming (v. 23): Christ alone now, the rest to follow. In Paul's mind, then, to deny the future resurrection is in effect to deny and nullify the resurrection of Christ, because the two are a unity.

Since death came through a man, the resurrection of the dead comes also through a man begins the first of two Adam-Christ analogies (vv. 21-22; cf. vv. 44-49). These brief statements have been called "the high point of the whole chapter" (Gerhard Barth, cited by Thiselton 2000:1226) as well as a Pauline anthropology in miniature (Murphy-O'Connor 1979:142). How can Christ's resurrection embody everybody else's resurrection? Paul's answer: in the same way that the first human being, *Adam,* was both a historical individual and a representative, corporate person. The divine judgment on Adam's sin, resulting in his death, has become also the divine judgment on all human beings because of their sins (see Paul's later statement in Rom 5:12-21).

In an apparently unique view among those of his Jewish-rabbinic counterparts, Paul understands that in some real, not merely analogical or metaphysical, sense, all human beings are under the judicial sentence of death pronounced on Adam's one trespass. More than the fountainhead of our sins, Adam's free choice to sin brought the same condemnation—death—on all of us for our own sins. Paul does not elaborate specifically on this connection, and theologians have argued extensively for different theories.

Here without any elaboration Paul uses the Adam-Christ analogy to support both the universality of death by our participation or unity in

---

15:21-22 An excellent, fresh reexamination of the Adam-Christ typology of Paul that

the one man Adam and the universality of the resurrection from the dead by our participation or unity in the one man Christ. Paul's source for this analogy is not Philo, nor the myth of a primal man, but his own apocalyptic understanding of the human plight (the old order) and that only a divine act of new creation can provide a new order in which God will be all to all (Thiselton 2000:1227).

In Christ all will be made alive (v. 22); *those who belong to him* (v. 23) limits the resurrection to those who are the people of God through Christ. The resurrection is God's final triumph over the reign of death caused by Adam's sin in the Garden. But just as in God's older created order the human being, Adam, represented or mediated his humanity and actions to the whole human race, so Christ as the new creation's human representative or mediator, the "firstborn from among the dead" (Col 1:18; Rev 1:5) and "first to rise from the dead" (Acts 26:23), brings to all who are in him the same resurrection from the dead.

But there is a divine order in God's plan. First is *Christ, the firstfruits* (v. 23; see v. 20), his resurrection being the beginning and promise of the new creation and resurrection of *all who belong to him. Then [second], when he comes* (v. 23) clearly links the resurrection of all the dead in Christ to Christ's parousia, his second advent, which for Paul has emphatically not happened yet.

Then the end [telos] will come (v. 24) refers not to the "rest of the dead" (Rev 20:5) but to the eschatological end of God's redeeming purposes through Christ in the earth. Debate has surrounded the question whether this final sequence allows for a millennial kingdom on the earth as Justin Martyr (d. 165), Irenaeus (d. 202) and many other early church fathers believed. Admittedly it is difficult to get an earthly millennial kingdom into this scheme, since the resurrection of the righteous dead is connected with the return of Christ, which in turn is linked to the final completion of the reign of Christ (1 Cor 15:25-26).

However, as Bruce points out, "the temporal adverb *eita* [then] implies an interval of indeterminate duration between the parousia and the *end,* when Christ hands his dominion back to God," which could

---

helpfully modifies traditional Reformed views is Blocher 1997.

allow for the millennial kingdom. But, Bruce adds, "the context suggests the interval is short" (1971:147). Yet does not Paul connect the defeat of the final enemy, death, with the resurrection, and the resurrection with the return of Christ? If so, then there doesn't seem to be any space for the millennium after Christ returns (the premillennial position). Still, this would not rule out the postmillennial view, where Christ returns and the resurrection takes place after the millennial rule is completed.

When he hands over the kingdom to God the Father after he has destroyed all dominion, authority and power (v. 24) defines more specifically what the end *(telos)* involves. *Dominion, authority and power* refers to mediatorial beings (angelic and demonic) or structures that are part of God's creation order but are in rebellion against God's rule (cf. Gal 4:3; Eph 6:12; Col 2:12, 15, 20).

For he [Christ] must reign until he has put all his enemies under his feet (v. 25) is an allusion (not a quote) to Psalm 110:1, "The LORD says to my Lord: 'Sit at my right hand until I make your enemies a footstool for your feet;'" and Psalm 8:6, "You made him ruler over the works of your hands; you put everything under his feet" (cf. Heb 2:5-9; 10:12-13). "The mention of some of Jesus' actions at his coming is not an unnecessary digression; it serves and sustains Paul's argumentation against the Corinthians' [wrong] understanding of life after death" (Holleman 1996:46).

When Jesus comes he will do two things, as described in verse 24: he will defeat all his enemies, and he will hand over his rule to God the Father. That this subjection of Jesus' enemies and thus his lordship and kingdom have already begun is evident first in the resurrection of Jesus himself from the dead and his exaltation—enthronement as Lord (cf. Rom 1:4; Heb 10:12-13). *The last enemy to be destroyed (katargeō,* made ineffective; see 1 Cor 13:8-11) *is death* (15:26). Paul makes the defeat of death the finale of Christ's rule in behalf of God. "Death will

---

15:28 Recent evangelical attempts to argue for the eternal subordination of the Son to the Father in the Trinity to justify the subordination of women to men in their roles is effectively addressed and rejected as heretical by a study of evangelical Australian scholar Kevin Giles (2002). Also, evangelical theologian Thomas F. Torrance comments: "The notion of a hierarchy within the Holy Trinity was repudiated by

be overcome only through the resurrection or transformation at the end of time, when Jesus comes. Then death will be destroyed for ever" (Holleman 1996:65).

It is clear that this does not include God himself, who put everything under Christ (v. 27). Why is Paul so concerned that God not be included in the everything subjected to Christ's messianic kingdom? How is this related to the context? I can only briefly sketch the highlights. One rather oblique explanation is that Paul is countering here the Roman *Pater-Patriae* imperial eschatology propaganda, which stressed that the emperor was both divine and the "father of the fatherland" (Witherington 1995:304-5). Presumably in this approach Christ defeats all the lesser lords and subjects them to the true Father of all. Though this sheds light on the historical situation, the context requires further explanation.

Joost Holleman seems to catch the right nuance: "Yet the idea behind the image [Ps 110:1] is that the king and God are so closely related that, although the king is the actual ruler, it is God who exercises his power through the king. . . . Although it is Jesus who actually destroys every rule, authority, and power, it is God who acts through Jesus. Jesus acts on behalf of God so that God's reign is established and then Jesus will hand over his kingdom to God" (1996:60). The "except God" clause reaffirms the centrality and inclusiveness of God. It also protects the "sole monarchy" of God (the Trinity) and avoids ending with two rival deities and two kingdoms.

The second action of Jesus according to verse 24 is that *after* he has annulled the last enemy, death, by raising the dead, *he hands over the kingdom to God the Father* (v. 24). Christ does this by submitting himself to the Father: *then the Son himself will be made subject to him who put everything under him, so that God may be all in all* (v. 28). The purpose of the messianic interim rule of Christ is to bring the full fruits of Christ's saving work (death, burial, resurrection) to bear on the full

---

Gregory Nazianzen, Epiphanius, and Cyril of Alexandria particularly, and of course the Ecumenical Council of Constantinople in its authorization of the Nicene-Constantinople Creed. Basil and his brother Gregory tended in a subordinationist direction to the horror of Gregory Nazianzen, and it has been rejected by Orthodox Theology. See my *Trinitarian Faith*, pp. 239ff., and also *Trinitarian Perspectives*, pp. 125ff on

redemption of the world (Heb 10:12-13; Rev 11:15). Paul's own expression for this ultimate triumph of God through his Messiah's kingdom is that *God may be all in all*. This is not a pantheistic expression identifying God with the sum of all things, but rather an affirmation of the absolute lordship of God over all creation and human life in particular. Romans 11:36 captures this term thus: "For from him and through him and to him are all things. To him be the glory forever! Amen."

But what of the Son's being *made subject to* the Father? Is this not an expression of what the church has rightly come to brand and reject as a "subordinationist Christology" (Hays 1997:266)? I believe Hays is misled at this point. The delicate theological balance in the trinitarian involvement in our salvation that Paul has already shown (1 Cor 12:4-7) should alert us that what these verses are describing is not the ontological relation between the Father and Son in the being of God, but the incarnate, obedient Son's mission as the "second man," who will subjugate all God's enemies, including death, to the lordship of the triune God, and then, as man, will remit into the Father's hand the authority given him for his mission as the messianic King (15:21, 44-49).

Gregory of Nazianzus (d. 390) captures the true relationship of Father to Son in pointing out that "as the Son subjects all to the Father, so does the Father to the Son, the one by his work, the other by his good pleasure" (in Bray 1999:164). We must emphatically deny any notion of subordinationism in the Trinity itself, which would clearly lead into heresy, as Gregory of Nazianzus, Cyril of Alexandria and Augustine all understood. To read this passage, which concerns the mediatorial office of Christ in his incarnation for our salvation, back into the eternal relations of Father and Son in the Holy Trinity would be to overthrow the Trinity (Torrance 1996:179-80).

Often John 14:28, "the Father is greater than I," is connected with 1 Corinthians 15:28 as evidence of the "lesser" nature of Christ relative to the Father, or at best as a reference to a hierarchical ordering of the Father over the Son in the Trinity. Augustine addresses this misunderstanding

---

the Monarchy, in which the Orthodox and the Reformed reached complete agreement. See also *Theological Dialogue Between Orthodox and Reformed Churches,* vol. II, 1993, pp. 219ff, and my book *The Christian Doctrine of God,* p. 115ff.

"The notion of a hierarchy in the Trinity is really a Roman Catholic Idea—even

as well: "If the Son is equal, how is the Father greater? For the Lord himself says, 'because the Father is greater than I.' However, the rule of the Catholic faith is this: when Scriptures say of the Son that he is less than the Father, the Scriptures mean in respect to *the assumption of humanity*. But when the Scriptures point out that he is equal they are understood in respect to his *deity*" (in Bray 1999:164).

Here in 1 Corinthians it is important to note that Christ voluntarily hands over the kingdom to the Father by submitting himself to the rule of God as the representative last Adam of the new creation (vv. 21, 45). That the lordship and exaltation of Christ never end is amply attested in other writings of Paul (Phil 2:9-11). Christ's kingdom will be blended into the eternal kingdom of God when he returns.

Finally, "any 'evangelical' exploitation of the notion of an hierarchy in the Holy Trinity, in order to justify some sort of subordinationism between men and women, and in the ministry, is simply unbiblical, and heretical!" (Torrance 1998; see also note 15:28).

Otherwise Hope, Suffering and Faithfulness Are Pointless (15:29-34) In this section Paul makes a final attempt to persuade the Corinthians that there will be an end-time resurrection from the dead. His approach is to appeal to their own experiences (vv. 29, 33-34) and also to Paul's and the other apostles' sufferings (vv. 30-32) in a contrary-to-fact mode: why do this if there is no resurrection?

Verse 29, *baptized for the dead,* has been called the most difficult and obscure verse in the Bible. Certainly it holds the record in this epistle. Thiselton counts no fewer than forty different explanations (2000:1240); Ralph Martin suggests two hundred is closer to the truth (1984:118). I am tempted to skip it altogether! But what does it mean, and how does it support Paul's argument in the context for a future bodily resurrection from the dead? To begin, I will try to categorize the major interpretations.

1. Vicarious (or surrogate) baptism for the dead is the most frequent view encountered in the commentators. This means that some living

---

Barth seems to have had an element of subordinationism in the Trinity, but no notion of an eternal hierarchy. Any 'evangelical' exploitation of the notion of an eternal hierarchy in the Holy Trinity, in order to justify some sort of subordinationism between men and women, and in the ministry, is simply unbiblical, and heretical!!" (1998).

believers were being baptized *for* or in the interests of those who had died. This may have taken different forms, such as baptism for those who died without it, baptism for pagan family members who died before the gospel reached them, or baptism for pagans for the sake of their reunion with departed Christian loved ones. It might be objected that if this proxy baptism was in fact the case in point, why didn't it continue in the church (except among early Marcionites and now Mormons)? Why doesn't the New Testament mention it elsewhere?

2. Martyrdom as baptism changes the meaning of *baptized* from the sacrament to sufferings and death (Mk 10:38-39), a sort of baptism in blood; they were being baptized with a view to death. Paul's point then would be to call attention to why they would be willing to so suffer if there was no hope of resurrection awaiting them. This is all unlikely and strains the sense of the preposition *hyper (for)*.

3. *For the dead* is a reference not to a third party but to the ones who are getting themselves baptized. They are being baptized for the sake of their own dying bodies (Chrysostom). If the wholly dead (corpses) are not to be raised, what would they gain by being baptized? This view suffers from a deeply strained sense of "the dead" as meaning first our dying bodies and in the next verse a reference to the wholly dead.

4. Those who get themselves baptized do it to join their departed family members (the dead). For example, a dying mother may win her son to the faith with the appeal "Meet me in heaven!" (so Thiselton 2000:1248; Bruce 1971:149). This assumes that (1) baptism and conversion to Christ are linked and (2) baptism de facto implies future bodily resurrection. But while this might assure one of being reunited to a loved one after death, how is it an argument for the resurrection of the body?

While some of the above views are more attractive than others, none of them seems to fully satisfy. What is important to Paul's argument is that some Christians at Corinth were practicing baptism in such a way (whether approved by Paul or not) as to express belief and hope in the final resurrection. Otherwise what they were doing would not make sense. That much we can with confidence affirm.

And as for us, why do we endanger ourselves every hour? I die every day (vv. 30-31) presents ad hominem arguments for the resurrection of the dead. Paul's and the other apostles' (*us . . . we,* see v. 11) own experiences in fulfilling his (their) call to preach the gospel (2 Cor 1:8-11; 11:23-33) would be unexplainable, illogical, not worthwhile if there were no resurrection. We put our lives at risk, and day to day we are at death's door. Why would we do this, he reasons, if there were no expected hope of resurrection from the dead for us and others to motivate us in the midst of such a bleak and suffering-filled life? Luther's great hymn says it well:

Let goods and kindred go, this mortal life also;

The body they may kill; God's truth abideth still;

His kingdom is forever.

As I write these words we have just learned of the brutal death of missionary Martin Burnham, killed by a radical Islamic group in the Philippines. Those who take Christ to the unevangelized still face the daily threat to life and safety that Paul describes. Of the early apostles Reginald Heber writes,

A glorious bond, the chosen few

On whom the Spirit came.

Twelve valiant saints, *their hope they knew,*

And mocked the cross and flame;

They met the tyrant's brandished steel,

The lion's gory mane,

They bowed their necks the death to feel:

Who follows in their train? (italics mine)

I glory over you in the modern idiom would be an affirmation based on something of ultimate importance to them: "I swear by all that I hold dear" that this is true.

Paul continues with his own experience in his missionary travels of fighting *wild beasts in Ephesus.* Paul was in Ephesus in 53-56, during which time he wrote both 1 Corinthians and 2 Corinthians. Was he imprisoned there? Did he face the Roman circus there? Or is the reference metaphorical of his life-threatening battles with city officials or other hostile persons there? Later he speaks of "many who oppose me" in Ephesus (1 Cor 16:9). Since in normal, nonanarchic times Roman citizens could not be condemned to the arena without first being stripped of their citizenship, and Paul much later still had his (Acts 22:25-29), most commentators opt for the metaphorical sense of "grave danger" or "deadly opposition" (cf. Ps 22:12-16; Acts 19:9; 19:23—20:1; 2 Tim 4:17).

Often, not without significance, the early church father Ignatius (d. 110) is cited as evidence of this sense: "From Syria to Rome, by land and by sea, night and day, I am fighting with wild beasts. I mean *these soldiers*, to whom I am bound, for they are like ten leopards" (*To the Romans* 5.1). Also: "Shall I encounter wild beasts only then at length when I arrive in Rome? No, I am assailed by them every hour throughout my journey" (*To the Romans* 5.3). *For merely human reasons* is in the Greek simply *kata anthrōpon,* which can mean "from a human perspective" or "after the manner of a human" (that is, those who have no hope in resurrection).

If the dead are not raised, "Let us eat and drink, for tomorrow we die" shows how disbelief in the future resurrection of the dead could seriously affect our ethical conduct. The quotation is usually understood to come from Isaiah 22:13 (cf. Is 56:12; Song 2:6), although Paul does not formally indicate that it is a quote, leaving room to understand it as a popular saying. If from Isaiah, the words are a pathetic expression of the inhabitants of Jerusalem as they faced the imminent invasion of the Assyrians. Instead of repenting and weeping, they chose to "party like there was no tomorrow" (Hays 1997:268). On the other hand, the saying may simply express either a pro-Epicurean or an anti-Epicurean exaggerated sentiment intended to denigrate the life of pleasure.

Whatever the source, Paul seems to suggest that without the resurrection of the dead, life is reduced to bodily pleasure seeking as the logical course to follow, since death ends all. The following quote taken by Strabo (4 B.C.) from an inscription written by Sardanapallus, the founder of the city of Tarsus, for his own tombstone, shows such an advocacy of pleasure seeking in the light of human mortality.

Sardanapallus . . . built Anchiale and Tarsus in one day. *Eat,*

15:32 Ralph Martin refers to a study of G. S. Duncan to the effect that there was social anarchy in Corinth in A.D. 54 (Martin 1984:122).

15:32-34 I am indebted for some thoughts in this section to Bruce Winter, who helpfully posits that 1 Corinthians 15 may have aimed to combat widespread belief in the

drink, and *play,* because all things else are not worth this. . . . Well aware that you are by nature *mortal,* magnifying the *desire of your heart,* delighting yourselves in *merriments,* there is no *enjoyment* for you after death. For I too am dust, though I have reigned over Ninus. Mine are all the *food* I have eaten, and my loose *indulgences,* and the *delights of love* that I have enjoyed; but those numerous blessings have been left behind. This to mortal man is wise advice on how to live. (italics mine)

This is close to the advice given by the modern hedonist Hugh Hefner in his Playboy philosophy of life!

The old adage certainly sums up the spirit of the current age. Some would say that this is true of every age. We all seek pleasure, to maximize happy times and minimize pain. A modern television beer commercial puts it this way, "Go for the gusto! You only go around once!" Sean Flynn, son of the late Errol Flynn, once asked a Santa Monica court, "What's wrong, nowadays, with a young man specializing in pleasure?"

Somewhat more crass is the statement of a potential candidate for the Hell's Angels motorcycle group. "I have tried marriage, and the home and the kids, and it ain't hitting on nothin'. What I like about the 'Pagans' is that every night you can get drunk, have a blast, and enjoy yourself. Broads and booze and everything they got to offer." Not too far from Aldous Huxley's *Brave New World:* "Never put off until tomorrow the fun you can have today."

For Paul the denial of a life centered on pleasure, rather choosing to put one's life constantly in harm's way (vv. 30-32), is perfectly understandable if there is a resurrection of the dead and a consequent new creation life when Christ returns.

I want to return momentarily to the maxim of verse 32. Literature of ancient Greece and Rome makes a connection between eating, drinking and play (*paizō*) that involved sexual intercourse after dinner. The Strabo

---

immortality of the soul, and that belief's implications for ethical conduct may have had more to do with the problems at Corinth than an overrealized eschatology with no place for the resurrection of the body (2001:96-103).

quote is evidence of this, but Paul's next words again seem to quote a popular saying or may indicate his direct knowledge of a line from Meander's lost comic play *Thais*. The context of the line is quite revealing:

Loose-bridled [woman]? Pest! Methinks, though I have suffered this, that none the less I'd now be glad to have *her*. Sing to me, goddess, sing of such a one as *she:* audacious, beautiful, and plausible withal: *she* does you wrongs; *she* locks *her* door; keeps asking you for gifts; *she* loves none, but every makes pretence. *Evil companionship corrupts good character.*

The language here is that of sexual companionship. We should recall Paul's earlier reference to the incident of the Israelites with the golden calf, when eating and drinking was associated likewise with sexual "play" (*paizō*, 10:7; see comments there).

This behavior may also be related to the individual-freedom emphasis of some at Corinth ("I have the right to do anything"—6:12; 10:23), which led to the problem of eating and drinking in pagan temple dining rooms, followed by sexual indulgence (cf. 6:13-20). Combine this with the "status" and "maturity" enjoyed by those who exercised such freedoms.

When a Roman boy came of age, his father gave him a special robe *(toga virilus),* and when it was put on he recited the words, "I have the right to do anything," to show he had entered into his majority. Something of this spirit was apparently at work in those who, adopting the Greek concept of the soul's eternal separation from the body at death and denying the future bodily resurrection, felt free to pursue whatever they desired and go wherever their desires took them.

So Paul warns them about self-deception: *Do not be misled* (v. 33; cf. 6:9-10) into a lifestyle of sensuous pleasure seeking in the name of freedom. That would avoid the denial that make true Christian service possible. Our bodies now belong to the Lord (cf. 6:13-20; 2 Cor 5:10); therefore *come back to your senses,* wake up (or sober up after drunkenness) to God's righteous use for our bodies, *and stop sinning* by denying the resurrection and pursuing pleasure.

Ignorant of God, or having an utter lack of knowledge of God, is called by Barth the secret mystery behind the whole epistle; he translates it as "to have no inkling of God!" "All things are these: correct doctrine, an upright faith, moral earnestness—but with all this not to have [personal, relational] knowledge of God—which makes everything vain, empty and nugatory." The words "Some have no inkling of God," Barth says, should be emblazoned on pulpit steps and similar places, so that pastors may be reminded every time they address a congregation (Barth 1933:18, 190-91).

Shame or disgrace (v. 34) would be felt by those who boasted of their knowledge and high status (8:1-2) but are now charged with utter ignorance of God. "Paul's aim is not to humiliate them (so he names no names) but to bring them to a better frame of mind" (Bruce 1971:150). He earlier had shamed them for going to non-Christian arbiters with petty internal disputes (6:5).

Resurrection Means a New Creation of the Body (15:35-58) Having argued that Christ has been raised from the dead, that every believer will likewise be raised when Christ returns and that disbelief in this truth concretely affects our present moral life, Paul now addresses the second major problem the Corinthians had with the resurrection, their aversion to resuscitated corpses. Their questions express the impossibility and inconceivability to them of a resurrection *body*.

Paul first shows the conceivability of the resurrection body by pointing to illustrations from the present creation: seeds that die and then emerge in new God-given forms, how God gives bodies different kinds of flesh, and how there are all kinds of different earthly and heavenly bodies that God has created with diverse splendors. In a similar manner God will create new bodies for us that are sown natural bodies and raised spiritual bodies. The natural body we have is because we belong to Adam's race. The spiritual body we will have in the resurrection is like the resurrected body of Jesus (vv. 35-49). There are allusions to Genesis 1-2, creation renewed.

Second, Paul argues for the possibility of the resurrection body because God will act in an awesome transformation of our perishable dead bodies, and of the mortal flesh of those who are alive, into imperishable new-creation bodies like Christ's. This will happen because our bodies are inseparably united to Jesus Christ and will participate in God's final victory over sin and death (vv. 50-57).

Therefore *let nothing move* us away from Christ. *Give yourselves,* in the light of this glorious future resurrection, fully to the service of Christ, because now you understand that your self-effacing labor to others in this body in him is worth it all (v. 58).

The Conceivability and Possibility of the Resurrection Body (15:35-49) So, someone listening to Paul might say, if there is to be a future resurrection as you say, how can dead, decomposed, rotting corpses come back to life? What kind of bodies will they have? (v. 35). The questions express puzzlement at best and challenge at worst to Paul's arguments in the previous sections of the chapter. Isn't a resurrection body inconceivable? Aren't dead corpses coming back to life impossible to imagine? His response to the first question *(how)* is given in verses 50-57, to the second *(what kind of body)* in verses 36-49.

1. The seed analogy (15:36-38). *How foolish!* is literally, "You fool!" (cf. Lk 11:40; 12:20); this may be a standard rhetorical device to belittle the questioner before a revelation of knowledge is offered (Snyder 1991:205; cf. Ps 14:1). *With what kind of body will they come?* is first answered with a seed analogy. A farmer plants a *seed* in the ground, *it dies* (not actually but figuratively), then God brings it back to life and *gives it a body* that he has chosen; *to each kind of seed he gives its own body* (v. 38). This latter shows the contrast, differentiation and variety without loss of identity that God accomplishes in plant bodies.

The *seed* corresponds to our perishable, rotting body that must die first, whereas the embodied life that emerges from death represents our new resurrection body. The perishable body that is laid in the ground in death is not the same body that emerges in new life, but the seed image strongly implies continuity of identity. Somehow we will know ourselves to be ourselves in the new body, and we will know others in their new bodies as the same persons we knew in their perishable bodies (cf. Lk 24:30-35; 36-42).

The following extended quote from Merrill Tenney, former dean of the Wheaton Graduate School, deserves special notice for its lucidity and judicial balance. He begins with a report about the decomposed body of the Rhode Island Baptist minister Roger Williams:

When the body of Roger Williams, founder of the Rhode Island colony, was exhumed for reburial, it was found that the root of an apple tree had penetrated the head of the coffin and had followed down Williams' spine, dividing into a fork at the legs. The tree had absorbed the chemicals of the decaying body and had transmuted them into its woods and fruit. The apples, in turn, had been eaten by people, quite unconscious of the fact that they were indirectly taking into their systems part of the long-dead Williams. The objection may therefore be raised: How, out of the complex sequence of decay, absorption, and new formation, will it be possible to resurrect believers of past ages, and to reconstitute them as separate entities? . . .

When a grain of wheat is dropped into the ground, its husk quickly decays, and even the live core disintegrates. The life of the seed, rather than its material substance, provides the continuity of existence. As the rootlets begin to grow, they draw nourishment from the earth, and by the chemistry of sun and rain the small seed soon becomes a large plant. The plant bears no external resemblance to the seed, nor is the bulk of its tissue drawn from the seed; nevertheless, the continuity is undeniable. There is persistence of type, because a given seed will always produce its own kind. Identity of type is not incompatible with discontinuity of substance. Continuity of individuality is assured by the persistence of the personality, which God will reclothe with a body. Jesus' statement, "all that are in the tombs shall hear his voice, and shall come forth; they that have done good unto the resurrection of life; and they that have done evil, unto the resurrection of judgment" (Jn 5:28-29), assumes the preservation of individuality, since those that have been buried will be restored to life. The restoration, however, is not a reconstitution of the original body that was interred, but a new structure patterned on the resurrection body of Christ. "As we have borne the image of the earthy, we shall also bear the image of the heavenly" (1 Cor 15:49). (quoted by Harris 1990:411-12)

2. The flesh analogy (15:39). *All flesh is not the same* presents another analogy to the resurrection body. The different types of fleshes (skin) that cover the present creation's human and animate bone structures provide another example of the rich diversity of God's creation. The argument is from the lesser (human flesh, animals, birds, fish) to the greater (the new creation of the resurrection body).

3. Differences in form and character of earthly and heavenly bodies (15:40-41). Again Paul points to the variety of God's creation of different *earthly* and *heavenly bodies* and to the different *splendor* (*doxa*, "honor," "glory," "radiance," "excellence") each has. Not that resurrection bodies will have different degrees of honor, but if God is so imaginative in creating bodies in this present creation, how much more can he create a resurrection body that is unimaginably glorious!

Something of that future event's character is captured in the refrain of Charles Gabriel's (1856-1932) hymn:

O that will be glory for me,

Glory for me, glory for me:

When by His grace I shall look on His face,

That will be glory, be glory for me.

4. The imperishable *spiritual body* of the resurrection (15:42-49). Paul now applies these analogies directly to *the resurrection of the dead* by returning to the seed language that combines continuity with radical transformation (vv. 42-44). The resurrection body is a mirror image of the present body; everything is reversed (Murphy-O'Connor 1979:147).

Now	Then
perishable (v. 42)	*imperishable*
dishonor (v. 43, humiliation)	*glory*
weakness (v. 43)	*power* (increased capacities for splendor or service)
natural body (v. 44)	*spiritual body*

Here the emphasis is more on discontinuity (but see at v. 53) between the present body and the future body. "What is *sown* is not identical to what is *grown,* though it is related to it" (R. Martin 1984). Paul now turns to a further focus on the human body.

Natural [psychikon] body . . . spiritual [pneumatikon] body (v. 44) has produced considerable discussion. The *-ikos* ending on the adjective signals an "ethical or dynamic relation, not a material one" (Harris

---

15:44-49 A controversy in evangelical circles has emerged over the exact nature of

1990:402). So the words denote "not substances but modes of being" (Thiselton 2000:1275). Therefore the proper distinction between the two types of embodiments is not material or physical versus immaterial or nonphysical but a body suited for the mere functioning of the *psychē*, the life principle, a body destined because of sin to die and to corrupt (Gen 3:19), in contrast to a body suited for the full functioning of the Holy Spirit, the imperishable resurrection body.

The future *spiritual body* is not a mere physical body (resuscitation) but a new creation of God that befits the transformation of our character into the pattern of life in Christ effected by the Holy Spirit, a body suited for the full expression of love (chap. 13). As Christ's resurrection body exhibited identity, communicability and communion, so also will ours. "The transformed body is not composed of 'spirit'; it is a body adapted to the eschatological existence that is under the ultimate dominance of the Spirit" (Fee 1987:786; also Thiselton 2000:1277; Wright 2003:348-53). As William Blake observes about each species having a body suited to its environment even in the present creation: "Robin Redbreast in a cage puts all heaven in a rage."

The first man Adam became a living being (v. 45) refers to Genesis 2:7, with Paul's addition of *first*, which prepares him to refer to Christ as the *last* Adam (cf. 15:21-22; Rom 5:12-19). The nature of the body of the resurrected Christ is described as *a life-giving spirit* (v. 45), *pneuma zōopoieō*, "Spirit that gives life" from the dead. Probably this is a reference to both the salvation experience of the Corinthians and the power of life in the future resurrection of the dead that is mediated through Christ (v. 21).

The order of *the natural* first, then the *spiritual* (v. 46), helps us keep Adam's significance in proper perspective to Christ and his importance to the human plight and God's triumphant reversal. Only when the natural with all its limitations and qualifications has been laid down in death can the Spirit fully transform our body and allow us to give full expression to the indwelling Spirit of Christ.

The first man was of the dust of the earth, the second man from heaven (v. 47) is possibly an allusion to both Genesis 2:7 (man from

the resurrection body (see Harris 1990).

dust) and Daniel 7:13-14 (man of heaven). Both seem to be individuals that also incorporate groups into their being. *As . . . the heavenly man, so also . . . those who are of heaven* argues that the archetype of each group grounds the character and nature of all who belong to the archetype. *As we have borne (phoreō,* "wear," "bear") *the likeness (eikōn,* "image") *of the earthly man [Adam], so shall we bear [or "wear"] the likeness of the man from heaven [Christ]* in the resurrection (v. 49). This is a clear statement that the resurrection archetype is the resurrected Christ himself. Paul beautifully states this same truth in a later letter: "But our citizenship is in heaven. And we eagerly await a Savior from there, the Lord Jesus Christ, who, by the power that enables him to bring everything under his control, will transform our lowly bodies so that they will be like his glorious body" (Phil 3:20-21). Hallelujah!

Both the Dead and the Living Will Be Changed at Christ's Coming (15:50-58) This final section seems to address an unstated question that may have arisen after readers have followed Paul's argument to this point. What about those who are alive and have not suffered death when the Lord returns? Do they have to die first and then be raised? Or do they simply migrate as they are into the new creation? Paul's answer is *transformation.*

I declare (v. 50) is a strong assertion that *flesh and blood cannot inherit the kingdom of God, nor does the perishable inherit the imperishable.* Paul wants it to be very clear that those who are living in earthly, natural bodies now (like himself) cannot inherit the kingdom of God or eternal life as they are. His words should not be taken, as they often are, as a denial that physical bodies will be in the eternal state. This would be to deny all that Paul has taught in the preceding sections. *Flesh and blood* is a Semitic idiom for human nature as it is now in its frailty, its perishability. What the strong assertion means is that "neither the living nor the dead can take part in the reign of God *as they are,* i.e., *without salvific transformation*" (Thiselton 2000:1275).

15:49 *So shall we bear the likeness (phoresomen,* future tense) is probably the correct text, but other primary witnesses read "let us bear the likeness" (hortatory subjunctive).

15:51-52 *We will not all sleep, but we will all be changed* is almost certainly the cor-

Mystery (v. 51, *mystērion*) means a divine truth formerly not disclosed but now revealed. *We will not all sleep [die], but we will all be changed.* Since this is a previously undisclosed truth *(mystērion)*, it could not be the same truth revealed by Paul earlier to the Thessalonians (1 Thess 4:13-18). What is different here is the transformation *(allassō,* to make different, change, alter, exchange) of the living at the coming of Christ (1 Cor 15:52-57). Paul pictures this change at length in 2 Corinthians 5:2-4 as the putting on of a new garment of immortality. In Philippians 3:21 the change involves nothing less than transformation into Christ's own risen being, his "glorious body," which is already taking shape in the Christian through the Spirit (Gal 4:19; 2 Cor 3:18; Eph 4:24).

This will take place at the coming of Christ (1 Cor 15:23), *in a flash* *(atomos,* "instant"), *in the twinkling of an eye* *(rhipē,* not "twinkle" but "blink"), *at the last trumpet* (v. 52). The *last trumpet* here is the apocalyptic victory signal that in the Qumran Dead Sea communities heralded the ultimate victory of God (1QM 18:3-4) but in the New Testament is associated with the return of Christ, the resurrection of the dead and the beginning of the new creation (Is 27:13; Mt 24:31; 1 Thess 4:16; Rev 10:7; 11:15). Some of the excitement of this great event is captured in the hymn "My Hope Is Built on Nothing Less" by Edward Mote (1834):

When He shall come with trumpet sound,

O may I then in Him be found,

Dressed in His righteousness alone,

Faultless to stand before the throne.

At this moment *the dead will be raised imperishable* *(aphtharsia,* "cannot wear out," "incapable of dying"), *and we [the living] will be changed* (v. 52). Paul no doubt included himself *(we)* in the hope that he would be among those alive at Christ's coming, not having to die before he was transformed into the new creation body. *Perishable* to

---

rect text, but there are several other interesting variants that reflect theological concerns: "we shall not all sleep, nor shall we all be changed" (p[46]); "indeed we shall all sleep, but we shall not all be changed" (A); "we shall all sleep, but we shall not all be changed" (Aleph); "we shall all be raised, but we shall not all be changed" (D).

imperishable most likely refers to those who have died, while *mortal* to *immortal* refers to the living who *must* (*dei,* apocalyptic necessity) be radically changed into *imperishable* bodies. This is a picture of radical transformation with continuity of identity. If, as some argue, there can be no continuing identity without continuing existence, then some form of continuing existence between death and resurrection seems to be necessary (see Lk 23:43; Rom 8:38-39; 2 Cor 5:8-9; Phil 1:23).

"Death has been swallowed up in victory" (v. 54) is a loose quotation of Isaiah 25:8 that agrees with neither the LXX or the Hebrew (the LXX versions of Aquila and Theodotion have the word *victory—nikē*). But the context in Isaiah does refer to the "shroud that enfolds all peoples" (Is 25:7), which commentators take as a reference to death. To swallow up something is to completely do away with it. *Victory* indicates the complete defeat of an enemy (v. 26); formerly *death* had the victory, but now Christ conquers it, swallowing it up forever with all the evils that attend it, in the stupendous event of the resurrection of the dead. "God will wipe away every tear from their eyes" (Rev 7:17; 22:4; Is 25:8).

Where, O death . . . is again a loose quotation from Hosea 13:14 and likewise departs from the LXX and Hebrew by replacing "plagues" with *victory* and "destruction" with *sting.* As several commentators have noted, these two prophecies (Is 25:8; Hos 13:14) seem to be the only Old Testament prophecies quoted by Paul that remain unfulfilled. *Sting* (*kentron,* "stinger," "goad") refers to the deadly stinger of a scorpion (Rev 9:10). *The sting of death is sin* recalls the earlier "as in Adam all die" (vv. 21-22), for Adam's sin and condemnation of death have affected all human beings. In Paul the *law* increases or intensifies *(power)* sin (and its sting) by provoking our sinful flesh to disobedience and thus exposing us to the death sentence for sin (Rom 6:23; 7:7-13).

Thanks be to God! He gives us the victory through our Lord Jesus Christ is the whole chapter in a nutshell! "Death's sting—its power to evoke fear and inflict suffering (cf. Heb. 2:14-15)—is therefore already plucked out, like the stinger of a malevolent insect, by Christ's resurrection from the grave" (Hays 1997:276).

Therefore, my dear (*agapētoi,* beloved) *brothers* (and sisters, TNIV), *stand firm* (cf. 15:1-2; 16:13). *Let nothing move you. Always give your-*

selves fully to the work of the Lord, because . . . your labor in the Lord is not in vain—because Christ is risen from the dead and God will raise us in him (15:58). This is the conclusion for all of chapter 15. "The resurrection [of the dead] is the necessary foundation for faithful action in the world" (Hays 1997:277). *Work of the Lord* is almost certainly labor directed toward the gospel proclamation, the growth of Christians, and ministries of love toward others in the name of Christ. Paul's exhortation is highly emotional at this point.

I conclude with an extended quote from one commentator who precisely targets this chapter's relevance for today's pastors.

In a culture that evades telling the truth about death, the teaching of the resurrection comes as a blast of fresh air. If asked, "What do we hope for after death?" many devout Christians would answer with sentimental notions of their soul going to heaven and smiling back down on the earth. Such ideas have virtually no basis in the Bible, and those who exercise the teaching office in the church should seek to impress upon their congregations that the predominant future hope of the New Testament writers is precisely the same as the hope presented here in 1 Corinthians 15: resurrection of the body at the time of Christ's *parousia* and final judgment.

I have never forgotten a conversation I had with a young woman in my church years ago. I will call her "Stephanie." Her eighteen-year-old sister (whom I will call "Lisa") had been killed in a car accident. All the members of her family were saying things like "Lisa is so much happier now in heaven; she was always such an unhappy child here" or "God must have wanted her to be with him" or "I just know that Lisa is watching us now and telling us not to be sad."

Stephanie was infuriated by such sweet, pious talk, for it seemed to deny both the reality of Lisa's death and its tragedy. Yet Stephanie felt guilty, because as a Christian she thought she ought to believe the pious things her family was saying. Thus, it came as a liberating word to her to learn that Paul speaks of death as a destructive "enemy" that will be conquered only at the end of this age. First Corinthians 15 enabled her to acknowledge soberly that Lisa was now really dead and buried in the ground, while at the same time realizing that she could hope to hold Lisa in her arms again, in the resurrection.

Obviously, such matters must be handled with the greatest pastoral sensitivity, but we need to find ways to communicate these matters more clearly in the church. The resurrection of the dead is, after all, the classical teaching of the New Testament and the Christian tradition; we might find that such teaching would go a long way to promote healthier attitudes towards death and life in our congregations. (Hays 1997:279)

□ Final Matters and Conclusion of the Letter (16:1-24)

It is a relief to pass into this clear, rather uncontroversial, but highly practical and interesting window into the day-by-day matters of one of the earliest New Testament churches. Compared to chapter 15, on which perhaps over forty times as many research articles have been written, chapter 16 is refreshingly free from scholarly disputes and has relatively few exegetical and theological conundrums.

In a nutshell, the chapter emphasizes themes of mutuality, hospitality and love. More specifically Paul takes up two remaining questions posed by the Corinthians' letter to him: a special offering for the people of God in Jerusalem and the plans of Apollo (vv. 1-12), He then gives them advice and instruction and sends greetings from those in Ephesus, where he has written the letter (vv. 13-18). Finally, Paul adds his own handwritten warning, eschatological prayer, wish for grace and expression of love for them (vv. 21-24).

Not a mere appendage, this chapter connects back to themes in the previous chapters, chapter 15 in particular. Responsibility for sharing material goods picks up on the importance of bodily acts in the previous chapter and elsewhere in the letter. That the Corinthians should share their wealth to promote the gospel links well with their indebtedness to the first church in Jerusalem to proclaim the resurrection of Christ. Themes such as mutuality, hospitality, reciprocity of love and generosity run through the epistle. Paul has just emphasized abundance and faithful action because of the resurrection of the dead through Christ the Lord. What better motivation for generous sharing of our goods with others than the fact they are part of the same hope?

The chapter is also very interesting for a number of subthemes it touches on: Sunday versus sabbath worship, how pastoral wisdom in financial matters is crucial for credibility, a theology of giving, Paul's evangelistic methods and follow-up, the dating and place of origin of the letter, respect for coworkers and leaders, Paul-and-Apollos relations, Paul's personal interests, models for wealthy Christian patrons, and the substance of the earliest Christian prayer recorded.

Early Mutuality and Hospitality (16:1-12) Christian love expressed in concrete actions underlies especially this early section of the chapter. Such love expresses itself in mutuality and hospitality. There are three matters Paul brings up: the special offering (vv. 1-4), his own travel plans (vv. 5-9), and Timothy's visit and Apollos's plans (vv. 10-12).

The Special Offering (16:1-4) Often the sharing of material goods has bound diverse Christian groups together in solidarity. A few years ago we visited a large church in the Chicago suburbs. It was just after a powerful hurricane wreaked widespread devastation in Honduras. An appeal had been made from the pulpit the previous Sunday for members to bring boxes of canned goods and nonperishables to the church. We witnessed a tremendous outpouring of material love as people stacked their boxes of food behind the trunks of their cars in the parking lots. While we worshiped, volunteers loaded semi trucks with the gifts. To our sheer amazement, the following week we learned that twenty-four thousand tons of food was collected and later that week airlifted to Honduras! What abundance of love, what joy and thanksgiving to God arose!

Five years ago our own small church seized an opportunity to help a small Korean congregation near us with financial gifts for its new church building. That congregation joined with ours a few Sundays later, and the Korean pastor preached for us with amazing power and blessing. Wonderful mutuality and community-building resulted, binding us together across racial, cultural and economic lines.

But we must be careful that our understanding of stewardship does not tempt us into becoming benefactors (patrons) who create dependency rather than foster true mutuality and the joy of equal membership. "As one considers the evils of welfare systems, racism, sexism, and economic imperialism, it can be said that dependency is the common thread. Any system is evil if it makes one person or one group dependent on another. For the Christian the death and resurrection of Jesus Christ creates mutuality or *koinōnia* rather than dependency" (Snyder 1991:218). It may be better to dig wells in the Sudan than to send food or money indefinitely for the starving.

Now about (*peri de,* similar to 7:1, 25; 8:1; 12:1) signals another question in the Corinthians' letter to Paul. *The collection* (*logeias,* offerings) occurs only here in the New Testament but frequently in the papyri for financial collections, especially ad hoc offerings. This was not a tax or a tithe but a freewill offering. Paul calls it a *gift* (v. 3, *charis*), stressing generosity (cf. 2 Cor 8:7). Other places Paul calls the same fund a "service" (*diakonia,* 2 Cor 8:4, 7), a "fellowship" or "sharing" (*koinōnia,* Rom 15:26) or a "priestly service" (*leitourgia,* 2 Cor 9:12). This could form the basis of a helpful theology of giving.

The same collection is evidently referred to also in Acts 24:17 (also Rom 15:25-27; 2 Cor 8-9; Gal 2:10). From these additional passages we learn that the collection was for famine relief (cf. Acts 11:27-30) and was a material way for Gentiles to show their indebtedness to the Jews into whose Abrahamic covenant stock they had been grafted through the Messiah, Jesus. But more, it was a way of uniting Jewish believers with Gentile Christians, since for the Jews to accept the gift would have in that culture signaled that they were accepting the Gentiles as equal partners in the gospel. "The collection was a key way of uniting the Gentile Christians with the Jewish Christians. Paul did not allow the Gentiles to become dependent on the Jerusalem church. He empowered the Gentiles to become equal partners" (Snyder 1991:217).

But would Jerusalem accept the gift? Perhaps Paul was quite concerned about this very matter as he planned to take the gift. "Pray that I may be kept safe from the unbelievers in Judea and that the contribution I take to Jerusalem may be favorably received by the believers there" (Rom 15:31 TNIV).

The first day of every week (v. 2) was not the sabbath (Saturday) but Sunday, the day of the resurrection (Acts 20:7; Rev 1:10), when presumably the Corinthian church gathered for worship, as did other early churches (Acts 20:7). However, this is not certain.

But how did the Jewish sabbath get eventually transferred to Sunday in many church traditions? Today many call the Lord's Day (Sunday) "the Christian sabbath" and transfer some of the Mosaic sabbath restrictions, including complete rest from work, to it. It appears that such "sabbatarianism" did not actually begin until medieval times, rather than in the New Testament or patristic period (Carson 1982:287).

The Corinthians were to set aside privately a sum of money, each *in keeping with his income* (v. 2, *euodoō*). The word can also mean "how you may fare" or "whatever you can afford" or "as each can spare." The NIV rendering is a bit too modern but not wrong (Fee 1987:814). *Saving it up* seems strange. Did they not have any church treasury?

It should be noted that Paul exercises wise pastoral steps in this whole process of the special offering. First, the process is highly participatory and democratic. Everyone, young and old, wealthy and poor, slave and free, Jew and Gentile, male and female, educated and illiterate, can have a part. This defuses the motives of those who wanted to be recognized as the patrons or benefactors of the poor and thus increase their status with their "clients."

Second, giving according to one's ability, in private, eases the competitive spirit and puts all on an equal footing, something the Corinthians needed desperately. Third, Paul wisely indicates that he *will give letters of introduction to the men you approve* (v. 3), not ones chosen by him—Gentiles, not Jews! Fourth, if they think it *advisable* (v. 4) in light of the circumstances at Jerusalem (see Rom 15:25-32), Paul will go also, accompanied by those chosen.

Handling money and other donated goods wisely, with utter integrity and accountably, is as important to the success of the gospel as any preaching or witness may be. Lack of financial accountability plagues the church in the Western world as well in Third World countries.

Paul's Plans and Christian Hospitality (16:5-9) In my late teens, shortly after I found Christ as my Savior, I traveled to the San Francisco area for basic U.S. Air Force training at Parks Air Force Base. Alone, away from home, a new Christian, on my first leave I was invited by a Christian family in San Francisco to spend the weekend with them in a real home. Their love and open home were a God-sent gift that refreshed and encouraged me memorably. Little did they know what a great impact this kindness would have in my life in the days to come. My own practice of hospitality to the stranger and to the lonely Christian was often a flashback to this early experience in my life.

Hospitality was quite important to the early church as well. In the *Didache* (second century) Christians are exhorted to entertain visiting leaders for three days. After that they were to work or to move on! Early the church began to select leaders who could and would show hospitality (1 Tim 5:10; *Shepherd of Hermas; Similitudes* 9.27). This led eventually to the medieval practice of "sanctuary" (Snyder 1991:214). Paul, as 1 Corinthians 9 revealed, deliberately refused support from the churches, choosing to work to avoid criticism (the Cynics were traveling leeches). However, he did expect that the churches would support his travel to the next place on his itinerary and that they would with Christian hospitality welcome him into their fellowship as long as he could stay (v. 6).

Paul is currently in Ephesus (spent three years there—Acts 19:1-41), and because there is a great opportunity for him to teach and proclaim Christ, he plans to stay awhile longer, until Pentecost (v. 8). After he leaves Ephesus he plans to pass *through Macedonia* (north of Greece), where he had founded churches five years earlier (A.D. 49-54). Then he plans to visit with the Corinthians (v. 5). This was planned as his second visit but turned out to be his third (2 Cor 12:14; 13:1). The first was when the church was established on his second missionary journey (Acts 18:1-17); the second, "painful" visit we know little about (2 Cor 2:1-2, 12:14, 21; 13:1-2). His plans did not go exactly as he had projected (see introduction), and the Corinthians accused him of misleading them (2 Cor 1:15-24; 2:12-13).

Timothy's Visit and Apollos's Plans (16:10-12) Timothy was a regular associate of Paul in his missionary travels and seems to function

---

16:9 The *many who oppose* Paul at Ephesus could be the same as the "wild beasts" of 15:32. A short time later a mob gathered in the twenty-four-thousand-seat amphitheater to stir up hostility against Paul (Acts 19:23-41).

16:10 *If Timothy comes* has presented a harmonization problem with 4:17-21 where Paul is committed to sending Timothy, only the timing is in question. Some com-

now as Paul's representative to the Corinthians, a sort of apostolic ambassador. He may have also, along with the three men mentioned in verse 17 (Stephanas, Fortunatus and Achaicus), carried this letter back to Corinth. Why should he have *nothing to fear* (v. 10) or be treated with contempt (v. 11)?

Timothy was relatively young and inexperienced (1 Tim 4:12), a biracial Jew and Gentile (Acts 16:1), a "nobody" compared to Paul, Peter and Apollos. But more likely these factors were outweighed in Paul's mind by the fact that Timothy would fully represent him, *for he is carrying on the work of the Lord, just as I am* (v. 10). Whatever reception Paul might have anticipated for himself after his letter was read to the Corinthians might now be experienced by Timothy. So they are exhorted to treat him with Christian hospitality and care and to send him back with *peace* (not hostility) to Paul, who is *expecting him* (v. 11).

Now about [peri de] our brother Apollos (v. 12) probably signals Paul's response to the last question from the Corinthians' letter (see 7:1, 24; 8:1; 12:1; 16:1). Did the Apollos party (1:12) at Corinth especially want him back to bolster their pride and status? Or was there concern that Paul had prevented him from returning? We really don't know. Paul does affirm that he and Apollos (he is probably with Paul at Ephesus in 52-54) are friends and not in competition (see 3:5-9). Paul also disclaims any responsibility for Apollos's delay in coming to Corinth.

Advice and Greetings (16:13-20) The traditional Roman letter form ended with some occasional remarks, last words of advice, final more specific greetings, and salutations. Paul modifies this standard form with Christian content. Reconciliation and love pervade the remaining parts of the letter.

Words of Advice (16:13-14) This is similar to the brief Christian catechisms (teachings) given to other churches at the end of Paul's other letters (cf. Rom 13:8-14; 2 Cor 13:11; Eph 6:10-20; Col 4:2-5; 1 Thess

---

mentators have argued that the *if* particle *(ean)* can be translated "when" or "whenever" (TNIV; Danker 2000:268). But the evidence for this is slender, and Paul can certainly use "whenever" *(hotan)* when he means that (vv. 3, 5, 6). But the better explanation is given by Hays: in 4:17-21 Paul issues a warning, whereas 16:10 is the actual travel plan (1997:287).

5:12-22; 2 Thess 3:6-15). Four ingredients in general characterize these catechetical endings:

1. Put aside the life of the "old age" (e.g., 2 Cor 7:1).
2. Watch for the age to come (1 Cor 16:13).
3. Be subject to appropriate persons (1 Cor 16:15-16).
4. Stand firm in your faith (1 Cor 15:58; 16:13).

"The first Christian catechism called for a Christian lifestyle which rejected the values of the old age, pointed toward the new, yet did not call for a deliberate break with local laws and customs" (Snyder 1991:215).

Be on your guard may be a warning call for vigilance against misleading doctrines and behaviors such as in chapter 15, or it may be an eschatological call to watch *(grēgoreō)* for the Lord's coming (1:6; 15:23; 16:22; Hays 1997:288). The NIV rendering seems preferable here but not certain. *Stand firm in the faith* echoes 15:1-2. Again the NIV rendering is preferable, since it emphasizes the body of truth called "the faith" rather than one's personal exercise of faith, important as that is.

Be men of courage is *andrizesthe,* "be brave, play the man," but the emphasis is not on maleness or masculinity but on maturity (13:11) and courage. "Show mature courage" would capture this thought. As in chapter 13, Paul can summarize his catechism with a call to love: *Do everything in love* (v. 14) is a central theme of the whole epistle.

What wonderful verses! They would make a beautiful statement over the doorway of a church or on a fireplace mantel of a home to remind all of the essence of Christian living. When I am working in Cambridge, England, I frequently pass the striking courtyard entrance to Selwyn College. Above its curved, beautifully carved arch are cut in the stone the words of verse 13 in Greek. Few in those learned halls today can read them, much less identify with their meaning. Note well that these exhortations are directed to the community of believers, and to individuals only as its participatory members.

Instructions (16:15-18) At this point Paul turns to an important model of new community leadership that he wants to commend to the church for their emulation and respect. With Paul, as part of the three-man delegation sent by the Corinthians to the apostle with their letter, was a certain man named *Stephanas,* and his *household,* described as the *first converts* ("firstfruits," cf. 15:20, 23) *in Achaia* (where Corinth was located). From an earlier reference to this same man and his household (1:16) we may infer that he was a man of wealth and belonged to the class of Roman people known as "patrons."

In the ancient Roman world there was an elaborate system of patronage. "Patrons" (wealthy owners) were served by "clients" (artisans, teachers, businesspersons), who promoted the social status of and were rewarded by the patrons, who saw themselves as benefactors. No doubt some at Corinth were attempting to bring this social system into the Christian community.

What Paul does here in elevating the exemplary behavior of this former patron, Stephanas, is nothing less than revolutionary. He abolishes client-patron relations among Christians by urging the other believers to become benefactors themselves by working and giving. Patrons should become servants of others, after the model of Stephanas and his household, who *devoted themselves to the service of the saints* (TNIV *God's people;* v. 15). The word Paul uses for *devoted themselves to* is *tassō,* "to bring about an order of things by arranging, arrange, put in place" (Danker 2000:991).

What seems to be implied is that Stephanas and his household put themselves in the position of service to the people of God. Seeing the need of this ministry, they appointed themselves to it. This is Paul's concept of leadership. Those who see the needs of the gospel ministry and appoint themselves to labor to meet them are the true leaders of the community. People volunteer to serve and thereby gain the community's esteem.

John Bunyan, the seventeenth-century English lay pastor and author of the famous Christian classic *Pilgrim's Progress,* found great encouragement from verse 15 for confirming his own calling into the pastoral ministry, though it cost him twelve years in prison. In another of his great classics penned in prison, *Grace Abounding,* he wrote:

> By this text I was made to see that the Holy Ghost never intended that men who have gifts and abilities, should bury them in the earth, but rather did command and stir up such to the exercise of their gift, and also did commend those that were apt and ready so to do. "They addicted themselves to the ministry of

the saints." This Scripture, in these days, did continually run in my mind, to encourage me, and strengthen me in this my work for God. (quoted in Hinson 1978:290)

Such men [as Stephanas, Fortunatus and Achaicus] deserve recognition (v. 18), and the people of God should "yield" *(hypotassō,* "submit") to them. Also they should yield *to everyone who joins in the work, and labors at it* (v.16), including women who model this same labor-in-service. Paul elsewhere commends Euodia and Syntyche, women he calls his "coworkers" (Phil 4:2-3); Phoebe is another example of a patron who became a servant *(diakonia)* of the church at Cenchrea (Rom 16:1-2).

E. A. Judge has captured well the radical change in social values brought by the love engendered through the gospel. "The Corinthian letters show him [Paul] in head-on confrontation with the mechanisms [of patronage] by which it imposed social power. . . . His positive response to this collision was to build a remarkable new construction of social realities that both lay within the fabric of the old ranking system and yet transformed it by a revolution of social values" (quoted by Winter 2001:184).

In the Roman period, owners often named a slave for a virtue. In contrast to the customary two to three names for patrons/owners, slaves had only one name (Snyder 1991:216). The Latin name Fortunatus means "fortune," and Achaicus reflects the name of the province where this person was perhaps born. Both were likely slaves (or freedmen) and may have been part of the *household of Stephanas* (v. 15). For patron and slaves to be engaged together in loving service to others for the sake of the gospel was quite socially revolutionary!

Together they *refreshed* Paul's *spirit,* and the Corinthians as well, by having *supplied what was lacking* from the Corinthian church (v. 17). This could mean that Paul is mildly rebuking the Corinthians for not having met his needs as Stephanas has. But it probably means that these men's presence with Paul filled the hole left in his heart by the

---

16:19 According to the Roman historian Suetonius, the emperor Claudius had by an edict forced the Jews out of Rome in A.D. 49 ("since the Jews constantly made disturbances at the instigation of Chrestus, he expelled them from Rome," *Claudius* 25.4; see Acts 18:2). "Chrestus" is undoubtedly a misspelling of Christus (Christ), and the

absence of other Corinthian brothers and sisters. Stephanas and the others brought him a little bit of the Corinthian fellowship in Ephesus. Notice Paul's diplomatic handling (infused by love) of his absence from them, as well as the way he elevates Stephanas as a model of Christ's self-sacrificing service-love in action that he has urged upon them throughout the letter.

Greetings (16:19-20) *Aquila and Priscilla . . . and the church that meets in their home* send warm greetings to the Corinthian church, thus again emphasizing their acceptance, love and unity with the Corinthians. This Jewish married couple were significant partners and co-laborers in the gospel with Paul. In a great tribute to them he mentions that they "risked their lives" for him and that "all the churches of the Gentiles are grateful to them" (Rom 16:3-4). It is likely that this risking of their lives occurred during the three years Paul was in Ephesus with them. This counters some mythical views of Paul as an unlovable, awkward misogynist, for it is hard to imagine Priscilla risking her neck for someone who puts down women.

Priscilla and Aquila established a church in their home just about everywhere they went (Ephesus, 1 Cor 16:19; Rome, Rom 16:5). This would surely indicate they had some amount of wealth (thus patron status) and yet gave themselves to serving rather than being served by "clients." They stayed in Corinth with Paul and worked at tentmaking after they and other Jews were expelled from Rome by Emperor Claudius in the wake of public disturbances regarding Christ (Acts 18:1). They were also responsible for the initial theological education of Apollos, whom they met in Ephesus (Acts 18:24-26). So this couple had many ties with Corinth.

Yet so as not to mention only these more prominent believers, Paul adds, *All the brothers and sisters here send greetings* (v. 20). Great mutuality and equality are expressed in these greetings.

What about the *holy kiss* (v. 20)? It is commanded some five times in the New Testament to be shared by all Christians as a mark of love, ac-

---

disturbances were probably caused by agitation and rivalry between Jewish Christians and nonbelieving Jews in the synagogues of Rome as Christ was preached as Messiah and Lord. As believing Jews, Aquila and Priscilla were expelled and went to Corinth, where they met Paul.

ceptance, reconciliation, mutuality, equality of status and oneness of identity (Rom 16:16; 2 Cor 13:12; 1 Thess 5:26; 1 Pet 5:14). How are we to understand the *holy kiss* or Peter's "kiss of love"? Early in the second century the "kiss of peace" was practiced as a part of the Communion service, after the general prayers and before the Eucharist (Justin Martyr, A.D. 150, *Apology* 65). Many have supposed Paul's reference here is also liturgical (part of the worship service's order). But there is no reason to think that the holy kiss here and elsewhere in the New Testament is anything more than familial (as in Gen 50:1). However, the kiss on the lips was most likely exchanged when Christians met, including their gathering for worship. Ambrosiaster says, "The holy kiss is a sign of peace, doing away with discord" (in Bray 1999:190). If we see that such a kiss was also a recognition or sign between Christian churches (such as the different house churches in Corinth) of their mutuality, reconciliation, love, respect and equality, we will be closer to the New Testament usage.

What about *holy?* Often it is understood to point to a "pure" kiss instead of one that is impure and sexually motivated. However, it may be better understood as Peter describes it, not a kiss of peace but a kiss of love (1 Pet 5:14). It is *holy* because it is a greeting of love between God's people, a holy kiss for the holy people of God (Thiselton 2000:1346). John Chrysostom is more specific and says: "Having bound them together by his exhortation, Paul goes on to bid them to set the seal on their union by means of a holy kiss, which unites and produces one body. The kiss is holy when it is free of deceit and hypocrisy" (in Bray 1999:190).

16:20 In Greco-Roman culture, equals kissed on the mouth, nonequals but socially close on the cheek, social inferiors on the feet (cf. Lk 7:38). Families in the privacy of their homes kissed on the mouth; the betrothal kiss done in public was the one exception. In the few references in the New Testament the kiss is either familial or the unconventional and countercultural practice of Christians exchanging a "holy kiss" when they were in another disciple's presence. Jesus seems to have begun the practice with his disciples as a mark of unity with him (Lk 7:45; Acts 20:17, 37). The holy kiss on the lips was likely also a pneumatological sign of communicating not "love" or "peace" *per se* but the Holy Spirit (cf. Jn 20:22).

In the second to third centuries all the Christians present gave the holy kiss to the newly ordained bishop. Further the bishop extended the kiss of peace first to the newly baptized Christians, and then all the Christians present extended the same kiss to the new converts. Finally, the holy kiss became a sign of reconciliation extended

Paul's Postscript in His Own Hand (16:21-24) As in all his letters (see 2 Thess 3:17) Paul here picks up the pen from the secretary who writes the letter (an amanuensis, Sosthenes, 1:1?) and adds his personal greetings and further comments (Rom 16:23; Gal 6:11; Col 4:8; Philem 19). Such a practice serves to authenticate the letter, if his handwriting is recognized, but its main purpose is to put a personal touch, a sign of affection, on it (both effects lost to us today). Perhaps it adds a sense of importance to the words and of Paul's authority.

There follow three succinct, connected verses: pronouncement of a curse, a prayer, a benediction and an affectionate goodbye. There is no good reason to see these verses as liturgical, despite their early use in this fashion (cf. *Didache* 10.6).

The Curse and the Prayer for Christ's Return (16:22) *If anyone does not love [phileō] the Lord* puts clearly the difference between belief and unbelief in Jesus and the gospel. The Christian community is not infinitely inclusive (Hays 1997:291). Everyone is not included in God's saving grace. Only those who respond in kind to God's gift of love in Christ are included in his elective purposes (Rom 8:28). "Not loving Christ is the ultimate sin" (Witherington 1995:323). To not love Jesus is to show utter disrespect not only to him but also to God, who gave his Son for us.

A curse be on him is the sanction (at least in part) for unbelief and presents great difficulty for the modern reader because of our emphasis on religious tolerance and pluralism. The word Paul uses for *curse* is *anathema* and may mean either "devoted to a deity" or "devoted to

---

to lapsed Christians who repented of their defection from Christ during times of persecution.

In the fourth to fifth centuries Ambrose taught that the holy kiss infuses grace, and that one kisses Christ in receiving the Spirit. Augustine indicates that following the Lord's prayer in the service Christians say to one another, "Peace be with you" followed by a holy embrace and kiss: "This is a sign of peace; as the lips indicate, let peace be made in your conscience" (Augustine 1959:197-98). Western cultures today may have difficulty restoring the early church's practice of kissing on the lips with its pneumatological significance. We may well wonder if today's Western handshake or embrace could ever serve in the same way as a radical enactment of Christian unity. Nevertheless, some countercultural sign that represents equality and unity between Christians without regard for kinship or friendship should be consistently practiced (Phillips 1996:36).

destruction, cursed" (Danker 2000:63). In this latter sense it occurs numerous times in the LXX, translating the Hebrew *herem* (Num 21:3; Deut 7:26; Josh 6:17; 7:12). In the New Testament it is used almost exclusively by Paul (Rom 9:3; 1 Cor 12:3; Gal 1:8), though Jesus uses the word once in the positive sense (Lk 21:5, "dedicated to God"). The verbal form is found in Mark 14:71 ("call down curses") and several times in Acts 23:12, 14, 21 ("solemn oath").

The basic sense in which Paul uses the term is "delivering up to the judicial wrath of God" (Behm 1964:354). There does not seem to be a case of discipline in the history of the church where this formula was used against heretics. It does occur, however, in some ancient creedal formulations as forms of "denials" corresponding to "affirmations" (cf. *The Anathemas of the Second Council of Constantinople,* A.D. 553). To understand further Paul's use of the curse, the next expression in the verse needs to be examined.

Come, O Lord (v. 22) is most probably a prayer. In fact it may be the earliest known prayer of the church (Snyder 1999:217; R. Martin 1974:32). In the Greek text we find a transliterated (untranslated) Aramaic expression, *maranatha,* with two possible meanings. If we construe the construction as *Maran atha,* the translation would be "Our Lord is coming"; if *Marana tha,* the sense is "Our Lord, come!" The consensus and preferable rendering is the second, a prayer addressed to Jesus, for him to return. Similar language is found in Revelation 22:20, "Amen. Come, Lord Jesus."

In both cases this prayer should not be reduced here in Paul or in Revelation 22 to a mere liturgical invocation for Jesus to be present at the worship service. Rather Paul uses it in its full eschatological sense of the Lord's soon return to the world at "the end" (1:8; 4:5; 11:26; 15:23). But how does it link with the imprecatory curse of the preceding line?

16:21-24 These verses should not be taken as a liturgical text but as originating with Paul (Thiselton 2000:1349-50).

16:22 *Come, O Lord!* is the Aramaic *mara* (Lord), *na* (our) and *tha* (imperative, "come!") and is given untranslated in the Greek text. The early use of this prayer in connection with the eucharistic service in the *Didache* (10.6) should not be seen as the only use of it in the churches founded by Paul or as limited to an invocation of

Paul has indicated the seriousness of disrespecting Jesus by failing to respond in love to the love he has shown in giving his life for our sins (15:3); upon such persons the eschatological, judicial wrath of God will come. It will come when Jesus returns. He will judge the world with justice and truth (Jn 5:22; Acts 17:31). Jesus alone, when he comes, will effect the "curse" of God's just and true judgment of all. He will show who are his true followers, expose and judge every false system, and bring in everlasting righteousness to the world.

Until that time we who follow Christ must not, dare not, take that judgment into our own hands. We must be tolerant of others, of other faiths, of other claims to truth outside the Christian faith. This will not mean that we will forsake evangelism or Christian argumentation for the truth claims of Christ as we understand them. But it will mean we must be tolerant, respectful, nonviolent toward other faiths until the One who alone will settle all these claims comes and judges justly and with truth.

Since he will be utterly intolerant of injustice and untruth, we must be tolerant now. Our temptation is to be impatient and to forcefully, violently, abusively, unilaterally judge and condemn others presumptively before the Lord comes. But Paul could say earlier that even he does not even judge himself, though his conscience is clear. Instead we must "judge nothing before the appointed time; wait till the Lord comes. He will bring to light what is hidden in darkness and will expose the motives of men's hearts. At that time each will receive his praise from God" (4:3-5; cf. 13:9-12).

Grace and Love (16:23-24) *Grace* . . . is a benediction that closes most of Paul's letters and that brings this epistle full circle (cf. 1:4). Grace has been an emphasis throughout the letter, and now Paul wants it to continue in the community (see 2 Cor 13:14; Gal 6:18; Eph 6:24; Phil 4:23; Col 4:18; 1 Thess 5:28; 2 Thess 3:18; 1 Tim 6:21; 2 Tim 4:22;

Jesus' presence at the meal. Cullmann correctly sees the prayer as having in the church's tradition a threefold temporal sense: past, Christ's appearance on the day of his resurrection; present, Christ's presence with the community at the eucharistic meal; and future, the presence of Jesus at the end (Cullmann 1953:14).

Credit for the idea of Christ's intolerance in the future and our consequent tolerance now is given to John Piper's 2002 commencement address at Wheaton College.

Tit 3:15). Martin Rinkart (1636) reminds us of this in his classic hymn "Now Thank We All Our God":

O may this bounteous God through all our life be near us,
With ever joyful hearts and blessed peace to cheer us;
And keep us in his grace, and guide us when perplexed,
And free us from all ills in this world and the next.

My love to all of you in Christ Jesus (v. 24) is quite amazing in light of the stormy letter Paul has just written. It reveals his true heart and concern for all in the congregation, even toward those he has had to rebuke sternly and scold. They are not his opponents but his dear, loved brothers and sisters in Christ, even if they are errant. *Love* is the final word! *Amen* (let it be so!).

Now should anyone draw profit from reading this treatise, let him give thanks to God and ask for Christ's mercy upon my sins. But if anyone deems what I have written superfluous or impractical, let him pardon my unhappy position whose occupations forced me to put limits on the thought I could give to this meditation. (Aelred of Rievaulx, d. 1167)

Bibliography

Agnew,
Francis H. C. M.

1986   "The Origin of the New Testament Apostle Concept: A Review of Research." *Journal of Biblical Literature* 105:75-96.

Augustine,
Bishop of Hippo

1959   *Sermons on the Liturgical Seasons.* Translated by Mary Sarah Muldowney. Fathers of the Church 38. New York: Catholic University of America Press.

Aune, David

1983   *Prophecy in Early Christianity and the Ancient Mediterranean World.* Grand Rapids, Mich.: Eerdmans.

Baird, William

1964   *The Corinthian Church: A Biblical Approach to Urban Culture.* New York: Abingdon.

Bandstra, Andrew J.

1971   "Interpretation in 1 Cor 10:1-11." *Calvin Theological Journal* 6:5-21.

Barrett, C. K.

1968   *The First Epistle to the Corinthians.* New York: Harper & Row.

Bartchy, S. Scott

1973   Μαλλον Χρησαι: *First-Century Slavery and the Interpretation of 1 Corinthians 7:21.* Atlanta: Scholars Press.

Barth, Karl

1933   *The Resurrection of the Dead.* New York: Fleming H. Revell.

1958   *Church Dogmatics* 4.2. Edinburgh: T & T Clark.

Bassler, Jouette M.

1982   "1 Cor 12:3: Curse and Confession in Context." *Journal of Biblical Literature* 101:415-18.

Becker, Jürgen
1993   *Paul: Apostle to the Gentiles*. Louisville, Ky.: Westminster
                John Knox.
Bedale, Stephen
1954   "The Meaning of *kephalē* in the Pauline Epistles." *Journal
                of Theological Studies* n.s. 5:211-15.
Behm, Johannes
1964   "ἀνάθεμα." In *Theological Dictionary of the New Testa-
                ment,* 1:354-55. Edited by Gerhard Kittel and Gerhard
                Friedrich. 10 vols. Grand Rapids, Mich.: Eerdmans.
Beker, J. Christiaan
1984   *Paul the Apostle: The Triumph of God in Life and Thought.*
                Philadelphia: Fortress.
Belleville, Linda L.
2003   "Thorny Issue of Headcovering in 1 Corinthians 11:2-16."
                In *Paul and the Corinthians: Studies on a Community in
                Conflict: Essays in Honour of Margaret Thrall.* Edited by
                Trevor J. Burke and J. Keith Elliott. Leiden; Boston: Brill.
Bengel, John Albert
1971   *New Testament Word Studies.* Vol. 1. A new translation by
                Charlton T. Lewis and Marvin R. Vincent. Grand Rapids,
                Mich.: Kregel.
Berding. Kenneth
2000   "Confusing Word and Concept in 'Spiritual Gifts': Have We
                Forgotten James Barr's Exhortations?" *Journal of the Evan-
                gelical Theological Society* 43:37-52.
Bieringer, R.
1996   *The Corinthian Correspondence.* Leuven, Belgium: Leuven
                University Press.
Bilezikian, Gilbert
1985   *Beyond Sex Roles.* Grand Rapids, Mich.: Baker.

Bittlinger, Arnold
1967   *Gifts and Graces: A Commentary on 1 Corinthians 12-14.*
                Translated by Herbert Klassen, supervised by Michael
                Harper. London: Hodder & Stoughton.
Blattenberger, David E.
1997   *Rethinking 1 Corinthians 11:2-16 Through Archaeological
                and Moral-Rhetorical Analysis.* Studies in the Bible and
                Early Christianity 36. Lewiston, N.Y.: Edwin Mellen.
Blocher, Henri
1997   *Original Sin: Illuminating the Riddle.* New Studies in Bib-

Bloesch, Donald

2004

lical Theology. Downers Grove, Ill.: InterVarsity Press.

Statement from Donald Bloesch by telephone, January 2, 2004. Used by permission.

Blomberg, Craig

1994

1 Corinthians. NIV Application Commentary. Grand Rapids, Mich: Zondervan.

Bockmuehl, Markus N.

2000

Jewish Law in Gentile Churches: Halakah and the Beginning of Christian Public Ethics. Edinburgh: T & T Clark.

Boff, Leonardo

1986

Ecclesiogenesis: The Base Communities Reinvent the Church. Maryknoll, New York: Orbis Books.

Boring, Eugene

1992

"Prophecy (Early Christian)." In *The Anchor Bible Dictionary* 5:495-502. Edited by David Noel Freedman. 6 vols. New York: Doubleday.

Bray, Gerald, ed.

1999

1-2 Corinthians. Ancient Christian Commentary on Scripture New Testament 7. Downers Grove, Ill.: InterVarsity Press.

Bruce, F. F.

1971

1 and 2 Corinthians. New Century Bible Commentary. Grand Rapids, Mich.: Eerdmans.

1990

The Acts of the Apostles: The Greek Text with Introduction and Commentary. Grand Rapids, Mich.: Eerdmans.

Brümmer, Vincent

1993

The Model of Love. Cambridge: Cambridge University Press.

Brunner, Emil

1947

The Mediator. Philadelphia: Westminster Press.

Bunyan, John

1978

Grace Abounding. In *The Doubleday Devotional Classics,* 1:199-314. Edited by Glenn E. Hinson. New York: Doubleday.

Bynum, Caroline Walker

1995

The Resurrection of the Body in Western Christianity, 200-1336. New York: Columbia University Press.

Cadbury, Henry J.
1934   "The Macellum of Corinth." *Journal of Biblical Literature*
               53:134-41.

Caird, G. B.
1956   *Principalities and Powers: A Study in Pauline Theology.*
               Oxford: Clarendon.

Calvin, John
1960   *The First Epistle of Paul the Apostle to the Corinthians.*
               Translated by John W. Fraser. Edited by David W. Torrance
               and Thomas F. Torrance. Calvin's Commentaries. Edin-
               burgh: Oliver and Boyd.

Carson, D. A.
1987   *Showing the Spirit: A Theological Exposition of 1 Corin-
               thians 12-14.* Grand Rapids, Mich.: Baker.

Cervin, R. S.
1989   "Does *kephalē* Mean 'Source' or 'Authority Over' in Greek
               Literature? A Rebuttal." *Trinity Journal* 10:85-112.

Cheung, Alex T.
1999   *Idol Food in Corinth: Jewish Background and Pauline Leg-
               acy. Journal for the Study of the New Testament* Supple-
               ment Series 176. Sheffield, U.K.: Sheffield Academic.

Clark, Stephen B.
1972   *Building Christian Communities; Strategy for Renewing
               the Church.* Notre Dame, Ind.: Ave Maria Press.

Clarke, Andrew D.
1991   *Secular and Christian Leadership in Corinth: A Socio-his-
               torical and Exegetical Study of 1 Corinthians 1-6.* Cam-
               bridge: Cambridge University Press.

1993   *Secular and Christian Leadership in Corinth: A Socio-his-
               torical and Exegetical Study of 1 Corinthians 1-6.* New
               York: E. J. Brill.

Clarke, Andrew D.,
and Bruce W. Winter,
eds.
1991   *One God, One Lord in a World of Religious Pluralism.*
               Cambridge, U.K.: Tyndale House.

Cole, R. Alan
1973   *Exodus: An Introduction and Commentary.* Downers
               Grove, Ill.: InterVarsity Press.

Colet, John
1985   *John Colet's Commentary on First Corinthians: A New Edi-
               tion of the Latin Text, with Translation, Annotations and*

Introduction. Translated and edited by Bernard O'Kelly and Catherine A. L. Jarrott. Medieval & Renaissance Texts & Studies 21. Binghamton, New York: Medieval & Renaissance Texts & Studies.

Conzelmann, Hans

1969   *Outline of the Theology of the New Testament.* New York: Harper & Row.

1975   *1 Corinthians: A Commentary on the First Epistle to the Corinthians.* Hermeneia. Philadelphia: Fortress.

Cowman,
Mrs. Charles E.

1925   *Streams in the Desert.* Los Angeles: Cowman Publications.

Cranfield, C. E. B.

1979   *A Critical and Exegetical Commentary on the Epistle to the Romans.* 2 vols. Edinburgh: T & T Clark.

Cullmann, Oscar

1953   *Early Christian Worship.* London: SCM.

1956   *The State in the New Testament.* New York: Scribner.

1972   "Oekumenismus im Lichte des biblischen Charismabegriffs." *Theologische Literaturzeitung* 97:812.

Cunliff-Jones, Hubert

1978   *A History of Christian Doctrine.* Philadelphia: Fortresss.

Dahl, Nils Alstrupp

1977   *Studies in Paul: Theology for the Early Christian Mission.* Minneapolis: Augsburg.

Danker,
Frederick William

2000   *A Greek-English Lexicon of the New Testament and Other Early Christian Literature.* Chicago: University of Chicago Press.

Davis, James A.

1984   *Wisdom and Spirit: An Investigation of 1 Corinthians 1.18–3.20 Against the Background of Jewish Sapiential Traditions in the Greco-Roman Period.* Lanham, Md.: University Press of America.

Dawes, Gregory W.

1998   *The Body in Question: Metaphor and Meaning in the Interpretation of Ephesians 5:21-33.* Biblical Interpretation 30.

Leiden, Netherlands: E. J. Brill.

Deissmann, Adolf

1927   *Light from the Ancient East*. Translated by L. R. M. Stra-
        chan. London: Hodder & Stoughton.

1957   *Paul: A Study in Social and Religious History*. New York:
        Harper.

Denney, James

1911   *The Way Everlasting*. London: Hodder and Stoughton.

Dunn, James D. G.

1975   *Jesus and the Spirit*. Philadelphia: Westminster Press.

Edwards, Jonathan

1989   *The Ethical Writings*. Edited by Paul Ramsey. New Haven,
        Conn.: Yale University Press.

Ellis, E. Earle

1957   *Paul's Use of the Old Testament*. Edinburgh: Oliver and
        Boyd.

1978   *Prophecy and Hermeneutic in Early Christianity*. Grand
        Rapids, Mich.: Eerdmans.

Engels, Donald W.

1990   *Roman Corinth: An Alternative Model for the Classical
        City*. Chicago: University of Chicago Press.

Erdman, Charles R.

1928   *The First Epistle of Paul to the Corinthians*. Philadelphia:
        Westminster Press.

Fee, Gordon D.

1980   "*Eidōlothyta* Once Again, An Interpretation of 1 Corinthians
        8—10." *Biblica* 61:172-97.

1987   *The First Epistle to the Corinthians*. New International
        Commentary on the New Testament. Grand Rapids, Mich.:
        Eerdmans.

1994   *God's Empowering Presence: The Holy Spirit in the Letters
        of Paul*. Peabody, Mass.: Hendrickson.

Findlay, G. G.

1908   *St. Paul's First Epistle to the Corinthians*. Vol. 2 of *The Ex-
        positor's Greek Testament*. Edited by W. Robertson Nicoll.
        Grand Rapids, Mich.: Eerdmans.

Fitzmyer, Joseph A.

1989   "Another Look at *kephalē* in 1 Cor 11:3." *New Testament
        Studies* 35:503-11.

1992   "*Kephalē* in 1 Cor 11:3." *Interpretation* 47:32-59.

Flanagan, N. M.,
and E. H. Snyder
1981   "Did Paul Put Down Women in 1 Cor 14:34-36?" *Biblical Theology Bulletin* 11:10-12.

Foerster, Werner
1964   "δαίμων κτλ." In *Theological Dictionary of the New Testament*, 2:1-20. Edited by Gerhard Kittel and Gerhard Friedrich. 10 vols. Grand Rapids, Mich.: Eerdmans.

Forbes, Christopher
1995   *Prophecy and Inspired Speech in Early Christianity and Its Hellenistic Environment*. Wissenschaftliche Untersuchungen zum Neuen Testament. Tübingen: Mohr, 1995.

Fowl, Stephen E.
1998   *Engaging Scripture: A Model for Theological Interpretation*. Challenges in Contemporary Theology. Oxford: Blackwell.

Furnish, Victor Paul
1988   "Corinth in Paul's Day." *Biblical Archaeology Review* 15:14-27.

Gaffin, Richard B., Jr.
1996   "A Cessationist View." In *Are Miraculous Gifts for Today? Four Views*. Edited by Wayne A. Grudem. Counterpoints. Grand Rapids, Mich.: Zondervan.

Gagnon, Robert A. J.
2001   *The Bible and Homosexual Practice: Texts and Hermeneutics*. Nashville: Abingdon.

Gardner, Paul Douglas
1994   *The Gifts of God and the Authentication of a Christian: An Exegetical Study of 1 Corinthians 8–11:1*. London: Eurospan.

Geisler, Norman L.
1988   *Signs and Wonders*. Wheaton, Ill.: Tyndale.

Giles, Kevin
2002   *The Trinity and Subordinationism: The Doctrine of God and the Contemporary Gender Debate*. Downers Grove, Ill.: InterVarsity Press.

Gill, David W. J.
1990   "The Importance of Roman Portraiture for Head-Coverings in 1 Corinthians 11:2-16." *Tyndale Bulletin* 41:245-60.
1992   "The Meat-Market at Corinth (1 Cor. 10:25)." *Tyndale Bulletin* 43:389-94.
1993   "In Search of the Social Elite in the Corinthian Church." *Tyndale Bulletin* 44:323-37.

Glatzer, Nahum N.
1969   *The Passover Haggadah*. New York: Schocken.

Godet, Frederic
1957   *Commentary on St. Paul's First Epistle to the Corinthians*. 2 vols. Grand Rapids, Mich.: Zondervan.

Grosheide,
Frederik Willem
1953   *Commentary on the First Epistle to the Corinthians*. New International Commentary on the New Testament. Grand Rapids, Mich.: Eerdmans.

Grudem, Wayne
1982   *The Gift of Prophecy in 1 Corinthians*. Lanham, Md.: University Press of America.
1985   "Does *kephalē* Mean 'Source' or 'Authority Over' in Greek Literature? A Survey of 2336 Examples." *Trinity Journal* 6:38-59.
1990   "The Meaning of *kephalē* ('Head'): A Response to Recent Studies." *Trinity Journal* n.s. 11:3-72.
2001   "The Meaning of *kephalē* ('Head'): An Evaluation of New Evidence, Real and Alleged." *Journal of the Evangelical Theological Society* 44:25-66.

Gundry, Robert H.
1966   "'Ecstatic Utterance' (NEB)." *Journal of Theological Studies* 17:299-307.

Gundry-Volf, Judith
1997a   "Gender and Creation in 1 Cor 11:2-16: A Study in Paul's Theological Method." In *Evangelium, Schriftauslegung, Kirche: Festschrift für Peter Stuhlmacher,* pp. 151-71. Edited by Jostein Ådna, Scott J. Hafemann, and Otfried Hofius. Göttingen, Germany: Vandenhoeck & Ruprecht.
1997b   "Gender Distinctions, Discrimination and the Gospel." *Evangelical Review of Theology* 21:41-50.
1997c   "Christ and Gender. A Study of Difference and Equality in Gal. 3:28." In *Jesus Christus als die Mitte der Schrift: Studien zur Hermeneutik des Evangeliums,* pp. 439-77. Edited by Christof Landmesser, Hans-Joachim Eckstein and Hermann Lichtenberger. Beihefte zur Zeitschrift für die Neutestamentliche Wissenschaft und die Kunde der älteren Kirche 86. New York: Walter de Gruyter.
1999   "Putting the Moral Vision of the New Testament into Focus: A Review." *Bulletin for Biblical Research* 9:277-88.

Hanson, Anthony
1982   "1 Corinthians 4:13b and Lamentations 3:45." *Expository Times* 93:214-15.

Harnack, Adolf von
1908   *The Mission and Expansion of Christianity in the First Three Centuries.* Volume 1. New York: G. P. Putnam's Sons.

Harrill, J. Albert
1995   *The Manumission of Slaves in Early Christianity.* Hermeneutische Untersuchungen zur Theologie 32. Tübingen, Germany: J. C. B. Mohr.

Harris, Murray J.
1990   *From Grave to Glory: Resurrection in the New Testament, Including a Response to Norman L. Geisler.* Grand Rapids, Mich.: Zondervan.

Hauerwas, Stanley
1991   *After Christendom: How the Church Is to Behave If Freedom, Justice and a Christian Nation Are Bad Ideas.* Nashville: Abingdon.

Hays, Richard B.
1997   *First Corinthians.* Interpretation. Louisville, Ky.: John Knox.
1999   "Wisdom According to Paul." In *Where Shall Wisdom Be Found?* Edited by Stephen C. Barton, 111-23. Edinburgh: T & T Clark.

Hendricks, Howard
2001   "Discipline." In "Wisdom from 'Prof': Letters by Howard G. Hendricks Reflecting on Fifty Years of Ministry at Dallas Theological Seminary." Typescript, Dallas Theological Seminary.

Héring, Jean
1962   *The First Epistle of Saint Paul to the Corinthians.* London: Epworth.

Hill, David
1979   *New Testament Prophecy.* Atlanta: John Knox.

Holleman, Joost
1996   *Resurrection and Parousia: A Traditio-historical Study of Paul's Eschatology in 1 Corinthians 15.* Supplements to *Novum Testamentum* 84. Leiden, Netherlands: E. J. Brill.

Hooker, Morna D.
1963-1964   "'Beyond the Things Which Are Written': An Examination

of 1 Cor 4:6." *New Testament Studies* 10:127-32.

1990   "Authority on Her Head: An Examination of 1 Cor 11:10." In *From Adam to Christ: Essays on Paul,* 113-20. Cambridge: Cambridge University Press.

Horsley, Richard A.

1998   *1 Corinthians.* Nashville: Abingdon.

House, H. Wayne

1983   "Tongues and the Mystery Religions of Corinth." *Bibliotheca Sacra* 140: 135-50.

Hull,
Gretchen Gaebelein

1987   *Equal to Serve: Women and Men in the Church and Home.* Old Tappan, N.J.: Revell.

Hurley, James B.

1981   *Man and Woman in Biblical Perspective: A Study in Role Relationships and Authority.* Leicester, U.K.: Inter-Varsity Press.

Ilan, Tal

1996   *Jewish Women in Greco-Roman Palestine: An Inquiry into Image and Status.* Peabody, Mass.: Hendrickson.

Instone-Brewer, David

2002   *Divorce and Remarriage in the Bible: The Social and Literary Context.* Grand Rapids, Mich.: Eerdmans.

Johnson, Luke T.

1992   "Tongues, Gift of." In *The Anchor Bible Dictionary,* 6:596-600. Edited by David Noel Freedman. 6 vols. New York: Doubleday.

Keener, Craig S.

1992   *Paul, Women and Wives: Marriage and Women's Ministry in the Letters of Paul.* Peabody, Mass.: Hendrickson.

Kent, John H.

1966   *The Inscriptions, 1926-1950,* vol. 8, pt. 3, *Corinth.* Princeton, N.J.: American Schools of Classical Studies at Athens.

Kim, Seyoon

2003   "Imitatio Christii (1 Corinthians 11:1): How Paul Imitates Jesus Christ in Dealing with Idol Food (1 Corinthians 8—10)." *Bulletin for Biblical Research* 13, no. 2: 193-225.

Kistemaker, Simon J.

1996   *Exposition of the First Epistle to the Corinthians.* New Testament Commentary. Grand Rapids, Mich.: Baker.

Kittel, Gerhard, and
Gerhard Friedrich, eds.
1964-1976   *Theological Dictionary of the New Testament.* 10 vols. Grand Rapids, Mich.: Eerdmans.

Knight, George W.
1985   *Role Relationship of Men and Women: New Testament Teaching.* Phillipsburg, N.J.: Presbyterian & Reformed.

Knox, R. A.
1950   *Enthusiasm; A Chapter in the History of Religion.* Oxford: Oxford University Press.

Leith, John H.
1973   *Creeds of the Churches: A Reader in Christian Doctrine, from the Bible to the Present.* Richmond, Va.: John Knox.

Lewis, C. S.
1988   *The Four Loves.* New York: Harcourt Brace Jovanovich.

Liefeld, Walter A.
1986   "Women, Submission and Ministry in 1 Corinthians." In *Women, Authority and the Bible,* pp. 134-53. Edited by Alvera Mickelsen. Downers Grove, Ill.: InterVarsity Press.

Liefeld, Walter L.,
and Ruth A. Tucker
1987   *Daughters of the Church: Women and Ministry from New Testament Times to the Present.* Grand Rapids, Mich.: Zondervan.

Lightfoot, J. B.
1981   *The Apostolic Fathers: Clement, Ignatius, and Polycarp.* Part Two: Ignatius and Polycarp. Volume 2. Grand Rapids, Mich.: Baker (from the Macmillan edition of 1889-1890).

Litfin, Duane
1994   *St. Paul's Theology of Proclamation: 1 Corinthians 1—4 and Greco-Roman Rhetoric.* Cambridge: Cambridge University Press.

MacArthur, John F., Jr.
1992   *Charismatic Chaos.* Grand Rapids, Mich.: Zondervan.

Marshall, Peter
1987   *Enmity in Corinth: Social Conventions in Paul's Relations with the Corinthians.* Wissenschaftliche Untersuchungen zum Neuen Testament 23, Reihe 2. Tübingen, Germany: J. C. B. Mohr.

Martin, Dale B.

1995   *The Corinthian Body*. New Haven, Conn.: Yale University Press.

Martin, Ralph P.

1974   *Worship in the Early Church*. Grand Rapids, Mich.: Eerdmans.

1984   *The Spirit and the Congregation: Studies in 1 Corinthians 12-15*. Grand Rapids, Mich.: Eerdmans.

McGill, Arthur C.

1982   *Suffering: A Test of Theological Method*. Philadelphia: Westminster.

McGinn, Sheila E.

1996   "*Exousia echein epi tēs kephalēs:* 1 Cor 11:10 and the Ecclesial Authority of Women." *Listening: Journal of Religion and Culture* 31:91-104.

McGrath, Alister E.

1988   *The Mystery of the Cross*. Grand Rapids, Mich.: Zondervan.

1997   *Christian Theology, An Introduction*. 2nd ed. Oxford: Blackwell.

Meeks, Wayne A.

1982   "'And Rose up to Play': Midrash and Paraenesis in 1 Corinthians 10:1-22." *Journal for the Study of the New Testament* 16:64-78.

1983   *The First Urban Christians: The Social World of the Apostle Paul*. New Haven, Conn.: Yale University Press.

Mercadante, Linda

1978   *From Hierarchy to Equality: A Comparison of Past and Present Interpretations of 1 Cor 11:2-16 in Relation to the Changing Status of Women in Society*. Vancouver: G-M-H/ Regent College.

1979   "The Male-Female Debate: Can We Read the Bible Objectively?" *Crux* 15:20-25.

Mitchell, Margaret Mary

1991   *Paul and the Rhetoric of Reconciliation: An Exegetical Investigation of the Language and Composition of 1 Corinthians*. Hermeneutische Untersuchungen zur Theologie 28. Tübingen, Germany: J. C. B. Mohr.

Moffatt, James

1938   *The First Epistle of Paul to Corinthians*. London: Hodder & Stoughton.

Moiser, Jeremy
1983   "A Reassessment of Paul's View of Marriage with Reference to 1 Cor 7." *Journal for the Study of the New Testament* 18:103-22.

Moltmann, Jürgen
1997   *The Source of Life: The Holy Spirit and the Theology of Life.* Minneapolis: Fortress.

Moore, George Foot
1962   *Judaism in the First Centuries of the Christian Era, the Age of the Tannaim.* 2 vols. Cambridge, Mass.: Harvard University Press.

Morris, Leon
1958   *The First Epistle of Paul to the Corinthians: An Introduction and Commentary.* Tyndale New Testament Commentaries. Grand Rapids, Mich.: Eerdmans.

1985   *The First Epistle of Paul to the Corinthians: An Introduction and Commentary.* 2nd ed. Tyndale New Testament Commentaries. Grand Rapids, Mich.: Eerdmans

Murphy-O'Connor, Jerome
1979   *1 Corinthians.* Wilmington, Del.: Michael Glazier.

1983   *St. Paul's Corinth: Texts and Archaeology.* Good News Studies 6. Wilmington, Del.: Michael Glazier.

1996   *Paul: A Critical Life.* Oxford: Clarendon.

Nestle, Erwin, ed.
1957   *Novum Testamentum Graece.* Edition vicesima tertia. Stuttgart, Germany: Hergestellt in den Werkstatten der Privileg. Wurtt. Bibelanstalt, Stuttgart.

Niccum, C.
1997   "The Voice of the Manuscripts on the Silence of Women: The External Evidence for 1 Cor 14:34-35." *New Testament Studies* 43:242-55.

Nygren, Anders
1969   *Agape and Eros.* New York: Harper & Row.

Odell-Scott, D.W.
1987   "In Defense of an Egalitarian Interpretation of 1 Cor 14:34-6." *Biblical Theology Bulletin* 17:100-103.

Osiek, Carolyn,
and David L. Balch
1997   *Families in the New Testament World: Households and House Churches.* Louisville, Ky.: Westminster John Knox.

Outka, Gene
1972   *Agape: An Ethical Analysis.* New Haven, Conn.: Yale University Press.

Padgett, Alan
1984   "Paul on Women in the Church: Contradictions of Coiffure in 1 Cor 11:4." *Journal for the Study of the New Testament* 20:69-86.

1994   "The Significance of *Anti* in 1 Corinthians 11:15." *Tyndale Bulletin* 45:181-88.

Payne, Philip B.
1995   "Fuldensis, Sigla for Variants in Vaticanus, and 1 Cor 14:34-35." *New Testament Studies* 41:240-62.

Perriman, A. C.
1994   "The Head of a Woman: The Meaning of *kephalē* in 1 Cor 11:3." *Journal of Theological Studies* 45:602-22.

Phillips, L. Edward
1996   *The Ritual Kiss in Early Christianity Worship.* The Alcuin Club/Grove Liturgical Studies Series #36. Cambridge, U.K.: Grove Books.

Phipps, W. E.
1982   "Is Paul's Attitude Toward Sexual Relations Contained in 1 Cor. 7:1?" *New Testament Studies* 28:125-31.

Rengstorf, Karl H.
1964   "ἀπόστολος." In *Theological Dictionary of the New Testament,* 1:407-47. Edited by Gerhard Kittel and Gerhard Friedrich. 10 vols. Grand Rapids, Mich.: Eerdmans.

1972   "ὑπηρέτης κτλ." In *Theological Dictionary of the New Testament,* 8:530-44. Edited by Gerhard Kittel and Gerhard Friedrich. 10 vols. Grand Rapids, Mich.: Eerdmans.

Robertson, Archibald,
and Alfred Plummer
1929   *A Critical and Exegetical Commentary on the First Epistle of St. Paul to the Corinthians.* International Critical Commentary on the Holy Scriptures of the Old and New Testaments. Edinburgh: T & T Clark.

Rogers, Cleon L., III,
and Cleon Rogers Jr.
1998   *The New Linguistic and Exegetical Key to the Greek New*

Testament. Grand Rapids, Mich.: Zondervan.

Rosner, Brian S.
1999   *Paul, Scripture and Ethics: A Study of 1 Corinthians 5-7.*
            Grand Rapids, Mich.: Baker.

Routledge, Robin
2002   "Passover and Last Supper." *Tyndale Bulletin* 53, no. 2:
            203-21.

Ruler, A. A. van
1958   *The Greatest of These Is Love.* Translated by Lewis B.
            Smedes. Grand Rapids, Mich.: Eerdmans.

Ruthven, Jon
1993   *On the Cessation of the Charismata: The Protestant Po-
            lemic on Postbiblical Miracles. Journal of Pentecostal The-
            ology.* Supplement 3. Sheffield, U.K.: Sheffield Academic.

Ryrie, Charles C.
1958   *The Place of Women in the Church.* New York: Macmillan.

Samarin, W. J.
1972   *Tongues of Men and Angels: The Religious Language of
            Pentecostalism.* New York: Macmillan.

Sanders, E. P.
1977   *Paul and Palestinian Judaism: A Comparison of Patterns
            of Religion.* Philadelphia: Fortress.

Schatzmann, Siegfried
1987   *A Pauline Theology of Charismata.* Peabody, Mass.: Hen-
            drickson.

Schmithals, Walter
1971   *Gnosticism in Corinth: An Investigation of the Letters to the
            Corinthians.* Nashville: Abingdon.

Schrage, Wolfgang
1991   *Der Erste Brief an die Korinther,* vol. 1. Evangelisch-
            Katholischer Kommentar zum Neuen Testament 7. Neu-
            kirchen-Vluyn, Germany: Neukirchener.

1995   *Der Erste Brief an die Korinther,* vol. 2. Evangelisch-
            Katholischer Kommentar zum Neuen Testament 7. Neu-
            kirchen-Vluyn, Germany: Neukirchener.

1999   *Der Erste Brief an die Korinther,* vol. 3. Evangelisch-
            Katholischer Kommentar zum Neuen Testament 7 Neu-
            kirchen-Vluyn, Germany: Neukirchener.

Shanor, Jay
1988   "Paul as Master Builder: Construction Terms in 1 Cor." *New
            Testament Studies* 34:461-71.

Shogren, Gary S.

1997   "Christian Prophecy and Canon in the Second Century: A Response to B. B. Warfield." *Journal of the Evangelical Theological Society* 40:609-26.

Smedes, Lewis B.

1978   *Love Within Limits: A Realist's View of 1 Corinthians 13.* Grand Rapids, Mich.: Eerdmans.

Snyder, Graydon F.

1985   *Ante Pacem: Archaeological Evidence of Church Life Before Constantine.* Macon, Ga.: Mercer University Press.

1991   *First Corinthians: A Faith Community Commentary.* Macon, Ga.: Mercer University Press.

1999   *Inculturation of the Jesus Tradition: The Impact of Jesus on Jewish and Roman Cultures.* Harrisburg, Penn.: Trinity Press International.

Stendahl, Krister

1984   "Paul at Prayer." In *Meanings: The Bible as Document and as Guide,* 151-61. Philadelphia: Fortress.

Still, E. Coyle, III

2002   "The Meaning and Uses of EIDŌLOTHYTON in First Century Non-Pauline Literature and 1 Cor 8:1–11:1." *Trinity Journal* n.s. 23:225-34.

Synan, Vinson

2001   *The Century of the Holy Spirit: 100 Years of Pentecostal and Charismatic Renewal, 1901-2001.* Nashville: Thomas Nelson.

Talbert, Charles H.

1987   *Reading Corinthians: A New Commentary for Preachers.* New York: Crossroad.

Theissen, Gerd

1982   *The Social Setting of Pauline Christianity: Essays on Corinth.* Philadelphia: Fortress.

1987   *Psychological Aspects of Pauline Theology.* Edinburgh: T & T Clark.

Thiselton, Anthony C.

1978   "Realized Eschatology at Corinth." *New Testament Studies* 24:510-26.

2000   *The First Epistle to the Corinthians: A Commentary on the Greek Text.* New International Greek Testament Commentary. Grand Rapids, Mich.: Eerdmans.

Thompson, C. L.

1988   "Hairstyles, Head-Coverings and St Paul: Portraits from Roman Corinth." *Biblical Archaeologist* 51:99-115.

Thrall, Margaret E.

1965   *The First and Second Letters of Paul to the Corinthians.* Cambridge: Cambridge University Press.

Tomson, Peter J.

1990   *Paul and the Jewish Law: Halakah in the Letters of the Apostle to the Gentiles.* Philadelphia: Fortress.

Torjesen, Karen Jo

1993   *When Women Were Priests: Women's Leadership in the Early Church and the Scandal of Their Subordination in the Rise of Christianity.* San Francisco: HarperSanFrancisco.

Torrance, Thomas F.

1975   *Theology in Reconciliation: Essays Towards Evangelical and Catholic Unity in East and West.* Grand Rapids, Mich.: Eerdmans.

1996   *The Christian Doctrine of God, One Being Three Persons.* Edinburgh: T & T Clark.

1998   Personal letter to Gary M. Burge (February 5, 1998). Used by permission.

Turner, Max

1996   *The Holy Spirit and Spiritual Gifts: Then and Now.* Carlisle, U.K.: Paternoster.

Walvoord, John F.

1977   *The Holy Spirit.* Grand Rapids, Mich.: Zondervan.

Warfield, B. B.

1918   *Counterfeit Miracles.* Carlisle, Penn.: Banner of Truth Trust.

Welborn, L. L.

1987   "On the Discord in Corinth." *Journal of Biblical Literature* 106:85-111. The following entry contains a revised version of this article on pages 1-42.

1997   *Politics and Rhetoric in the Corinthian Epistles.* Macon, Ga.: Mercer University Press.

Williams, J. Rodman

1989   *Renewal Theology,* vol. 1. Grand Rapids, Mich.: Zondervan.

1990   *Renewal Theology,* vol. 2. Grand Rapids, Mich.: Zondervan.

1995   *Renewal Theology,* vol. 3. Grand Rapids, Mich.: Zondervan.

Willis, Wendell Lee

1985   *Idol Meat in Corinth: The Pauline Argument in 1 Corinthians 8 and 10.* Dissertation Series. Chico, Calif: Scholars Press.

1987   "Eating and Others: Pauline Ethical Arguments," pp. 1-42. Unpublished paper presented at the Society of Biblical Literature annual meeting.

Wimbush, Vincent L.

1987   *Paul, the Worldly Ascetic: Response to the World and Self-Understanding According to 1 Corinthians 7.* Macon, Ga.: Mercer University Press.

Wink, Walter

1984   *Naming the Powers.* Philadelphia: Fortress.

1986   *Unmasking the Powers.* Philadelphia: Fortress.

1992   *Engaging the Powers.* Minneapolis: Fortress.

1998   *The Powers that Be: Theology for a New Millennium.* New York: Doubleday.

Winter, Bruce W.

1988   "Secular and Christian Responses to Corinthian Famines." *Tyndale Bulletin* 40:86-106.

1994   *Seek the Welfare of the City: Christians as Benefactors and Citizens; First Century Christians in the Graeco-Roman World.* Grand Rapids, Mich.: Eerdmans.

2001   *After Paul Left Corinth. The Influence of Secular Ethics and Social Change.* Grand Rapids, Mich.: Eerdmans.

2002   *Philo and Paul Among the Sophists: Alexandrian and Corinthian Responses to a Julio-Claudian Movement.* Grand Rapids, Mich.: Eerdmans.

Wire, Antoinette Clark

1990   *The Corinthian Women Prophets: A Reconstruction Through Paul's Rhetoric.* Minneapolis: Fortress.

Witherington, Ben, III

1988   *Women in the Earliest Churches.* Society for New Testament Studies Monograph Series. Cambridge: Cambridge University Press.

1990   *Women and the Genesis of Christianity.* Cambridge: Cambridge University Press.

1993   "Not So Idle Thoughts About Eidolothuton." *Tyndale Bulletin* 44:237-54.

1995   *Conflict and Community in Corinth: A Socio-Rhetorical Commentary on 1 and 2 Corinthians.* Grand Rapids, Mich.: Eerdmans.

Wright, N. T.
2003   *The Resurrection of the Son of God.* Minneapolis: Fortress.

Yeo, Khiok-Khng
1995   *Rhetorical Interaction in 1 Corinthians 8 and 10: A Formal Analysis with Preliminary Suggestions for a Chinese Cross-Cultural Hermeneutic.* Interpretation 9. Leiden, Netherlands: E. J. Brill.